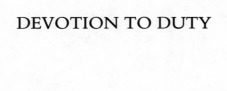

DEVOTION TO DUTY

DEVOTION TO DUTY

A Biography of
Admiral
Clifton A. F. Sprague

JOHN F. WUKOVITS

Naval Institute Press   Annapolis, Maryland

© 1995 by John F. Wukovits

Library of Congress Cataloging-in-Publication Data
  Wukovits, John F., 1944–
    Devotion to duty : a biography of Admiral Clifton A. F. Sprague /
  John F. Wukovits.
      p.   cm.
    Includes bibliographical references (p.   ) and index.
    ISBN 1-55750-944-1 (alk. paper)
    1. Sprague, Clifton A. F., 1896–1955.   2. Admirals—United States—
  Biography.   3. United States. Navy—Biography.   I. Title.
  E746.S67W84   1995
  359'.0092—dc20
  [B]   95-14270
                                                            CIP

Printed in the United States of America on acid-free paper ∞

02 01 00 99 98 97 96 95   9 8 7 6 5 4 3 2
First printing

To
Mom and Dad,
Amy, Julie, and Karen,
Tom and Fred,
and Terri

➜ CONTENTS ⬅

→ MAPS ←

✦ FOREWORD ✦

U nlike other professionals, career naval officers train and prepare for a service they may never be called upon to perform. That is, the officer of the line is a sea warrior, trained to fight battles upon the oceans, but such battles occur infrequently in modern warfare. Consider the limiting conditions: two fleets, both willing to fight, are required; and both combatants must be confident of victory. The Battle of the Philippine Sea illustrates the point. Usually, however, one fleet is inferior to another, and that lesser fleet will avoid sea battle with a stronger antagonist unless it is forced to defend a vital interest whose value is greater than the ships at risk. The Battle of Midway is a prime example.

Sea battles are consequently rare and usually brief. Hence, aggressive naval officers who have prepared themselves to do battle will normally become involved in one merely by chance and circumstance; and in a war, they may miss combat altogether. Among flag officers, the chances are fewer still. For every admiral's flag flying over a battle group, a score more will never see action.

An officer's peacetime reputation does not foreshadow how he or she will behave in combat. War is risk, but risk taking is not characteristic of peacetime. Naval commanders are, by nature, conservative; they avoid risks, for they have been conditioned to preserve their ships from such hazards as collision and grounding, weather and accident. In war the dangers are magnified by enemy action. A ship can be lost in an instant, like HMS *Hood* against the *Bismarck,* or the Japanese carriers at Midway destroyed by American bombs. As a warship requires years to build at enormous expense, such losses are often irreplaceable; only the most resolute commanders can balance aggressiveness with prudence.

The great naval commanders have had divergent attributes and personalities, and their styles of leadership have varied, often widely. Yet they each have possessed a *fighting spirit,* the determination to persevere, to press on against the enemy regardless of obstacles—not blindly and without reason, but with intelligence. It was fighting spirit that made the Royal Navy such a great naval power: its captains, like those under Nelson, were expected in the absence of other orders to place their ships alongside those of the enemy. The U.S. Navy was younger, but it too applauded a fighting spirit: Jones at Carrickfergus, Perry at Lake Erie, Farragut at Mobile Bay, Dewey at Manila.

The tradition—the *expectation*—of fighting spirit carried into the U.S. Navy of World War II. Its officers, whether Annapolis regulars or reservists, expected to take the war to the enemy and to win. No other outcome was imaginable. Many would fight bravely and well but would never be recorded in the war's written history. Clifton Sprague might have been among them, unknown except to those who were shipmates. By an accident of history, by circumstances he did not control, Sprague proved himself an American naval hero of the first rank.

Sprague fought his majestic battle under improbable odds, not inconsistent with the way the entire war would be fought, misunderstood from the beginning. The prewar Naval War College taught that the battleship would be the ship of the line; its guns and armor would decide the outcome of the ultimate decisive battle between the United States and Japan. All other ships—carriers, cruisers, destroyers, and submarines—would be auxiliaries to the battle line.

Once the war began, the fast carrier emerged as the principal strike force, and with it went the glamour and the glory. The escort carrier was an expedient: a small, slow flight deck for antisubmarine patrols in both oceans or for close air support during amphibious assaults. Grunt work. Never, not for a moment, did naval strategists envision the escort carrier fighting Japanese battleships and cruisers, for they would smash the fragile carriers like they would a bug. And yet at Leyte Gulf the unimaginable happened. The escort carriers and their escort destroyers fought and won a decisive fleet action.

Sprague commanded the task group of escort carriers and destroyers that took on the Japanese battle group at Leyte. The choice assignments, leading to three- and four-star promotions, had gone to his contemporaries commanding the fast carrier task groups, the muscle and power of the Pacific Fleet. But Halsey had taken those carriers with him on a wild-goose chase, and with him also the fast battleships whose main batteries would never fire upon a Japanese battleship or cruiser throughout the war. It was a cumulative blunder shared by all levels of the high command, including the Joint Chiefs of Staff, Nimitz, Halsey, and Kinkaid. Sprague and his men were stuck with the consequences.

What manner of man was Clifton Sprague? We will see that he was enterprising and ingenious, ready to fight the Japanese with whatever was at hand. At Pearl Harbor his doughty seaplane tender fought harder, and was more battle ready, than any other ship in port. He was prepared, if ordered, to steam his little tender unescorted to Wake Island to relieve the Marine garrison, where the large combatants feared to tread. Sprague was the quintessential professional naval officer; whatever his command—none were ever what we now call "high profile"—it would be ready to fight.

And so it was with Taffy 3 off Samar. Sprague fought the Japanese warships with everything he had, in a battle unprecedented in the Pacific war. Pilots trained for stationary land targets now dived upon swerving men-of-war. The little carriers dodged salvos of huge enemy projectiles. The destroyers unlimbered their unused torpedo tubes, rushed into their smoke screens, and emerged wraithlike alongside the enemy, like terriers attacking bulls. An extraordinary leader was this composed rear admiral in the roar of battle, his ships—the last barrier to the helpless supply ships off the beaches—in danger of annihilation.

Sprague was one of the great heroes of the war. He saved many of his own ships; he saved the transports off Leyte; and he broke the will of the Japanese admiral and forced him to withdraw. With a handful of jeep carriers and destroyers, he did what Halsey should have done with the entire Third Fleet. Nimitz suppressed any controversy and thereby deprived Sprague of the credit he should have received. For this and other self-evident reasons, this biography is needed, timely, and appropriate.

John Wukovits is extraordinarily well qualified to write this essential biography of Clifton Sprague. He is gifted with a profound love for naval history and a burning desire to share his knowledge with others through his lucid writing. His research is thorough and comprehensive, but he goes well beyond the written record. His contacts with Sprague's family and colleagues have been exhaustive. Wukovits has a singular sensitivity to the people he interviews; he understands them and their place in history, and they trust him and willingly share their experiences with him. The result is a written work that is exceptionally authentic and credible.

Sprague was devoted to duty in the finest traditions of the U.S. Navy. Now we shall know him as never before. We who love and serve that navy are grateful and indebted to John Wukovits for this splendid work of scholarship and literature.

Thomas B. Buell

✦ INTRODUCTION ✦

W hen I was asked to write a biography of Clifton Sprague, I knew little more about the man other than that he had performed admirably off the Philippine Islands in 1944. That action alone would not justify a full-length biography, so I deferred my answer until I had a chance to investigate Sprague's credentials.

They were impressive. I learned that far from being a one-day flash, Sprague compiled a lengthy list of accomplishments in his naval career that spanned thirty-four years. During the 1920s and 1930s, Sprague contributed to advances in aircraft carrier arresting-gear systems and helped popularize naval aviation by teaching the basics of flight to Annapolis midshipmen. Before his triumph at Samar, Sprague commanded a seaplane tender at Pearl Harbor that shot down three enemy planes during the 7 December raid, organized Atlantic antisubmarine efforts, and captained an *Essex*-class carrier in the Battle of the Philippine Sea. Following the war, he participated in the Bikini atom bomb tests and became the first admiral to fly over the North Pole.

The more I delved into his life, the more it appeared to me that Sprague stood among that second generation of naval aviators who took the knowledge gained from pioneer aviators and expanded it to newer areas, especially aircraft carriers. In the personal realm, he achieved notice of sorts by marrying the sister of the acclaimed American novelist F. Scott Fitzgerald.

What most piqued my interest, however, was something I observed in speaking with men who served under Sprague. Almost unanimously, they poured out praise for their World War II commander and claimed, sometimes heatedly, that he had not received the honors due him. For some, it has become a mission to see that Clifton Sprague not be forgotten. Why, I wondered, did these men retain such deep loyalty? What qualities emanated from Clifton Sprague that inspired an affection that has lasted half a century?

I wanted to answer that question, as well as to examine the role he played in naval aviation from 1914 to 1951. Research has taken me down many roads that have finally merged to produce this book. Along the way, numerous people have helped me. Clifton Sprague's family was very gracious, not merely in sharing their memories and giving me unlimited access to Sprague's papers, but also in allowing me free rein to interpret material the way I saw it. Daughters Courtney Sprague Vaughan and Patricia Sprague Reneau warmly opened their homes and fulfilled every request. Sprague's sister Dorothea, at the time of printing a sprightly 91-year-old, graciously shared an afternoon discussing her brother.

Staff members at the Naval Historical Center, especially Dean Allard, Edward Marolda, and the invaluable Michael Walker, always seemed able to locate exactly what I needed from the center's vast accumulation of documents. Personnel at the Admiral Nimitz Library at Annapolis offered a friendly hand whenever needed.

Veterans and veterans organizations assisted me. Though I undoubtedly will omit a name that deserves to be included, a few warrant mention. Henry Pyzdrowski, of the Heritage Foundation of the U.S.S. *Gambier Bay* and VC-10, Inc., was a conduit of helpful information and contacts. William Mercer provided eyewitness material and lists of names from crews of the *Johnston* and *Hoel;* H. Whitney Felt of the *Samuel B. Roberts* was always available to answer questions; Everett Fulton sent a first-person account of his time on the *Wasp;* Robert P. Daly helped me better understand Sprague's eight months on the *Wasp; Tangier* crew members Richard Fruin and Wesley Larson kept me on the right track with Pearl Harbor; Rear Adm. E. H. Eckelmeyer cast light on Sprague's tenure with VP-8; while Adm. James Russell proved a treasure of information about aviation's early days and Sprague's time on the *Yorktown.*

Others helped with the writing process. Frank Uhlig, longtime editor of the *Naval War College Review,* offered wise suggestions. Family members and friends read various portions and shared their impressions. Robert Kalvaitis and Kyle Westberg of CAD CAM Inc., in Farmington Hills, Michigan, crafted the fine maps that accompany the text.

I want to single out two men, in particular, whose advice, assistance, and encouragement helped me complete this biography. Bernard Norling, professor emeritus of history at the University of Notre Dame, nurtured my desire to write by sending lengthy letters filled with exhortations and suggestions, proofread not only this book but practically every other major piece of writing I crafted, and showed an interest in a former student that helped spark his first steps toward writing. I shall never forget him for this.

Many readers of this biography will know the other man, for he has already established a stellar reputation among naval historians and biographers. In 1984, Thomas Buell offered me my first research assignment. Since then, our professional association has grown, usually by his recommending my name to someone in need of a writer, but frequently by long discussions on the telephone or through the mails. I value his advice, partly because I know he will be brutally honest, but mainly because I respect the man. In his work he is conscientious, determined, thorough, and intelligent; in his life he is honest, caring, and friendly. His beauty as a writer is surpassed only by his decency as a human being. Tom Buell inspired me far more than he probably realizes, and I will always be in his debt.

My family too deserves a word of thanks. For three years my daughters, Amy, Julie, and Karen, endured with a grin my preoccupation with Sprague. Time that could have been theirs, was not. Instead of anger, which high school and college-age offspring can easily produce, they offered support. For that I am not only thankful, but deeply proud. Finishing this book has also taken time from another person. Terri, thank you for your encouragement and for patiently waiting.

→ CHRONOLOGY ←

8 January 1896	Born in Dorchester, Massachusetts
June 1914	Entered Naval Academy
28 June 1917	Graduated one year early due to World War I; finished forty-third out of 199
July 1917 to October 1919	World War I duty on the gunboat *Wheeling*
December 1920 to March 1922	Student aviator at NAS, Pensacola
11 August 1921	Designated Naval Aviator No. 2934
March 1922 to October 1923	Pilot and section leader, VS-1
November 1923 to February 1926	Catapult experimentation at Philadelphia Naval Aircraft Factory; flight officer and executive officer, NAS, Anacostia, D.C.
24 April 1925	Married Annabel Fitzgerald
March 1926 to February 1928	Experimental work on the *Lexington* and *Saratoga* to develop arresting gear
March 1928 to April 1929	Flight deck officer and assistant air officer on the *Lexington*
January 1929	Fleet Problem IX

May 1929 to November 1931	Executive officer of VN-8-D5 at the Naval Academy
10 June 1930	Promoted to lieutenant commander
December 1931 to April 1934	Squadron commander, VP-8 in Panama and Hawaii
February 1934	Became the first naval aviator to complete the 2,650-mile, round-trip flight from Hawaii to Midway Island
May 1934 to July 1936	Air operations officer, NAS Norfolk
July 1936 to June 1939	Air officer, *Yorktown*
December 1937	Promoted to commander
June 1939 to November 1939	Student at Naval War College
November 1939 to June 1940	Commanding officer, *Patoka*
June 1940 to July 1940	Student at Naval War College
July 1940 to June 1942	Commanding officer, *Tangier*
7 December 1941	Attack on Pearl Harbor
3 January 1942	Promoted to captain
June 1942 to March 1943	Air officer, Gulf Sea Frontier, Miami

April 1943 to October 1943	Commander, NAS Seattle and Naval Air Center, Seattle
24 November 1943 to 23 July 1944	Commanding officer, *Wasp*
May 1944	The *Wasp* participated in the Marcus and Wake Islands raids
June 1944	The *Wasp* participated in the Mariana Islands campaign
18–20 June 1944	Battle of the Philippine Sea
9 July 1944	Promoted to rear admiral
23 July 1944	ComCarDiv 25
September 1944	Commander, Task Unit 77.1.2: Supported Morotai landing; rescue at Wasile Bay
25 October 1944	Battle off Samar Island
February–March 1945	ComCarDiv 26: Supported Iwo Jima operation
March–April 1945	Supported Okinawa operation
April–August 1945	ComCarDiv 2
15 August 1945	V-J Day
February–July 1946	Commander, Joint Task Group 1.1.2 and commander, Navy Air Group for Operation Crossroads
August 1946 to April 1948	Chief of Naval Air Basic Training, Corpus Christi

16 January 1948   Redesignated commander, Naval Air Advanced
                       Training, Corpus Christi

May–October 1948   ComCarDiv 6: Duty in the Mediterranean

January 1949 to   Commander, Naval Air Bases, Eleventh and
February 1950   Twelfth Naval Districts, San Diego

March 1950 to   Commandant, Seventeenth Naval District, and
October 1951   commander, Alaskan Sea Frontier

12 November 1950   Flight over the North Pole

1 November 1951   Retirement from active duty; advanced to vice
                       admiral

11 April 1955   Died at Naval Hospital, San Diego, California

DEVOTION TO DUTY

CHAPTER ONE

"The Crowd Will Cheer"

I ronically for a future admiral and military hero, Clifton Sprague's roots begin with two individuals who possessed neither a love of the sea nor an affection for military conformity. His paternal grandparents, Frederick and Hedwig Sprague, fled Prussia around 1860 to avoid prosecution for opposing military conscription. After settling in one of New York City's poorer sections, Frederick labored in a city hospital while Hedwig sewed clothes to earn extra money. The young couple sorely needed the funds as the first of seven children, Henry Bruno, arrived ten days before Christmas, 1865. In rapid succession, two sets of twins and two more boys—Fred and Albert—joined the burgeoning family. Sorrowfully, only the three boys survived the host of deadly diseases that plagued children of poorer background in those times.[1]

Unlike most families with a Prussian heritage, Hedwig dominated her husband and sons. Remembered by a granddaughter as possessing a very strong jaw that shook vehemently when espousing her political views, Hedwig rarely allowed tenderness to peek through her iron façade, even later in life with grandchildren.

"I felt like I was a piece of the furniture," recalled granddaughter Josephine Heinzelman. "I can never remember ever having her show any interest or affection toward me." She exhibited grit even into her seventies. Told

1

by doctors she probably would not survive the required amputation of a badly infected leg, the gutsy woman lived another ten years before dying of pneumonia in January 1929, at the age of eighty-three.[2]

Not much is known of the childhood of her son Henry, later to become Clifton's father, other than that he delivered packages for Stewart's Department Store in New York. After moving to Boston, Henry fell in love with a stunning immigrant from Nova Scotia, Hazel Williams Furlow, and married the twenty-year-old on 2 June 1894 in Boston's Anglican Church of the Ascension.[3]

By July the newlyweds had moved into their first home, a wooden structure sporting narrow windows and a steep roof located at 22 Grant Street in Dorchester, a small town south of Boston. Eighteen months later, on 8 January 1896, Henry and Hazel welcomed the first of their four children, upon whom they bestowed a regal-sounding sobriquet, Clifton Albert Frederick Sprague, apparently out of Hazel's admiration for the English royal family's penchant for lengthy names. Two daughters, Hazel Louise Alma Marguerite, born in 1899, and Dorothea ("Dora") Salome Ester Evelyn, born in 1903, and a second son, Edwin Dexter Wadsworth, born in 1907, brought the family to six.[4]

Also in 1896, 31-year-old Henry embarked upon a successful business career by founding the Sprague-Nugent Company along with his close friend George Nugent. The firm, one of the earliest in the blossoming field of outdoor billboard advertising, quickly established a solid reputation as it fended off challenges from its main rival, the Donnelly Advertising Company. George and Henry carefully expanded their business, and the two families became almost inseparable. Clifton and the other children responded with glee whenever Uncle George and Aunt Kathryn stopped by to visit.[5]

Henry exemplified the stereotypical businessman of his day. A fervid Republican, he acted according to the Puritan code of ethics that rewarded hard work and fair play. Henry "was very honest," according to Dorothea. "He would never cheat anyone." Gradually, though, George's interests drifted toward sporting events and European travel, which increasingly dumped the business's burdens on the hardworking Henry. In 1914, rather than continue what had turned into an unworkable situation, the partners sold out to Donnelly.[6]

The rift depressed Henry for a time, but he soon started a second firm with business associate Lester Bates, selling heating units and ice boxes to construction companies. He remained with this Boston firm, called the

Sprague-Bates-Place Company, until his retirement at age sixty-nine in 1934, when he concentrated on developing real estate holdings and contributing to various civic groups.[7]

In 1903, when Clifton was seven, Henry Sprague moved his family to a larger home in Milton, Massachusetts, three miles south of Dorchester. The structure at 214 Highland, a tidy, two-story clapboard house containing four bedrooms, rested on ample land for the youngsters to explore. Always the astute entrepreneur, Henry later ordered a road constructed near his land, christened it Clifton Road after his son, then sold lots along it. Visitors to Milton can still see it winding peacefully among modest homes.[8]

As with most children, summertime offered the highest level of enjoyment for Clifton and the other three children, for then the family packed up and moved to their eleven-room summer cottage at Rockport, Massachusetts, a resort town perched at the tip of Cape Ann, thirty-five miles northeast of Boston. Here the children swam and fished in the cold ocean waters and hunted fossils in nearby granite quarries.

"I have fond memories of my childhood, especially Rockport," mused Dorothea in 1992. "Clif loved it." Though frequently absent during his military school years, Clifton adored the seaport community and could usually be found along the shore, searching for crabs with his sister or fishing from a huge rock that protruded into the water while his thoughts drifted seaward. One summer, while the Nugents toured Europe, Clifton helped take care of their family dog, an Irish setter named Buster. Family members recalled that Buster loyally sat near the rock and watched while Clifton reeled in fish after fish. A love for the sea and all it held captivated the young boy.[9]

He and Dora used to walk along Rockport's beaches searching under rocks for tiny crabs that Sprague used as bait. "I'd go with him and turn over my rocks," mentioned Dorothea, "but I would always call for him to actually pick up the crabs. I wouldn't touch those things. Clif would stop what he was doing and come get my crabs, and he would never complain."[10]

Sprague retained his love for the sea late into his life. Son-in-law Daniel Vaughan, with whom Sprague shared many thoughts about his career in frequent conversations, recalled that because Sprague so loved the sea "he had to be near it. He wanted to smell the salt air and have the ocean near him. When he'd come visit us in San Jose, he felt like he was in the desert when the ocean was only fifteen miles away! He felt at home on the ocean."[11]

Summers by the sea formed only a portion of the easy lifestyle available to the Spragues, whose income had risen to the high-middle-class level through Henry's business acumen. The Sprague children felt safe and secure in the world created by caring parents who avoided harsh reprimands and strict discipline.[12]

Henry and Hazel's parental instincts flowed along similar paths on all notions save one—organized religion. The two parents held radically differing views, though these were never a source of bitterness or argument. "Mother went to church all the time, but she never tried to get Dad to go," stated Dorothea in words that would be repeated years later by Clifton's own daughters. Hazel stressed regular attendance at church services for her growing brood, who attended Sunday school classes at the Episcopal church in neighboring Mattapan. When older, the four children trekked into Boston with their mother for weekly service at the elegant Church of the Advent on Beacon Hill, first riding on a streetcar to Mattapan, then switching to a second streetcar that transported them to West Roxbury, and finally hopping aboard an elevated train to Boston. A short walk across Boston Commons brought them at last to the church.

A picture of Clifton as an altar boy illuminates distinguishing features. Wide, circular eyes, already deep and penetrating at age eight, dominate and lend the youthful face a studious, thoughtful air. Straight, dark hair, parted almost in the middle, falls toward protruding ears. A quiet seriousness leaps out at the observer, something Sprague developed because, as he once mentioned to a family member, "his father talked so much."[13]

While his family donned their finest clothes and marched off to church, Henry remained behind. "Father never went to church. I mean never," emphasized Dorothea. Instead, Henry placed importance on living a decent life every day and "knew the Bible from beginning to end." He cringed at so-called "respectable" people who attended church on Sunday yet disregarded their fellowman Monday through Saturday. As an example, he pointed to a wealthy lawyer in the neighborhood who shamelessly bilked a hapless client out of a large sum of money.[14]

While Henry disparaged organized religion, he constantly emphasized the value of a college education. All four of his children graduated from prestigious institutions—Clifton from the Naval Academy, Hazel from Smith College, Dora from what would become Pembroke College, and Edwin from Harvard.[15]

Milton's Consolidated Grammar School handed Clifton Sprague his first taste of education. Little is known of these years, but the young boy early exhibited an inclination toward the military. His sixth-grade teacher, Miss

Wilcox, recalled assigning a composition to Sprague and his classmates, asking them to explain what they wanted to be when they were older. Sprague wrote of his dreams to attend West Point and to so succeed that "when I ride down the street on my horse, the crowd will cheer and say, 'There goes General Sprague!'" He received his first taste of public acclaim on the night of 20 June 1910, when Sprague recited F. Marion Crawford's "The Making of the City" to assembled parents, friends, and forty-five classmates at the eighth-grade graduation ceremonies.[16]

After graduating from Milton at the age of fourteen, Sprague moved on to Highland Military Academy, a tiny private school in nearby Worcester, Massachusetts, that combined an emphasis on developing students' character with a rigorous schedule and military discipline. According to its history, Highland hoped to "send out its graduates, not merely as educated men, but as true gentlemen" and bluntly warned in its *General Regulations* that a prospective candidate need not apply if he "does not intend to be a gentleman" or "will be an unfit associate for good boys."

An intense schedule left little time for misbehavior. Starting with thirty minutes of study at 6:30 A.M., Sprague followed breakfast with fifteen minutes of prayer in accordance with Highland's rule that "All cadets will study and recite a Bible lesson," then embarked on three and a half hours of classes. Forty-five minutes of military drills ended with lunch, which was followed by one and a half hours of classes and two and a half hours of sporting endeavors. After the 6:00 P.M. dinner cadets had an hour of study and an hour of recreation before they plopped on their beds for lights out at 9:15.[17]

Starting with his years at Highland, Sprague rarely spent much time at home. He "was like an absentee brother," declared Dorothea. "Clif was always off at school and never home as a young boy." A lengthy Navy career that frequently separated Sprague from his wife and daughters produced similar sentiments from his children years later.[18]

Unfortunately, Highland Military Academy closed in 1912, forcing Sprague to complete his senior year at Roxbury Latin School in West Roxbury, Massachusetts, where he rejoined many of his Milton classmates. Opening in 1645, Roxbury is the nation's oldest private school in continuous operation and most of its students go on to Harvard. It counted among its distinguished graduates Revolutionary War General Joseph Warren, who died in the struggle for Bunker Hill.[19]

Though records before 1918 are sparse since the school employed only part-time secretaries, we receive the best image yet of the maturing Sprague from a handful of official documents, school publications, and classmates' correspondence. Academically, Sprague quickly blended into the undistinguished middle mass of students as he accumulated mainly Bs and Cs in a curriculum heavily oriented toward science. Beginning with an A in Latin, Bs in advanced mathematics and chemistry, and Cs in English and physics, by June 1913 Sprague had dropped one letter grade in three of his subjects while holding his own in mathematics and physics. Although mediocre in academics, Sprague sparkled in conduct, earning As in every area from deportment and attention to fidelity and neatness. Not once did a faculty member issue a warning to Sprague, nor was the punctual high schooler tardy for any class until a sole exception in June.[20]

Fellow classmates remember Sprague with respect and fondness. Harold P. Drisko, secretary of Sprague's class since 1913, claimed that Sprague "was extremely popular" with everyone, while the graduation issue of the school publication, *The Tripod,* opened its summary of Sprague with the assertion "Oh! he sits high in all the people's hearts." Both Drisko and *The Tripod* hinted that the young Sprague, up to now showing only a shy, introspective side, frequently employed a dry wit to gently agitate his classmates. "His sense of humor, as we call it," cautiously characterized *The Tripod,* "has kept us on edge at all times." Drisko attributed Sprague's popularity directly to "his wit and humor."[21]

Sprague's lifelong love of sports also flourished at Roxbury, where he anchored the infield defense as shortstop. Known as a fine fielder, the quick Sprague earned the appellation "Rabbit" from his coach, Leighton Thompson, because the lanky infielder could range deep into the hole or scamper far toward third base to gather in slippery ground balls with his stubby, padded glove.[22]

During his short stay at Roxbury, Sprague seems to have set his path for the future. Combining a deep love of the sea with his childhood military fantasy of riding through the streets to the acclaim of fellow townsmen, Sprague openly declared his intention to attend the Naval Academy at Annapolis. Sprague, wrote Drisko, "was with us for only our senior year, and it was a foregone conclusion that he was going to Annapolis and was simply marking time. . . ." Unfortunately, Sprague failed the hearing test during candidacy examinations in the highly competitive Massachusetts section and failed to win appointment in his first attempt.[23]

Disappointed yet undeterred, Sprague quickly shifted gears and states to wrest his bruised dream from the trash heap. After graduating from Roxbury with a certificate of attendance rather than a diploma because his Highland Academy curriculum failed to meet the more rigid Roxbury standards, Sprague enrolled at Norwich University, a military academy in Northfield, Vermont. Founded in 1818 by Capt. Alden Partridge, a former West Point superintendent, the school maintained an excellent military tradition and offered an early version of the Reserve Officers' Training Corps (ROTC). Only fifteen years before Sprague first walked onto Norwich's grounds, one of its distinguished students, Commodore George Dewey, steamed into Manila Bay and naval glory by soundly humiliating the Spanish fleet during the Spanish-American War.[24]

Sprague switched to Norwich for nothing more complicated than to establish residency in Vermont, a state far less competitive than Massachusetts in selecting candidates for the Academy. The midshipman-hopeful improved his overall academic record in the fall term until he stood sixth in his class, again showing more aptitude for science and mathematics than the literary courses.[25]

During the fall term, the Sprague family contacted Vermont Representative Frank Plumley, who agreed to nominate their son as first alternate for appointment. In December, Sprague received a lengthy communication from Rear Adm. Victor Blue, chief of the Navy's Bureau of Navigation, requesting his appearance at 9:00 A.M. on 21 April 1914 at the Montpelier, Vermont, post office, "for examination as to your mental qualifications for such appointment." Admiral Blue asked Sprague to confirm his desire to take the test and to obtain a birth certificate and parental consent form allowing him to join the Navy.[26]

By March 1914, one month before his exhaustive entrance examinations, Sprague's chances of gaining admittance to the Academy improved when Vermont Senator Carroll Page named Sprague his principal candidate. On 7 April, after inspecting Sprague's portfolio, an impressed Page told his candidate the material "has the right kind of ring and I feel sure that you are going to win out. Work hard to do it." Figuring his tenure at the Academy would soon begin, Sprague withdrew from Norwich University before the spring term ended.[27]

Sprague traveled to Montpelier for the grueling three-day examinations, which focused on mathematics, geometry, and history. Unprepared or unconfident candidates might have recoiled in shock at first sight of such questions as "Reduce 19 rods and 4 feet to the decimal part of a mile" or "Write a theme of about 300 words on how [your] State has recently shown its patriotism," but Sprague experienced few problems. Unfortunately, he had to wait until 20 May—one agonizing month—before learning from Senator Page that he had "satisfactorily passed your mental examinations." Sprague outdistanced his nearest competitor by over one hundred examination points, registering high scores in mathematics and history, and now awaited the next stop along the complex path to Annapolis—the June physical examination. "I advise that you devote yourself assiduously to such exercises," recommended Page, "as will best fit you to take the physical examination, as it will be too bad, after having passed the mental, to fail in the physical test."[28]

Sprague passed the physical examination and received notice that he would be admitted to the United States Naval Academy. Family and friends joined in celebration at this achievement, particularly Sprague's father, Henry, who practically elevated his son to hero status. Before truly earning his father's approbation, however, numerous ordeals, fascinating experiences, and an amazing range of assignments home and abroad awaited the plebe from Massachusetts.[29]

CHAPTER TWO

"A Friend Once, a Friend Always"

T he young man could hardly have selected a more opportune time to embark upon a naval career. After years of neglect during which American naval power diminished compared to other nations, a massive shipbuilding program erupted as America entered the twentieth century. Naval victories in Cuba and the Philippines during the Spanish-American War boosted pride in the service, while the 1901 elevation of Theodore Roosevelt to the presidency handed the Navy a steadfast friend. The dynamic young chief executive, who had avidly devoured Capt. Alfred Thayer Mahan's monumental *The Influence of Sea Power upon History, 1600–1783* and who had written his own book on naval history at age twenty-four, quickly convinced Congress to approve funds for one new battleship a year and for expansion of the Naval Academy.[1]

A coinciding boom in young adult literature produced novels that romanticized both the sea and the Naval Academy. Such authors as Edward L. Beach and H. Irving Hancock wrote about fictional midshipmen and their trials and triumphs at Annapolis. Rarely had a service academy received such widespread acclaim, particularly among younger people, than did the Naval Academy in the first twenty years of the new century. This renewed interest paid dividends, as most of the men who guided the Navy through the epic World War II sea clashes with Japan attended the Academy during these years, including Ernest J. King, Chester W. Nimitz, Raymond A. Spruance, William F. Halsey, and Marc A. Mitscher.

Approximately ten years later, Sprague's class yielded its own share of men whose abilities propelled them to such mid-grade World War II commands as carrier task units and task groups, where their talents contributed significantly to victory.[2]

In June 1914 Sprague arrived at Annapolis, a quiet town with cobblestone streets and buildings dating to colonial times. Founded in 1845, the Naval Academy rests at the mouth of the Severn River as it flows into Chesapeake Bay, an ideal location for an institution dedicated to training professional seamen. Appropriately, sailing craft of various sizes dotted the Academy's Santee Basin, situated on the eastern edge of campus. The 338-acre enclosure, called the Yard, included massive Bancroft Hall, an enormous granite and gray brick structure that housed every student.[3]

One by one, classmates arrived from around the nation to join the eighteen-year-old Sprague. Forrest P. Sherman appeared from Sprague's home state of Massachusetts. Joseph J. Clark represented Oklahoma. Even a second Sprague—Thomas L.—traveled from Ohio to give the Academy an unlikely duo of unrelated Spragues.

After taking the oath swearing him into the U.S. Navy, Midshipman Sprague deposited $280.64 with the pay officer for "Outfit and Text Books," then received from the storekeeper his "white works"—white baggy trousers, a white blouse with his name stenciled across the chest, a black neckerchief, and a white sailor's cap edged in blue.[4]

If Sprague possessed any illusions that Academy life would be a snap, one look at his spartan room demolished them. Simple, utilitarian, and sparsely furnished, the room contained wooden table desks for his roommate and him, unpainted desk chairs, a plain mirror, wash basin, narrow iron beds, and a clothes closet without doors. After meeting his roommate, Jesse "Cy" Perkins of Missouri, Sprague joined other new midshipmen for their first drills before walking to the tailor's to be measured for uniforms.[5]

Before that initial day ended, the incredible array of rules and procedures that govern the military cascaded upon Sprague. A book titled *Regulations of the United States Naval Academy* was thrust into his hands with the admonition to master every page, especially "Conduct and Discipline," an imposing twenty-two pages of small print listing hundreds of infractions ranging from fifty demerits for "Indecorous or ungentlemanly conduct" to three demerits for "Smiling in ranks."[6]

Sprague's conduct record reflected his quiet nature. He avoided serious offenses and compiled a short list of one-demerit infractions such as "Bed carelessly made" and "Hat adrift." Only once in his three years, when he was late returning to ship during the 1916 summer cruise, did Sprague receive more than ten demerits.[7]

Later in the summer, Sprague and his fellow classmates participated in the annual midshipman summer cruise. No other group of plebes could boast of going on cruise, as that was normally reserved for upper classmen, but to mark the one hundredth anniversary of the writing of "The Star-Spangled Banner" by Francis Scott Key, a special cruise had been arranged.[8]

"Those few weeks of life on board gave us something to be proud of, for no other class has been so fortunate," boasted the 1915 *Lucky Bag,* the Academy's yearbook. Three battleships from the fleet anchored off Annapolis to board the entire Academy contingent, then steamed into Chesapeake Bay for the voyage, called the Centennial Cruise. Eleven years later Sprague would marry Annabel Fitzgerald, a descendant of Francis Scott Key.[9]

During these days and nights, veteran officers and sailors hammered the intricacies of life at sea into the midshipmen's brains, from the complicated machinery secured deep in the ship's bowels to the colorful signal flags snapping in the salty breeze. Since these youthful students would one day command men at sea, so the notion went, they should at least understand what each job required. Though difficult to endure at times, this and Sprague's two other summer cruises introduced Sprague to the life he had chosen and tested his seaworthiness.[10]

They also exposed him to different lands and expanded his horizons. With Sprague on board the battleship *Ohio,* ships of the 1915 summer cruise steamed through the recently opened Panama Canal and headed north to San Diego, where former President Theodore Roosevelt addressed the assembled midshipmen with evident envy in his eyes. "Young gentlemen," stated Roosevelt, "if I could, I'd trade places with any one of you."[11]

Sprague served on board another battleship, the *Missouri,* on the 1916 summer cruise, where he learned that Navy discipline can sometimes hurt in unintended ways. While on liberty in Portland, Maine, Sprague became preoccupied and failed to return to his ship on time. He received fifty demerits for this offense and was restricted to the ship on its next stop. Normally that might not be too severe a penalty, but as the *Missouri*'s next destination was Rockport, Massachusetts—the locale of the Sprague summer cottage—the punishment's sting was compounded. While a boatload of jovial midshipmen enjoyed the lobster feast planned by Sprague's mother to mark the return of her son, Sprague had to remain on board the battleship.

Typically, the penalty failed to dampen Sprague's spirits. The *Lucky Bag* alluded to this humorous incident and remarked with admiration that "No one saw him downcast for long—even when restricted on board ship within a stone's throw of his Rockport home." [12]

By anyone's standards, Annapolis placed its midshipmen on a rigid schedule that permitted Sprague few moments of relaxation. Reveille came at 6:30 A.M. At 8:00, every midshipman marched to morning classes, which ended at 12:15. After lunch came another two hours in the classroom, one hundred minutes of drills, and ninety minutes of free time. Supper was followed by the two-hour evening study sessions. From 9:30 until lights out at 9:55, Sprague could relax with Jesse Perkins and other plebes. [13]

Since a midshipman's future rested upon the decks and bridges of fleet ships, his education at the Academy stressed a thorough knowledge of vessels and their workings. The curriculum leaned heavily toward machinery, electrical systems, seamanship, and ordnance, while skimping on literature, philosophy, and inquisitiveness. [14]

Academy education did not encourage a willingness to challenge antiquated ideas. The midshipmen were expected to quietly pay attention in class and never volunteer information for fear of making classmates look bad by comparison. Instruction depended mainly on memorization of time-worn solutions to problems thrown at midshipmen since the Civil War, conducted (rather than taught) by officers bearing few outstanding academic credentials. Though imparting abundant information and facts to the students, this system failed to stimulate the mind, to challenge midshipmen to plunge into unexplored areas and develop bold, new ways to implement naval strategy or evaluate situations from fresh vantage points. During those moments of crisis in the Pacific conflict when Sprague calmly assessed the situation and responded correctly, he exhibited not so much what he absorbed at the Academy as mental capabilities and command talent that he possessed long before entering Annapolis. [15]

At the end of his first year, Sprague stood sixty-sixth out of 255 members, enjoying most of his success in courses emphasizing logical evaluation of problems, such as science and mathematics. Classmates Forrest Sherman and Thomas Sprague, destined for lofty Pacific command in World War II, finished second and tenth respectively. By graduation two years later,

Sprague rose to the top 22 percent of his class (forty-third out of 199), surpassing marks achieved by Thomas Sprague, who slipped to forty-fifth, and other future Pacific luminaries such as Joseph "Jocko" Clark (forty-seventh) and Adm. William F. Halsey's chief of staff, Miles Browning (fifty-third).[16]

Though Academy education suffered in comparison to that of contemporary universities, three facets influenced Sprague's career. Ever since American naval forces charged into Manila Bay to wrest Pacific holdings from Spain during the 1898 Spanish-American War, Japan had been considered America's primary threat in the Pacific. Annual war games and fleet exercises targeted Japan, and during the intervening years an American naval response evolved to counter any Japanese offensive. Most strategists regarded the Philippines as the likely Japanese objective and thus based their response upon such an assault. Since instruction at the Academy reflected this viewpoint, Sprague considered Japan a rival, a nation to be regarded with a high degree of suspicion. In the immense Pacific waters surrounding the Philippines was where the colossal naval actions of the future would be staged and where a naval officer could make his mark.[17]

The writings of Alfred Mahan emphasized the aggressive employment of sea power and provided a philosophy absorbed by Sprague and Academy graduates of his time. The eminent historian depicted the impact that naval power wielded on various world events, particularly the French Revolution, and he illustrated through historical examples how command of the sea effectively neutralized an enemy possessing superiority on land. Sprague, as well as graduates from Nimitz to classmate Forrest Sherman, employed Mahan's theories to guide their actions through the hectic World War II years.[18]

The third Academy influence on Sprague, one that would affect his career thirty years in the future, evolved from a controversy that nearly shattered the Navy. Following a splendid naval victory at Santiago, Cuba, during the Spanish-American War, supporters of the two principal American commanders on the scene, Commodore Winfield Scott Schley and Acting Rear Adm. William T. Sampson, claimed their man was responsible for the triumph. Recriminations bounded from side to side as each camp dug in to boost its candidate. Even an official Court of Inquiry failed to bridge the chasm that split the Navy. Soon, fueled by reports printed in the nation's newspapers, the Navy became a public laughingstock. Finally, President Theodore Roosevelt stepped in and clamped a lid on the bubbling cauldron by stifling further discussion of the matter.[19]

One Academy student hated watching his Navy openly air its dispute before the American public. Future Fleet Admiral Chester W. Nimitz, Class of 1905, vowed that if he ever became commander, he would never permit a similar controversy to shatter his forces' morale. In 1944, when presented with such a situation, Nimitz quickly suppressed excessive criticism of one commander and adulation of another. His steps affected the careers of both officers—William F. Halsey and Clifton A. F. Sprague.[20]

Sprague's quiet manner, which directly contrasted with the far more abrasive personalities that bounded about the Yard, made him one of the most popular members of his class. Called at various times "Peanut," "Liz," "Clifting," and "Ziegie" by his nickname-crazed Academy classmates, the small but powerful Sprague excelled in almost every sport, particularly base-ball, which he played each year. According to the 1918 Lucky Bag, Sprague's unique way of zigzagging down corridors with "his seagoing 'Rockport roll'" made him look "rough as a file, hard as nails," and probably gave rise to his most common nickname, Ziggy. Every portion of his five-foot nine-inch wiry frame appeared in motion, from his "tousled hair swinging fore and aft" to his legs and arms jutting wildly in all directions when in a hurry.[21]

Yet his classmates respected Sprague not so much for his physical talent and agility as for the inner qualities he possessed. He loved fast, furious verbal putdowns with opponents who thought they could deflect his cutting wit, contests he rarely lost. Often the defeated challenger walked away with-out realizing he had been targeted for Sprague's amusing game, for as the 1918 Lucky Bag stated, "His apparently harmless ejaculations contain 'hid-den' meanings" that only a close scrutiny of "that merry twinkle in his eye" could detect. "And such eyes!—fringed with long silken lashes that look innocent, but aren't." Friends at the Academy, and associates with whom he worked later in his career, loved being around his razor-sharp mind because they knew no matter what, they could count on departing with a smile.[22]

Sprague typified that Annapolis seaman they all hoped to be—physically able, quick-thinking, honorable, and above all, loyal to country, class, and service. Associates drew closer to him because he shared good times yet remarkably hid his bad times "beneath an exterior of happiness." Since they rarely saw him depressed, friends felt free to seek him out when going through rough times of their own. "All in all, Clifton is a living example of a true-blue comrade with all that term implies," summed the 1918 Lucky Bag. "A friend once, a friend always, particularly in need."[23]

Although Sprague's friendly nature endeared him to most classmates, that same quality tended to impede his rise to the highest leadership spots at the

Academy and later in his career. Sprague lacked a ruthless edge, that killer instinct that propelled many officers to the upper crust of command. He hated playing the "political" game of establishing ties with influential people and building a base of support with which he could advance his own career. A man's work spoke for the man, he believed, and rather than promote himself he allowed his record to present his case.[24]

While popular and funny with his male classmates, Sprague felt uncomfortable with women. Though dancing was popular, Sprague stayed away from the frequent hops and balls more often than he participated. During his final year at Annapolis, his classmates selected Sprague to the Hop Committee—the group overseeing dances—as a lark, since he never dated anyone.[25]

Sprague's correspondence during this stage of his life exhibits the subtle sense of humor that became a Sprague trademark. After receiving a care-package from his sister Dora, he started one early note to her with the teasing manner that many older brothers convey to their sisters. "Well, double-ugly, I got your dates, and they certainly were good." He followed that backhanded compliment by relating that out of "fear that you had them doped with gun cotton, I invited all the first classmen on the corridor in to taste them so we would all suffer." Like many students away from home, Sprague pled for "cake, doughnuts, etc. In fact, we invite your worst experiments for our sampling."[26]

In another letter to Dora, Sprague crafted a story to make his point rather than simply declare he wanted some candy. "Once there was a little homely girl who had a lot of candy, and this homely girl had a fine melagorgeous brother. The dear boy liked candy but the ugly girl never made any for him. Well this brother knew all the fairys [sic] so he sent a dozen to swipe the taste from double-ugly, so now all candy tastes like castor oil to her. Ain't that awful."[27]

As Sprague moved into his third year at the Academy, storm clouds from Europe cast an ominous shadow on the horizon. War had broken out in 1914, causing concern in neutral Washington, D.C., that the nation would be dragged into the affair by combatants from either the Central Powers (Germany, Austria, Italy) or the Allies (France, England, Russia). Slowly, President Woodrow Wilson's administration adopted military measures in case the predicament worsened.

Some of those steps affected Sprague's class. Sensing a need for additional naval officers in case of war, in February 1916, Congress increased the number of midshipmen from almost eleven hundred to over seventeen hundred. A gigantic naval appropriation six months later ignited a mad scramble to construct the ten battleships, six battle cruisers, fifty destroyers, and numerous other vessels needed in three short years. The United States, lagging far behind other naval powers when the war began, threw its incredible industrial might into closing the naval gap.[28]

Rarely has opportunity for a naval officer knocked so loudly as it did for Sprague and his classmates in 1916–17. With war a distinct possibility, the Class of 1918 might actually leave Annapolis and sail directly to a combat zone. No group of midshipmen had been that fortunate since the Spanish-American War eighteen years earlier. With a sense of urgency, eagerness, and high hopes, Sprague attacked his third-year classes.

Opportunity came much faster than he expected. In an effort to rush new officers to the fleet, the Class of 1917 was graduated in March rather than June. Sprague's class learned that it would graduate in September 1917, almost one full year ahead of schedule. To compensate for the loss of instructional time, drills were drastically reduced so that classes could be lengthened.[29]

References to possible entanglement in war dampened Sprague's usual lighthearted correspondence, though even there he injected levity. When Dora quizzed him on the 1917 Army-Navy football game, he explained he would not be there, and the contest might not be held, because of the European conflagration. "If we have a football game next year, I won't get to see it, you goof, since I'll be out in the fleet in command of the First Division."[30]

Despite emphatic warnings from President Wilson, Germany resumed unrestricted submarine warfare on the open seas. In retaliation, Wilson severed diplomatic relations with Germany on 3 February. An inflammatory German note to the Mexican government, seeking aid in the event of war with the United States in return for the land Mexico lost in the 1840s— Texas, New Mexico, and Arizona—further enraged the American populace. Passions bubbled over the walls of restraint during February and March when German submarines sank eight American vessels, including three on 18 March.[31]

President Wilson, who had hoped to avoid war, could hold back no longer. In one of American history's most famous speeches, on 2 April he asked Congress to declare war. "The world must be made safe for democracy," he uttered in a phrase destined to ring throughout the land. As the weary leader stepped down from the podium to the raucous cheers of assembled politicians, he pondered the coming years. "Think of what it was they were applauding. My message of today was a message of death for our young men. How strange it seems to applaud that." Four days later Congress overwhelmingly voted to begin hostilities with Germany.[32]

Sprague learned of war that same day when the Academy's superintendent, Capt. Edward W. Eberle, canceled spring athletic contests and posted an announcement that "a state of war exists between the United States and Germany. . . ." Sprague and the Class of 1918 were heading for war.[33]

For the normally calm, controlled Sprague, Annapolis must have been exceedingly attractive during these early emotional days of war fervor that swept the nation. He wrote his mother in May: "I imagine the excitement around Boston over the war is pretty great. This place here is about the calmest in the country." Other than "one whole company on duty for twenty-four hours," Academy life varied little from its already accelerated pace. He now commanded one machine gun squad posted to protect the Academy against any riot, he informed her, but quickly allayed any fears she might have by adding, half-jokingly, "as there are three Germans out in town—and they are under Secret Service observation, I don't guess there will be much trouble." Sprague ended his letter by switching to a lighter topic—that Annapolis females had vowed to salute every man in uniform—then exhibited the deep love and dependency he carried for his mother with words that could have been penned by a grade-school child. "I hope you become a nurse, and I am shot in the back, so you can nurse me. I'd even let you feed me chicken with spuds and peas and ice cream." The future admiral closed with "Yum, yum. With love, Clif." Underneath his signature, Sprague added in giant capitals the letters "U.S.A."—totally made out of hand-drawn stars.[34]

Shortly before graduation, a controversy angered Sprague's entire class. With a headlong rush to prepare additional naval officers in full swing, the Navy Department expanded the naval reserve program. If all progressed as planned, the initial contingent of almost a thousand reserve officers would graduate from the abbreviated sessions and join the fleet before the Class of 1918, meaning that Sprague and his classmates would be shoved down a thousand numbers in the seniority system. Such fury arose from the midshipmen that their graduation, at first scheduled for September 1917, was advanced to 28 June.[35]

Thus, on that June day, Sprague and 198 classmates received their diplomas at Dahlgren Hall after listening to speeches by Superintendent Eberle and Secretary of the Navy Josephus Daniels. Jocko Clark, Forrest Sherman, and Thomas Sprague, among others, joined Sprague in embarking upon careers that spiraled to the Navy's upper echelon. Now earning the annual sum of $1,500, the untested ensign departed Annapolis and headed for his first assignment, a duty sure to challenge him in ways Annapolis never could.[36]

→ CHAPTER THREE ←

"A Pleasure to Serve"

Ensign Sprague barely had enough time to organize belongings and say good-bye to family before heading to Tampico, Mexico, where he boarded his first ship as a naval officer. Though not as glamorous as the battleships that most Academy classmates preferred, the gunboat *Wheeling* actually benefited Sprague more than duty on a larger ship. A capital ship may have appeal, but Sprague would have been only one of many officers, each vying for distinction as a leader of men. On the *Wheeling,* where only nine officers oversaw the operations of ten chief petty officers and 153 men, Sprague had an easier time gaining recognition and learning the intricacies of command. In a little over two years on the gunboat, he acquired experience in four separate posts—gunnery, communications, navigation, and executive officer.[1]

The *Wheeling*'s main purpose was to escort supply and troop ships to the fighting areas. Her main foe—German U-boats—had terrorized European waters since the war's start, but their effectiveness had been dramatically reduced by the successful implementation of the convoy system. The 189-foot-long gunboat brought six 4-inch guns, four 6-pounders, two 1-pounders, and one Colt machine gun to the line. Boasting a top speed of just under thirteen knots, the *Wheeling* had earlier supported American troops fighting in the Boxer Rebellion and in the Philippine insurrection.[2]

Three of Sprague's classmates also started their careers on board ships providing escort duties. Jocko Clark and Tommy Sprague served on cruisers, while the classmate who eventually rose highest in the Navy—Forrest Sherman—like Sprague saw action in a gunboat. The four were fortunate they had graduated so quickly from the Academy, then headed directly to a combat zone that, for those who proved their mettle, was the chief avenue of advancement in the military.

The *Wheeling,* with Sprague on board, left Tampico on 10 July and headed for New Orleans for repairs and supplies. After two weeks in dry dock, the gunboat sailed east to Key West, Florida, then up the Atlantic coast to Hampton Roads, Virginia. Two days later—8 August—the ship's skipper, Comdr. Edward Watson, pointed the *Wheeling* across the Atlantic toward Ponta Delgada, Azores, 750 miles due west of Portugal.[3]

After two days at sea, the *Wheeling* returned to the United States after the edges of a hurricane snapped off both top masts, damaging every boat and a few of the guns. Though no men were lost, the *Wheeling* required eighteen days of repair at the New York Navy Yard, during which time Comdr. H. W. Osterhauss relieved Commander Watson.

The repaired gunboat headed for Delaware on 29 August, where the destroyers *Whipple* and *Truxtun* joined her for the trip across the Atlantic. Finally, on 16 September, Sprague and the *Wheeling* arrived at Ponta Delgada to begin seven months of convoying ships between the Azores and the Madeira Islands off the northwest coast of Africa. The *Wheeling* never engaged in any action during this segment and rarely used her guns except for practice, but the monotonous duty provided Sprague a chance to get accustomed to life on board a ship at sea and begin learning how to lead men under his supervision.[4]

Sprague's style of leadership quickly appeared. The men warmed to his smile and soft nature, which permitted them to perform their duties without constant harassment. They learned that Ensign Sprague treated them like men rather than as underlings to boss around. Sprague based his leadership on respect rather than fear, a technique that produced results, since he received high marks from his superiors and rose to lieutenant (jg) then to lieutenant during the war.

The men could approach him and, at least in one instance, gently tease him without fear of disapproval. At this time the youthful-looking Sprague attempted to grow a mustache, but he could cultivate nothing more than a sprinkling of light-hued hair that hardly inspired awe among the crew. One stout seaman sporting a bushy mustache, Quartermaster Woods, used this to the men's advantage whenever Sprague tried to pound home some deficiency to the division. In the midst of Sprague's lecture to his assembled men, Woods would suddenly ask permission to grow a mustache, almost ensuring that the now-smiling ensign could no longer maintain a stern attitude.[5]

Sprague experienced his first combat action in May 1918, when the *Wheeling* joined the American Mediterranean Patrol Squadron based at Gibraltar. As the ship escorted a convoy off the northern coast of Algeria in the predawn hours of 11 May, the German submarine *U-52* crept up and launched a torpedo into the side of the Norwegian vessel *Susetta Fraisinette,* located about thirteen hundred yards off the *Wheeling's* starboard quarter. Though Sprague did not actually participate in any offensive action, since the *Wheeling* was ordered to remain with the convoy while other ships chased the U-boat and rescued survivors, he had witnessed the black side of war for the first time.[6]

He received a more complete introduction six days later when German U-boats descended on his convoy. At 1848 hours, the British vessel *Sculptor* took a torpedo amidships from *U-39,* which caused her to veer directly into the convoy. The *Wheeling* began corraling the dispersed convoy, but turned to the offensive when a lookout spotted a submarine on her starboard bow at 1915. Rushing to the area, the *Wheeling* dropped a calcium light to mark the sighting, then dropped six depth charges in a sweeping arc about the light. Two other escorts also dropped depth charges, but no debris floated to the surface to indicate a kill. The next day, however, the three American escorts seemed to receive confirmation their attacks had succeeded when the damaged *U-39* limped into port.[7]

The *Wheeling* charged after her second U-boat within an hour when at 2016 another explosion rent the night behind her. She turned sharply to aid the stricken vessel, the British steamer *Mavisbrook,* but had to slow down to avoid crashing into debris from the ship and running over floating survivors. Since her primary responsibility lay in protecting the convoy, the *Wheeling* could not stop to pick up the survivors, but men on the ship tossed overboard a large number of life rafts and life belts. Sprague, bothered that his ship had to steam by helpless victims, took some solace that the *Wheeling* signaled another ship to come to their aid.[8]

The *Wheeling's* long day was not yet over. Shortly before midnight a third U-boat approached the convoy. Ships scattered and escorts darted after the submarine, but the *Wheeling* remained at its station to safeguard the convoy's port flank.[9]

Sprague remained on escort duty with the *Wheeling* until early June, when the ship entered dry dock at the Gibraltar Navy Yard for three weeks of repairs. This gave Sprague a chance to unwind from the constant tension of serving on board a floating target for U-boats. He visited cities in Portugal, Spain, and Italy and purchased gifts he mailed to his mother and other family members. Though Sprague enjoyed his respite from the war, the 17 May incident where his ship had to pass by survivors from the torpedoed *Mavisbrook* so nagged at him that he wrote of his anguish to his sister Dora. "He wrote that they could do little more than throw things overboard for the men to cling to," explained Dora. "That bothered him a lot." [10]

Sprague served out the war escorting supply vessels about the Mediterranean. Monotonous stretches of routine duty were frequently interrupted by real or supposed submarine sightings, but his ship avoided serious damage. U-boats sank twenty-two merchant ships on Sprague's twenty convoy trips, so there was always plenty of danger around, but the *Wheeling* was never officially credited with a kill. Doubt even shrouded her role in damaging *U-39* when pilots of two British aircraft claimed they hit the submarine during an 18 May attack. [11]

Sprague remained with the *Wheeling* until October 1919, when the ship was decommissioned and his first naval posting officially ended. Two years in a war zone provided the young officer the valuable opportunity to find out how well he could lead men during the stress of battle, and Sprague illustrated his competence under fire. He made such an impact on his men that twenty-five years later, one former *Wheeling* seaman wrote to then-Vice Admiral Sprague, "It would be a pleasure indeed to serve again under your command." [12]

Sprague remained with the *Wheeling* until October 1919, when he became the reserve commanding officer on board the destroyer *Manley.* Two months later he joined other officers to begin training a crew for a new battleship, the *Tennessee,* and assumed the duties of the sixth Broadside Battery Officer upon the ship's commissioning. For almost a year, Sprague supervised the crew of the sixth mounted gun emplacement along the battleship's side. [13]

But a new horizon beckoned. Though battleships remained the linchpin of the Navy, an infant arm began attracting a few hardy souls, summoned by the call of adventure and the excitement of challenging an untested frontier. Lieutenant Sprague turned his gaze toward aviation.

→ CHAPTER FOUR ←

The Emerging Commander

Just as Sprague entered the Academy at the height of his nation's renewed interest in naval affairs, his introduction into naval aviation in 1920 was equally well timed. Struggling to overcome an ignored infancy and haphazard growth, aviation established itself in the 1920s and 1930s as a permanent feature in the Navy's arsenal. Lieutenant Sprague, barely three full years removed from his academic training at Annapolis, recognized before most of his classmates that aviation offered a speedy path to higher command and he became embroiled in every aspect of this thrilling yet dangerous field. Starting as a student pilot in Pensacola, Florida, by the end of the 1930s he had risen to his own seagoing command and had unmistakably linked his name with that of naval aviation.

Lieutenant Sprague reported to Pensacola on 3 December 1920, carrying orders for duties "involving actual flying in aircraft including dirigibles, balloons and airplanes. . . ." He joined thirty-three other student aviators, including Academy classmate and close friend Thomas Sprague, in getting an initial glimpse at their new surroundings.[1]

Eventually to expand into an important hub of aviation, the former naval base at Pensacola had been reopened in 1914 by Lt. John H. Towers and Capt. Washington Irving Chambers, two of the Navy's aviation pioneers, who believed Pensacola's warm climate and large, sheltered bay provided an ideal spot for year-round flying and experimentation.[2]

Sprague spent almost half his time in the classroom, listening to instructors as they guided the students through the intricacies of flight. The remainder of the time was divided between hangars, where Sprague learned to take apart and reassemble the planes and their engines, and the air. Like all students, Sprague learned to fly in seaplanes and soloed for the first time only five weeks after arriving at Pensacola when he piloted an N-9 craft for twenty minutes on 11 January 1921. Torpedo planes, dive-bombers, and observation planes came next, followed by instruction with flying boats and fighters.

Since planes carried few instruments, Sprague learned to fly by "feel," to estimate speed by how the controls responded or by the sounds the wires emitted. Sprague mapped routes according to known landmarks and maintained a level course by watching the horizon. After a rigorous eight months of training, Sprague earned the designation Naval Aviator No. 2934 on 11 August 1921 and joined the sparse ranks of approximately three hundred active naval officers who knew how to fly.[3]

Sprague loved everything about the air, from listening to the engines roar to life to feeling the wind swirl about his head in the open cockpit. His daughter Patricia recalled that her father "was absolutely nuts about flying" and was drawn by the spirit of adventure attached to it. "Sprague saw right away that planes were special," explained Daniel Vaughan. "He knew they were the future and he wanted to be a part of it."[4]

The neophyte pilot logged fifteen flights within two months of receiving his certificate, including a five-hour fifty-minute jaunt from Charleston, South Carolina, to Fort Lauderdale, Florida. He became so proficient at flying that his superiors named him commanding officer of Squadron 3 at Pensacola.[5]

Sprague climbed into his aircraft fully understanding that in these adolescent days of flying, serious injury or sudden, violent death loomed as distinct possibilities. A pilot could easily soar above the clouds, but he could just as quickly crash from a mid-flight malfunction. Unreliable planes and unpredictable weather challenged the pilot's skills and transformed routine flights into frightening journeys. Though aviation had progressed from those earliest days when undertakers eerily parked their hearses at the edges of runways, crashes, injuries, and death lurked in the shadows.[6]

"The flying machine of fiction may be a very formidable monster, but the real thing is feeble enough, the sport of wind and a hundred mischances," summed a 1910 aviation article about open-cockpit planes assembled from wood, wire, and fabric. Many people, in and out of the military, considered aviators crazy. Sprague learned that while in flight a wise pilot always searched the ground for level plots of turf upon which to land in case of emergency. When, not if, a cohort died in a crash, Sprague and other aviators blamed the fatal accident on pilot error rather than admit what they knew to be true—that the violent end most likely occurred because of the flimsy craft.[7]

Sprague's Flight Log reflects the hazards he faced. Less than two months after he soloed, Sprague recorded two flights and gave their purposes as "To Crash of 855" and "To Crash Lt. Sloman." On 17 January 1923 he brought down his own plane because of "Forced landing."[8]

His first serious brush with death occurred in the fall of 1922, when he and a junior officer flew from Washington, D.C., to Providence, Rhode Island, to visit his family. Sprague's father and sister drove the aviators back to the landing strip, which was little more than an ordinary field. With the younger officer at the controls, the plane lifted off, then careened to the ground in an ear-splitting crash. Though neither was injured, Sprague, as senior officer, was responsible for the badly damaged plane and had to answer to an investigative board, which eventually cleared him of all wrongdoing. Sprague "was very upset" at the crash scene, according to Dorothea, who maintained her composure until a few hours later when "I couldn't stop trembling."[9]

The death of one of Sprague's closest friends in a plane crash less than one year later so affected him that, according to Dorothea, he "cried like a baby." Though Sprague lived with the daily possibility of death, as do most military personnel, he never forgot that human beings flew planes, manned ships, aimed weapons. Some commanders forget that their decisions in battle translate into life or death for large numbers of people, but Sprague always kept this in mind.[10]

In the late 1940s, Sprague examined his aging Pensacola class picture and noted that eight of the thirty-four classmates, almost one-fourth of the group, had died in aviation accidents. Insurance companies either flatly denied coverage or charged such exorbitant prices that much of a pilot's flight pay was used up. Sprague accepted these risks simply because, like most aviators, he loved to fly.[11]

Sprague battled adverse elements on the ground as well. After a promising start that included a 1914 proclamation by Secretary of the Navy Josephus Daniels that "Aeroplanes are now considered one of the arms of the

Fleet, the same as battleships, destroyers, submarines, and cruisers," naval aviation stumbled on difficult times. From a wartime high of three thousand officers and thirty thousand enlisted men, the naval air arm plummeted 90 percent by the time Sprague earned his pilot's certification in 1921. Bitter criticism erupted from older, conservative admirals weaned on battleships who resented the appearance of any new force that threatened their long-standing dominance of the Navy's hierarchy. Chief of Naval Operations Adm. William S. Benson dismissed aviation as "just a lot of noise" and appointed a lowly lieutenant (jg) to oversee its affairs.[12]

A siegelike atmosphere surrounded airmen who, having shared the dangers of their occupation, banded together in a sort of occupational elite that extended even to their families. Years later, his daughter Courtney remembered Sprague's pride in aviation and added, "I had the feeling that 'we' were the best, that naval aviators couldn't be beat."[13]

Naval aviators frequently had to defend themselves from people who were angry over the intrusion of something new and strange to their world or wanted all Army and Navy air components merged into one air force. Most naval aviators, including Sprague, argued that only a naval aviator understood problems unique to the sea and to fleet maneuvers.[14]

"The antagonism to aviation has become so intensely acute that I am more disgusted than ever," wrote Rear Adm. William A. Moffett in 1929. Aviators longed for the chance to prove the offensive capabilities of the air arm and show doubters that aviation offered the path to the future.[15]

"A naval air service must be established, capable of accompanying and operating with the fleet in all parts of the world," urged a 1919 Naval General Board report supporting the development of a strong naval air arm. Two years later the Navy created the Bureau of Aeronautics under the able Admiral Moffett. Additional impetus came in 1925 when a special naval board recommended an increased number of airplanes, the construction of an aircraft carrier, and more thorough aviation training for Naval Academy students. Another board suggested that naval aviators receive a higher proportion of air commands, such as aircraft carriers, and positions on command staffs than they currently held, moves that were implemented by the 1926 Naval Aircraft Act.[16]

Besieged by activists for a united air force on one side and dwindling military budgets on the other, naval aviators like Sprague had to do what they could to promote their cause. At least twice—in April 1924 and October 1925—Sprague's Log records airspeed tests at Anacostia, where numerous distance and speed records were shattered by Navy pilots. Air races captivated audiences while gaining publicity for naval aviation and helped spur revolutionary developments in engine and plane design. Sprague participated as a backup pilot in one race—the 1925 Detroit *News* Air Transport Trophy Race held at Mitchell Field in Long Island, New York.[17]

Sprague's most valuable contribution in promoting aviation occurred during 1929–31 when he returned to the Naval Academy as a flight instructor. Concerned over a lack of knowledge about aviation among Academy graduates, the Secretary of the Navy ordered that midshipmen receive basic flight instruction. For two years Sprague taught flying to hundreds of students, who represented the coming wave of officers, and helped solidify a spot for naval aviation alongside surface ships and submarines as an integral portion of the Navy.[18]

Comprising aircraft squadron VN-8 D5, nine officers and forty-two enlisted men, commanded by Lt. Comdr. D. C. Ramsey and executive officer Sprague, reported for duty in the first week of June 1929. Squadron personnel were quartered aboard the *Reina Mercedes,* a captured relic from the Spanish-American War that normally housed midshipmen serving confinement as punishment for various infractions.[19]

On Monday, 10 June, Ramsey and Sprague welcomed the first twenty of four hundred eighty midshipmen from the Academy's second class (junior year) scheduled to be trained that summer. Ramsey assigned four midshipmen to each of the five aviators, including himself, Sprague, and Lt. (jg) J. C. Waldron, who would later fly to fame as squadron commander of Torpedo 8 at the Battle of Midway, where he led fifteen planes in a suicidal attack on Japanese carriers that helped determine the battle's outcome.[20]

Sprague assembled his four midshipmen at Santee Landing near Luce Hall at 0750 on Tuesday for two days of training. For an hour he explained the basics of flight to the midshipmen, then spent one hour in the air. He repeated this process with a second group of four from 1000 until 1210. Though no midshipman was permitted to actually pilot the aircraft, Sprague gave each student exposure to four key duties—navigator, observer, gunner, and mechanic. Sprague ran a new group of midshipmen through the identical schedule on Thursday and Friday, then repeated the process throughout the summer. Within two months, all the midshipmen left Santee Landing with an increased understanding of aviation. Sprague and the others educated future officers to the possibilities of aviation and paved the way for increased acceptance of that field among Navy circles. Results two years later showed the program's effectiveness. Of the four hundred graduating midshipmen, more than two hundred volunteered for aviation training at Pensacola, a spectacular improvement over recent years.[21]

One of Sprague's students would later reenter his life in dramatic fashion. Capt. William Halsey, stationed on board the *Reina Mercedes* until June 1930 as its commanding officer, constantly pestered Ramsey and Sprague to take him into the air. They accommodated him whenever a chance arose, and soon "I was eating, drinking, and breathing aviation," wrote Halsey. "I flew as often as Duke or 'Ziggy' Sprague would give me a ride." Sprague's Flight Log, for instance, indicates he flew Halsey to Norfolk and back on 25 June 1929, a total of three hours and twenty minutes together in the air. Teacher Sprague and student Halsey had few subsequent encounters until October 1944 off Leyte, where Halsey's debatable actions endangered thirteen ships and thousands of men commanded by then-Rear Admiral Sprague.[22]

Especially during the 1920s, Sprague alternated field assignments with duties as a test pilot and in research and experimentation for the Navy's pride and joy—its powerful new aircraft carriers. From March 1922 to November 1923 Sprague flew aircraft with VS-1 Aircraft Squadron, Atlantic Fleet, where he directed scouting functions while based on the seaplane tender *Wright*. He followed that with two and a half years at the Anacostia Naval Air Station, just outside Washington, D.C., where he served as operations officer and executive officer.[23]

These two decades saw incredible, fast-paced movement in naval research and experimentation, even though military budgets stagnated. Innovations appeared with stunning regularity, often replacing equipment that had barely moved off the planning board. Creativity and utility ruled the times, and Sprague contributed to each.

Sprague's experimental and scientific research work, carried out chiefly as a test pilot, helped produce advancements for aircraft carriers. While working at the Naval Aircraft Factory in Philadelphia in 1923, Sprague contributed to developing aircraft carrier catapult systems. His more important work, however, came with inventor Carl Norden of bombsight fame while Sprague was stationed at the Hampton Roads Naval Air Station, Virginia, from March 1926 to February 1928. Eager to possess an effective method of landing airplanes on relatively small aircraft carrier flight decks, the Navy asked Norden to improve its current arresting gear. At first aircraft carriers had thick ropes stretched across the decks and weighed down with sandbags, but this proved ineffective. With Sprague's assistance, Norden developed the Mk-1 arresting gear for the *Lexington* and *Saratoga,* then under construction. The precursor to the hydraulic arresting gear, which the Navy eventually adopted, Norden's Mk-1 relied on cross-deck wires to snare the plane and longitudinal wires to prevent it from swerving from one side to the other.[24]

Sprague complemented Norden's laboratory work by testing various arresting gear designs on experimental flight decks. Entries such as "Landed on deck," "Practice Precision Landings," and "Taxiing on Exp. Deck" dominate his Flight Log for 1926–28, as Sprague tested a succession of ideas that flowed from Norden's mind. While Sprague's work helped save airmen's lives by making carrier landings safer, his test work, which produced numerous sudden, jarring halts as his aircraft hit the wires, inflicted permanent dental damage. Sprague suffered from what was called "instrument face"— loosened teeth and a flattened nose. His daughter Patricia remembered her father experiencing such "terrible trouble with his teeth that he ate a lot of sardines." Eventually, Sprague had to replace most of his teeth.[25]

A number of sources through the years credit Sprague with developing arresting gear, starting with wartime newspaper interviews and continuing to as recent a source as Kenneth Poolman's 1988 book, *Allied Escort Carriers in World War Two in Action,* which stated that Sprague "invented the flight deck arrestor gear system which had saved the lives of many aviators." Government records are less clear on the issue. A biographical file in the Naval Historical Center declares that Sprague "had additional duty in connection with the arresting gear on the landing platforms of the aircraft carriers *Lexington* and *Saratoga*," while Clark Reynolds stated in his 1978 book, *Famous American Admirals,* that Sprague served at Hampton Roads "for developing arresting gear for the Navy's new aircraft carriers." Sprague never boasted of his role, so it is no surprise that doubt exists as to his precise contribution. What is certain is that Sprague, at a minimum, played an active part in developing early arresting gear systems and deserves partial acclaim for the gear's eventual effectiveness.[26]

The knowledge that he helped improve pilot safety for fellow aviators would suffice for Sprague. At the same time, Sprague's reticence to publicize his own accomplishments hurt his career. If an officer wanted to rise to higher command, he had to promote himself. Sprague refused to engage in something he considered inappropriate and thus avoided playing the political game. Instead, he allowed his work to do his speaking.

Sprague's activities as a test pilot spoke loud and clear. An aviator did not survive the ordeals of flight's early days, let alone those of a test pilot, without excellent instincts and quick reflexes. Sprague was blessed with both and they, as well as a small measure of luck, allowed him to develop trust in his skills and judgment. No room existed in those years for doubts or second-guessing. A pilot had to believe he could cope with any emergency in the air. Sprague emerged unharmed because he knew in a tough spot he could rely on certain talents.

Near the end of the 1920s, Sprague began a series of assignments that gradually gave him greater responsibilities and led to his first commands. In early 1928 he received orders to join the new *Lexington* as flight deck officer. With a 36,000-ton displacement, 180,000-horsepower engines, an 888-foot flight deck capable of handling seventy-two aircraft, eight 8-inch guns, a crew of over two thousand, and a top speed of 33 knots, the *Lexington* combined power with grace. Any aviator worth his salt longed for an assignment on board the *Lexington,* where he could work with torpedo planes, dive-bombers, and fighters in stretching the offensive limits of aircraft carriers and test theories of carrier warfare never before implemented.[27]

In carrying out his responsibilities as flight deck officer, and then as assistant air officer, Sprague accumulated a solid core of knowledge about managing an aircraft carrier. Sprague coordinated aircraft movement on the flight deck, a difficult task with the small space available and the variety of tasks assigned his aircraft. All planes had to be shifted aft for launchings, then forward for recoveries or refueling. Since any movement of planes could hamper other operations if not done properly, Sprague had to plan each shift carefully to minimize disruptions and to ensure that the proper aircraft remained available for emergencies. To help organize the frequent changes, Sprague used a scale-model flight deck and scale-model planes set up in the Ready Room.[28]

During his year with the *Lexington,* Sprague joined the elite of young aviators whose work established the frontiers of naval aviation and helped create tactics that would be used against Japan in the 1940s. In June 1928, after the *Lexington* established a new speed record from San Francisco to Hawaii of seventy-two hours and thirty-four minutes, Sprague participated in an exercise that foreshadowed the 1941 attack on Pearl Harbor. With aggressive Rear Adm. Joseph "Bull" Reeves and his flag on board, the *Lexington* carefully approached Hawaii at night and, when 250 miles away, launched her planes for a dawn attack that stunned the surprised defenders on Oahu. Thirteen years later, Sprague remembered this exercise as his ship bobbed in the quiet December waters of Pearl Harbor.[29]

The following year Sprague participated in Fleet Problem IX, where all three carriers—*Langley, Lexington,* and *Saratoga*—executed an attack on the Panama Canal. Sprague and other aviators looked to this exercise as a chance to prove that naval aviation could deliver an offensive punch of its own. One advocate, Eugene E. Wilson, recalled that "we felt a certain sense of urgency; now was the time to show the battle wagons what we could do, and thus 'sell aviation to the fleet.'"[30]

Sprague's *Lexington* and the *Langley* defended the Canal as part of the Blue Fleet while the *Saratoga,* hosting Rear Admiral Reeves's flag, operated with the attacking Black Fleet. After receiving permission from his commander to operate the *Saratoga* independently from the main force, Reeves took the carrier a thousand miles south of the Canal to the Galapagos Islands to elude the opposing Blue Fleet. On 25 January 1929 he turned north and approached to within 150 miles of the Canal, where he launched sixty-nine aircraft for a dawn attack on the locks at Pedro Miguel and Miraflores. While Army defenders ate their breakfast, the surprise assault swept in and succeeded in theoretically destroying their target.[31]

Carrier tactics received a critical boost with Reeves's stunning strike. The commander of the Black Fleet, Adm. W. V. Pratt, praised the carrier's assault as "the most brilliantly conceived and most effectively executed naval operation in our history," and switched his flag to the *Saratoga* for the ride home as a way of honoring the outstanding achievement.[32]

In December 1931 Sprague, a lieutenant commander since June 1930, took command of VP-8 Patrol Squadron, a scout squadron attached to the seaplane tender *Wright* at the Norfolk Navy Yard. The following April he led the squadron on the lengthy trip down to the Panama Canal for duty in defending that vital waterway. A. Lincoln Baird, the officer on board Sprague's plane who handled navigation charts, possessed a deep respect for charts, which stemmed from his days as assistant navigator with the battleship *Colorado.* Baird always carefully marked the charts and then "folded and unfolded them the same way with due regard to creases." Baird recalled, however, handing Sprague "a chart carefully opened to the pertinent location, and he'd hand it back all rumpled up like a piece of junk." Sprague's main task—safely flying the squadron thousands of miles across water and land to Coco Solo—occupied his attention, not whether a chart was neatly folded.[33]

Since VP-8 was Sprague's first command, we get a glimpse of how the emerging commander handled situations that any successful leader had to master. From the start, Sprague placed a premium on practice and preparation. According to squadron member E. H. Eckelmeyer, who would also rise to rear admiral, "as soon as we were settled" on the base, Sprague ordered gunnery practice, though his was only a temporary post until the regular naval defense squadrons returned from a fleet problem.[34]

One day during such practice, a mishap almost occurred. The squadron shooting area stretched over the Caribbean, just to the western side of the Canal entrance, and required planes to fly directly in front of an Army coastal artillery fort. The local Army commander alerted Sprague that his artillery would be shooting on this particular day and that the naval aviators should avoid his fort's vicinity. Sprague passed the warning to his squadron.

After Eckelmeyer completed his turn at the gunnery area, Sprague ordered him to his office. Without asking any questions, Sprague snapped, "You flew directly in front of the batteries at the fort despite their warning to stay clear. I want you to give me a written statement of your activities."

Eckelmeyer knew he had not been the guilty party, but returned to his quarters to pen a reply. Just before he began, Eckelmeyer glanced at the "yellow sheet," a form listing any nonworking parts of the aircraft as well as takeoff and landing times. This form proved that Eckelmeyer had not jumped into the air until fifteen minutes after the plane had erroneously flown past the Army artillery.

Eckelmeyer hastened back to Sprague's office with the form. "Ziggie gave a big gulp," related Eckelmeyer, "glared at me again and, without further words, dismissed me. He knew I was absolved but now had to look for another culprit."

Sprague realized he had accused the wrong officer. Instead of taking out his frustrations on the young subordinate or saving face with a blustery harangue, Sprague quietly dropped the matter.[35]

Eckelmeyer remembered Sprague as "a serious man who didn't say much. He seemed to be always quietly thinking about whatever was on his mind. He wasn't the sort of man we junior officers could get very close to, so we had to watch our p's and q's. We didn't fear him, we just respected him and tried to do what he wanted. He was a fine skipper and we all liked him. I'm proud to have served with him." Baird summed up Sprague as "very fair. If there was a difficult job to be done, he would do it first."[36]

Even when off duty, Sprague thought and observed. During one visit to Sprague's home, Daniel Vaughan watched his father-in-law stare out the front window for a few minutes. Vaughan wondered what had intrigued Sprague because nothing but a few cars had sped by the house. He was amused when Sprague turned to him and said, "Do you realize that seven

Chevrolets in a row just went by?" As Vaughan stated, Sprague's "mind was working on something all the time and was quietly observing people all the time." [37]

Sprague received his first glimpse of a post that would later play an important part in his career when the squadron was transferred to Pearl Harbor in 1933. He kicked off his new assignment in impressive fashion with a 2,650-mile round-trip flight to Midway Island in February 1934. While top-ranking naval officers cruised on board the *Wright* and the seaplane tenders *Avocet* and *Pelican* patrolled the expected route in case of mechanical difficulties, Sprague guided three seaplanes of VP-8 from Hawaii to the small speck of dirt over thirteen hundred miles to the northwest. He became the first naval aviator to complete the trip, which lasted close to thirteen hours.[38]

As senior squadron commander, Sprague bore the responsibility for preparing and dispensing operational orders covering search and patrol for any local war games. During one of the first such exercises after his arrival, Sprague released orders written by Baird, who was Sprague's operations officer. A storm of protest quickly arose from other squadron commanders since Baird's apparently vague orders caused confusion among the aviators. Baird was then completing a correspondence course on strategy and tactics from the Naval War College, which Sprague used as a way out. He gave each officer the same reply—that the orders had been prepared by a War College student and they would be corrected shortly. This ruse deflected the steamed commanders from pursuing the matter and allowed Baird to breathe a sigh of relief as he watched each commander depart "without a further word." [39]

New orders returned Sprague to Norfolk as air operations officer in April 1934. A young ensign who commanded a naval reserve squadron at Norfolk, Dorris Gurley, heard disconcerting rumors about the toughness of the incoming officer and wondered how the initial meeting with Sprague would go. His fears evaporated when Sprague gathered his officers and, rather than change everything around to his own liking, asked each man what Sprague could do to improve conditions at the station. A relieved group left Sprague's office with far more confidence in their new boss.[40]

Sprague's responsibilities as air operations officer ranged from the complicated coordination of heavily congested air traffic to relatively minor affairs involving public relations with the nearby community. Within a few weeks of Sprague's arrival his commanding officer, Capt. Aubrey Fitch (who would also achieve fame in the Pacific), handed Sprague the enormous task of coordinating the arrival, servicing, and departure of numerous aircraft carrier squadrons flying in from the Fleet Air Department on their way to San Diego. For almost three months, Sprague opened the field, its hangars and service personnel, and barracks to pilots swarming in from the fleet. Overworked mechanics labored nonstop in crowded hangars to service the aircraft, whose pilots impatiently demanded takeoff or landing times at the inundated field. In that short span, Sprague coordinated the movement of more squadrons operating from a single naval air station than had ever been accommodated before.

Such a strain can cause short tempers and low morale, but Sprague pulled it off. The commander, Aircraft, Battle Force, sent a letter to Captain Fitch praising the entire base for its "excellent operating effectiveness and the high state of morale of that Station under the strain of very unusual requirements." Fitch, in turn, congratulated Sprague for his "careful planning, sound judgment and efficient administration," and for diplomatically dealing with countless fleet aviators with a "ready spirit of cooperation" and "tactful discretion." [41]

In 1937, Sprague received his largest responsibility to date when he was posted as air officer on board a newly constructed aircraft carrier, the *Yorktown*. In this duty, Sprague controlled five divisions of men and joined the select group of senior officers who served as chief advisers to the commanding officer (the executive officer, navigator, gunnery officer, communications officer, and engineer officer were the others). [42]

"Sprague's main duties would cover everything that pertained to the air on board the ship," explained Adm. James Russell, USN (Ret.), the *Yorktown*'s flight deck officer under Sprague. "Since the main purpose of the carrier was to fly airplanes, that made his job an important post." Sprague commanded all aircraft on or near the carrier, and in that role he had to ensure proper servicing, arming, and fueling of planes; coordinate thorough and clear mission plans for the pilots; direct fighter defense of the carrier; and organize launches and recoveries. He had at his disposal a squadron each of fighters, bombers, scout planes, and torpedo planes—as well as numerous pilots and service personnel. [43]

In November 1937, Sprague piloted the first two landings ever made on the *Yorktown*, partly for the honor, but mainly because he did not want his men to carry out a mission he had not completed. Admiral Russell recalled when the ship's hangar catapult, which could propel planes to either port or starboard directly through the hangar door opening, had to be tested. "With the ship moving ahead, the plane would go from a still-air situation into a crosswind as it emerged from the barn door on the side, and we didn't know what effect this would have on the machine. Ziggy could have ordered someone else to do it, but he wanted to be the first one off."

As officers and men checked the catapult, Sprague climbed into the aircraft and announced he was ready to be shot off. However, the catapult officer had not completed his check below, and when Sprague's craft sped into the air, the officer stormed up and demanded who ordered the launch.

"When he signaled he was ready to go," explained Russell, "and I knew we were not ready for him, I said to myself, 'I hope everything holds together,' because Ziggy didn't realize we were still checking the catapult. But it worked fine.

"Ziggy could sympathize with the troops and was a good shipmate. He did not want any of us to do something that he had not done. We appreciated that."[44]

Along with her sister ship, the *Enterprise,* the *Yorktown* conducted a series of Atlantic Ocean maneuvers stretching from Virginia to the coast of Cuba into early 1939, hoping to demonstrate an offensive capability for naval aviation. In February the *Yorktown* participated in Fleet Problem XX in the Caribbean, where she successfully practiced tactics in convoy escort, antisubmarine defense, and offensive air thrusts. These operations gave Sprague experience for similar missions he would later supervise against Japan and Germany.[45]

Adm. George W. Anderson, USN (Ret.), the landing signal officer under Sprague at the time, recalled one hectic day in the South Atlantic when Sprague juggled seventy-five airborne planes as deteriorating weather set in. In stormy seas that swayed the flight deck sixty-five feet up and down, Sprague, worried over his pilots' safety, lit cigarette after cigarette to relieve the tension. "It was the only time I saw one person smoking three cigarettes at one time," related Anderson. Fortunately, every pilot landed without mishap.[46]

Anderson claimed that the *Yorktown* possessed "a splendid" air department because of Sprague, who dished out a wide range of responsibilities to his officers. "He gave us his full support, but held us fully accountable to produce good results."[47]

Russell marveled that Sprague could achieve results without losing his composure. "He never had to yell at people to get the job done. He was very reasonable and a smooth operator. Even though I never saw him get mad, there was no question who was in charge of the air department. We liked him very much."

Russell observed two other qualities at which Sprague excelled. "He informed himself on *everything*. Sprague was a very thorough guy. I can't remember any time we had something to do when I thought he was doing the wrong thing. He always seemed to do what was right." Sprague also mastered the trick of cultivating familiarity with the men he led while maintaining authority. Russell mentioned that although Sprague was not a great conversationalist nor a person who easily engaged in small talk, he employed a sense of humor and was "very close to being a jolly fellow. We knew, though, he was the boss."

Russell gave an example of Sprague's quiet humor. During one stint, Sprague was nominated by his fellow officers to handle the food budget, which was not a position many officers eagerly sought. With a wry smile, Sprague announced to his compatriots, "You're not going to like this, but I love rice." Then followed such a steady stream of rice dinners, pud- dings, and casseroles that within a short time Russell and other officers despised the sight of it. "We decided that we'd had enough rice. Ziggy did it to razz us." [48]

Ominous rumblings in world affairs helped Sprague, a commander since December 1937, land his first seagoing command. Ordered to the Naval War College in Newport, Rhode Island, in June 1939, Sprague spent three months in study. Because of increasing tensions in both Europe, where Adolf Hitler disturbed the peace, and the Pacific, where Japan threatened to overrun European and U.S. holdings, the Roosevelt administration or-dered an increase of active-duty ships and transferred to seagoing posts ap-proximately half the naval officers attending either the Postgraduate School or the Naval War College. One of those ships—the twenty-year-old oil tanker *Patoka*—was paired with one of those naval officers—Clifton Sprague. [49]

Constructed in 1919, the *Patoka* gained distinction as the only vessel in U.S. naval history to tender for dirigibles. Sporting an awkward 125-foot mooring mast at her stern, the *Patoka* serviced the dirigibles *Shenandoah, Los Angeles,* and *Akron* in the 1920s until fatal air crashes pushed the Navy into eliminating such aircraft from its roster. [50]

Six years later, on 10 November 1939, two months after Hitler's vaunted armies swept into Poland to ignite World War II, Commander Sprague stood on the *Patoka's* after deck to begin his first seagoing command. Usually a singular occasion in every naval officer's career, Sprague's initial moments unfolded ingloriously. The ship was hardly the type to satisfy an ambitious officer, yet here Sprague stood, in Puget Sound on board the *Patoka* with an ungainly and irrelevant mooring tower, about to address ten officers and 242 men in an afternoon ceremony. Suddenly, as Sprague began speaking, a steady rain started that never relented until after the program's end.[51]

It got worse from there. Twice Sprague attempted to guide the *Patoka* out of Puget Sound for its journey down the western coast, but in a foretaste of what the voyage would be like, twice the engines quit. Finally, on the third attempt, the awkward *Patoka* burst forth into Pacific waters and pounded its way south.[52]

George S. Hausen, yeoman 2d class on the *Patoka,* summed up the ship's maiden voyage under Sprague. "Yes, we had all kinds of engine problems from the time we left the yard. It seems that every time we'd reach a port we'd have to have major repairs." Sprague could do little with his ship but wait while service personnel tried to correct its troubles. Though many in the crew found humor in the predicament, Sprague saw nothing but frustration.[53]

On 5 February, the ship finally left San Diego and headed for the Canal Zone, arriving on 19 February. After one week's stay in Balboa, Sprague took the ship through the Canal to Colón in preparation for a refueling exercise in the Caribbean. The mission called for Sprague to head to preselected landing areas where the *Patoka* would refuel a flight of PB-1s from Puerto Rico, but the ship's terminally slow pace—its feeble engines could crank up to only about eight knots—put it behind schedule. The planes arrived one day before the *Patoka,* waited for a time, then departed.[54]

Despite the voyage's shortcomings, Sprague made an impact on his crew. Gunner's Mate Frank Stewart thought Sprague was a fine commanding officer who "ran and required a taut ship." Hausen claimed few people disliked the new commander, who had "friends calling on him and inviting him ashore in every port we hit."[55]

"I feel sure [Sprague] was rather frustrated at having command of an old WWI oil tanker, converted to a sea-plane tender at 8 knots," wrote Stewart. "Him being a naval air officer, I'm sure he was use [*sic*] to a much faster pace, and, with the problems we had with keeping the engines running."[56]

After a second cruise to Panama and Puerto Rico, Sprague received orders returning him to the Naval War College to complete the course begun one year earlier. Once again, his studies would be interrupted, this time by a seaplane tender headed for Pearl Harbor.

* * *

Sprague's personal life in the 1920s and 1930s contained an equal measure of high and low points. Tragedy struck first, when his mother died from breast cancer on 24 October 1923. Her death deeply moved Sprague, who was always close to her despite numerous absences for school and the military.[57]

Another woman shortly entered the picture. Born in 1901, Annabel Fitzgerald received from Washington society the deference accorded the family of a world-renowned novelist. In fact, her brother's "first certain memory" of his life was "the sight of [Annabel] howling on a bed." So wrote author F. Scott Fitzgerald, Annabel's older brother, who quickly soared to the literary world's zenith as chronicler of the Jazz Age.[58]

In 1924, while Sprague helped run the Anacostia Naval Air Station, Annabel and her parents lived at the Highland Apartments in nearby Washington, D.C. On Christmas Day, 1924, she attended a party hosted by a young naval officer, Wallace "Gotch" Dillon and his wife, Mary. Two of Dillon's Navy friends also attended—the eligible bachelors Knefler "Sock" McGinnis and Clifton Sprague.

Sprague, normally ill at ease with women, was instantly captivated by Annabel. Though McGinnis had already asked Annabel to dance, Sprague surprised McGinnis by cutting in, spent the rest of the party in her company, then offered to drive her home.[59]

"Clif was not normally bold," explained his sister Dorothea, "but he met Annabel and almost instantly determined he would marry her." Later that night, Sprague confided his intentions to a close friend.[60]

"He trusted his instincts," explained Daniel Vaughan. "He had the ability to grasp the entire picture and to see right away she was right for him, so he made his decision."

Vaughan, a fine amateur golfer, frequently played with Sprague and marveled at his father-in-law's hasty pace, even in such a minor matter. "He played golf in a hurry. He would just walk up to his next shot and hit the ball. His mind was made up quickly. Some golfers line up a putt from three sides, but not him. He'd just do it."[61]

The Reverend Edward L. Buckey from Washington's St. Matthew's Cathedral officiated at the marriage in the presence of family and very close friends. Notable by his absence was F. Scott Fitzgerald, whose roaming lifestyle typically made him unavailable for family affairs. The bride wore a powder-blue chiffon dress and carried a bouquet of Killarney roses; the groom stood proudly in his dress blues. With melodies flowing from a rented harp, and Gotch and Mary Dillon as witnesses, Clifton and Annabel became Lieutenant and Mrs. Sprague.[62]

The newlyweds embarked on a thirty-day honeymoon immediately following the ceremony. After taking a train to Boston, they headed for Milton and Rockport. Bitter weather forced them from the seaside home and into the Cambridge apartment of Sprague's older sister Hazel, where they spent the remainder of their honeymoon. They then returned to Washington, where the young couple occupied a small home in Cleveland Park for five months before renting an apartment at 16th Street N.W.[63]

Within two and one-half years, the Spragues produced two daughters—Courtney on 5 April 1926 and Patricia on 16 December 1927. With each birth, a pattern arose that plagued the family as long as Sprague remained in the Navy. Sprague had just started a new post at the Hampton Roads Naval Air Station when Courtney was born. Though he hastened back as quickly as possible, Sprague missed his first daughter's birth. When labor pains announced the arrival of daughter number two the next year, Sprague rushed Annabel to St. Vincent's Hospital. Once again, though, duty tore him away from family when Sprague received orders to meet an arriving delegation of influential people at the base. The Navy vied with family for Sprague's attention frequently, and often sadly, over the next three decades. Sprague may not have liked the turn of events, but his philosophy was to put other considerations out of his mind and get the job done. "The Navy was his life, and it came first," explained Courtney. "It never entered our minds that the Navy didn't come first."[64]

Marriage to the sister of a popular author did not change Sprague's manner of living since the two men rarely met over the years. Never a close brother-sister duo, Scott and Annabel gradually grew farther apart throughout the late 1920s and into the 1930s, partly because of the famed brother's travels about the world but mainly because the devout Annabel disapproved of Scott and his wife Zelda's fast-paced life. One time, when Sprague taught aviation at the Academy, Scott and Zelda's daughter, Scottie, came for a short visit. Accompanied by a French governess, the young girl of seven or eight remained for three days and, by her behavior, showed she existed in a world far different from that of her relatives. While Annabel normally served ample portions of food, dinner remained an informal occasion for family chatter. Scottie, however, appeared with an accordion-pleated pink chiffon dress, and her governess sported a floor-length black velvet sleeveless dinner dress. Annabel later remembered how stunned everyone was. "I didn't know what to do so I went in and changed to more formal attire. . . ."[65]

Sprague met Scott during the funeral of Annabel's father. Ill at the time, Annabel remained in Annapolis while Sprague traveled to Washington for the service. Though Scott had flown in from Europe and undoubtedly chatted with Sprague, the naval officer had little to say about it later. In his own manner, Sprague attempted to make both wife and brother-in-law comfortable while remaining in the background over the family rift. He quietly supported his wife, but never tried to make the author feel shunned whenever the two men met.[66]

The family chasm widened following the death of Annabel and Scott's mother on 2 September 1936. Though Annabel and Clifton attended the funeral, they did not get a chance to speak to Scott, who missed the service because of an arm injury. However, over the next few months Annabel's correspondence with her famous brother escalated, since her mother had named Annabel executor of an estate containing money that the heavily indebted author sorely needed. Scott told an associate that his mother's estate was "the luckiest event of some time," and he deluged Annabel with entreaties to get at the funds.[67]

Eight days after his mother's death, Scott wrote Annabel a lengthy letter outlining his woes. "Since a year ago last February I have succeeded in getting myself into more debt than you can imagine . . ." explained the author, who claimed his doctors had ordered him to take six weeks' rest from work, else "I would either be dead or be a jibbering nervous wreck in some sanitorium. . . ." He tried to borrow money from his publisher and agent, but neither would lend any more funds until the author produced some publishable stories. His health, he added, did not permit him to write on a full schedule.

Acknowledging his past and current battles with alcohol and that Annabel frowned on his drinking excesses, the author asserted she would achieve no purpose "reproaching me for past extravagances nor for my failure to get control of the liquor situation under these conditions of strain." He wrote when he could, and that "with no help but what can be gotten out of a bottle of gin."

Scott requested that the estate be settled as quickly as possible, since he bore enormous financial burdens imposed by Zelda's hospital stays, his daughter's exorbitant bills from exclusive schools, and their free-wheeling lifestyle. "I want you to talk this over with Cliff [sic]," mentioned the author, who appeared to seek Annabel's sympathy by adding, "This story of becoming a nervous wreck at forty is not pretty . . ." but he saw "no reason why in decent health I couldn't write myself out of this mess, being still under forty and having the necessary connections and reputation." He suggested if he only had two months to write without any financial worries besetting him, he could turn conditions around. His mother's money could enable him to do this. As he had earlier borrowed heavily from his mother, Scott suggested the debts be set aside and that Annabel and he equally divide the estate.[68]

To his chagrin, Maryland law required a six months' wait until the funds could be dispersed, thus there was little Annabel could do about freeing the approximately $23,000 due her brother, even had she been willing. That was unlikely, as by now Annabel rarely mentioned her brother's name around the house. "F. Scott Fitzgerald was never talked about in our home," explained Courtney. "I have vague recollections of Mom saying to Dad that Scott has a story in some magazine, but that's about it. I really didn't know who he was until we got into high school and read one of his stories. Then I knew he was famous."[69]

Annabel gave away every signed first-edition novel that Scott mailed her and threw out each letter he wrote to her. So upset did she become that in one letter she castigated his writings and drew a quick retort from Scott. "Don't tell me I can't write," wrote Scott. "It's like telling Cliff he can't fly." In fact, the author held her husband in high esteem and even wondered in a 1940 letter to a cousin "whether Clifton Sprague has become a great power in the Navy."[70]

For one of the rare instances of his life, Sprague stepped into a family squabble and told Scott to keep still about the money. He reminded his brother-in-law that before he received his inheritance, the money he borrowed from his mother would be subtracted. Only then could he have what remained of his share.

"He couldn't imagine anyone being that dishonest," said Daniel Vaughan of Sprague's reaction to Scott's wanting the borrowed money forgotten.[71]

Annabel and her brother had few contacts from that time on. Scott died in Hollywood from his third heart attack on 21 December 1940, a broken and tired man. Not surprisingly, neither Annabel nor her husband attended the small Maryland funeral service for the author.

An expanding family; a rising career. That is where Sprague stood as the 1940s beckoned. Having established a solid reputation in naval aviation, Sprague stepped into a decade that would bring opportunity amid destruction, advancement amid death.

→ CHAPTER FIVE ←

"All Right for My Money"

I n July 1940, Sprague returned to the Naval War College. Once again the family packed its belongings and headed toward another temporary home, this time a rented house in Newport. As though reflecting the fast-paced world events then transpiring in Europe and the Pacific, the Spragues lived in Newport less than one month when the Navy abruptly transferred him to Oakland, California, to take command of the USS *Tangier,* a two-year-old cargo ship that was being converted into a seaplane tender.

"To say the least, the new orders came as quite a shock to the family," recalled Sprague's daughters. Both girls accepted this move, and the many previous ones, as part of their father's life, but the constant shifting proved hard. "I always adjusted, but it was tough," related Patricia. "I felt I was the new kid on campus at any school and was always the last one chosen for games because nobody knew me."[1]

On one occasion Courtney balked at going to a new school. Sprague fired off a missive that imparted a basic tenet of his personal and professional life. "I believe you are more like me than any one in the family, and some of the traits both you and I have are not always good. In the first place we are painfully bashful, reserved, and retiring and it has always been a handicap to me all my life . . . Even now I find it an ordeal to meet people and go out and give these speeches BUT I'VE GOT TO DO it and you have got to pull up your socks and pitch in with your share."[2]

Sprague "felt a deep sense of responsibility," added Patricia. "He very much believed that if it's your job, you do it, and if no one else is there, you still do it." The past year must have been particularly trying, though, since the frequent moves imposed by the Navy forced the Spragues to enroll the girls in four different schools.[3]

A cross-country train bore Sprague to his West Coast destination while Annabel and the girls redirected furniture and personal belongings. To ease his family's transition, as he headed west Sprague penned a flurry of humorous postcards describing his journey. A 29 July postcard from Washington, D.C., facetiously boasted that he spent "lunch with Franklin [Roosevelt]. He and I both decided it was darned hot. We both had a schooner of beer . . . Got a wire from MGM wanting me for a part in their new picture *Only A Moth with a Broken Wing*. I'll think it over on the way out." A 1 August postcard informed Annabel of his arrival in Salt Lake City, and on 11 August Sprague could finally write from San Francisco, "Look where Daddy is!"[4]

With Sprague's arrival, conversion of the *Tangier* at the Moore Dry Dock Company in Oakland kicked into high gear. As relations with Japan deteriorated, more tenders were needed to service the expanding number of PBY Catalinas used to scout the approaches to Pearl Harbor. Sprague's superiors thus applied heavy pressure to complete the conversion, but hammering the product into final form proved harder than expected. Blueprints changed frequently. Crew members either joked about the *Tangier*'s ultimate look or outright doubted the work would ever be finished. For more than one year, as many as eight hundred workmen labored to transform the *Tangier* into a tender. Leon J. Kehoe, Sprague's yeoman, recalled that "day and night the sound of air hammers, drills and cutting torches never ceased."[5]

Recalcitrant area union workers posed a second problem for Sprague. He controlled his own crew, but he could not simply order civilian laborers to work overtime. The only man who could—Sprague's superior—refused to stir up a controversy and allowed the forty-hour week to continue. "Union standards which have this area sewed up," he wrote in a 30 April 1941 letter to his friend Comdr. D. Ketcham, "have much to do with the Commandant's [his superior] attitude in this matter."[6]

At length, workers applied the final touches, and the reconstituted *Tangier* stood ready for sea trials. Her complement of just over four hundred officers and men moved on board the 492-foot-long tender, now refurbished with machine shops, cavernous storage spaces for the engine parts, fuel, and bombs she would provide for her seaplanes, and quarters and mess room facilities for officers and men. "The *Tangier* was a Floating Air Station," declared Kehoe of the former cargo ship, now able to cruise at a top speed of eighteen knots. For protection, the *Tangier* sported one 5-inch gun and two 3-inch antiaircraft guns aft, two more 3-inch antiaircraft guns forward, and eight .50-caliber machine guns positioned along the deck—not a potent arsenal but one that could hurt an approaching enemy.[7]

With only a limited number of carriers available, Sprague knew those posts would go to senior officers, so he was not disappointed in getting a seaplane tender. He would have to bide his time and hope that he performed creditably enough to warrant his own carrier one day. Marc Mitscher started in a seaplane tender, and classmate Thomas Sprague currently commanded the seaplane tender *Pocomoke* with the Atlantic Fleet, so this post was certainly not an undesirable one. Besides, Sprague, infused with an aviator's offensive philosophy, intended to train his crew to be ready for more than simply repairing aircraft. If the occasion arose, as was likely in the turbulent Pacific, his men would fight as if they served on board a cruiser or battleship. Under Sprague, the *Tangier* would be a very aggressive tender.[8]

Soon after the *Tangier*'s commissioning on 25 August 1941 an incident almost ruined Sprague's career. Sprague had just taken the ship out on her shakedown cruise when he anchored in Carquinis Bay, ten miles from San Francisco, to load ammunition and fuel. An eight-knot current strained the anchor chain and threatened to drag the anchor. When Boatswain Wesley L. Larson came off first watch (2000 to 2400) as officer of the deck, he warned his relief to carefully track the ship's position because of the dangerous conditions.

As Larson prepared for bed, Sprague's orderly knocked on Larson's door to tell him that the captain wanted to see him on the bridge. Larson hastened to the bridge, where Sprague muttered, "Larson, I think we are dragging anchor." Dropping a second anchor failed to prevent the ship from drifting into the mud. Both the ship and Sprague's career wallowed in the sticky grasp of Carquinis Bay.

After crewmen unloaded fuel oil the next day to lighten ship, a destroyer steamed alongside and created a wake that rocked the *Tangier* free from the mud's suction. Since the *Tangier* suffered no damage, and since Sprague's superiors realized he commanded a large number of new reserve officers who were more apt to err in their duties, no disciplinary action was taken. Besides, with the perilous world situation heating up in both Europe and the Pacific, the Navy needed experienced officers for its rapid expansion, not another ex-commander staring from the sidelines.[9]

Sprague continued the *Tangier's* shakedown cruise on 29 August, heading out of the San Francisco area to Bremerton, near Seattle, to load torpedoes. He then took the ship to San Diego and San Pedro before turning west in late October for Pearl Harbor to join Fleet Patrol Wing Two. Sprague used the shakedown to implant his system of command among officers and crew, which consisted of Navy veterans supplemented by a large number of fresh recruits and reserve officers. Of forty officers listed on the ship's 1 December 1941 roster, twenty-one were reserve.[10]

"Many of our officers were just out of college, ninety-day wonders who had never been to sea before," explained Lt. (jg) Richard L. Fruin, the ship's junior medical officer. "They were as innocent as a farm boy from Illinois." With so many inexperienced men, Sprague spent most of his time off the bridge, observing crewmen and officers so he could chart their progress and notice flaws. "You saw Sprague a lot on the shakedown. He was always around," mentioned Seaman 2d Class Joseph Mapes.[11]

Since he commanded so many raw seamen, Sprague led with a loose hand rather than rigidly enforce each regulation. As long as officers or men completed their tasks properly and on time, Sprague never pushed or prodded anyone or dished out extra duties. Seaman 1st Class Leonard Barnes, the radio operator, claimed Sprague was "likeable and had an air about him that he knew what he was talking about. You got no bullshit from Sprague. He always seemed to say logical things that we could relate to. Some officers gave us orders just to give them, but if everything was clean and neat, Sprague wouldn't order you to do more." On the other hand, the executive officer, Comdr. J. F. Wegforth, and the ship's navigator, Comdr. R. W. Bockius, continually irritated the crew by putting men on report for minor infractions, a habit that angered Sprague and led to Wegforth's transfer shortly before Pearl Harbor.[12]

Sprague liked to give great amounts of responsibility to his officers. He normally outlined their duties in general, then allowed them to work out the details. Though he monitored his officers and was quick to spot flaws, Sprague hoped they would learn from each duty. If an ensign performed poorly, Sprague refrained from berating the man, but instead might casually mention a particular book that could yield valuable information for the young officer.[13]

"Commander Sprague would never jump on anyone and yell at them for doing something wrong," recalled Ens. John J. Hughes, a *Tangier* officer.

"He was very soft-spoken and easy to talk to. We respected him, but we didn't fear him."[14]

Sprague treated the crew in similar manner. He was apt to tell sailors that liberty awaited them if they finished their jobs properly and on time. Petty Officer 3d Class Robert Isacksen said the soft-spoken Sprague commanded a happy ship because the crew admired Sprague's fairness in all matters. "He was the best. He had the respect of all the personnel. Sprague didn't lord it over you. The crew always did what he wanted them to do, but no one minded because of the way he said it. Almost a question; not like barking out an order."[15]

One man, out on a raucous liberty the night before the *Tangier* headed to sea for Pearl Harbor, ended in jail and missed the ship's departure. After the Shore Patrol caught up with the *Tangier* the next morning and delivered the tardy sailor, Sprague asked him to explain what went wrong. Terrified that his commander would throw the book at him, especially since a naval officer from a different ship was involved in the fracas, the sailor haltingly related his version of events while a quiet Sprague listened. "You should be a little more careful," responded Sprague after the sailor finished. "You're green and need to spot danger areas. You are confined to the ship for thirty days." As the *Tangier* had yet to cross the immense Pacific on its way to Pearl Harbor, the sailor could serve a large portion of his penalty while at sea. Sprague dealt out retribution while, at the same time, acknowledging the sailor's version of events with a relatively mild punishment.[16]

Mild. Calm. Fair. In control. These are the words used repeatedly by those who served under Sprague on the *Tangier*. One time Sprague donned his white uniform to go ashore. As he left, a sailor swabbing the deck directly above hit the edge of the signal bridge and directed a torrent of water onto Sprague. Without muttering a single word or even looking up to determine the guilty party, the drenched commander returned to his quarters, changed his uniform, and resumed his outing. "There was no yelling or anything," mentioned Barnes. "But then, I *never* saw Commander Sprague lose his composure. When he spoke, we listened, like a grandparent who walks into the room gets respect from his family. We did our best to please him."[17]

Years later, Sprague's daughter Courtney reflected on her father's career and believed, of all the ships he commanded or posts he held, Sprague best loved the *Tangier*. Sprague thought nothing of walking into the ship's radio shack after midnight, dressed only in a robe and slippers, to share a cup of coffee and chat with whomever had the duty. Fruin recalled seeing Sprague frequently watching the men play touch football on the deck. "He loved to watch us play. I liked Sprague for this. He seemed to be one of us and almost acted like he wished he were younger and could join us. Other officers, like Bockius, would have found fault and made us quit, but not Sprague. Sprague was like a father proudly watching his sons." [18]

Like a father, though, Sprague also expected the best from his crew. Aware both that Japanese militarists threatened aggressive actions in the Pacific that would likely involve the United States and that he commanded an inexperienced crew, Sprague conducted seemingly endless drills as the *Tangier* steadily steamed across the Pacific toward the Hawaiian Islands. The constant drills, though vastly improving the ship's efficiency, naturally failed to meet with universal approval from the men. After one sluggish exercise, Sprague rebuked his crew over the ship's speaker because it took almost two minutes for everyone to man their battle stations. "It took you too long to respond," barked Sprague. "The real thing is going to happen one day and you've got to be ready." [19]

The *Tangier* arrived in Pearl Harbor on 3 November. Sprague granted liberty to the crew so they could secure housing for wives and children planning to follow. Sprague, however, told Annabel to wait until after the first of the year to bring the girls over. "I don't like the looks of things." [20]

Across the Pacific in Japan, events occurred with lightning rapidity as November waned. One month before Japan's surprise attack, Adm. Isoroku Yamamoto, commander in chief of the Combined Fleet, issued "Operation Order No. 2," selecting 7 December for his daring raid on Hawaii. Nine days later, Japan's six largest, most modern aircraft carriers departed Japan and headed for the Kurile Islands to the north, maintaining strict radio silence to mask their movement from American traffic monitors. On 26 November, Adm. Chuichi Nagumo led the entire strike force to sea—an armada consisting of the 6 carriers bearing 423 combat planes and escorted by 2 battleships, 2 heavy cruisers, 1 light cruiser, 9 destroyers, and 3 fleet submarines. The inexorable countdown toward war had dwindled to a mere twelve days. [21]

Sprague used the final days of peace to ready his ship. In the two weeks before 7 December, most of the Pacific Fleet steamed out of Pearl Harbor for a huge Pacific Fleet Problem, but the *Tangier* remained at her berth. Sprague canceled liberty for his crew during the Fleet Problem, blacked out the *Tangier* at night, continued intensive drills, and ordered his men to be at battle stations on a four-hours-on, eight-hours-off schedule. He recalled Admiral Reeves's successful 1928 sneak attack on Pearl Harbor and wanted his men alert.[22]

"We were more than ready for Pearl Harbor because of all our training," recalled Isacksen, and Sprague agreed. With the end of the two-week Fleet Problem, Sprague granted liberty on 5 December.[23]

In the meantime, Adm. Husband E. Kimmel, commander of the Pacific Fleet, received an alert from Washington on 27 November: "THIS DIS-PATCH IS TO BE CONSIDERED A WAR WARNING . . . AGGRES-SIVE ACTION EXPECTED BY JAPAN IN THE NEXT FEW DAYS." However, Washington believed a Japanese attack somewhere in the Far East—the Philippines, Kra Peninsula, or Borneo—was far more likely than a thrust deep into the Pacific at Pearl Harbor.[24]

The officers gathered that evening at the Pearl Harbor Officers Club for a farewell party for Wegforth who, in a move welcomed by the crew, was being replaced as executive officer by Comdr. G. H. DeBaun. To greet the arrival of his new executive officer and to familiarize DeBaun with the Tangier's readiness, Sprague ordered a lengthy series of drills on 6 December. Weary after two weeks at battle stations, the resentful crew went through the motions. The drills were a shambles.

Afterwards, Sprague assembled the officers in the wardroom, where anger erupted through his customary composure. "We're not prepared," he emphasized. "We can't trust the Japanese. How do you know the Japanese won't attack tomorrow?"

Still agitated as he left, Sprague turned to his orderly, Seaman 2d Class Robert Munroe, and asked him the location of his battle station. When Munroe answered, Sprague cautioned, "You may have to use it some day soon."[25]

Nagumo's force silently moved closer to Hawaii even as Sprague chided his officers on 6 December. On the same day, President Roosevelt learned with certainty that Japan would soon strike when codebreakers handed him the Japanese rejection of his latest peace efforts. Though the president could not pinpoint the hour or location, he knew the Japanese response would shatter twenty-three years of peace for his countrymen. Dejected, he quietly turned to his adviser, Harry Hopkins, and muttered, "This means war."[26]

A few miles from Pearl Harbor's entrance, five midget submarines separated from their larger, parent I-boats in the early morning hours of 7 December to begin a hazardous journey toward the harbor. Three hours later, Japanese pilots toasted the mission's luck with sake, draped thousand-stitch good luck belts across their shoulders, and entered carrier operations rooms for a final briefing. On board Nagumo's flagship, the aircraft carrier *Akagi*, Comdr. Mitsuo Fuchida studied a blackboard listing Pearl Harbor ship positions as of the day before. "I have confidence in you," stated Nagumo to Fuchida. At 0600, as the *Akagi* turned into the wind less than two hundred miles north of Oahu, Fuchida led the first wave of forty-nine level bombers, forty torpedo planes, fifty-one dive-bombers, and forty-three fighters into the air. Sprague and the *Tangier* had under two hours before Japanese bombs invaded their peaceful berth.[27]

Luxuriant sun and brilliant blue skies greeted the *Tangier* on 7 December as she rested at berth F-10 along Ford Island's northwest side, a berth normally used by aircraft carriers but now given to Sprague because the carriers were at sea. Closely behind the *Tangier*, spread out one by one, sat three other warships. The battleship *Utah*, employed primarily as a target ship, lay directly astern, followed by the light cruisers *Raleigh* and *Detroit*. Across Ford Island to the *Tangier*'s port side, seven mighty battlewagons floated majestically on the calm waters of Battleship Row, sparkling as the sun's morning rays filtered down. Other cruisers, destroyers, and tenders gently swayed at their moorings throughout the harbor. On shore and on board ship, sailors and soldiers leisurely began their relaxed Sunday morning routines.[28]

Technically, the first American action in the Pacific war occurred at 0645 when the destroyer *Ward* attacked and sank one of the enemy's midget submarines two miles from the harbor's entrance. Fifteen minutes later a PBY Catalina, a flying patrol boat, sank a second midget submarine one mile from Pearl Harbor. Sprague and other ship commanders in Pearl Harbor were unaware of these actions, however, and though the U.S. Navy inflicted the war's initial punches, the remainder of the day favored the Japanese.[29]

Fuchida opened the battle at 0749 by signaling all pilots to begin their descent—dive-bombers toward Pearl Harbor's airfields and ships; torpedo planes against Battleship Row. He then notified Nagumo that surprise had been achieved against the seventy combat and twenty-four auxiliary ships in Pearl Harbor with the prearranged message, "TORA, TORA, TORA." Seven minutes later the first Japanese bombs ripped into Hawaiian targets, in that instant changing the destinies of sailors, soldiers, and civilians and setting in motion a lengthy chain of events that would take Sprague from a minor seaplane tender commander in one of the nation's worst military debacles to the key task force admiral determining the outcome of one of the Navy's most glorious moments. Along both sides of Ford Island, speeding airplanes and exploding bombs quickly shook sailors from their Sunday morning lethargy.[30]

Lieutenant Fruin had just gone out to the deck when he noticed a group of airplanes heading toward Ford Island from the wrong direction. One week earlier, superiors chastised a Navy pilot for flying in unauthorized areas, so Fruin assumed that speedy retribution awaited this group of reckless souls. His thoughts abruptly ended when the planes, clearly bearing a red circle, passed overhead and dropped a string of bombs on Ford Island. Fruin rushed to his battle station, the aft Battle Dressing Station, to prepare for possible casualties.[31]

The *Tangier*'s officer of the deck, Boatswain Larson, stood on the gangway alongside Ford Island when he noticed bombs falling from an airplane. He first thought the bombs came from an American plane attempting to widen the channel leading into Pearl Harbor, but soon discarded that notion when the plane buzzed overhead and he "saw the red circle under the wings." Quickly turning to the bugler, who was about to sound First Call for morning colors, Larson ordered him to instead sound General Quarters.[32]

From all sections of the *Tangier,* sailors and officers scrambled to their battle stations. Sprague bolted out of his quarters and dashed up to the bridge, where he instantly went on the speakers—something he normally did not do—and barked "Quarters! Quarters! Dammit! Hurry!" Storekeeper 3d Class C. A. Wilkinson followed Sprague's heels, dressed only in pants, shoes, and a T-shirt instead of the regulation battle gear that covered head, arms, and legs for protection from powder burns. Radio operator Barnes had just finished breakfast "when all hell broke loose." He ran to his station in the radio shack a few decks up as explosions rumbled and the ship vibrated. Seaman Mapes scrambled down to the mess hall hollering, "They're bombing us! They're bombing us!"[33]

By 0800, only two minutes after the Ford Island control tower commander broadcast the official alarm—"AIR RAID PEARL HARBOR, THIS IS NOT A DRILL"—the *Tangier*'s 3-inch antiaircraft guns had already begun firing at Japanese targets, spraying metal shell casings that clanked against the decks. Sprague believed *Tangier* gunners returned fire at the Japanese before any other ship in Pearl Harbor, but he tempered that in his official report where he claimed it was his "impression that this ship was the first to open fire or surely among the first" in Pearl Harbor, a view that is difficult to substantiate with the myriad activities occurring simultaneously in different parts of the harbor. What is beyond doubt is that the *Tangier* crew's speed placed all men at battle stations within minutes of the first enemy bombs, the direct result of Sprague's penchant for drills and training. "Everyone knew his job and went where he was supposed to," explained Barnes.[34]

On the bridge, a silent Sprague watched Japanese planes speed by the *Tangier's* port side at an altitude of four hundred feet on their way to blast the Ford Island Naval Air Station. A string of bombs plunged downward, demolishing a hangar packed with American PBYs. Sprague estimated he saw forty to fifty enemy planes charging at targets as he scanned Pearl Harbor.[35]

The unpopular navigator, Commander Bockius, ran to the bridge to assume his battle station at this time, but Sprague ordered him below, explaining "Larson and I have got it." The two men remained on the open bridge until almost midnight, when Sprague headed for a brief respite in his quarters and permitted Larson to be relieved.[36]

While Sprague's gun crews filled the sky with antiaircraft fire, three Japanese torpedo planes approached the *Tangier's* starboard quarter from the north at 0803 and released their torpedoes at the *Utah*, directly behind the *Tangier*. At least two torpedoes tore into the old battleship and produced an explosion that blew ladles and other hanging equipment in the *Tangier's* galley off their racks and knocked cooks off-balance. The *Utah* sank bottoms up only eight minutes later. Sprague noticed that none of the attackers released their torpedoes until flying by White Spar Buoy No. 1, marking the harbor's depth at thirty-seven feet or more. Sprague later concluded that this tactic was no accident: "The Japanese must have had the most detailed information about this harbor. . . ." Though two more torpedo planes completed runs against the *Raleigh* and *Detroit*, sinking the *Raleigh* by the stern, the *Tangier* escaped notice in this initial flurry, although a torpedo reportedly barely missed the ship's stern. After releasing their missiles, the Japanese planes veered right and retired north over Pearl City.[37]

Battleship Row absorbed the heaviest attacks. A pillar of dark red smoke spiraled high into the air above the mortally damaged *Arizona*, then billowed across Ford Island to envelop the *Tangier* in a protective haze. "Thank God it did," exclaimed Ens. John F. Dore, the *Tangier's* assistant navigator, "because we were loaded with torpedoes and would've gone up right away if we'd been hit."[38]

Other ships of the line billowed smoke as Japanese bombs transformed their once proud structures into twisted metal coffins. Ninety percent of the damage inflicted on the U.S. Navy occurred during this first phase of the assault, which lasted until 0825. According to earlier orders from Admiral Kimmel, Sprague began preparations to steam out of the harbor and seek the open sea, but he delayed departure so that larger ships, with greater firepower, could try to leave first.[39]

Sprague gave few orders that day. Officers and crew, accustomed to Sprague's penchant for popping up anywhere during drills, saw their commander quietly watch from the bridge as they executed their duties. Confident his men would perform well, Sprague hoped to show his absolute faith by remaining on the bridge and interfering as little as possible. Radio operator Barnes marveled at how cool Sprague stayed throughout the long day, "but then, he always was cool. At Pearl Harbor, he acted like he'd thought everything out. Sprague knew just what to do, like he was born to command during a crisis." Sprague realized that sometimes the most effective leadership exerts itself in knowing when *not* to step in.[40]

Sprague elected to stay on the bridge for another reason. His inexperienced crew faced death at the hands of an enemy for the first time, an ordeal that can produce a variety of reactions, particularly among men who fight from exposed gun positions. Sprague could have opted for a protected bridge one deck below, but he deliberately remained on the open bridge— in plain sight of many of his men—to lend moral support at a time when their spirits most needed a boost. The men he had trained earlier now battled for their lives; he would not at that crucial moment descend to more protected quarters. "All those men on the main deck and above it, at one time or another as they fought," recalled Ensign Hughes, "could see Sprague calmly standing there throughout the battle. That impressed us officers and encouraged the men."[41]

A slight lull occurred in Japanese bombing and strafing from 0825 to 0840, allowing *Tangier* crewmen to check watertight doors, hatches, ports, ammunition supplies, and hoses. Men were moved about as needed, but executive officer DeBaun found that few changes in the *Tangier*'s response had to be made. The intensive prewar training was paying off. During this pause, *Tangier* boats were dispatched to rescue survivors from the sunken *Utah*.[42]

* * *

Action resumed at 0843 when a Japanese midget submarine appeared eight hundred yards off the *Tangier's* starboard bow. The forward antiaircraft gun fired six shells in rapid succession while the tender *Curtiss,* positioned west of the *Tangier* near Pearl City, joined with its 5-inch gun. The submarine launched a torpedo at the *Curtiss,* which missed the target and exploded against a dock at Pearl City. Two minutes later the destroyer *Monaghan,* heading out to sea from the East Loch, changed course toward the submarine, avoided a second Japanese torpedo that detonated harmlessly on shore, rammed the pint-sized submarine, then dropped two depth charges for good measure.[43]

As Sprague followed the brief, action-filled encounter from the bridge, a seaman manning the radio watch in the same room became sick, most likely from the emotions of battle. Sprague glanced over, noticed what happened, then said calmly, "Let me take over." He yielded his "temporary" post a few minutes later when the bridge had been cleaned and the boy returned to his job.[44]

A minor controversy evolved over who should receive credit for sinking the midget submarine. Though official records cite the *Monaghan,* most *Tangier* officers and crew believed their ship sank the submarine. Fruin claimed the *Tangier* opened fire first. DeBaun asserted that when gunnery officers later raised the enemy craft, they discovered a single 3-inch shell hole through the conning tower, and the *Tangier* "was the only 3" gun ship in that part of the harbor." Larson, who watched the struggle with Sprague on the bridge, added that an officer in Pearl Harbor, who did not know that Larson served on the *Tangier,* passed along the same information about the 3-inch shell hole to him later during the war. Sprague, who realized a 3-inch shell through the conning tower alone does not sink a submarine, agreed that his ship might have a claim but omitted the *Tangier's* role from his official report because of the uncertainty. He warmly praised the *Monaghan's* commander for "a fine piece of work and the Commanding Officer of the *Monaghan,* in my opinion, should be commended for an excellent and rapid action."[45]

Nagumo's second wave of eighty dive-bombers, fifty-four level bombers, and thirty-six fighters appeared overhead around 0840. Since all eight battleships either lay on Pearl Harbor's bottom or coughed clouds of black smoke, this second wave focused on undamaged cruisers and destroyers as well as on ships along Ford Island's north side where Sprague and the *Tangier* sat. Fuchida's aircraft from the second flotilla, in Sprague's words, "made deliberate bombing attacks on the *Tangier*," though they caused little damage to any ship compared to the violent first wave because of ferocious anti-aircraft fire from a more prepared American fleet.[46]

"All ships in the harbor are setting up a terrific antiaircraft barrage . . . ," scribbled Radioman 1st Class R. A. West in notes taken at his station on the bridge. When one Japanese plane flew abeam to starboard of the ship, the 3-inch forward battery ripped off the entire tail section while .50-caliber machine gun bullets peppered the plane's side. The doomed plane crashed in the Middle Loch, directly behind the *Curtiss* and the repair ship *Medusa,* northwest of the *Tangier's* position.[47]

While the battle raged, Sprague periodically sent information to men who served below decks. Sweating in the oppressive heat of the engine room or carefully patching up the wounded, sailors and officers laboring in the ship's bowels could not follow the battle's progress. Frequent explosions rattled their ship and heightened their emotions, but they had no way of knowing what happened above decks. Sprague did not forget them. Fireman 2d Class Walter F. Hamelrath claimed, "To one who was frequently on duty in the confines of the engine room this was a definite morale booster."[48]

Five minutes after warding off the first attacker, *Tangier* gun crews sighted a second Japanese dive-bomber approaching from the northeast. Accurate fire caused it to veer out of control and crash on the shore at Beckoning Point, due west of the ship. At the same time, the 3-inch battery hammered without effect at a squadron of level bombers as they came in from south to north at twelve thousand feet. These bombers dropped their payload on the Waipio Peninsula off Ford Island's western edge.[49]

Sprague watched a third attacker charge the *Tangier's* port side around 0910 but *Tangier* gun crews, Sprague later commented, pumped "a veritable storm of lead" at the invader and destroyed it before it did any harm. Machine gun bullets ripped into the plane and started a fire in the fuselage directly in front of the dead pilot, whose head visibly lolled from side to side. The Japanese observer desperately attempted to extricate himself from the rear seat by pulling the ripcord of his parachute and shoving it out of the plane, hoping that a gust of wind might yank him free from the doomed craft. Before he succeeded, the dive-bomber swerved sharply to the right and crashed into the *Curtiss,* damaging its near after stack, its boat crane, and an antiaircraft gun station while starting a large fire.[50]

In rapid succession, five dive-bombers took aim at the *Tangier.* Geysers

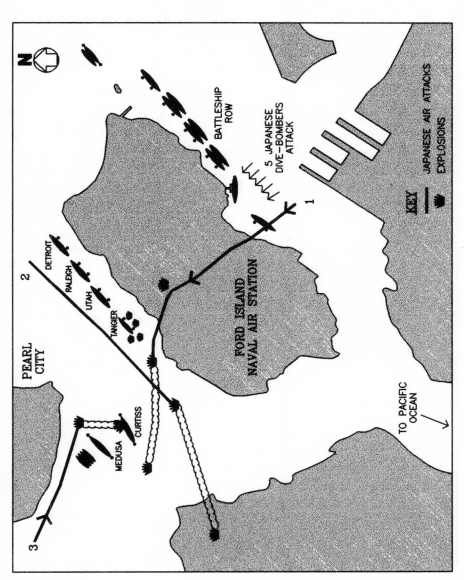

MAP 1. Attacks on the *Tangier* at Pearl Harbor

erupted off the ship's bow and bomb fragments shattered windows on the protected bridge, but not one bomb touched the *Tangier*. Fruin patched up wounded sailors at his post below decks and recalled the terrifying feeling that coursed through him and those who worked nearby. "We couldn't see what was happening from down below, but when the ship vibrated you knew the bombs were getting close. The only thing you could do was try to put all those thoughts out of your mind."[51]

The first enemy pilot released his bomb short of the *Tangier* onto Ford Island, in Sprague's opinion because "the pilot of this plane did not press home his attack as the other pilots`did and dropped short before turning away." The other Japanese fliers remained on their runs longer and released their missiles from three hundred feet in a shallow dive. Sprague followed the bombs, which he estimated to be about three hundred pounds, as they plummeted from the planes directly toward the *Tangier* and "felt sure they were going to be hits. . . ." Two splashed into the water fifteen and twenty feet off the starboard side and two hit twenty and forty feet aft. Sprague braced for shuddering explosions, but only a dull thud reverberated through the ship. Sprague later reported he "was surprised that after they missed that there was no more damage to the ship than what took place," but he concluded the bombs must have burrowed into the harbor's mud before exploding, thereby muffling the detonation and minimizing any damage.[52]

Bomb fragments struck the *Tangier* in forty-two separate places, slightly wounding three crewmen, but none caused serious damage and none penetrated below the ship's water line. Sprague later claimed the reason the Japanese missed his ship, "and some came damn close, was that the volume of our fire was so great they couldn't complete their dive." According to De-Baun, who found bomb fragments in his bathrobe pocket the next day in his room, the *Tangier*'s seven guns spread out such a protective curtain of antiaircraft fire around the *Tangier* that it "expended more .50-caliber ammunition per gun than any ship present" at Pearl Harbor and stood among the top few in expending total numbers of shells, even though most ships carried a larger number of .50-caliber guns.[53]

While Sprague tended to his ship in the debris-littered harbor, Fuchida circled above, experiencing a "warm feeling" as he inspected the devastation below. Finally, with the last of his pilots departing about 1000, Fuchida turned his plane away from the blazing warships and headed toward the *Akagi*.[54]

From all appearances, Japan had inflicted a stunning blow on its surprised enemy. Once-proud battleships rested on the harbor bottom. Almost two hundred twisted airplanes blanketed Pearl Harbor airfields like crushed metal bugs. Overworked physicians labored in area hospitals to treat the wounded, while funeral arrangements would have to be started for 2,403 soldiers and sailors. Only a small handful of ships, including Sprague's *Tangier*, emerged relatively unscathed in the worst debacle ever suffered by the Navy. Against this incredible tally, Fuchida counted only twenty-nine airplanes and fifty-five men lost. When he returned to the *Akagi*, Fuchida strongly urged Nagumo to launch a third strike against oil farms and repair facilities, but a cautious Nagumo feared American counterattacks and ordered a withdrawal to the Marshalls. Nevertheless, in one short, vicious attack, Fuchida had shown the whole world the offensive capability and frightening destructiveness of air power.[55]

Sprague took advantage of the respite around 1100 and sent his men below in small groups to don protective dungarees. Cooks dished out ham sandwiches, cake, and coffee to men at their battle stations, while some crew members jumped into boats to rescue survivors struggling in the harbor. Sprague sent two medical officers to assist another ship in handling the wounded, and when a banging noise emanated from inside the overturned *Utah*, Sprague dispatched a cutting outfit to crack a hole in the warship. Cautiously scaling the *Utah*'s slippery hull, *Tangier* sailors cut an eighteen-inch opening and shouted to whomever was inside to step away while they pounded in the weakened plating. Within minutes, a grateful Fireman John Vaessen emerged from his temporary tomb. Later that afternoon, the ship's printer distributed special postcards so each man could inform loved ones back home he was safe.[56]

Rumors of enemy sightings filled the following jittery hours. *Tangier* crewmen heard that an invasion convoy of four troop transports neared Hawaii. Ninety miles to the southeast, so another rumor claimed, a Japanese naval armada closed in. Regrettably, according to Radioman West's notes taken on the bridge, reports that "boatloads of men are being taken from the battleships badly burned" proved true, as was the visible evidence of fire, smoke, and destruction that mingled with the frequent "explosions heard from direction of Air Station and burning battleships."[57]

Reports circulated that Japanese parachute troops had landed at Barbers Point while other enemy contingents, astonishingly said to be wearing blue coveralls with red insignia, already infested northern Oahu. In response, Sprague sent Ensign Dore and ten crew members armed with rifles and pistols to Admiral Kimmel's office, where they were to receive further orders concerning the alleged parachutists. After enduring a scary harbor ride past nervous sentries likely to shoot at anything that moved, Dore arrived at the commander in chief's office. There he found Admiral Kimmel all alone, pacing from one end of the room to the other and repeating over and over, "Goddamn Japs! They caught us with our pants down!" Kimmel canceled the order, since he had learned the report was erroneous, and instead diverted Dore's group to the mainland to help with the wounded.[58]

Inevitably, as day wound down to night, apprehension rose among the sailors. Boatswain's mates on board various ships challenged small boat operators as they searched the waters for survivors or bodies. Sprague sent a boat to the shore around 2000 to investigate and extinguish the sudden appearance of two bright lights. Periodic antiaircraft outbursts transformed the night into, as West remembered, "a mass of tracer fire and flashes from three and five inch guns" as tired gunners imagined squadrons of enemy fighters swooping in. Unfortunately, four *Enterprise* dive-bombers on their way to a Pearl Harbor base drew fire from practically every gun below, including the *Tangier,* reminding Fruin of a quiet church service where one person starts coughing, another joins, "and soon, it would seem, almost everyone in the church would be coughing. Tracers zoomed in every direction." The four aircraft crashed amid a flurry of American shells.[59]

An astonished Lt. James R. Pace, in charge of the *Tangier* after battery, asked one gun crew, "What in God's name are you shooting at?" A gunner pointed to a hole in the clouds and, as Pace gazed at it, asserted: "I don't know what the rest of the guys are firing at, but any son of a bitch coming through that hole will have had it. That's what I'm shooting at."[60]

For a ship bearing only seven guns and manned largely by a green crew, Sprague's *Tangier* performed amazingly well on 7 December. Since DeBaun had arrived the day before and had no role in training the crew, he could judge Sprague and his crew more objectively than other participants, and he called their performance "one of the bright spots of a very sad day. I do not see how any one of them could have done his job better than he did, and . . . they should be commended on their performance of duty and their preparation for battle." He added that the *Tangier's* guns continuously blazed away at the attackers and only halted "when their ammunition was expended."[61]

Sprague praised his crew in the official report for downing three enemy planes, hitting and possibly destroying two more, plus participating in the attack on the midget submarine. His gun crews expended 217 rounds of 3-

inch .50-caliber shells, 198 rounds of 3-inch .23-caliber shells, and 23,000 rounds of .50-caliber machine gun bullets, leading Sprague to state that the "conduct of the officers and crew was excellent throughout." Sprague recorded "suitable entries" in each man's service record.[62]

Sprague recommended that three individuals receive the Legion of Merit with V "for their bravery and skill while under attack" on 7 December— Lt. Samuel P. Thwing, commanding the forward battery; Lt. James R. Pace, directing the aft battery; and Boatswain Wesley L. Larson, officer of the deck when the Japanese struck, who "grasped the situation so quickly and sounded the general alarm so promptly that this ship was as a direct result, the first to open fire, or I shall say the first the Commanding Officer could observe open fire." Larson initially received only a letter of commendation, but continuous prodding over the next five years by Sprague finally resulted in the Bronze Star with Combat V for Larson in 1946 and a permanent citation two years later.[63]

A more accurate image of Sprague's feelings came in personal letters, where he could be more frank. The attack on Pearl Harbor, he wrote his sister Dora, two months later, "was a cooler but the Tangier did fine. I was proud of my boys. Everybody did their job and considering it was a complete surprise on a Sunday morning we have a lot to be proud of." Sprague asserted in a letter to one crewman that, although he felt the Tangier never received adequate recognition for being the first to open fire and for her role in sinking the midget submarine, the officers and men "were outstanding, they worked like dogs, willingly, cheerfully," and "if we are satisfied in our own minds with what we accomplished what does that [no recognition] matter." To his own crew, he movingly wrote seven simple words that spoke volumes in a memo posted 8 December, "You are all right for my money."[64]

Sprague's crew reciprocated the feelings. "It isn't by coincidence we were the only ship tied up at Ford Island not to get hit," boasted Joseph Mapes. "It was because of Sprague's training and drills." They contended the Tangier was the first ship to open fire on the Japanese, but claimed senior officers— all nonaviation—did not want to acknowledge that a ship commanded by an aviation officer had outperformed them. Sprague, in fact, received his first Battle Star for demonstrating "a high degree of alertness and readiness for battle."[65]

While her husband battled for his ship's life thousands of miles away, Annabel organized personal belongings for another trek across the country.

First hearing the news on San Francisco radio with the girls at 11:22 A.M., Annabel thought the report was another hoax, similar to Orson Welles's famous Martian invasion of 1938 that terrified large portions of the nation. As in the aftermath of Welles's prank, rumors and incredulous "sightings" of a Japanese assault force off California shores bounded along the West Coast. Nightly blackouts became the norm, giving rise to even more fantastic tales of Japanese carrier planes flying over San Francisco. Three times during the war's first night, sirens blared in the Bay Area. Lt. Gen. John L. DeWitt, commanding officer, Fourth Army and in charge of the Western Defense Command, exclaimed to those who doubted the planes' existence, "There are more damned fools in this locality than I have ever seen. Death and destruction are likely to come to this city [San Francisco] at any moment."[66]

A bit flustered by the commotion and separated from her husband by half an ocean, Annabel pondered what to do. When Dora offered her home near Chicago as a temporary haven, Annabel quickly accepted the chance to extricate the family from what might become a war zone.[67]

At least Annabel knew Clifton had survived. A Navy postcard dated 8 December, which prohibited the sender from adding anything besides the standard phrases already printed, arrived on 12 December: "I am well. Am getting on well. Letter follows at first opportunity." She dashed off a Western Union telegram to Dora in Glencoe, Illinois: "VERY HEAVILY CENSORED PRINTED CARD FROM CLIFTON WITH HIS OWN SIGNATURE SAYING I AM WELL CAME AIR MAIL."[68]

In a matter of weeks, however, as the war scare tempered, Annabel and the girls returned to San Francisco, news that piqued Sprague's devilish side. In a February 1942 letter to Dora, Sprague mentioned he had heard that the Bay Area had experienced another alert a few days before, so Annabel and the girls "may have fled to Denver. Some more of that and they better make it Reno. Annabel evidentally [sic] was as nervous as a cat on a tin roof."[69]

The momentous first day of war stands out as one of those rare times in history when little is the same afterwards as it was before. The day emitted shock waves of change that rippled through nations, military services, and individuals and left in its wake a vastly altered world. One nation rose from the ignominy of Pearl Harbor to the pinnacle of world power while its opponent, victorious on 7 December, plummeted to the ashes of atomic annihilation. Families from every inhabitable continent endured separation, pain, and heartbreak.

The U.S. Navy experienced a basic transformation as well. In the years before Pearl Harbor, battleship advocates held power. Fleet doctrine placed a small number of battleships at the top of the naval arsenal, while all other branches inhabited secondary roles. Now, the once-potent Pacific Fleet, centered around those battleships, rested on Pearl Harbor's bottom. In its place would eventually float a revised Navy whose offensive punch originated from bombs and torpedoes delivered by aggressive carrier air squadrons rather than from the cumbersome barrels of static battleships. Though many in the Navy refused to admit it, the battleship-dominated fleet died at Pearl Harbor while aviation came of age, courtesy of Yamamoto's carriers and Fuchida's aircraft.

Tragically for the United States, it took an enemy to prove that what Sprague and other aviators had been insisting throughout twenty years of tests, fleet problems, and debates was indeed correct. Naval aviators never doubted that aviation was the wave of the future, but they could not totally convince its detractors until aviation "showed its stuff" in actual wartime conditions. Pearl Harbor offered that opportunity and resoundingly answered aviation's critics with an awesome display of air power.

Few naval aviators occupied such a central seat as Sprague did that December morning. He certainly gazed in horror and anger as the enemy maimed fellow countrymen, but in some way he must have felt wonderment and fascination, for here was occurring the very event he and other aviators argued could happen. At Pearl Harbor, the battleship was forcibly shoved off center stage right before Sprague's eyes. Neither Jocko Clark, Forrest Sherman, nor Thomas Sprague could claim as much.

Sprague had compiled an impressive list of assignments previous to the *Tangier,* but at Pearl Harbor he showed his true worth as a commander. Sprague endured bloodshed, death, violence, and destruction without wavering. Despite the incredible noise, the billowing black smoke pouring from ships in their death throes, the enemy aircraft charging his ship, the fear reflected in cohorts' eyes, and the complete astonishment that his Navy had been caught flat-footed, Sprague emerged as a successful leader of men under fire and one of the few officers who could wrench even a tiny amount of pride from the "day of infamy."

The assault propelled Sprague along a series of promotions that resulted in his presence in a key command at Leyte Gulf as the Japanese Navy threw its final desperate challenge at the advancing Americans. Ironically, the Japanese also provided the tool Sprague would use to defeat them in the Philippines—the aircraft carrier. Since Fuchida's torpedo planes and dive-bombers had removed the U.S. Navy's battleships from the war, American planners focused on developing aircraft carrier tactics. Carrier task forces and escort carriers would dominate the Pacific conflict, a situation ready-made for an aviator like Sprague.[70]

→ CHAPTER SIX ←

"We Might Have Made It"

Japanese carrier air power shattered all sense of order in Pearl Harbor and, as in most major calamities, created a vacuum into which flooded additional rumors, fears, and reported sightings of enemy forces. Americans braced for a Japanese attack and apprehensive eyes spotted enemy plots in any suspicious movement. A fire in a cane field near the ammunition depot became "a perfect beacon for enemy planes." *Tangier* sailors circulated a supposed sighting of an enemy submarine received, of all places, from an "officer in station wagon on beach." Anxious men on watch spotted a submarine in the harbor confines moments before Radioman R. A. West scribbled in his notes that "something passed us on the starboard beam." In the attack's immediate aftermath, any person or object moving about the harbor's waters drew suspicious glances from edgy sailors. "For the next few days," recalls *Tangier* engineer Henry Frietas, "whenever I moved about in the *Tangier's* boat, particularly at night, I got shot at by nervous sentries." [1]

In one five-minute span, Sprague received orders from headquarters to (1) commence firing at reported enemy aircraft, (2) cease firing, (3) disregard the order to cease fire, and (4) "fire at will" at a different group of supposed enemy aircraft. The shooting accomplished little more than forcing men stationed at the *Tangier's* bow to seek shelter from errant American bullets zipping by.

Sprague tried to calm his jittery crew. He informed the Ford Island Naval Air Station their fire "was coming too close to our bow." He sent ashore two crew members to investigate a plane, rumored to be an American fighter, that had earlier crashed near town. The duo extracted a Very pistol from the downed aircraft to prove "beyond a doubt it was one of our planes," and handed it to Sprague.[2]

In the midst of fear and doubt, West recorded two events on the same page of his typewritten notes that symbolized the end of one era and the start of another—the arrival of the aircraft carrier *Enterprise,* and the extinguishing of the deadly inferno that took so many lives on board the battleship *Arizona.* In a sense, these actions represented the passing of a torch from old to new—from the surface-oriented battleship advocates who fought World War I to the air-minded naval aviators who would play such a crucial role in World War II. As the ship typifying the past settled to her permanent resting spot on the harbor bottom, the weapon pointing to the future arrived to take up the burden with its fighters and bombers.[3]

Amid the confusion and uncertainty of the war's earliest days, one voice attempted to calm the American population, remind them that trying times lay ahead, and rouse their spirits with thoughts of eventual victory. In Roosevelt's Fireside Chat on Tuesday, 9 December, which Sprague broadcast to his entire crew over the ship's speaker system, the president branded the Japanese assaults on American possessions "sudden criminal attacks" by gangsters who "have banded together to make war on the whole human race." Roosevelt warned that "We must share together the bad news and the good news, the defeats and victories . . ." and he explained that Japanese forces would most likely seize Guam, Wake, and possibly Midway. While Sprague and his men searched the skies for the very enemy Roosevelt castigated, for the *Tangier* stood on yet another air-raid alert even as their president spoke, he cautioned that "We must be set to face a long war against crafty and powerful bandits." Referring to the embarrassing 7 December debacle, the president concluded, "Not only must the shame of Japanese treachery be wiped out, but the sources of international brutality, wherever they exist, must be absolutely and finally broken."[4]

One way American forces could eradicate shame was to relieve beleaguered Wake, a V-shaped group of three tiny islands located approximately twenty-one hundred miles west of Hawaii that had been attacked mere hours after Fuchida turned away from Pearl Harbor. Wake soared to world acclaim when its undermanned and poorly supplied force of five hundred

Marines successfully repelled a far superior Japanese contingent on 11 December. This first defeat of a seemingly invincible enemy inflated American home front morale and gave birth to the patriotic cry "Wake Up!" Newspaper headlines proudly proclaimed "MARINES KEEP WAKE," while the *Washington Post* predicted that Wake would become a "stage for an epic in American military history. . . ."[5]

Stirring cries and optimistic news did little to aid the weary Marine defenders facing a determined enemy. Ammunition, weapons, planes, and men counted for more. Some were available, but how could the Navy, reeling from the attack on Pearl Harbor, get the needed reinforcements and supplies to Wake while fending off the strong Japanese naval forces that prowled the nearby seas? Most of Kimmel's Pacific Fleet lay on Pearl Harbor's bottom, and the main weapons available to him—three aircraft carriers—could not be carelessly expended. The American people, though, clamored for a victory to avenge the humiliation suffered on 7 December, and Kimmel and other naval leaders could not stand by and allow America's first heroes to be taken without a relief attempt.[6]

"We felt good, almost cocky," wrote the commander of the sixty-nine naval personnel on Wake, Comdr. Winfield Scott Cunningham, after the war. "Surely help would come from Pearl Harbor any day now, and meanwhile we could wait it out." In fact, even before the war Kimmel had foreseen action off Wake, where an American naval force might have an opportunity to engage the Japanese fleet. Comdr. Edwin T. Layton, the Pacific Fleet's intelligence officer, recounted that at an 11 December staff meeting, one officer strongly argued in favor of reinforcing the Wake garrison, rather than allow it to be evacuated or overrun by the enemy. Records do not indicate who this officer was, but many of the *Tangier* crew believed it was Sprague. Sprague attended a meeting at Kimmel's headquarters on that day and, according to word on the *Tangier*, he was asked by Kimmel how to best evacuate Wake. Supposedly Sprague objected. "We won't evacuate it. We'll reinforce it." After listing his reasons favoring reinforcement, so claimed *Tangier* crew members, Sprague offered to take a contingent of Marines directly to the threatened island.[7]

Kimmel issued orders forming Task Force 14, commanded by Rear Adm. Frank Jack Fletcher. The aircraft carrier *Saratoga,* three heavy cruisers, nine destroyers, the oiler *Neches,* and Sprague's *Tangier* would rush additional supplies and Marines into Wake while diversionary forces built around the carriers *Enterprise* and *Lexington* harassed Japanese forces elsewhere and guarded the approaches to Hawaii. The bold plan could result in a disastrous fiasco should stronger Japanese forces appear, but the shot in the arm to American military and home front morale outweighed the negative factors. Kimmel ordered the force to depart Pearl Harbor as soon as the *Saratoga* arrived from California with a Marine fighter squadron.[8]

Sprague, delighted that he was about to embark on the first offensive wartime thrust by a carrier force in U.S. history, prepared the *Tangier* for a sudden influx of Marines, ammunition, and supplies. Since earning his wings in 1921, Sprague had worked to boost naval aviation's importance as an offensive weapon, and he now was one of the few aviators given the chance to prove the assertion.

After Sprague took the *Tangier* from her normal mooring to a pier near the supply and ammunition facilities, Marines of the 4th Defense Battalion began loading matériel on board the *Tangier* on the morning of 12 December. For three days without letup, Sprague watched a continuous stream pour by: 5-inch shells, antiaircraft shells, a 3-inch antiaircraft battery, a 5-inch battery, beach mines, wire, grenades, one of the few radar sets to arrive in the Pacific, aviation spare parts, millions of rounds of machine gun ammunition, and the Marines themselves. Other military personnel swarmed to the pier to wish their departing comrades good luck, while Marines who could not accompany the *Tangier* yelled to those who were going, "Goodby and give 'em Hell!"[9]

For two more days Sprague and the *Tangier,* bursting with war supplies and eager Marines, waited impatiently for the *Saratoga* to arrive from California. Four days had elapsed since Wake's defenders had repelled the Japanese, who would undoubtedly mount a second attempt at any moment. If the men on Wake were to be saved, Fletcher's task force must head to sea without delay, so when the *Saratoga* appeared early 15 December, Kimmel ordered Sprague and the oiler *Neches,* accompanied by a handful of destroyers, to get under way. The *Saratoga,* escorted by the cruisers *Minneapolis, Astoria,* and *San Francisco* and Destroyer Squadron 4, would depart the next day when fueling had been completed.[10]

The *Tangier* crew peered west with apprehension. Somewhere, the men assumed, all or part of Nagumo's carrier force waited. Enemy submarines were said to be off Midway, Johnston Island, Hawaii—rumors placed the Japanese practically everywhere. Most crew members accepted the fact that at some point during the mission, the task force would engage a more powerful enemy in a melee from which the *Tangier* would most probably not return. Even before the *Tangier* left Pearl Harbor, sailors and workers on shore offered no better than a hundred-to-one odds that the *Tangier* would survive.[11]

"Most of us didn't expect to come back," mentions Storekeeper 1st Class Norris G. Edwards. "We felt it was the end of the war for us. When we took on all those Marines, we knew we were going somewhere undesirable." As the *Tangier* exited Pearl Harbor into the immense Pacific, Edwards's shipmate, C. A. Wilkinson, walked topside and gazed at the tropical paradise as it receded. "I looked at it as long as I could because I did not think I'd ever see any more American land ever."[12]

Sprague read the *Tangier*'s orders over the speaker system. The ship was to disembark the Marine reinforcements on Wake and take out as many of the island's civilian construction workers as space would allow. Should the small American force be attacked or should Wake be in imminent jeopardy of being overrun, Sprague was to run the *Tangier* aground on Wake to guarantee delivery of the men and supplies. The stark order fell hard on the crew, for unspoken was the reality that if Sprague had to beach his ship, he would strand the *Tangier* crew and himself on Wake at a very inopportune moment.[13]

When the refueled *Saratoga* caught up with the *Tangier* and *Neches* on 17 December, Task Force 14 for the initial time sallied as an entire unit. Comprising the first American westward thrust of the war, the task force carried enough power to seriously harm the enemy, but it had to reach Wake before the Japanese overwhelmed the tired garrison. A frustrating race with time began, a race in which Fletcher's ships were handicapped by the plodding oiler *Neches,* which could steam no faster than 12.75 knots.[14]

In the meantime, while daily bombing raids further reduced Wake's ability to resist, Marines on board the *Tangier* prepared for battle. Youthful privates and veteran gunnery sergeants studied terrain maps, sharpened bayonets, and constantly took apart and cleaned their rifles, all the while hoping their comrades on Wake could hold out for a few more days. The *Tangier* machine shop altered machine guns so they could be easily fired even while being unloaded from the ship. Navy pilots James J. Murphy and H. P. Ady brought welcome news to the besieged men on 20 December when they landed a PBY in Wake's lagoon and informed Cunningham of the relief expedition's expected arrival on Christmas Eve. The Marines "felt pretty good that night," stated Maj. James P. Devereux, Marine commander on Wake.[15]

Confusion set in the very next day. Cunningham notified Fletcher that carrier-borne dive-bombers had attacked Wake, meaning that Nagumo's flotilla steamed relatively close by. Vice Adm. William S. Pye, the acting commander in chief of the Pacific Fleet until Adm. Chester W. Nimitz arrived to assume control from the already relieved Kimmel, was reluctant to risk any of the three remaining Pacific aircraft carriers in an uncertain situation, and he worried that enemy carriers might swing around Task Force 14 and again hit Hawaii. However, Pye also faced heavy pressure from Navy and Marine circles to rescue the Wake garrison.

Rather than commit to a clear-cut course of action, Pye vacillated, a lackluster strategy that bewildered Fletcher, Sprague, and other task force commanders. He first ordered Fletcher to take the *Saratoga* within two hundred miles of Wake to search for the enemy. Pye quickly canceled that order and issued a second directive sending Sprague ahead of Task Force 14, *without escort,* to evacuate everyone on Wake.[16]

Fletcher reluctantly relayed the order to Sprague, who moved the *Tangier* ahead of the task force. The sight of the huge *Saratoga* disappearing over the horizon unsettled a number of the crew, whose dim hopes of returning now seemed crushed. Fletcher agreed with that dismal sentiment. On Sprague's personal copy of the order sending the *Tangier* ahead, Sprague wrote that Fletcher told him in Seattle later in the war that "he felt like he was putting a pistol to my head."[17]

Pye canceled this order shortly after Sprague broke away from the *Saratoga,* spreading relief among the *Tangier* crew but causing more unease among Task Force 14 commanders. Do they advance to Wake? Do they pull away? No one steaming the Pacific waters between Pearl Harbor and Wake knew exactly what was going on. Sprague supported an immediate advance to reinforce Wake, but real and imagined dangers stalemated the cautious Pye, undoubtedly shaken from watching his flagship *California* descend to Pearl Harbor's bottom on 7 December. Thus, as the *Saratoga* and *Tangier* slowly churned toward a Wake garrison begging for assistance, a frustrating 21 December wound to an indecisive finish. Forced to steam westward at the exasperatingly tepid pace of 12.75 knots set by *Neches,* by 1000 the task force remained a distant six hundred miles from Wake.[18]

The following day was worse. Fletcher, concerned that his destroyers might have to engage the enemy without enough fuel, decided to refuel in the morning, an operation that required the task force to reduce speed by as much as six knots and steam north into strong tradewinds. By dusk, with only half of the eight destroyers topped off, Task Force 14 had moved only a hundred miles closer to its destination. Pye's indecision and the lengthy refueling angered Sprague, who saw his chance to help the Marines and to take part in the first carrier offensive of the war dissipating before his eyes.[19]

Marines on Wake were too occupied to think about relief, as Japanese invasion forces swarmed onto the island early on 23 December (22 December in Pearl Harbor). Though the weary men fought valiantly, the rested and better-equipped enemy quickly seized huge sections of the American outpost. As Sprague waited for his superiors to stiffen their resolve, Cunningham radioed Pye around 0500 a disheartening message, "ENEMY ON ISLAND—ISSUE IN DOUBT." After conferring with key members of his staff, Pye concluded that Wake could no longer be saved and that further attempts to draw the enemy force into a sea battle should be called off. At 0911, with Sprague and Task Force 14 still more than four hundred miles from Wake, Pye recalled the ships.[20]

Reactions from surprised leathernecks, task force members, and *Tangier* crew ranged from bitterness to elation. One *Enterprise* officer scathingly concluded, "It's a war between the two yellow races." Admiral Fitch fled his own bridge to avoid hearing near-mutinous talk from officers. Even Nimitz sadly commented that Pye had "great brains but no guts."[21]

Some in the *Tangier* crew castigated Pye's recall as cowardly. Marines angrily agreed. "Here we were, loaded for bear with a carrier and cruisers, and we didn't go in!" mentioned Fruin. "Everyone was distressed." Even though the assignment asked them to steam directly into harm's way, something few men or officers eagerly sought, the crew would have overwhelmingly voted to continue because, as Frietas added, "It was wartime. We would have gone in."[22]

Some historians claim Pye missed a golden opportunity to inflict serious damage on unescorted Japanese cruisers and amphibious forces at Wake—a sentiment Sprague shared—while others assert that Pye had no recourse but to rein in his ships. In all likelihood, the most Task Force 14 could have accomplished was to disrupt the Japanese invasion attempt, since most of the enemy's cruisers and carriers had already steamed away. But even this would have been welcome news to a victory-starved nation and revenge-minded military. Until Coral Sea some six months later, the U.S. Navy would shy from taking the initiative while it rebuilt its shattered fleet and protected vital supply lines to Australia. These were important tasks, but hardly the stuff to boost morale.[23]

In the United States, a public still reeling from Pearl Harbor was kept blissfully ignorant of the Wake Island expedition and recall. Across the ocean, Tokyo Rose taunted her opponent over the air waves, "Where, oh where is the United States Navy?" Five hundred miles from Wake, Sprague sadly concluded, "We might have made it." [24]

Pye's indecision bothered Sprague. The situation demanded bold, determined leadership, yet Sprague saw only hesitation and caution from above, which affected every person down the chain of command. Each crucial event possesses its own precise moment when one can either seize the initiative and reap huge benefits or let it slip away and gain little. Perils envelop that moment, but few advantages in wartime are attainable without gamble. Sprague believed Wake was worth the risk and he would have gone in.

Fletcher's task force dissolved into separate components. While the carriers steamed back to Pearl Harbor, Sprague turned the *Tangier* toward Midway Island, 1,025 miles northeast of Wake, where he was ordered to deposit his Marine contingent. Little excitement broke the monotonous routine of maintaining the tender and gazing skyward for the enemy. One day Ensign Dore thought he spotted a Japanese plane, but two other officers claimed they could not see a thing. When Dore insisted something was there, Sprague, who had been following the discussion from near the bridge, stepped over.

"Where the hell is this plane, Dore?" asked Sprague.

"It's right above us, sir."

After a quick skyward inspection, Sprague claimed he could find nothing.

"Captain," replied Dore, "if you'll come down where I am, maybe you'll see it."

Sprague stepped below to join Dore and made a second sweep of the sky. Suddenly Sprague burst out laughing. "By God, that *is* something, Dore. Hell, that's a star!" Impressed that his officer could spot a star during daylight, Sprague commended Dore before returning to the bridge. [25]

The *Tangier* observed Christmas in the traditional Navy manner with a sumptuous meal of turkey and dressing, baked ham, mashed potatoes, peas and corn, apple pie, and ice cream. To accompany the meal, Sprague issued a simple Christmas message to his crew.

"I wish to take this means of wishing my officers, crew and the Marine Detachment, a Very Merry Christmas.

"I also wish to express my appreciation of the behavior of the crew of the U.S.S. *Tangier,* during these trying times, and am sure should the occassion [sic] arise, that they will 'come through' as they have in the past." [26]

The *Tangier* arrived at Midway early in the morning of 26 December and immediately began disembarking its load of supplies and Marines, which Sprague figured would take two days and nights to complete. He had not counted on the incredible energy of the huge civilian construction work-force on Midway, who had received plenty of impetus to get off the island from the threat of being overrun by the Japanese. Since they could go no-where until the *Tangier* put ashore the final crate of ammunition, the work-ers readily pitched in to quicken the process. Before dawn broke the follow-ing morning, every box earmarked for Midway had been taken off the ship. When Larson woke Sprague to tell him the *Tangier* could be ready to leave by 0600, he could hardly believe it.[27]

Sprague gave the order to board the civilians. Larson watched such a continuous stream of men file onto the ship that it "seemed they were running out of our ears." The *Tangier* crew might have been concerned over sharing limited living space with a group of sturdy construction workers, but their guests quickly became fair game for "unauthorized" gambling sessions, especially for the old-timers among the crew who were veterans of infamous Asiatic Station craps and black jack games. As much as $1,500 changed hands in a single deal of black jack, while one member of the crew walked away with $5,000 of the construction workers' salaries in games that Frietas labeled as "civilized, clean, very honest. No fighting broke out."[28]

Gambling on board a ship, especially during wartime, had long been prohibited by the Navy, but under the unusual circumstances Sprague turned a blind eye toward the infractions. His crew had experienced the shock of Pearl Harbor, the elation of heading out to save Wake's garrison, and the dismay at Pye's recall—all within three weeks. To avoid more seri-ous problems during the return journey to Pearl Harbor, Sprague decided it would be more advisable to let both his crew and the civilians blow off steam with gambling rather than let them mill around and dwell on the precariousness of their situation.

"This was very smart of Sprague," asserted Mapes. "We had so many civilians aboard, and this was just a way to relax. If we had been standing around after our work was done or had no form of relaxation, that could have caused problems. What the hell, it didn't matter if you lost anyway, because you could be dead the next day."[29]

The *Tangier* encountered no difficulties on the trip back, other than a possible submarine sighting and overworked evaporators that barely man-aged to produce enough fresh water for cooking and drinking. Personal bathing or cleaning of clothes thus had to be done in salt water, leading one crew member to smile, "being clean was indeed a luxury." The construction workers gradually became accustomed to sailors scampering to General Quarters, for Sprague called emergency drills several times each day. On the final day of 1941, Sprague guided his packed tender and exhausted crew into a Pearl Harbor alive with the sounds of repairmen and mechanics trying to patch up the damage sustained on 7 December.[30]

While workers repaired and replenished his ship for the next month, Sprague caught up on letters to relatives back home who, because of Sprague's role in the secretive Wake expedition, had heard nothing of his whereabouts. In a lengthy letter to his sister Dora, who had married businessman Fred Harvey and with whom she was about to open the first in an eventually large chain of department stores, Sprague mixed lighthearted chitchat with somber statements. Referring to Dora's business venture, Sprague hoped she and her husband would succeed beyond their wildest dreams, but warned, "don't work yourself to death doing it." He mentioned that Courtney and Patricia had apparently become very popular with the boys in San Francisco and mourned that—"I can see where father isn't going to get the front room in his slippers or bare feet any longer which is a hell of an oath." As to life on the *Tangier,* he described it as "hotter than hell out here. The ship soaks up the heat during the day and it isn't until about midnight that it cools off." Since every ship was blacked out at night, "we go groping around bashing our shins and cursing." He concluded the letter in a positive tone with a postscript for his nephew. "Tell Rick we're doing all right after a bum start."[31]

As a result of his leadership since Pearl Harbor, the 46-year-old Sprague was elevated to the rank of captain in a simple ceremony on board the *Tangier* on 3 January 1942. Early the next month, he received orders to sail for New Caledonia, a French possession in the South Pacific off Australia's eastern coast. Realizing his family would again hear little from him during the operation, Sprague wrote Annabel on 9 February that "It will be quiet [*sic*] some time before you'll hear from me but don't worry. Kiss the babies for me."[32]

The *Tangier* departed without escort on 11 February, bound for Tutuila, Samoa, 2,276 miles southwest of Hawaii, carrying a full load of aviation gasoline, ammunition, and bombs for the Catalinas it would tend, plus 10 Army trucks, 1,500 Army bombs, 6 Army officers, 86 Army enlisted personnel, and 73 civilian workers. After arriving in Samoa and discharging the Army and civilian personnel and their equipment, the *Tangier* sailed the same day for Suva, Fiji, seven hundred miles southwest. Though cruising to the South Seas, the voyage was far from pleasant. One crewman moaned that "endless drills by day was our steady fare," something that would not abate until the *Tangier* arrived in New Caledonia. After an eight-day stay in Suva, the *Tangier* headed toward New Caledonia on 28 February and completed the 734-mile segment the morning of 3 March, when it steamed into Noumea to relieve the tender *Curtiss* and begin servicing six Catalinas based out of the island.[33]

A destructive typhoon swept down on Noumea and the *Tangier* only two days later, hurling winds of up to 100 mph before it tore the ship's aerometer off the mast. Deadly gales blew ships aground in the harbor, a fate Sprague averted by dropping both anchors and firing the engines to 60 rpm to keep the ship pointed away from the beach. His efforts almost went for naught when powerful gusts of wind shoved a nearby American destroyer close to the *Tangier* and entangled the destroyer's anchor chain with the *Tangier*'s. Both ships were slowly being dragged toward the beach, but fortunately the storm abated before either ship ran aground. Luckier than most vessels at Noumea, the *Tangier* suffered slight damage that required minimal repairs.[34]

When the *Curtiss* departed the next day for Pearl Harbor, Sprague's ship assumed the duties as tender for the six Catalinas, which flew long-range searches north of New Caledonia to the Solomons as part of the Navy's protection of the vital American supply route to Australia. In addition, as the sole American naval vessel in New Caledonia, the *Tangier* acted as Station Ship and flagship for the commander of Patrol Wing Two, housed visiting admirals, and served as fleet post office.[35]

Thus isolated on the outer fringes of the American defense line, Sprague enjoyed a freer hand than other officers of similar rank stationed elsewhere. Like his ship, Sprague balanced a variety of duties at this French-dominated island—diplomat, representative of his nation, host, commanding officer, improviser, and liaison with the Army. This gave him an opportunity to exercise command and learn how to coexist with other military services and nations.

He performed well. Sprague realized that most of his crew had never been placed in such a far-flung outpost, so distant from speedy help and familiar surroundings. To combat fear and homesickness, Sprague eased rules and regulations, limited inspections, kept the galley and mess hall open around the clock, again overlooked gambling, and relaxed the uniform requirements.[36]

Sprague treated foreign powers in New Caledonia and members of his own military in similar fashion. After some of his men were almost killed by gunfire in Noumea, Sprague sent a blunt message to the leaders of the Free French and Vichy French on New Caledonia who were fighting for control of the island. They could shoot at each other all they desired, but if any man from the *Tangier* was harmed, he would retaliate immediately. Though the *Tangier's* few guns could inflict only minimal damage, Sprague wanted the French groups to clearly understand his stance. *Tangier* personnel experienced few problems ashore afterwards.[37]

Not long after U.S. Army forces arrived in New Caledonia in March, the commander of Army aircraft in Noumea informed Sprague that a planned training mission would take his planes over the *Tangier* at 1000 one day. Sprague replied that his gunners would hold their fire. When no aircraft appeared at the appointed time, Sprague waited four hours for the truant planes before angrily contacting his Army cohort. He chewed out the officer and reminded him that if enemy planes had attacked the *Tangier* during that four-hour stint, his men would have held their fire and thereby exposed the ship to great damage. Sprague coldly told the officer to cancel plans for future missions because the *Tangier* would shoot down any plane flying overhead.[38]

Not wanting to order aloft any of the *Tangier* planes without some semblance of protection, Sprague had wooden guns mounted on each. On 12 March, while on patrol one pilot spotted a Japanese observation and patrol bomber. Instead of turning away, he charged the enemy aircraft and succeeded in chasing it off, apparently because the Japanese pilot thought he faced a fighter.[39]

Shortly before American and Japanese naval forces clashed in history's first carrier duel twelve hundred miles to the northwest in early May at the Battle of the Coral Sea, Sprague left the *Tangier* for a new assignment— operations officer on the staff of Rear Adm. James L. Kauffman, commander of the Gulf Sea Frontier in Miami, Florida. The trip home followed six of the most crucial and exciting months in the Pacific theater that provided an invaluable training ground for the young commander. He arrived in Florida with an assurance that develops only from experience. While fellow Miami officers wondered what actual fighting was like and whether they would carry out their responsibilities with courage and confidence, Sprague was one of a small handful of naval officers who had already commanded in combat in this war. He had logged more miles at sea than most compatriots and had successfully dealt with soldiers of another nation. None of his Academy classmates, and few naval aviators, could point to such an active war record after only six months. Forrest Sherman would soon play a major role in the Coral Sea, and Jocko Clark had participated in January raids against the Marcus and Gilbert Islands, but Tommy Sprague had yet to see combat.

The *Tangier* crew already recognized that Sprague stood on a fast track to higher command. Though the ship had been embroiled in bitter fighting at Pearl Harbor and had suffered through agonizing disappointment at Wake, Sprague never allowed morale to sag. Thirteen years after Pearl Harbor, one man who fought four years in the Pacific war under different commanders was so impressed with his few short months with Sprague that he wrote to the Chief of Naval Operations, "Under fire and in any emergency he remain[ed] cool and his fighting spirit was unbeatable, no matter what the odds were against him. He had a keen sense of humor and during the attack at Pearl Harbor and other emergencies which followed, his little jokes and disregard of personal danger made us all forget our fear of what might happen and with such a leader, we couldn't but help to win." [40]

"We always felt safe with him," stated another crewman forty-six years after the war started. [41]

As Sprague headed to Miami in 1942, though, he viewed conditions with more concern. In a letter to his sister he wrote, "I'm afraid this war is going to be a long one unless the japs [*sic*] suddenly collapse which I doubt." [42]

CHAPTER SEVEN

Atlantic Interlude

S prague's war almost ended before he left Pearl Harbor. As the PB2Y2 seaplane taking him to the mainland lifted out of the water on 6 May, Sprague glanced out the window and noticed that the plane was flying too low to clear the mast of one of the sunken battleships still littering the harbor from 7 December. A sudden jolt smacked the plane back toward the water as it clipped the protruding mast, forcing Sprague to scurry out a rear entrance to safety. Though a small boat plucked Sprague out of the harbor in minutes, he lost most of his personal gear. Ironically, after safely enduring the attack on Pearl Harbor, the perilous Wake Island relief expedition, and three hectic months in the South Pacific, Sprague narrowly avoided death during a routine takeoff. He gathered what remained of his gear and boarded a destroyer headed for the United States when he learned that no other air transportation was available.[1]

While Sprague slowly approached the west coast of the United States, the Navy hurriedly scraped together a makeshift defense to fend off another potential disaster—the German U-boat campaign in the Atlantic. Commencing 12 January 1942 when *U-123* sank a British steamer three hundred miles east of Cape Cod, the German submarine offensive, called Operation Paukenschlag (Roll of the Drums), had terrorized shipping along the eastern coast. Within two weeks German torpedoes destroyed thirteen Allied vessels. In the Gulf Sea Frontier, Sprague's destination, U-boats sank sixteen ships inside Florida's territorial waters alone in three months and victimized almost one ship a day in May in the Gulf of Mexico.[2]

U-boat commanders feasted upon shipping in U.S. home waters during the war's first six months, frequently taking advantage of assistance handed to them by a naive and unprepared foe. One German commander, Peter Cremer in *U-333,* arrived off Miami on 4 May, shortly before Sprague's appearance, expecting to find the coast blacked out and the U.S. Navy on guard after half a year of war. Instead, "a mile-wide band of light" radiated from the Miami area, causing Cremer and his shipmates to stare in amazement. "Before this sea of light," he mentioned, "against this footlight glare of a carefree new world, were passing the silhouettes of ships recognizable in every detail and sharp as the outlines in a sales catalogue. Here they were formally presented to us on a plate: please help yourselves! All we had to do was press the button."[3]

When Adm. Karl Dönitz concentrated his German U-boat forces in Gulf Sea Frontier waters in May and June, the amount of sunken tonnage soared to alarming heights. Forty-one ships disappeared, mostly off the mouth of the Mississippi in the Gulf of Mexico. U-boat commanders inflicted more damage to the American war effort in the war's first six months than had been suffered at Pearl Harbor and in the entire Pacific for the same duration. Even worse, many of these lost ships were tankers that transported oil and vital supplies from South America to waiting American ports, and U.S. naval leaders had to digest the sober fact that the average 5,000-ton tanker carried the same amount of supplies as two freight trains of 150 cars each.[4]

Because of small prewar military budgets, most money had been poured into larger ships like cruisers and battleships rather than the unglamorous destroyer escorts needed to fight U-boats. Most available escort shipping streamed to the Pacific, leaving few resources along the Atlantic coast to harass Dönitz's boats. The Gulf Sea Frontier began operations with only two destroyers, twenty-five cutters, thirty-five aircraft, and an assortment of yachts and small craft—too small a force to implement the convoy system that had been so successfully utilized by the British.[5]

Without a convoy system to protect American coastal shipping, tankers steamed on their own schedules and braved the hazards alone, hoping that they could elude the deadly U-boats. As a result, the situation from January to June became, in the words of the Gulf Sea Frontier's official historian, "largely chaotic." Stopgap measures had to be used until a more efficient antisubmarine effort could be employed. On 22 May for example, the merchant vessel SS *San Pablo* came under attack south of the Yucatan Channel. Since there were no aircraft or surface forces available to come to her aid, a fake message was broadcast in plain English from the Gulf Sea Frontier Command that aircraft were on their way, a move, according to the Frontier's official historian, that was "the result of rather frantic desperation on the part of a command whose meager forces had long since been stretched beyond the breaking point." As they hoped, the U-boat captain intercepted the message and broke off the attack. In six and one-half months of war, American forces sank only eight U-boats, about what German shipyard workers produced in ten days.[6]

After arriving in Miami and learning the dismal facts of the U-boat situation along the eastern coast, Sprague must have wondered if fate had been playing a cruel hoax. His assignment to the Gulf Sea Frontier was not a demotion, since the Navy rushed in many excellent officers to quickly construct a defense system for the crucial Atlantic coast. However, six months earlier he had watched one enemy devastate Pearl Harbor. Now he worked in a different American sector while a second enemy inflicted what one historian has called "one of the greatest maritime disasters in history and the American nation's worst-ever defeat at sea." The fact that he faced an indefinite tour of duty combating U-boats from behind a desk compounded Sprague's consternation. He had gained valuable experience battling Japan's air attack on Pearl Harbor and commanding one component of a carrier task force, yet here he was thousands of miles away from the action, sitting in an office chair in sunny Miami. Rather than wasting his expertise—few officers could boast such an active war record—Sprague preferred the controls of an airplane or command of an aircraft carrier.[7]

But at least in Miami he could employ his considerable command talents, for over the next nine months Sprague faced a stern challenge, and if he performed well he could get one of those carriers that all aviators wanted. The nation's shipyards were busily forging hundreds of ships, including new aircraft carriers. The opportunity for higher command waited temptingly in the near future.

As operations officer he stood third in command at the Gulf Sea Frontier behind Rear Adm. James L. Kaufman and Kaufman's assistant commander. The Gulf Sea Frontier comprised a huge expanse of water stretching from northern Florida to Belize in Central America and had the responsibility of protecting Florida, much of the Bahamas and Cuba, and the entire Gulf of Mexico.[8]

Eleven assistants helped Sprague carry out his diverse duties that, in effect, handed him the day-to-day administration and coordination of all Gulf Sea Frontier air and surface forces as well as all naval bases in the region. In addition, Sprague commanded the Operations Center in Miami, planned offensive and defensive missions, organized convoy escorts, commanded rescue operations, and coordinated his forces with those of local defense forces and forces of Allied nations.[9]

From command headquarters on the sixth and seventh floors of the Du-Pont Building in downtown Miami, Sprague and his fellow officers began applying some sting to Atlantic coastal defenses. Within one month, the number of available aircraft almost doubled, most of them being Vought-Sikorsky OS2U-3 seaplanes stocked with depth bombs. Air ships helped maintain a watch on vital sea routes. Civil Air Patrols, derisively labeled the "yellow bees" by U-boat commanders after their bright red, blue, and yellow paint, eased the pressure on military aircraft by flying daylight patrols. Pilots of Pan American Airlines voluntarily attended submarine identification classes so they could radio any sightings as they cruised along their normal air routes to Central and South America.[10]

Thirty-five additional ships, including sixteen Coast Guard cutters, joined the Gulf Sea Frontier in May and June. Civilian craft again augmented military forces when auxiliary yachts and boats less than a hundred feet long were appropriated and organized into the "Hooligan Navy." Most often retaining the owner as skipper for each boat, these small vessels frustrated U-boat commanders who were forced to dive and remain under water to avoid being sighted and reported by the tiny craft. Within eight months, 550 yachts and boats peppered the Atlantic and Gulf coasts.[11]

The biggest single change implemented along the eastern shores proved to be the convoy system, where merchant ships gathered into large groups and steamed together under the protection of naval escort craft. Successfully employed by the British against German U-boats in Europe, the convoy system relied on carefully drawn schedules whereby convoys moved by day and anchored in protected bays by night. Because of a serious shortage of escort vessels, Sprague and other commanders could organize only sporadic convoys at first, but as more destroyer escorts rolled out of shipyards the system expanded until ships could steam in daylight under naval protection and berth in an entire network of anchorages that stretched along the coast from Canada to the Caribbean.[12]

Results of these moves, most implemented by Sprague, so dramatically improved defenses in the Gulf Sea Frontier that its historian wrote soon after, "It was unquestionably in August that the German undersea raiders were definitely defeated in the Gulf Sea Frontier." An effective combination of convoys, air and surface forces, radar-equipped night search planes, blimps, an improved communications system, sufficient air bases to place aircraft almost anywhere along the major shipping lanes within one hour, and valuable experience and training for defense forces turned the Atlantic coast into hazardous duty for U-boat commanders. Sprague also negotiated with the Mexican and Cuban governments for the inclusion of their aircraft and gunboats.[13]

Another officer stationed at Miami who worked closely with Sprague and succeeded him as operations officer, Capt. (later Rear Adm.) James R. Dudley, credited the speedy improvement in Gulf Sea Frontier defenses to Sprague. "The operations developed from almost no combat facilities" to include a multitude of bases, craft, and tactics, Dudley wrote after the war. "Most of this was developed under [Sprague's] supervision."[14]

What had once been deadly waters for American and Allied merchantmen now turned lethal for U-boats. The war diary for the U-boat High Command in Germany stated on 21 August that effective American defenses "must, if continued, lead to unsupportable losses, to a decline in successes and so to a decline in the prospects of success of the U-boat war as a whole." As a result, Dönitz began shifting his focus south to the Caribbean region.[15]

The number of U-boat contacts in the Gulf Sea Frontier dropped dramatically. Though fifty-nine contacts were recorded in August, only three vessels totaling less than ten thousand tons were lost. Contacts plunged to thirty in September, resulting in only one loss, which turned out to be the final ship sunk in the Gulf of Mexico. October saw so few contacts with U-boats—only one definite—that the Frontier's historian claimed "the enemy had given up the struggle." The next month underscored this assertion when Gulf Sea Frontier defenses logged not even one definite sighting of German U-boats. Submarine activity remained stagnant until just before Sprague left the Gulf Sea Frontier in March 1943, when a mere seven contacts occurred.[16]

Near the end of March 1943, having performed what Dudley labeled a "tremendous job . . . in getting defenses organized in the Gulf Sea Frontier," Sprague left to assume the duties of his next post—commander of the Naval Air Center in Seattle and of the nearby Naval Air Station at Sand Point. This duty was ideal for Sprague, since aviators came to Sand Point for advanced flight and carrier flight training. After recording successes with the *Tangier* and at Miami, Sprague was due to be given one of the sparkling new *Essex*-class aircraft carriers being constructed in the United States.[17]

By the time Sprague arrived in Seattle, he had been on shore duty for almost one year while other contemporaries participated in Pacific carrier actions in the Coral Sea, at Midway, and in the Solomon Islands. Classmate Forrest Sherman had already been given command of one carrier—the *Wasp*—which unfortunately sank in September 1942 off Guadalcanal. The same month Sprague assumed duties at Seattle, Jocko Clark took command of the new fast carrier *Yorktown* and participated in the Central Pacific's opening offensive against the Gilbert and Marshall Islands. Thomas Sprague received the fast carrier *Intrepid* in June 1943, and took her into Pacific combat shortly afterwards.[18]

Sprague remained in Seattle for only seven months. In that time, air squadrons were organized and commissioned for service in the Pacific, including VC-10, a squadron of torpedo and fighter pilots who would eventually wind up on board the escort carrier *Gambier Bay* and form part of Taffy 3, the division of escort carriers Sprague later commanded at Leyte Gulf. A pilot from that squadron, Henry Pyzdrowski, recalls that Sand Point hummed with aviation activity during that time and that Sprague oversaw "a very vital area" for naval aviation.[19]

Something larger beckoned, however. In October 1943, Sprague received orders to take command of the new fast carrier *Wasp,* then near completion in Massachusetts. Sprague hoped he could once again carry the name *Wasp* into battle and gain further glories to add to those already accumulated by prior captains, the last of whom was classmate Forrest Sherman.

CHAPTER EIGHT

Seek Out and Destroy
Our Foe

When Sprague arrived in November 1943 to take command of
the *Wasp,* yard workers were laboring around the clock to
complete her construction. Instead of sparkling new aircraft,
he saw riveters' cables, scaffolds, and tools on the partially completed deck.

Sprague's crew was as incomplete as his ship. Practically all of the 3,448-
man complement had filtered into the Boston area for training classes conducted by *Wasp* officers, but they were a crew in name only. Sixty percent
had never even been to sea, and few had ever served together. Sprague faced
an enormous challenge in molding his men into a first-rate fighting crew.
He had successfully accomplished a similar task with the *Tangier,* but the
Wasp dwarfed the tender in size and complexity.[1]

Sprague arrived as unceremoniously as possible. Instead of rank, he
wanted to emphasize work. Each man, from the oldest veteran to the green-
est recruit, had a duty to perform, and he intended to focus their energies
on that task. He hoped this attitude would permeate all levels of the carrier
and form an initial bond among his inexperienced crew.

It worked. Officers and crew were quickly impressed with Sprague's
quiet authority and realized their new captain was no ruthless officer bent
on speedy promotion nor an overly bombastic leader who relied on emotion to charge up his crew. A staff writer for the ship's newsletter, *Waspirit,*

wrote with some astonishment that Sprague "came in quietly and took over with so little fanfare that it was several days before the word got around. Though it was not realized at the time, the key-note for his command had been set. . . ."[2]

People, especially in a war zone, also need a purpose for enduring hardships they normally would shun. A vague rationale, such as defeating the enemy, fails to motivate as powerfully as specific reasons that reach down to touch the ordinary seaman. Sprague took advantage of the *Wasp*'s commissioning ceremony, at which he was scheduled to deliver a speech, to instill a purpose that could unite his crew.

Dignitaries traveled to Bethlehem Steel Company's Fore River Yard near Boston for the 24 November commissioning of the Navy's newest fast carrier, including Boston Mayor Maurice Tobin, Massachusetts Governor Leverett Saltonstall, and the principal speaker, Rear Adm. D. C. Ramsey, chief of the Bureau of Aeronautics. Shortly before commissioning day an unexpected guest announced her intention to participate. One of Sprague's officers happened to be Lt. John A. Roosevelt, the president's youngest son. A few days before the ceremony, communications officer Lt. Robert P. Daly quizzed each officer on the names of their guests. Lieutenant Roosevelt responded with a straight face, "My father's too busy and can't come, but my mother will be here."

Daly quickly relayed the news to Sprague. "Oh my God!" exclaimed the commander. "We're going to have to ask her to speak, and the programs are already printed." A hasty addendum solved that problem.[3]

Sprague, never comfortable with public speaking, nevertheless composed an effective oration for his first official address. Braving cold winds that chilled the numerous guests and naval personnel assembled on deck, Sprague gave roots to the neophyte crew, whom he called the "officers and men of the new *Wasp*," by linking them with the earlier *Wasp*s, whose men had established "a glorious name in naval tradition" by a list of courageous actions stretching back to the American Revolution. This placed a heavy burden on the current crew to carry forward such an honorable reputation. Sprague asserted that "a debt is to be repaid for the gallant officers and men of the previous *Wasp*s who were unsparing in their efforts to establish and maintain the everlasting greatness of the United States and her Navy." He told his listeners, though, that as a unit they faced opportunities unlike any that had occurred before. "The book lies open before us, and collectively, we will write the next chapters in *Wasp* histories . . . It is indeed an honor for all of us to be allowed to continue a great tradition."

He added that their nation had spared no expense in providing "as excellent a ship as naval construction can produce." Supported by the abundance of superb equipment and arms that poured out of American factories, he stated in words that stamped his own essence on that of the crew's, "we will face any foe with quiet confidence."

Sprague moved on to the crux of his speech, and his words no doubt brought a smile to the face of every aviator on board. "The air group is the only reason for the carrier's existence. Remember that," he emphasized. The air group's "comfort and efficiency is our major concern." At one stage of their careers, most aviators had served on carriers that had been commanded by nonaviators, and they had found the experience distasteful. Those commanders considered the air groups as only one of the weapons in their arsenals, rather than *the* weapon. With Sprague, the aviators of Air Group 14 knew their commander understood the dangers inherent in flying and would do everything possible not merely to send them into combat with the best-maintained aircraft, but to bring them back safely.

"A carrier, offensively, you know," Sprague continued, "is no better than the air group it supports." He wanted the *Wasp* to sport the best. One of Sprague's wartime aides, Lt. Comdr. Charles Cunningham, later attributed the love and affection Sprague's subordinates had for their commander to Sprague's "insistence of doing everything within his power for the pilots. Having been through the mill himself, he always felt that nothing should stand in his way to see that the boys get back to the ship safely."[4]

Sprague ended with unusually venomous words for his enemy, "whose cruelty is unparalleled in history; whose every so-called advancement in its civilization was obtained through treachery; whose cunning and deceit is particularly abhorrent to all Americans." Sprague then stated the single mission of the *Wasp:* "It is our mission and purpose, or aim, indeed, our privilege, to seek out this foe and destroy him wherever he may be."[5]

A staff writer on the *Waspirit,* writing as though the ship were speaking, mirrored the feelings of most officers and men by mentioning that although final judgment on the new skipper would have to wait until he took the *Wasp* to sea for her shakedown cruise, he earned points with his talk. The writer added that "with his cap sitting a little to one side, and his heavy overcoat worn with that rugged air of his, I had to admit to myself that he did look pretty salty."[6]

After delivering his speech, Sprague hosted a reception in his quarters for Mrs. Roosevelt, dignitaries, and family members. Though this aspect of his duties bothered him as much as giving speeches, the affair went smoothly.

Eleanor Roosevelt charmed the entire Sprague family with her friendliness and warmth, and once walked across the room to shake hands with Courtney and Patricia to make them feel a part of the festivities. Even die-hard Republican members of Sprague's family left with a favorable impression of the First Lady. Early the next month, after receiving a souvenir program of the commissioning from Sprague, she thanked him on White House stationery.[7]

It was now time to get down to serious preparations. On 10 January 1944 Sprague took the 872-foot-long *Wasp* and her escort of three destroyers out of Massachusetts Bay for her shakedown cruise. The shakedown, meant to iron out any wrinkles in the ship's construction and to train the air group and crew, formed a crucial segment in the carrier's development. Poor execution by Sprague, his officers, or men would cast a pall over the *Wasp* immediately prior to heading into the Pacific war zone.[8]

Once into Atlantic waters, Sprague turned the carrier south for Chesapeake Bay. From 11 to 28 January, he put his men through daily flight operations, anchoring each night in Old Plantation Flats.[9]

Cameramen from an organization called *Pathé* News, which ran news shorts in movie and newsreel theaters, accompanied the *Wasp* in its shakedown cruise, even though at first Sprague had denied their request to come on board because of the large amount of classified material on the carrier. He changed his mind after receiving a request to reconsider from Capt. Leland Lovette, director of the Navy's Office of Public Relations. Lovette explained that the film would be reviewed by his office and any sensitive material removed before its release to the general public. He added that "Scenes of routine life aboard a carrier" would not only be informative to the general public, but would be valuable as "an indoctrination film for Naval personnel . . . and as a positive aid to the accelerated aviation recruiting program."[10]

Sprague conducted almost daily flight operations as the carrier wound through the Caribbean to give his airmen and crew practice in launchings and landings. By the time the ship headed back to Boston in late February, a confident crew had emerged from the diverse conglomerate that had assembled the previous November. The crew believed in its air group; the air group knew it could rely on the crew. Mostly, air group and crew believed in their skipper.

According to the *Waspirit,* the shakedown cruise was "the first opportunity for many of the crew to see [Sprague's] now familiar figure on the bridge, directing the course of the *Wasp* . . . and all hands had that feeling of complete safety that comes only with utmost confidence in their leader." This confidence emerged from the impressive results logged by the ship and crew. They carried out their exercises without any major malfunction in equipment. No accidents hampered landings and launchings. Most important to both Sprague and his men, every pilot launched from the *Wasp* returned safely.[11]

"The fact that the *Wasp* had one of the best shakedown records of any aircraft carrier was largely due to the minute care and attention that the Captain gave to each detail of the operations," summed the *Waspirit* in words that could have been spoken by any crew member aboard the *Patoka* or *Tangier.*[12]

"It was on my shake-down cruise that I came to realize how lucky I had been in getting the Old Man," stated a *Waspirit* staffer, writing as if the carrier itself could speak. "I discovered that I had that rare combination of an airman who could handle a ship like Babe Ruth handled his bat." The president's son, Lieutenant Roosevelt, later wrote that Sprague "took a very green crew and molded us together into a unit that each and everyone of us had a personal pride in."[13]

"I breezed back into Boston feeling pretty doggone good about the whole thing," boasted the personified *Wasp,* "and I was rarin' to get a crack at those Japs." The ship would get its chance in less than three months.[14]

After six weeks of meetings, minor repairs to the ship, and leave for the crew, the *Wasp* departed Boston on 15 March for its three-week voyage to Pearl Harbor. Accompanied to the Canal by members of the print media—including a Time-Life reporter—who wanted a view of carrier operations, the *Wasp* enjoyed a fairly routine cruise south, although Sprague later reported with a touch of humor that jittery lookouts issued "a more than usual number of submarine warnings—one at [*sic*] which was evidently authentic. . . ." Five days later the carrier arrived at the Panama Canal, where Nimitz designated Sprague commander of Task Group 12.2, consisting of the *Wasp* and her destroyers, the *Bryant* and *McNair.* Sprague was ordered to proceed to San Diego to take on more supplies and a Marine contingent, then head to Pearl Harbor.[15]

The *Wasp* remained only two days in San Diego, loading an additional one hundred aircraft and twenty-eight hundred Marines into already cramped conditions. Sprague had cots placed underneath the wings of aircraft for the Marines, which alleviated the situation somewhat, but when the *Wasp* departed on 30 March, she rode much lower in the water than usual. Leaving before a group of high-ranking Navy officers and serenaded to the tune of "Anchors Aweigh" by the Navy Band, five tugboats helped guide the carrier out of San Diego. Sprague would not return to the United States for eight long months—months that would take the *Wasp* into two of the war's largest carrier clashes and would propel Sprague to flag rank.[16]

Since Sprague had not been back to the Hawaiian Islands for over a year, he must have wondered what the once-shattered anchorage looked like. Much to his surprise, when the *Wasp* arrived on 3 April, few signs of the December debacle remained. Instead, personnel swarmed about the busy docks around the clock, ferrying men and supplies to the many waiting ships that would transport American military and industrial might to the front lines of Pacific combat.[17]

With the time drawing nearer when he would take his carrier into battle, Sprague squeezed in as much training as possible. He spent most of April conducting gunnery exercises, nighttime and daytime flight qualifications, and launchings and landings. Fighters and bombers dove on and attacked towing spars pulled behind the *Wasp* to improve accuracy, while in separate drills gunnery crews fired at target sleeves pulled by *Wasp* airplanes. Sprague could enhance performance in practice runs and get a handle on his crew's efficiency, but he knew an accurate picture would not emerge until his crew faced actual combat conditions.[18]

Sprague's task force commander, Vice Adm. Marc A. Mitscher, also wanted to get extra practice for the green crews and new ships that supplemented his veteran flotilla of carriers. Before throwing them against the Japanese during a full-scale attack, Mitscher scheduled a sortie against Japanese-occupied Marcus and Wake Islands, two locales offering enemy targets that possessed little offensive threat. Sprague's aviators and crew would gain combat experience without being exposed to first-line enemy units.[19]

Fuel, ammunition, and provisions poured into the *Wasp* from 29 April to 3 May, as Sprague prepared his ship for her initial action. After granting the crew a brief liberty, Sprague took the *Wasp,* stocked with thirty-eight Grumman F6F Hellcat fighters, thirty-two Curtiss SB2C Helldiver dive-bombers, and eighteen Grumman TBF Avenger torpedo planes, out of Hawaiian waters on 3 May and headed for Majuro Atoll in the Marshall Islands, twenty-six hundred miles southwest of Pearl Harbor.[20]

Five days later, the *Wasp* entered Majuro Atoll, where Sprague reported for duty to Admiral Mitscher. Mitscher assigned him to Task Group 58.6, a unit of three carriers commanded by Rear Adm. Alfred E. Montgomery. Along with the carriers *Essex* and *San Jacinto*, Sprague was ordered to "destroy enemy aircraft, installations and surface craft" at Marcus and Wake Islands "by air strike."[21]

"This was Big Time," wrote crewman Marvin H. Bender of the attack on Marcus. "We had left the Bush Leagues far behind." Sprague would now be measured by standards already established by successful fast carrier captains.[22]

A tense atmosphere pervaded the *Wasp* on the night before her first combat action. Aviators and crew donned calm exteriors to mask nervous stomachs. Cooks prepared battle rations while men checked life jackets and flash-proof clothing. A Catholic chaplain heard confessions of men who would later scribble notes to parents and loved ones back home.[23]

The operation started at 0445 on 19 May, when Sprague launched four fighters to make a predawn reconnaissance sweep of the target. Almost four hours later, from 0803 to 0815, Sprague sent off Strike A of twelve fighters, fifteen Curtiss SB2C Helldiver dive-bombers, and eight Grumman TBF Avenger torpedo planes from ninety miles south of Marcus Island. He followed this with three other strikes, launched approximately every three hours and varying in numbers from twenty-two to thirty-three aircraft. After recovering all planes, Sprague took the *Wasp* that night to a spot ninety miles north of Marcus Island, its assigned launch position for the four strikes on 20 May. Two strikes hit Marcus that day before Montgomery canceled the remainder of the operation because accompanying destroyers were running low on fuel.[24]

While the task group headed for Wake, a thousand miles to the southeast, intelligence officers debriefed aviators and studied photographic reconnaissance to determine the effectiveness of the six attacks on 19–20 May. Sprague, who could examine information from an aviator's point of view, conducted his own interviews of pilots to see what improvements could be implemented at Wake.[25]

The results were disappointing. Though his pilots encountered no enemy aircraft, either on the ground or in the air, thick antiaircraft fire rattled the inexperienced pilots and threw them off their intended bombing runs. They damaged two gun emplacements and four buildings and littered the runway with thirty bomb craters, but Sprague could hardly justify results when compared to expenditures. Of 189 sorties that flew over Marcus Island, 29 (representing 15 percent) failed to deliver their load because of clouds or enemy fire. The other 160 succeeded in doing little more than rearranging clumps of dirt. If Wake was to be any better, enemy antiaircraft fire would have to be suppressed and his pilots would have to be more determined to maintain their run in at their target.[26]

Sprague's outlook brightened when he examined other aspects of the raid. Every plane landed without mishap after their missions. *Wasp* combat air patrol fighters shot down the sole enemy plane that came near the carrier on 19 May when they splashed what was most likely a Japanese reconnaissance bomber twenty-nine miles from the *Wasp*. Only two men were injured, both sustained when enemy flak tore into their aircraft. Mistakes made at Marcus Island could be addressed in time for Wake, which would be attacked by a more confident group of aviators because of the experience gained.[27]

Throughout the first two days, officers and men watched Sprague to see how he handled combat. According to those who were near the captain, he tried to keep everyone on the bridge loose by mixing in light chatter and laughter when possible. His signalman, Robert Carew, remembered Sprague talking to anyone within hearing range, officers and seamen alike, to ease the tension. "He wouldn't crack jokes on the bridge," said Carew, "but I heard him laugh plenty of times. I can never recall Sprague raising his voice to an officer over some mistake."[28]

In action, Sprague maintained the same steadiness as during the shakedown cruise. "During our first combat with the enemy," wrote the *Waspirit*, "when all of our previous months of training were put to the test, the Captain's leadership, and his cool and dispassionate manner as he handled the ship were an inspiration to all hands."[29]

They performed better at Wake. From seventy miles southwest of their destination, five strikes lifted off the *Wasp* and, against lighter antiaircraft fire, dropped seventy-two tons of bombs on gas tanks, buried ammunition and supply stores, and a radio station. They were credited with damaging gun installations and four enemy aircraft on the ground, one lugger, and probably destroying three to four barges. Again safely recovering all planes, Sprague and the *Wasp* headed for Majuro with the rest of the task group.[30]

In his action report, Sprague admitted his air group inflicted only minor damage when he stated that "the greatest value of the operation was the training and education afforded both ships and air group personnel" (which was, in effect, the main reason for conducting the mission). Though he wrote that his crew performed to "a high standard," he refrained from mentioning any individual outside the air group because his ship faced no enemy opposition.[31] Rear Adm. F. W. Wagner, on board the *Wasp* as commander of Carrier Division 5, submitted a much harsher report, claiming that the results, especially at Marcus Island, were "disappointing." *Wasp* aircraft carried almost five hundred bombs against Marcus, he added, yet less than one-third "hit dry land at the target." Though he attributed the poor results in part to inclement weather over Marcus and bomb rack malfunctions, the main portion of blame rested with "green pilots" who gave up on their runs too soon because of thick antiaircraft fire. Wagner recommended that in the future enemy antiaircraft fire had to first be eliminated before the strikes appeared. When they arrived over Marcus, the pilots experienced too much difficulty picking out their precise target from among the numerous similar objectives. He stated that Sprague's pilots succeeded in reducing antiaircraft fire at Wake, which secured improved results, and he urged that aviators be given more freedom to select their own targets once over the objective.[32]

Wagner's report must have pained Sprague, since he had always placed great emphasis upon preparation. Though Mitscher praised the task group on 25 May for accomplishing the mission "WITH GREAT CREDIT" and Nimitz wired a "WELL DONE" to the task group two days later, Sprague hoped to perform better when the *Wasp* got her second chance.[33]

Events in the Pacific quickly heated up. Having seized the Gilbert Islands in November 1943 and the Marshall Islands three months later, American military strategists next set their sights on the Mariana Islands group, located approximately fifteen hundred miles east of Manila Bay and thirteen hundred miles southeast of Tokyo. Controlled by Japan since 1920, these islands—particularly Saipan, Tinian, and Guam—had been gradually built into a major fueling and supply station for the Imperial Navy. Possession of these islands by the United States would hinder Japan's lines of communications, serve as a launching pad for subsequent assaults, and provide bases for the huge American B-29 bombers so they could commence their bombing of Japan proper.[34]

An enormous naval armada, commanded by Vice Adm. Raymond A. Spruance, supported the invasion. Spearheading the effort was Mitscher's Task Force 58, fifteen fast carriers broken into four task groups sporting nine hundred planes. Sprague's *Wasp* joined Admiral Montgomery's Task Group 58.2, along with the carrier *Bunker Hill* and light carriers *Monterey* and *Cabot*.[35]

Sprague, along with the other carrier commanders under Mitscher, was given four objectives. His air group was ordered to destroy "by repeated air strikes" aircraft and aircraft facilities at Tinian, Rota, and Guam that might hinder the 15 June invasion of neighboring Saipan. The *Wasp* was also to provide air support for the ground forces at Saipan, defend both land and sea forces from enemy air attack, and provide air support for the subsequent landings at Guam.[36]

Wasp aviators experienced a taste of combat at Marcus and Wake, but Sprague understood that the earlier raids might pale compared to what his fliers and crew could face in the Philippine Sea west of the Marianas. Providing adequate support for soldiers and Marines in the heat of battle would be tough in itself, but his ship also had to guard against enemy counterattack. Should the powerful Imperial fleet sail out for the first time since their losses at the Coral Sea and Midway two years prior, the next few weeks could provide a harder test for the *Wasp*—and for Sprague—than anyone realized.

On 6 June Mitscher's Task Force 58, including the *Wasp,* sortied from Majuro harbor in the Marshall Islands and headed for the Marianas. From his bridge, Sprague observed an impressive spectacle as nearly a hundred ships, which required five hours to leave the harbor, covered seven hundred square miles of ocean. One *Wasp* pilot recalled that "Ships of all classes may be seen in all directions as far as the eye can see," lending a feeling of confidence to the assembled aviators and crew. Would the Imperial fleet dare emerge to issue a challenge to such a powerful force?[37]

Exactly one week later the Japanese responded. On 13 June the commander of the First Mobile Fleet, Vice Adm. Jisaburo Ozawa, guided his fleet out of Tawi Tawi in the Sulu Archipelago off Borneo's northeast coast and headed northeast for the Philippine Sea to enact the Japanese plan called A-Go. This plan, involving two steps, was designed to crush American carrier air power. Land-based aircraft would first attack the American fleet from Mariana airfields and destroy one-third of its carriers before Ozawa even fired his first shots. Ozawa would then advance and, relying upon a hundred-mile advantage in attack range given him by his lightweight carrier aircraft, smash Spruance's remaining carriers before they had moved into strike range.[38]

Ozawa's flawed plan contained the seeds of disaster. He relied on five hundred land-based aircraft to remove a significant portion of his opposition, but what if they failed to do so? He also asked his aviators to fly against the best the enemy had to offer, yet because of combat deaths and attrition, his aviators were far less skilled than those who had commanded the skies in 1942–43. Ozawa took into aerial combat untested pilots with far less training than the American aviators they would soon face.[39]

Sprague started his first offensive action of the Marianas campaign on 11 June when, from 240 miles east of Tinian, he launched Air Group 14's planes in a sweep against Tinian airfields while aircraft from other carriers attacked similar targets on Guam, Saipan, and Rota. As part of Spruance's strategy to remove Ozawa's land-based air strength from his arsenal and gain local air supremacy for the United States, *Wasp* fighters destroyed thirteen Japanese aircraft on the ground while encountering no opposition in the air. *Wasp* aircraft flew more than two hundred sorties the following day, dropping almost seventy tons of bombs on Tinian Town, Gurguan Point runway, and Ushi Point airfield. In two days of heavy attacks, Spruance stripped Ozawa of most of his land-based aircraft and seriously impeded any chance Ozawa had of success. However, for some astounding reason the commander of the land-based aircraft, Vice Adm. Kakuji Kakuda, failed to inform Ozawa he had lost much of his offensive power. Ozawa sailed onward, ignorant that one of his two offensive arms had been removed.[40]

Sprague liked the performance of Air Group 14 in these raids. He believed the pilots controlled their nervousness better than at Marcus and Wake Islands and pressed home their attacks with more determination.[41]

During the night of 12–13 June Sprague moved his ship into launching position north of Saipan for further strikes on the Marianas. *Wasp* aircraft pounded Mariana airfields over the next four days as the invasion forces neared the jump-off point for their assault on Saipan. Air Group 14 flew a variety of missions as Sprague took the *Wasp* within ten miles of Saipan, sinking three enemy barges, conducting frequent fighter sweeps over Tinian, and blasting targets on Rota and Saipan. When Marines hit the invasion beaches on 15 June, Sprague's fighters flew overhead, prepared to strike enemy positions whenever called upon by their Marine compatriots.[42]

Signs were building that the Japanese fleet would soon arrive. American submarines had immediately reported Ozawa's 13 June sortie from Tawi Tawi. Two days later, as Marines stormed ashore on Saipan, Sprague received notice from official sources that the Imperial fleet had departed from the Philippines on its way to the Marianas, and that same day he listened to Radio Tokyo boast that its fleet would put the Americans to flight. By 17 June, when the American submarine *Cavalla* tracked Ozawa's fleet only eight hundred miles to the southwest, everyone on the *Wasp* knew that battle was imminent.[43]

Ozawa split his fleet as he moved east. Vice Adm. Takeo Kurita, a man Sprague would again encounter four months later off the Philippines in a more desperate situation, commanded an advance group of three aircraft carriers escorted by battleships and cruisers. One hundred miles behind steamed Ozawa's main force of six carriers and their escorts. Ozawa planned to entice Spruance west, using Kurita as bait. When Spruance came out to smash Kurita, Ozawa intended to throw his 340 aircraft on the unsuspecting American admiral.[44]

Ozawa might have had a feasible plan, but Japanese naval tactics were becoming predictable for perceptive American naval commanders. Yamamoto had unsuccessfully attempted to lure Spruance farther west at Midway so that he could engage him with superior forces while another Japanese group surprised the island in an end run. A document retrieved from a Japanese aircraft downed in the Philippines indicated that Japan would soon use empty carriers to draw American naval forces away from the beachhead. Consequently, Spruance decided to keep his ships close to Saipan's beaches and the large number of transports unloading precious supplies to the Army and Marine units ashore. In case of a decoy, Spruance wanted to be near Saipan to protect the beachhead.[45]

As the Japanese fleet moved nearer, Mitscher ordered long-range searches in hopes of locating the enemy before they located him. Sprague sent six Avenger torpedo planes on a 350-mile search in the early morning hours of 17 June and an entire series of scouting missions on 18 June, but failed to spot anything. Later that evening, he turned the *Wasp* back toward Saipan as part of Spruance's plan to protect the beachhead, disappointed that his aviators would not get a first crack at the enemy.[46]

At about the same time, Ozawa foolishly sent a signal to a land-based commander that was picked up at Pearl Harbor. It placed the Japanese fleet 355 miles to the southwest. Mitscher and most aviators in Task Force 58 saw this as their opportunity to launch a first strike at dawn, but when Mitscher requested permission from Spruance to head west so his carriers could be in position to attack, Spruance turned him down.[47]

Spruance's answer stunned Mitscher and his aviators, who now would be forced to sit still while Ozawa's carriers crept into strike range and launched a first attack. Capt. Arleigh Burke, Mitscher's chief of staff, moaned, "This we did not like. It meant that the enemy could attack us at will at dawn the next morning. We could not attack the enemy."[48]

Sprague voiced no opinion about Spruance's controversial decision. As an aviator, he strongly favored turning west and launching a full strike, but he never once expressed his views. His job was to carry out orders, not second-guess his superiors. As with the unpopular recall of the Wake Island relief expedition, Sprague would let history judge the decision makers.

The day of the expected battle, 19 June, found Sprague in position with the other three carriers of Task Group 58.2 at the southeastern end of Spruance's disposition, which formed an enormous floating "4" covering 270 square miles of ocean. Three task groups, each arranged in a four-mile-wide circular formation with the escorting cruisers and destroyers steaming on the outer fringes as protection, stretched across twenty-five miles of ocean in a north–south axis. Spruance placed Vice Adm. Willis A. Lee's powerful battle line of battleships and cruisers fifteen miles west of the carrier groups, while twelve miles north and three miles east of Lee sailed Mitscher's fourth task group. To get at American carriers, Ozawa's inexperienced pilots would have to elude American fighter interceptors, plunge through Lee's concentration of antiaircraft fire, and survive carrier task group antiaircraft fire.[49]

American carrier aviators were about to experience combat so lopsided that the twelve hours would be compared to a comfortable bird-hunting outing back home. By day's end, Sprague would know if his system functioned despite repeated aerial assaults, the staccato noise of antiaircraft guns, the apprehensive gazes cast skyward by nervous crewmen, and the fears and doubts that plague many at times of crises. With American shipyards producing carriers at a record pace, experienced aviators would be needed to command carrier task groups. Forrest Sherman in the previous *Wasp,* Jocko Clark in the new *Yorktown,* and Tommy Sprague in the *Intrepid* had successfully commanded fast carriers. A strong showing over the next few days would enhance Sprague's reputation and earmark him for one of those lofty posts.

The captain had done all he could to prepare his men for battle. On board a ship as large as an aircraft carrier, a captain maintains little actual control over the average seaman—that is delegated to subordinates. There are a few areas, however, in which a commander affects men serving underneath him. Whenever a meeting became bogged down in statistics or threatened to erupt in heated discussion, Sprague cut in with a humorous tale. As one current newspaper article stated, subordinates loved Sprague's stories and the "democratic informality" that dominated his meetings. "Short, stocky and athletic, [Sprague] has a face outlined with laugh wrinkles and a wide mouth that gives you the impression his whole face is opening when he laughs. Laughter is a habit with Sprague."[50]

Sprague had the fighter pilots of his air group ready to take off at short notice on 19 June as he, like most commanders, expected action any time.

Ozawa started the fast-paced day by launching sixty-nine aircraft at 0830, his first of four air raids against Mitscher's carriers. At 0955, from 100 miles west of Guam, *Wasp* radar picked up Ozawa's planes 150 miles out, and within one minute of receiving Mitscher's order at 1023 to launch Sprague had the first of his fighters aloft and on their way to intercept their adversary. To protect the remainder of his air group and to clear his deck for action, Sprague sent the dive-bombers and torpedo planes outside the carrier formation and ordered them to circle until further orders could be given.[51]

The first raid did little harm, as not a single Japanese aircraft came near either the *Wasp* or the task group. Hellcats took advantage of their opponents' inexperience and eliminated almost half the enemy planes before they reached Lee's advance battle line. Rather than immediately press their attacks before American fighters reached proper intercept altitude, Japanese pilots foolishly circled at twenty thousand feet to regroup. By the time they were ready to strike, Hellcats had set up a multitiered intercept formation miles ahead of Lee. Then, instead of remaining in formation, raw enemy pilots frequently attacked on their own or in small numbers and were easily deflected by veteran Hellcat pilots.[52]

American pilots or Lee's antiaircraft arsenal destroyed forty-two of Ozawa's sixty-nine aircraft, using information supplied by superbly trained American fighter-director officers, including one Japanese-speaking lieutenant who picked up over the radio every command given to the untested Japanese by their air coordinator. Sprague mentioned in his action report that "Numerous raids appeared on the radar screen during the [attack], but did not approach our disposition." Aviators, including four of his Hellcat pilots who recorded a kill, so manhandled the opposition that one *Lexington* pilot yelled to another after returning to their carrier, "Why, hell. It was just like an old-time turkey shoot down home!" From then on, the air battles of 19 June were tagged by American aviators as the Great Marianas Turkey Shoot.[53]

Ozawa's surviving pilots hastened back to their carriers at 1057. Sprague had little time to relax, as only ten minutes later Ozawa's second raid—128 planes launched at 0856—appeared on radar. The *Wasp* radar operator wondered if his screen—which showed over a hundred unidentified planes within a hundred miles of the *Wasp*—worked properly, but Sprague wasted no time getting every available aircraft into the air, changing the *Wasp*'s course, and diverting planes already aloft to intercept. He then ordered his officers to check that each man donned flash-proof clothing and helmets.[54]

Calm settled over the *Wasp* for a few moments while Sprague awaited word about the unidentified aircraft from his fighter pilots. Should this be the enemy, as appeared almost certain, he knew his aviators faced a harsher challenge in keeping the enemy away from the *Wasp* than in the initial raid, which contained less than one-third the number of aircraft in the current force. In that case, his gun crews would have to bear the brunt of defending the carrier. Though Air Group 14 had already seen action at Marcus-Wake and moments ago in the first raid, his gun crews had yet to operate under fire.

A thirteen-knot breeze wafted in from the east (95°) as anxious faces searched the cloudy skies for telltale signs of the enemy. Suddenly, Sprague heard over the radio that his pilots had engaged a large number of Japanese. Dogfights crisscrossed the skies as American aviators attacked. After spotting a group of four enemy torpedo planes, *Wasp* pilot Lt. William M. Knight dove, forced the planes to drop near the water, selected one target, and sent the aircraft careening into the sea with a well-aimed burst of fire. His squadron companion, Lt. Marvin R. Novak, started to line up one enemy dive-bomber in his sights when a second plane darted by in the opposite direction. He jerked his fighter around, closed on the quarry, and quickly sent it smoking toward the water. American aviators registered so many kills that downed enemy aircraft and pilots floated over a twelve-mile stretch of ocean.[55]

The American fighter intercept faced more Japanese planes than they could handle though, which meant that inevitably a number broke through. Additional numbers fell to Lee's battle line, but even it could not deter such a large group. At 1127 the surviving Japanese closed on Montgomery's task group, where they battled through American combat air patrols toward the carriers.[56]

When Sprague peered skyward, so many different kinds of aircraft dotted the skies—Japanese dive-bombers intermingled with American combat air patrols, antisubmarine patrols, and planes launched to clear carrier decks—that Sprague and his gun crews had trouble distinguishing friend from foe. According to pilot Everett Fulton, "planes were literally falling like flies. It was like seeing an exaggerated Hollywood production of an air battle—for real." Wherever he looked, Sprague saw three or four burning aircraft plummeting to the water and other planes exploding in a fury that spun detached airplane wings madly into the ocean. Tense *Wasp* antiaircraft gunners had to check their impulses to shoot at anything that zoomed into sight for fear of destroying one of their own planes. In fact, the commander of Task Group 58.3, Rear Adm. John W. Reeves, Jr., was so concerned over

American antiaircraft fire splashing his own planes that he signaled his ships earlier in the morning, "Try to avoid shooting down our own planes. They are our best protection."[57]

Uncertainty breeds error. Near 1200, four enemy dive-bombers swooped down on the carrier. Sprague quickly surveyed his men and noted with satisfaction that "all guns on the ship fired at the targets," but while his gun control concentrated on tracking enemy aircraft, another plane assumed to be friendly suddenly roared in on the starboard side and dropped a 550-pound bomb. Sprague watched the missile fall thirty feet forward of the port bow and explode with such force that shrapnel punctured holes in the hull and tore through the back and out the chest of Gunner's Mate 1st Class Alfred J. Bridges, killing him instantly while wounding four others. Because of confusion in the skies and doubt over proper identification, this plane was not spotted and identified as the enemy until it had a chance to drop its bomb. *Wasp* gunners zeroed in on the dive-bomber as it pulled away and splashed it into the water twelve thousand yards ahead.[58]

The second raid produced an even worse fiasco for Ozawa than the first, as a scant 31 planes out of 128 returned. He achieved little more with the 47 aircraft of his third raid, launched around 1015. Over half never located the American fleet, no plane came near the *Wasp,* and of the twenty that attacked, seven were shot down.[59]

Sprague used the calm to take stock of his situation. So far, *Wasp* fighters had contributed to what was turning into a slaughter in the skies. His gunners had deflected most planes that came near the carrier and shot down the one that managed to sneak through. So far, the men had performed well under the stress of their first major conflict.

The relative quiet was interrupted about 1330 when *Wasp* radar picked up the eighty-two aircraft of Ozawa's fourth raid. The ship's fighter-director officer guided *Wasp* Hellcats toward the incoming flight, which had drawn within fifty-three miles of the carrier by 1413. Seven minutes later the intercept shot down three enemy aircraft at an altitude of twelve thousand feet, but as most Hellcats were incorrectly positioned thirteen thousand feet higher, the bulk of the Japanese flew on toward Montgomery's task group untouched.[60]

At 1422, eight dive-bombers started runs on the *Wasp* that, along with the rest of the task group, was in the middle of a fifteen-degree left turn at twenty-two knots. Guns along both sides of the *Wasp* opened fire at 1426 and quickly knocked down five planes, but Sprague noticed another five enemy aircraft circling at about twelve thousand feet. Two dove on a different carrier, but one after another, the other three began their descent toward the *Wasp*.[61]

Despite thick *Wasp* antiaircraft fire, the three planes quickly closed the distance on their quarry. A bomb dropped from the first plane, followed by another from each of the trailing two dive-bombers.[62]

On the flight deck, Bender ran for cover as the bombs drew nearer. He found two other sailors huddled in a manhole under the flight deck, one crying and the other praying, expecting the bombs to tear into the *Wasp* at any moment. Bender wondered that if a single dive-bomber had barely missed earlier in the day, "how in the world can we survive three bombs and three planes? I thought this was it, and I started asking for God's help." Many others in the crew shared this pessimistic outlook, although on the bridge, Sprague's signalman, Robert Carew, at first dismissed the threat and thought the bombs would land some distance away.[63]

As the explosives plunged closer, even Carew worried that one of the bombs would hit. Suddenly, at almost the last moment, Sprague ordered a hard right turn. Bender felt the huge ship swerve to one side as the closest bomb crashed two hundred feet off the port bow, followed by the final two bombs, which exploded in the ocean less than two hundred fifty feet off the starboard quarter. His ship had been bracketed by the three bombs, but Sprague's hard right turn at the proper instant succeeded in dodging them.[64]

"I knew that our captain was practicing some real seamanship," mentioned Bender. "I thought to myself, if God didn't have his hand over us that time, then surely it was beyond any doubt a mystery to all of us." Carew was amazed that "Sprague saw that the bomb would come close to the ship and immediately made his decision. His judgment was much better than mine for sure."[65]

Sprague may have saved his ship with adept maneuvering, but not without a price. The first bomb sprayed the ship with shrapnel and flung one huge piece toward the port gun mount forward, injuring the control officer, Marine Capt. R. C. Rosacker, and three of his men. Rosacker, hit with such force in the left shoulder that his helmet and earphones were blown off, jumped to his feet, grabbed his errant helmet and earphones with his uninjured right arm, and continued directing gunfire. Fragments from one of the other two bombs also injured one man on the after part of the flight deck.[66]

Sprague had barely avoided these bombs when an incendiary cluster burst three hundred feet above the *Wasp* and showered the bridge and flight deck with pieces of flammable phosphorus. One piece fell to the bridge near

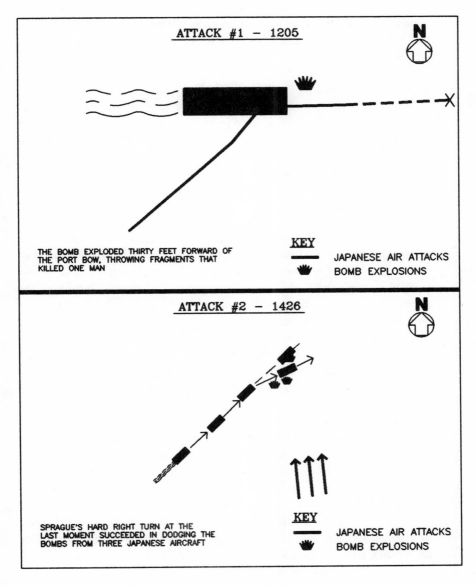

MAP 2. Japanese aircraft attack the *Wasp* during the Battle of the Philippine Sea.

Sprague. Executive officer Slattery smothered it with his foot, but the startled officer quickly kicked off his shoe when it ignited. Crew members rapidly extinguished any pieces that landed on the flight deck.[67]

The incessant Japanese attacks, which began shortly after 1000 and continued for eight hours, finally ended around 1845 when the last aircraft sputtered back to their carriers or to Japanese land bases in the Marianas, ending one of the most disastrous days for the Japanese in the war. Almost 250 of Ozawa's 374 aircraft had been shot down by American fighters or antiaircraft batteries, including eleven by Air Group 14 and five by *Wasp* guns. Morale soared on board the *Wasp* as she headed north to recover her planes, but as Bender recalled, one nagging question spoiled the jubilation—"where is that Jap fleet?"[68]

Three of Mitscher's four task groups, including Montgomery's 58.2, turned west at 2000 in an effort to shorten the distance with Ozawa for the expected battle the next day. While Sprague met with department heads to review the *Wasp*'s performance and plan for additional combat, crews worked through the night checking torpedoes, transferring bombs to the hangar deck, and installing extra gasoline tanks on scout planes that would be searching for Ozawa. Early in the morning of 20 June, Sprague launched the first of his long-range scout missions, then, along with the rest of his officers and crew, waited for the search planes to locate Ozawa. To pass the time, Sprague chatted with his exuberant aviators, who excitedly rehashed the smashing victory of 19 June and boasted that they would finish off the enemy fleet on 20 June.[69]

Until search planes picked up Ozawa, Sprague could do little on 20 June except ensure the readiness of every department. As usual, Slattery oversaw preparations so Sprague could be free to concentrate on major issues or be available to make those snap decisions often required of commanders.

"Sprague never left the bridge," mentioned Lt. Robert P. Daly, who as *Wasp* communications officer frequently stood near his captain. "Instead of going to his cabin, he'd have an orderly bring him fresh clothes or whatever he needed. Once in awhile he might go into the room next to the bridge for a quick nap, but he gave orders he was to be awakened at any course change that came in from Montgomery."[70]

Sprague engaged in a race with time as the long day unwound without word of Ozawa. If his aviators were to get a crack at the enemy fleet and return safely before dark, Ozawa must be located no later than 1200–1300. After that time, his pilots would be flirting with darkness on the way back and would, because of the threat of enemy submarines spotting light, have to land on a barely illuminated carrier at night, a feat few pilots wished to consider after a long round-trip flight and battle with the Japanese.

The morning slipped away with no word from search planes. Sprague left the bridge only long enough to attend the burial at sea of the first member of the ship's company to die in combat, Alfred Bridges, killed the previous day. Early afternoon arrived—still no sighting. Pilots sat impatiently in the Ready Room watching their golden opportunity dwindle by the minute.[71]

Sprague was ready to give up when American planes spotted Ozawa. At 1550, search planes located the retreating fleet steaming in four groups at twenty knots about two hundred seventy miles west of the *Wasp*. This presented a dilemma for every commander and aviator in Mitscher's three task groups—they knew where the enemy was, but could they get to them? The distance placed Ozawa at the extreme edge of American attack plane range. Could the fliers reach Ozawa, exhaust time and fuel in combat, and still have sufficient fuel to return safely to their carriers? Even if they could, the late sighting meant that planes would have to be launched immediately to hold a slim chance of getting to Ozawa and harming his forces before darkness settled in, but a prompt launching meant no time to replace bombs already attached to aircraft with extra fuel tanks. Finally, if they were to be launched, every carrier captain had to confront an operation few wanted or had experience in—a nighttime recovery of aircraft.[72]

Mitscher asked his operations officer, Comdr. W. J. Widhelm, if he thought the pilots could make it back to their carriers. "It's going to be tight," Widhelm replied. The benefits, however, outweighed the risks, and at 1610 Mitscher sent out the order to launch all planes. Eleven minutes later Sprague turned the *Wasp* into the wind with the ten other carriers of Task Force 58, and within ten minutes launched sixteen Hellcats, twelve Helldivers carrying one 1,000-pound and two 250-pound bombs each, and seven Avengers bearing four 500-pound bombs. By 1636, 216 aircraft sped toward Ozawa.[73]

Neither Sprague nor his pilots knew if there would be a return landing. Lt. (jg) Al Walraven lifted off in his dive-bomber with serious doubts that he carried enough fuel. Fellow dive-bomber pilot Lt. (jg) Everett Fulton "had a feeling it was going to be close." One *Lexington* pilot acknowledged the thumbs-up sign given him by his crew and sarcastically thought, "Thumbs up, hell! What they mean is 'So long, sucker!'" Lt. Comdr. Robert A. Winston of the *Cabot* believed his entire squadron would have to ditch.[74]

Hopes of a successful return dimmed shortly after takeoff when Sprague learned that the original position given by search pilots was short by sixty miles. This error added another one hundred twenty miles to the round-trip flight. He relayed this unwelcome news to *Wasp* pilots, who leaned out their fuel mixture as much as they dared to conserve fuel. Fulton barely spoke to his radio/gunner for the rest of the flight as "this was our most serious challenge and we met it with serious silence." Little chatter occurred on the *Wasp,* either, as Sprague and everyone else realized the air group would have less than thirty minutes to strike the enemy before darkness sheltered the Japanese ships from further harm.[75]

After flying almost three hundred miles, *Wasp* pilots sighted the Japanese fleet at 1840, just as the sun started its speedy descent below the horizon. Lt. Comdr. J. D. Blitch, commander of the *Wasp* bombers, spotted the east-ernmost group of Japanese ships, a group of oilers and escorting destroyers, but chose instead to lead his planes south in search of two reported carriers. A fruitless search only used up precious daylight and fuel, so Blitch turned his planes back toward the oilers that, if sunk, would at least deprive Ozawa of the fuel he needed to escape Mitscher.[76]

Just before he began his run against an oiler, Fulton and other *Wasp* aviators noticed that their fuel gauges had dipped below the halfway point. They now knew for a certainty that they could not possibly get back to the *Wasp* without ditching. Pushing the thought from their minds, Fulton and the other pilots dove against heavy antiaircraft fire and sank two of the six oilers while damaging a third. Afterwards, the pilots shot down five Zeros that tried to intercept them.[77]

The attack ended about 1935. When Fulton finished his run, night had blended with the blackness of the ocean to create an almost imperceptible velvet tapestry surrounding his plane. Worse, the tired aviator faced almost three hundred miles of flying to reach his carrier.[78]

Sprague figured his pilots carried enough fuel to remain aloft for about five hours, depending upon the wind, time over their targets, damage sus-tained, and fuel conservation measures. Since the final plane departed the *Wasp* around 1630, they would begin sputtering out of fuel and splashing into the ocean shortly after 2100, if not sooner. Sprague could do no more than hasten westward toward the fliers with the remainder of Mitscher's task force and hope for the best.[79]

* * *

Fulton was not optimistic. When he learned he had used 200 gallons to reach and attack the target and had only 120 gallons left for the 255-mile return trip, "the sickening realization of our hopeless lack of fuel to return to our ship hit me." He adjusted his fuel mixture controls to save gasoline, joined with aircraft from other ships that happened along, and continued flying into the night, fighting an exhaustion that was intensified by the calming drone of the engine in the still darkness.[80]

One by one, American planes dropped to the ocean. As they did, frequencies became jammed with pilots trying to announce their locations for search vessels and craft. Fulton noticed that "some [pilots] bordered on panic" in going down, and he finally shut off his radio when the numerous voices became indistinguishable. In the ocean below, a string of phosphorescent marks, telltale signs of splashdowns, increasingly dotted the water as Fulton and other pilots headed toward their carriers.[81]

Officers and operators in the *Wasp* radio room also listened to the frantic messages pouring in: "have ten minutes of fuel" vied for air space with "mine is on empty" or "I have to ditch." Some came from their own Air Group 14. Lt. Milton F. Browne went down with a punctured fuel tank only halfway to the *Wasp.* Lieutenant Walraven, flying alongside Browne, executed a soft landing in what he presumed was Browne's location because he thought they had a better chance for survival if they remained together.[82]

At 2015 first reports came over the *Wasp*'s radio that planes had arrived in the vicinity of the carriers. Harassed by enemy fighters and antiaircraft fire, wearied by the difficult flight out and back, and nearly hypnotized by the endless black expanse, *Wasp* pilots now had to locate what could be likened to a black aircraft carrier floating on a sea of ink. Because most aviators needed assistance if they were to land safely, one of the most remarkable episodes in the Pacific conflict occurred. Disregarding the very real possibility that an enemy submarine lurked nearby and would be aided by his action, Mitscher ordered every ship to light up the skies as brightly as possible.[83]

Suddenly, streams of light darted upwards from hundreds of sources. Carriers switched on red and green running lights while cruisers and destroyers pumped bright star shells to the heavens. Sprague lit up the *Wasp* to the fullest—landing and truck lights outlined its shadowy form; signal lights tapped out its position; brilliant searchlights bounced bright beams off hazy clouds. "We turned on all the searchlights we had and shot them straight up in the air so the pilots could see them on the clouds," mentioned the *Wasp* communications officer, Lieutenant Daly.[84]

"The Task Force presented an unusual sight to returning pilots," modestly wrote Sprague in his action report. Most aviators characterized the scene in more emotional terms. Fulton, with less than forty gallons in his tanks, spotted a small searchlight slicing through the clouds and immediately turned toward it. "What a beautiful sight," he later mentioned. "It was 'Be kind to aviators night' with all the lights turned on."[85]

It is a measure of the esteem in which Sprague was held by his officers and crew that when asked about that night, they claimed he illuminated the *Wasp* brighter than any other captain. Lt. Comdr. Charles Cunningham, a member of Sprague's staff, wrote years later, "Some skippers lighted up the minimum, fearing submarines, but [Sprague] lighted up the *Wasp* like a Christmas tree. . . ."[86]

Whether Sprague actually lit up the *Wasp* more than his counterparts on other carriers is unimportant. Each captain followed Mitscher's bold order. The sentiment, however, expresses the deep belief Sprague's officers and crew shared that, though he remained their commanding officer and often had to send them into battle, Sprague considered paramount the welfare of his men.

"The night landings? It was a wild night!" said Lieutenant Daly, who spent the time near Sprague on the bridge. Sprague noticed from the aircraft lights that, rather than falling into a landing pattern as was normally done, his pilots were descending in an unorganized fashion. Watching elsewhere on the ship, *Wasp* pilot Lt. Ray Heiden realized, "It was then we knew it was going to be a rather sordid affair."[87]

All eyes watched as the first aircraft approached the *Wasp* at 2046. A *Yorktown* dive-bomber touched down, then plowed into the crash barriers. Deck hands quickly ran out to extricate the pilot and shove the plane overboard to make room for following aircraft. A second plane landed smoothly, but a third crashed into the barrier and flipped over on its back. Red liquid gushed out of the demolished aircraft, causing some to think the pilot was bleeding to death, but after flight deck crews pulled him out, he shook his head and walked to the island structure. Because these barrier crashes tied up the *Wasp*'s deck, some following planes had to be waved off and had to ditch into the water alongside the carrier.[88]

For one of the few times in his career, Sprague showed emotion as he watched fellow aviators splash into the sea or smack into one of his barriers.

Lt. Walter D. Gaddis, the assistant gunnery officer, recalled that Sprague ran from one side of the bridge to the other trying to land more planes by saying, "Give that man a Charlie! Give that man a Charlie!" Normally wearing a cap that was slightly tilted upward to the right, Sprague this night dashed about hatless, stopping long enough only to check the wind or to run his hands through his hair.[89]

Fires from planes that crashed on board other carriers could be seen in the distance while circling pilots, according to Heiden, "were getting desperate and trying to land on anything that had lights showing. I have never seen such terrific confusion in all my life." Fulton, who landed safely on board the *Enterprise* with less than two gallons remaining, watched planes splash into the water, explode, and disappear. "We had just returned from defeating the Japanese fleet and destroying their air power. They were retreating, and here we were losing more planes than we had lost during battle!"[90]

Of the approximately eighty task force planes that were lost this night because of low fuel or landing accidents, Sprague's air group lost sixteen— eleven dive-bombers, three torpedo planes, and two fighters. Sadly, only five planes returned safely to the *Wasp,* though fifteen others landed on board nearby carriers. Sprague, in turn, recovered nine aircraft from other carriers—one each from the *Yorktown, Lexington, Bunker Hill,* and *Bataan,* and five from the *Enterprise.*[91]

The largest concern was over the fate of the twelve missing aviators and aircrewmen. They could be floating in a raft, aboard another carrier, or at the bottom of the Philippine Sea. All Sprague could do was wait for morning and the launch of search planes. "There was little sleep for any of us," stated a concerned Heiden.[92]

Spruance ordered Lee's battleships and cruisers, guarded by the *Bunker Hill* and Sprague's *Wasp,* to chase west after the retreating Ozawa. Sprague launched sixteen fighters, eight torpedo planes, and thirteen dive-bombers in a hurried attempt to locate the enemy, but even though Lee's force steamed at full speed for much of 21 June, it never closed the distance. Late that day, Spruance recalled the ships, thus ending an amazing three days.[93]

One bright note illuminated an otherwise dreary 21 June when Fulton and his radio/gunner, Larry Quinlan, landed on the *Wasp* after one day on board the *Enterprise,* and word arrived that another pilot had landed safely on a different carrier. Sprague's hopes that more pilots would return sank when Fulton explained that most *Wasp* planes flew back on their own rather than wait at the assigned rendezvous point. This meant the pilots and air-crew could have splashed anywhere at sea along an enormous axis, making rescue less likely. "It really is an unhappy squadron tonight," wrote dive-bomber pilot Heiden in his log.[94]

The next day Sprague learned that Commander Blitch had been rescued at sea, but he still knew nothing of the other downed aviators. Reluctantly, he ordered his commander of Air Group 14, Comdr. W. C. Wingard, to begin surveying the personal effects of each man.[95]

For the next five days, the *Wasp* headed toward Eniwetok for repairs and resupply. A *Wasp* fighter shot down a four-engined Japanese flying boat when it flew within forty miles of the carrier on 22 June, and two days later Sprague sent twenty-four fighters, twelve torpedo planes, and nineteen dive-bombers to destroy a runway on Pagan Island in the northern Marianas. The otherwise uneventful voyage ended when Sprague guided the *Wasp* into Eniwetok on 27 June.[96]

With his first major offensive action of the Pacific war concluded, Sprague enjoyed a bit of vengeance for the disaster at Pearl Harbor and the humiliation of Wake Island. From 11 to 24 June, he had launched 533 sorties, including 254 against Tinian, 148 over Saipan, and 35 against the Japanese fleet while losing 24 planes and 5 pilots missing and presumed dead. His ship had participated in one of the Navy's most thorough victories, one that so devastated Ozawa's 430 carrier aircraft that the forlorn Japanese admiral was forced to record in his 20 June log, "Surviving carrier air power: 35 aircraft operational." Ozawa's carriers lived to see battle once again but, stripped of their air arm, they functioned merely as decoys. Sprague was present when Japanese carrier air power stunned the U.S. Navy in Hawaii. It was only fitting that he participated in the battle marking the demise of his enemy's naval aviation.[97]

Two days after arriving at Eniwetok, Sprague submitted a report summarizing the *Wasp*'s role in the recent action. He commended the *Wasp*'s anti-aircraft battery for successfully warding off nine enemy bombers. "It was gratifying to note that all guns on the ship fired on the targets," Sprague commented. The accurate fire shot down five planes, recorded one probable kill, turned back two others, and permitted only one bomber to complete its run and get away. "By the accuracy and determination of the anti-aircraft fire," Sprague wrote, "the ship was saved from probable serious damage."[98]

Sprague singled out a group of individuals in the gunnery division, including the president's son, Lt. John A. Roosevelt, for its courageous leadership. He recommended Bronze Stars for Marine Capt. R. C. Rosacker for continuing to direct fire even when wounded; for the ship's gunnery officer, Lt. Comdr. George P. Huff, for successfully training his batteries and calmly directing them under fire; and for Marine 2d Lt. James H. Ayers because "His battery was the first to open fire due to alertness of himself and his crew under his leadership."[99]

Sprague praised the air group for "the skill and determination with which the attacks were executed," and cited the ship's company because "the resolute and consistent coolness of the recovery of aircraft [the night of 20 June] under most trying conditions indicate correct and thorough training of all personnel concerned."[100]

Sprague recommended a few changes. He strongly advocated increased aircraft recognition training. Since two of Sprague's planes were damaged by friendly antiaircraft fire, and one enemy aircraft was able to sneak in on the *Wasp* during the 19 June battles because of confusion over its identity, he believed "the importance of this subject cannot be overlooked." He also mentioned that pilots needed quicker dissemination of information on incoming enemy flights than they had received on 19 June. To achieve this, he recommended all officers handling such information be centrally located on carriers rather than berthed in separate positions and urged improved liaison between task group fighter directors.[101]

Sprague had to write another type of letter that, while hard for him to do, illuminated another side of the man. Whenever a member of the crew died, whether from accident or combat, Sprague wrote to his next of kin explaining the circumstances of their relative's death. He had already sent a handful before the ship first arrived at Pearl Harbor. On 3 January, he wrote Mrs. Lucy Clifton of Philadelphia of her son's death, Steward's Mate 2d Class Horace Williams. Rather than send a perfunctory letter, Sprague praised Williams for giving his life in the service of his country, then mentioned that Williams was "quiet, industrious, and attentive to his duties." Sprague emphasized, no doubt for the mother's benefit, that Williams "said his prayers each day, morning and evening. He read his Bible regularly, and had the reputation among all who knew him as being a good Christian lad." A letter the next month informed Mr. Walter S. Crawford of Bemis, Tennessee, that his son, Seaman 1st Class Richard D. Crawford, was missing at sea. Again, Sprague added a personal touch in relating that Crawford's shipmates "were unanimous in their high regard for Crawford. He was known as an industrious seaman who did his work conscientiously and well."[102]

After Gunner's Mate Alfred J. Bridges died during the 19 June battle—

the first member of the ship's company to die in action—Sprague sympathized with his wife, Mrs. Lyra Bridges of Long Island, New York, that "his devotion to duty will remain a splendid example to us all," and that she could take consolation in knowing "he gave his life for you, his family and his country. A man can make no finer sacrifice than that."[103]

Sprague earned high marks for his conduct in May and June. Though his action report of the Battle of the Philippine Sea modestly stated that when enemy aircraft attacked the *Wasp,* Sprague's order of a hard right rudder "probably saved the ship from being hit," the Navy awarded Sprague the Legion of Merit Medal. He even received notice back home. The New York *Herald Tribune* reported his receipt of the Legion of Merit, and the Philadelphia *Inquirer* called Sprague "one of the outstanding heroes" of the June action. His performance off the Marianas placed Sprague in line for flag rank and to receive command of one of the many new carrier task groups being rapidly formed.[104]

Words of praise from officers and crew meant more to Sprague than official recognition, and they were effusive after the Philippine Sea. The *Waspirit* claimed that Sprague's "cool and dispassionate" leadership steadied the *Wasp,* and "During the lulls that came between attacks, officers and men looked up at the familiar figure and were thankful for the confidence he inspired."[105]

Despite the smashing victory, American naval commanders, particularly Admiral Spruance, received bitter criticism from naval aviators who believed Spruance had allowed Ozawa's carriers to escape. They argued hotly that a more aggressive admiral would have headed west toward Ozawa on 18 June and crushed his forces, thereby shortening the war. Mitscher's own action report claimed "The enemy had escaped," and some officers urged that Spruance be relieved of command.[106]

Once again, as at Pearl Harbor and Wake Island, Sprague participated in a battle tarnished with controversy. The U.S. Navy had won, but according to critics, not won decisively enough by smashing the enemy's carriers. While Sprague characteristically kept his opinion to himself, one other naval commander, a student aviator under Sprague at Annapolis, noted the criticism Spruance received for allowing the Japanese carriers to get away. He promised if he had a similar opportunity, he would not make the same mistake. Adm. William "Bull" Halsey vowed he would chase after enemy carriers at first sight.[107]

* * *

The *Wasp* remained at Eniwetok for only a short time. On 30 June Sprague left, along with the rest of Task Group 58.2, to attack aircraft facilities and shipping at Iwo Jima before returning to support land operations at Guam.[108]

The task group hit Iwo Jima on 4 July. Sprague launched Air Group 14 in five separate raids during which they destroyed a variety of enemy aircraft while losing five of their own. Sprague later noted in his action report the absence of enemy aircraft flying out from Iwo Jima to challenge the *Wasp,* a surprising fact since his carrier struck within six hundred miles of the home islands from where fresh planes could easily be flown into Iwo Jima for an attack. He believed this could only be caused by either a serious deficiency of aviation gasoline or a catastrophic drop in trained aviators. The Japanese were indeed experiencing near-fatal shortfalls in both areas. As a consequence, they would shortly be forced to resort to a strategy of desperation as American forces, including Sprague, advanced against the Philippines.[109]

Sprague's tenure with the *Wasp* neared an end on 9 July 1944, when President Franklin D. Roosevelt appointed him to the flag rank of rear admiral alongside three illustrious classmates. Though Forrest Sherman had been promoted eight months earlier and Jocko Clark five months before, Sprague received his promotion the same month as Tommy Sprague and, at age forty-eight, became one of the youngest rear admirals in the Navy.[110]

Sprague continued to oversee *Wasp* support missions in the Marianas until relieved on 21 July by Capt. O. A. Weller. The next day, Sprague reported as commander, Carrier Division 25, comprising the escort carriers *Fanshaw Bay* and *Midway* (renamed *St. Lo* on 15 September) and four destroyer escorts. Similar to the inconspicuous manner in which he arrived on the *Wasp* eight months earlier in Boston, Sprague departed with little ceremony. Since air strikes were being launched, Weller could not muster the crew for an official send-off, but instead had the orders read over the speaker system.[111]

Sprague commanded the *Wasp* while she steamed 145,000 miles in two oceans. His air group flew 1,928 sorties against eight different Pacific targets in three months during which it dropped 607 tons of bombs, sank twelve ships, and destroyed seventy-three aircraft in the air or on the ground. In addition, his antiaircraft batteries knocked five aircraft out of the sky.[112]

Above all, Sprague's leadership of the *Wasp* proved his qualifications to lead men at that level. In nine months Sprague molded an unfinished carrier and a green crew into a highly prepared, trained unit capable of doing battle with an unyielding adversary. At his departure, he handed Weller a smooth-functioning ship blessed with a distinguished record and high morale.

Other people predicted a bright future for Sprague. Lieutenant Roosevelt wrote that "we were all happy that his fine quality of leadership had been recognized but, at the same time we felt a personal loss when he left the ship." In an article summarizing their first skipper's elevation, the staff of the *Waspirit* stated unequivocally about the entire crew, "there was no evidence that anyone was surprised at the announcement. Nor need they have been. The career of the USS *Wasp,* during the months since she first hoisted her commissioning pennant, was ample proof that Admiral Sprague's promotion was justly deserved. As a matter of fact, before shoving off from Pearl Harbor, the Supply Department wisely laid in a set of bars, shoulder boards and gold braid in anticipation of the coming event." [113]

Clifton Sprague at age six

Hazel Furlow Sprague instilled decency and fair play in her son.

Henry Bruno Sprague imparted a sense of responsibility to Clifton.

Though formal religion never became important in his life, Clifton Sprague developed a firm set of principles with which he conducted himself.

Clifton Sprague (*far right*), age fifteen, with his Highland Military Academy baseball team in 1911.

An eighteen-year-old Sprague, shortly before entering the Naval Academy

CLIFTON ALBERT FREDERICK SPRAGUE

Milton, Mass.

"Peanut" "Liz" "Clifting" "Ziegie"

Baseball Squad (3, 2, 1); Baseball Numerals (4);
Hop Committee (1); Buzzard

NICKNAMES are not always entirely appropriate. Take Liz for instance. He answers to a number of feminine titles, but when swinging down the corridor with his seagoing "Rockport" roll, looks rough as a file, hard as nails, and as non-reg as the Reina Squad, and certainly belying the name of "Sproggles," walks with every part of his body. His tousled hair swinging fore and aft, slender body rotating in all directions, legs and arms just everywhere—taken all in all gives the impression best described by his own words, "Tweet! Tweet! I am a simple harmonic pendulum." Liz utilizes the whole corridor when in a hurry, but will always stop gyrating in order to exchange verbal sallies with an acquaintance. In such conversations, he usually wins. His apparently harmless ejaculations contain "hidden" meanings that would probably go unnoticed if he could control that merry twinkle in his eye. And such eyes!—fringed with long silken lashes that look innocent, but aren't.

Liz has strength and agility that enables him to best many of the heavy eaters at the training-tables, being clever in nearly every sport. Only lack of weight or a man just a wee bit better has prevented him from being a regular member of several athletic teams.

But it is not for his gloom-dispersing ability, his ever-ready repartee, his athletic prowess, that we admire him. We like his type of manhood. Liz lets us in on his "ups" and then manfully cloaks his "downs" beneath an exterior of happiness. No one ever saw him downcast for long—even when restricted on board ship within a stone's throw of his Rockport home. All in all, Clifton is a living example of a true-blue comrade with all that term implies. A friend once, a friend always, particularly when in need.

Harrison: "Yes, sir, they raise mighty fine men in Missouri."
Sprague: "How are we to know?"

Sprague as portrayed by his classmates in the 1918 Naval Academy yearbook,
Lucky Bag

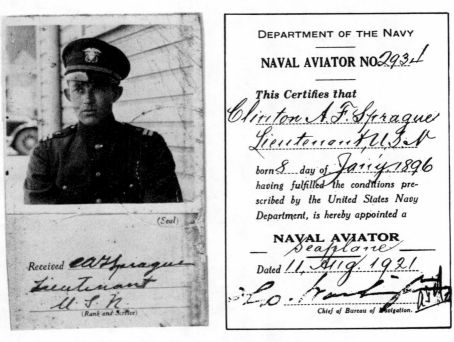

Sprague's 1921 Naval Aviator identification card

Sprague (*top row, third from left*) with his Pensacola classmates on 11 June 1921.
Other men who also rose to higher command in World War II are (*middle row*)
Donald B. Duncan (*second from left*), Samuel P. Ginder (*fifth from left*), Harold B.
Sallada (*sixth from left*) and (*top row*) Thomas L. Sprague (*second from left*),
V. H. Ragsdale (*fourth from left*).

Sprague (*tenth from the right and behind the Army general*) in Honolulu in 1933. Also pictured are Marc A. Mitscher (*fourth from right*) and Harry Yarnell (*ninth from right*).

Clifton Sprague in 1937

Sprague (*sixth from right*) sits to the left of Capt. Aubrey Fitch at the Norfolk Air Station in 1935.

The USS *Patoka* (A–9), Sprague's first seagoing command

Captain Clef wise Fox Murphy Au
Fitch

Commander Sprague on the bridge of the *Patoka* in 1940

Sprague at the beach
with daughters Courtney
(*far left*) and Patricia

Annabel, age twenty-one, in August 1922. Though here sporting the flapper look of the 1920s, Annabel never adopted the fast-paced lifestyle exemplified by her famous brother.

Sprague and Annabel on a California beach in 1941

The seaplane tender USS *Tangier* (AV-8), which Sprague guided through the attack on Pearl Harbor, the Wake Island relief expedition, and the South Pacific

Taken on board the *Tangier*, this photograph captures the *Utah* turning to port after absorbing a torpedo hit early in the battle. (*Courtesy Naval Historical Center*)

The *Utah* capsized, trapping some of her crew inside. The damaged seaplane tender *Raleigh* floats in the background. (*Courtesy Naval Historical Center*)

Sprague wrote on the back of this picture, taken from the *Tangier* as Japanese bombs hit close by, "Japanese bomb landing twenty feet off side of ship forward of bridge and exploding." (*Courtesy Naval Historical Center*)

L Z XG4 2ØØØ4ØN GX4 GR 228 BT

PARA 1 AND 2 AS P-ER CINCPAC OPORD 39 DASH 41 X TASKS X TASK UNIT
1411 UPON ARRIVAL POINT LOVE LAUNCH 14 VMF 18 SBD TO PROCEED AND
LAND AT WAKE X CARRIER AND PLANES GUARDS THEN OPERATE WITH TASK
UNIT 1412 X RECOVER SBD AT POINT ROGER UPON COMPLETION UNLOADING
TANGIER X TASK UNIT 1412 PROCEED FROM POINT LOVE AND OPERATE ABOUT
1ØØ MILES NORTH OF WAKE X TASK UNIT 1413 ESCORT TASK UNIT 1421
WITH 4 DDS FROM POINT LOVE TO WAKE COMMA FURNISH AA AND AS
PROTECTION WHILE ENROUTE AND UNLOADING PERIOD WHEN TANGIER UNLOADED
PROCEED TO POINT LOVE AT BEST SUSTAINED SPEED AND THEN SET COURSE
EAST UNTIL JOINED BY TASK UNIT 1412 PERIOD FURNISH 4 DDS TO SCREEN
TASK UNITS 1411 AND 1412 X TASK UNIT 1421 PROCEED WITH TASK UNIT
1413 UNLOAD AND EMBARK PASSENGERS AS QUICKLY AS POSSIBLE EVEN AT
RISK OF LOSING SOME SUPPLIES PERIOD RETURN TO POINT LOVE WITH
TASK UNIT 1413 X TASK UNIT 1422 PROCEED ACCORDANCE MY 2ØØØ2Ø X
(XRA-Y) IF TASK UNIT 1413 PASSES THROUGH POINT LOVE DURING
DAYLIGHT THIS FORCE WILL RENDEZVOUS THE-RE PERIOD OTHERWISE WILL
RENDEZVOUS TO EASTWARD THAT POINT X RADIO SILENCE X COMMUNICATIONS
WITH WAKE BY AIRCRAFT X POINT LOVE 15Ø MILES EAST OF WAKE X POINT
ROGER 1ØØ MILES NORTH OF WAKE X OPORD NUMBER ONE DASH FORTY ONE.

FROM: COMTASKFOR 14   *FAMOUS MESSAGE*
                            SENT BY ADMIRAL FLETCHER
TO : TASKFOR 14   *TO ME ON TANGIER*
                            FOR RELIEF OF WAKE

CAPT _____ EXEC _____ NAV ____ COMM ____ COL FASSETT _____

When I met him later in
Seattle he said he felt like
he was putting a pistol to
my head. The whole thing was
called off by Pye; Kimmel's relief
back at Pearl; might have
made it.

Sprague's handwritten comments at the bottom of Fletcher's dispatch sending
the *Tangier* ahead of the task force to Wake Island

Civilian construction workers on their way back to Pearl Harbor from Midway
walk about on board the *Tangier* on 28 December 1941.

Marines of the Fourth Defense Battalion embark on board the *Tangier* on 14 December for the Wake Island relief expedition.

Sprague shares a lighter moment at his *Tangier* farewell dinner. Two items always seemed present with Sprague—a smile and a cigarette.

Captain Sprague greets Secretary of the Navy Frank W. Knox (*middle*) and Vice Adm. Frank Jack Fletcher (*right*) at the Sand Point Naval Air Station in 1943.

Mrs. Eleanor Roosevelt addresses assembled dignitaries, crew of the *Wasp,* and families at the commissioning ceremony, 24 November 1943. Captain Sprague is seated at the far right.

Sprague escorts Mrs. Roosevelt from the stage after her dedication speech.

CHAPTER NINE

Prelude to Leyte

O n 18 August 1944, Sprague accompanied his good friend and classmate, Rear Adm. Thomas L. Sprague, on a flight from Manus Island in the Admiralties off the northern New Guinea coast to Woendi for briefings on the upcoming Philippines operation, the first large-scale assault in which Sprague would participate as a unit commander. Sprague learned that before challenging the Japanese Army and Navy in the Philippines, American forces would first seize the island of Morotai, lying halfway between New Guinea and Mindanao, which was the designated Philippine landing area for MacArthur's troops. Morotai offered a forward base for PT boats and landing field sites that could protect MacArthur's left flank. Sprague was ordered to take Carrier Division 25, consisting of his flagship, the *Fanshaw Bay,* and a second escort carrier, the *St. Lo,* protected by four destroyer escorts, to Morotai as part of Tommy Sprague's Task Group 77.1. There he was to provide support for the troops rushing ashore.[1]

The Spragues returned to Manus one day later to begin preparations for the mid–September assault. On 28 August, Sprague moved his flag on board the *Fanshaw Bay* after the ship returned from Pearl Harbor, where she had undergone repairs. Five days before the landings at Morotai, Sprague's Carrier Division 25 steamed out of Manus and set course for its island destination twelve hundred miles to the west.[2]

Army units pushed ashore against light opposition on 15 September. Though Sprague's two escort carriers were barely tested in this operation, Sprague played a prominent role in a daring air-sea rescue of a downed aviator on 16 September. On their way back to the escort carrier *Santee* from completing a mission, seven U.S. fighter pilots spotted three empty enemy barges anchored off the north shore of Wasile Bay, sixty miles south of Morotai. As they dropped down to strafe the targets, antiaircraft fire tore into one of the planes and forced its pilot, Ens. Harold A. Thompson, to parachute into the bay. A Catalina dropped Thompson a raft, but after he climbed in, the raft began drifting toward shore and a steady stream of Japanese machine gun fire. While the other six fighter pilots attempted to smother enemy fire, Thompson hurriedly paddled toward one of the barges two hundred yards away.

On the *Fanshaw Bay,* Sprague approved a rescue operation involving two torpedo boats manned solely by volunteers, and fifty aircraft, including fifteen from the *Fanshaw Bay.* Under cover of increased strafing and a smoke curtain dropped between shore and the barges, the PT boats ran a scary gauntlet of machine gun bullets and shells to Thompson's refuge. Two men plunged into the water to bring Thompson and his raft back to a PT boat, then both boats, constantly zigzagging to avoid shells, endured another twenty-minute run out, this time without air cover as the fighters had to return for more fuel. Thompson emerged relatively unharmed, although shaken by the eleven-hour ordeal.

In his report, Sprague attributed the mission's success to "the fine coordination between the air coverage and the PT boats." He praised all men involved, particularly the PT boat officers and men, and wrote in a letter that "The consummation of this rescue in the face of the tremendous odds is characteristic of the highest traditions of our Navy. The PT Squadron may well be proud of this act which is considered one of the most daring and skillfully executed rescues of the war." The commanding officer of the two boats, Lt. A. Murray Preston, received the Congressional Medal of Honor, and Navy Crosses were awarded to four other men.[3]

Since operations ashore continued smoothly, most escort carriers headed back to Manus in late September. Because of muddy conditions, however, Morotai airfields could not be readied for Army aircraft until the first week in October, so Sprague had to remain behind and provide air coverage until then.[4]

Sprague took advantage of the extra week on station to walk about the

Fanshaw Bay and familiarize himself with the men and operating conditions. To his dismay, he found an unhappy crew whose morale had taken a beating under his predecessor, Rear Adm. Gerald F. Bogan, who made no secret that he wanted to serve with the fast carriers. As a result, Bogan demanded the same quality of operations on the smaller escorts that officers expected with the more experienced crews on board fast carriers. When the relatively green escort crews failed to meet his high standards, he berated them for being "unreasonably slow" and condemned the carrier as "the worst ship [he'd] ever seen in any Navy." In Bogan's opinion, other than the air officer, "the entire complement was incompetent." Bogan later refused to attend ceremonies awarding the Presidential Unit Citation to ships of Taffy 3 because it included the *Fanshaw Bay*.[5]

Sprague started working on the ship's and unit's morale immediately. Just as high morale and efficient performance go hand in hand, so do low morale and haphazard performance. With his ships heading into a war zone, sloppy work could result in lost lives, and that was something Sprague wanted to avoid. Early one morning, ordnance workers laboring in the bomb bay of a torpedo plane were surprised to see Sprague walk up and ask them how things were going. According to crewman William Carson, the group complained that because they were undermanned, they had to work sixteen to twenty-two hours each day installing new aircraft rockets sent out by the Navy. Making matters worse, the rockets did not properly fit the aircraft, so each weapon had to be adjusted before it could be attached, a process involving hours of extra work. Sprague told Carson and the others they should "get as much sleep as possible between operations by flopping any place that was comfortable. He said that he would keep the Exec off our case and he did." That crew members felt free to complain to an admiral indicates the ease with which Sprague mixed with those in his command. Second, Sprague's effort to assist the weary seamen meant more than any words or pep talk could ever have accomplished. Carson added that "We really didn't get much more sleep, but what mattered was that someone cared and valued our really quite extraordinary efforts. That was typical of [Admiral Sprague]." In a relatively short time Sprague started turning around his unit's morale and transforming a once-jittery *Fanshaw Bay* into a smooth-running ship, just as he had achieved a similar feat with the *Tangier* and *Wasp*.[6]

Unfortunately, the week's delay involved Sprague's unit in one of the war's saddest cases of mistaken identity. At 0806 on 3 October, while Sprague's force steamed thirty-five miles off Morotai's northern coast, a torpedo churned by the *Fanshaw Bay's* port side. Two minutes later a second torpedo plowed into the side of the destroyer escort *Shelton,* sinking the vessel, killing thirteen crewmen and wounding twenty-two. Sprague ordered the destroyer escort *Rowell* to aid her fellow vessel and sent eleven aircraft to search for the enemy submarine.

Here is where the mixup occurred. To avoid depth charges being dropped on friendly submarines, a safety lane had been designated north of Morotai. Submarines cruising in that corridor were not to be attacked. Somehow, the pilots now scouring the seas had not been informed of this lane nor had word been passed to Sprague that the American submarine *Seawolf* was due in the lane at any moment.

One pilot, thinking he had spotted the enemy submarine, dropped bombs on the *Seawolf* as she cruised along the surface, forcing her to submerge. The *Rowell* sped over and added depth charges to the attack. When the *Seawolf's* commander tried to send sonar messages indicating her identity, Lt. Comdr. Harry A. Barnard of the *Rowell* dismissed them as an enemy attempt to jam his radar and continued firing depth charges. Amid a string of underwater explosions, an enormous air bubble broke the surface that spewed submarine debris across the waters. The *Seawolf* was lost with all hands.

A board of investigation later censured Barnard for ignoring the *Seawolf's* sonar messages, but conceding that such mishaps occur in war zones, recommended that no disciplinary action be taken. The board placed full blame on poor communications between different branches of the Navy.[7]

Later that day Sprague turned his task unit east toward Manus, which he reached on 7 October. Five days later he received command of Task Unit 77.4.3, another escort carrier division—the unit he would lead off the coast of Samar.[8]

An immense operation was brewing in the Pacific, one that had fermented in the mind of the brilliant but egocentric General MacArthur. Long yearning to again walk on Philippine soil, which he had left as the Japanese closed in on Bataan and Corregidor in the bleak 1942 days, Mac-Arthur urged the Joint Chiefs of Staff to implement a Philippine campaign under his guidance. So far, two independent American drives struck at the Japanese—MacArthur's Army-dominated Southwest Pacific campaign up the northern New Guinea coast, and Nimitz's Navy-dominated thrust through the Central Pacific. MacArthur proposed that the two arms unite—under his leadership, of course—for the sweep through the Philippines.

Nimitz and the Navy held a different view. Rather than advance toward Japan via the Philippine route, Nimitz wanted a direct leap toward Formosa—under his leadership, of course.

The infamous Army-Navy interservice conflict reared once again. MacArthur, who commanded the Southwest Pacific like a personal fiefdom, objected to the Navy intruding into his domain and balked at placing vast numbers of land troops under the command of a sea-oriented Nimitz. With equal vigor, Nimitz and Adm. Ernest King absolutely refused to let MacArthur control any of the Navy's newest and most potent offensive weapon—the fast carriers. The impasse begged for a firm decision.

President Roosevelt flew to Pearl Harbor in July 1944 to discuss future strategy with MacArthur and Nimitz. As a result of the meeting, the Joint Chiefs of Staff eventually selected MacArthur's Philippine drive as the next step. MacArthur received command of the Army units, plus the ships that would transport the men and provide air support for the invasion, but control of the fast carriers, who would have the responsibility of keeping the Imperial Navy off MacArthur's back, was left in Nimitz's hands. To appease both parties, the specter of divided command remained.

The American plan involved enormous forces and matériel. The Seventh Fleet alone, nicknamed "MacArthur's Navy" and led by Vice Adm. Thomas C. Kinkaid, contained 738 ships, including 430 transports to take the 174,000 men of Army Gen. Walter Krueger's Sixth Army into the Leyte beachhead, and 18 escort carriers, 6 of which would be led by Clifton Sprague. Other ships would ferry in the two million tons of equipment required on shore. For all practical purposes, Kinkaid controlled the largest armada in the world.[9]

But not the most destructive. That belonged to Halsey's Third Fleet, composed mainly of Vice Adm. Marc A. Mitscher's Task Force 38, sixteen fast carriers escorted by over eighty battleships, cruisers, and destroyers whose main task would be to engage the enemy fleet, should it appear. In its regular cruising formation, Task Force 38 stretched forty miles long by nine miles wide. According to the Joint Chiefs of Staff's decision, though, while Kinkaid answered to MacArthur, Halsey steamed under Nimitz's control.[10]

This led to confusion from the start. Kinkaid believed his mission was to land Krueger's troops and provide cover while they established a beachhead and started operations. While he was doing this, Halsey would watch his back in case the Japanese decided to use their fleet. Nimitz and Halsey, though, viewed things differently. Operation Plan 8-44 from Nimitz headquarters ordered Halsey to "cover and support forces of the Southwest Pacific" in its Philippine campaign and to "destroy enemy naval and air forces in or threatening the Philippine Area."[11]

Nimitz then added another directive stating that should the Japanese fleet appear, and should there be a likelihood of Halsey inflicting serious damage to it, "such destruction becomes the primary task" of Task Force 38. For an impetuous commander such as Halsey, itching for a crack at the enemy, this directive was tantamount to giving him free rein to ignore the beachhead and charge after the Japanese.[12]

Divided command might not have proved so disastrous had open lines of communication been established, but Halsey and Kinkaid could not easily get in touch with each other since they worked under different organizations. MacArthur maintained a tight hold on incoming and outgoing communications. During the entire operation, should Kinkaid want to contact Halsey, he would first have to send the dispatch to MacArthur's radio station at Manus in the Admiralties, which would then relay the message to Halsey. This process required time, something that might not be available should a crisis arise.[13]

Thus two errors weakened American planning for the assault at Leyte. The lack of an overall commander and its attendant confusion, particularly in regard to communications, and the differing views of Halsey's main responsibility held by Kinkaid and Halsey created a fissure that could be exploited should the enemy fleet appear in a desperate attempt to disrupt MacArthur's invasion.

Desperate plans had already made the rounds in Tokyo, where the Japanese Imperial High Command delineated the areas to which they would send their fleet should the U.S. Navy advance. Called Sho-Go (Operation Victory), the plan aimed to amass Japanese naval forces on the threatened area after land-based air power delivered a powerful first blow to the intruders. Sho-1 focused on the Philippines; Sho-2 earmarked Formosa, the Ryukyus, and southern Japan; Sho-3 defended central Japan; Sho-4 shielded northern Japan. If Japan controlled these areas, her tankers could still bring badly needed supplies from the East Indies to Japan. In American hands the supplies, particularly oil, would be cut off, drastically hindering Japan's ability to wage war.[14]

Adm. Soemu Toyoda, commander in chief, Combined Fleet, explained that if the United States seized any of these areas, "even though the fleet should be left, the shipping lane to the south would be completely cut off so that the fleet, if it should come back to Japanese waters, could not obtain its fuel supply. If it should remain in southern waters, it could not receive supplies of ammunition and arms. There would be no sense in saving the fleet" while expending the land.[15]

Toyoda's complex plan for the Philippines, Sho-1, depended on an intricate combination of deception and daring. As the enemy approached the islands, Japanese land-based air power would chip away at the American fleet in a series of raids. Three arms of a huge seaborne pincer action would then descend on the Philippines with the ultimate goal of crashing through American defenses to devastate Leyte Gulf shipping, disrupt MacArthur's invasion timetable, and sink enemy combatant ships. The plan's success depended upon one key event—the northern arm drawing Halsey's Third Fleet from Leyte Gulf to enable the two other arms to charge in on Kinkaid. For this purpose, Toyoda dangled what he knew would be irresistible bait—the four aircraft carriers and escorting ships of Vice Adm. Jisaburo Ozawa's Northern Force based in the Inland Sea between the home islands of Honshu and Shikoku. The carriers were without weapons, since American carrier air power had shorn the Imperial fleet of its air arm in major Pacific encounters, most recently in June at the Battle of the Philippine Sea. Toyoda hoped his American counterparts were unaware of this and that merely the appearance of Japanese carriers would lure Halsey north.

While Ozawa enticed the Third Fleet, Vice Adm. Shoji Nishimura's Force C of two old battleships, one heavy cruiser, and four destroyers would depart Lingga Roads near Singapore, cross the Sulu and Mindanao Seas, and steam through Surigao Strait, south of Leyte Gulf. Along the way, Vice Adm. Kiyohide Shima's Second Striking Force of two heavy cruisers, one light cruiser, and four destroyers would steam south from Formosa to form Nishimura's rear guard. Together these two units, comprising Toyoda's Southern Force, would swing north and attack Kinkaid's shipping from the south.

At the same time a fourth and vastly more powerful unit would head out of Lingga Roads. It, too, had no carrier air power to provide coverage. Vice Adm. Takeo Kurita's First Striking Force of battleships and cruisers would advance across the Sibuyan Sea, sweep through the San Bernardino Strait north of Leyte Gulf, then descend on Kinkaid from the north while Nishimura and Shima struck from the south.[16]

Toyoda pinned his hopes for victory on a plan that demanded too much. Three separate forces were expected to arrive simultaneously at Leyte Gulf after approaching from different avenues and most likely after encountering opposition along the way. This required precise navigation, communication, and luck. Toyoda needed a miracle, or some unforeseen blunder by the enemy, to succeed.

Another flaw existed. Kurita's chief of staff, Rear Adm. Tomiji Koyanagi, explained that most Japanese officers preferred to engage America's carriers. Troop and supply transports offered little more than substitute targets, since attacking them still left the enemy's rapidly expanding fleet of fast carriers to contend with. If Toyoda wanted to sacrifice ships and men, stated Koyanagi, "it should be for enemy carriers."

Only one element could make matters worse, added Koyanagi. Should some factor delay Kurita from reaching Leyte Gulf until after the transports had been emptied, the operation would have endangered valuable ships and crews for nothing. "It would be foolish to sink emptied transports at the cost of our great surface force!"[17]

When men and nations have their very survival at stake, strategy that once looked foolish suddenly appears more plausible. Reckless though the plan might be, Japan now had little choice but to challenge the U.S. Navy. Ozawa "expected complete destruction of my fleet" and Kurita predicted "more than half of our ships would be lost," but it was a gamble that had to be accepted.[18]

Not everyone agreed. Koyanagi stated that "This was a completely desperate, reckless, and unprecedented plan that ignored the basic concepts of war (carriers and their attending air groups should bear the offensive burden). I still cannot but interpret it as a suicide order for Kurita's fleet."[19]

Now that we have described the plans, it is time to meet three commanders, one Japanese and two American, who along with Sprague constituted the key players in the drama about to unfold. Unlike many other battles, this clash off Samar was dominated by personalities. To a large degree, its outcome depended on the training, experience, successes, failures, and mental characteristics of the men at the top. While taking nothing away from the raw courage exhibited by Sprague's Taffy 3—and bravery was certainly evident on board every ship and in each air group that day—decisions made or not made, and calmness shown or nervousness unmasked, swayed the prospects of victory from side to side throughout the long day. Let us meet these men—Admirals Kinkaid, Halsey, and Kurita.

Born in 1888, Thomas Cassin Kinkaid graduated from the Naval Academy in 1908. Speedily earning a solid reputation on battleships and cruisers, Kinkaid arrived at Pearl Harbor a scant five days after the Japanese raid and participated as an observer on the same frustrating Wake relief attempt that saw Sprague take his *Tangier* so close to the beleaguered island.

After leading Cruiser Division 6 at both the Coral Sea and Midway, Kinkaid commanded Task Force 16 on board the carrier *Enterprise,* where he covered the Guadalcanal landings and participated in the naval clashes at the Battle of the Eastern Solomons and the Battle of Santa Cruz Island. In early 1943 Kinkaid guided the North Pacific Fleet in its successful effort to stem Japanese aggression in Alaska and reoccupy the Japanese-held Alaskan islands of Attu and Kiska. Working closely with Army counterparts, Kinkaid so impressed the Joint Chiefs of Staff that they appointed him commander of the Seventh Fleet, the fleet attached to General MacArthur. The Joint Chiefs hoped that, unlike his predecessors at the Seventh Fleet, Kinkaid's diplomatic touch would enable him to construct a harmonious relationship with the difficult MacArthur and his even more irascible staff.

MacArthur liked Kinkaid right from the start, admiring Kinkaid's competence in battle and his willingness to speak his mind. For instance, when MacArthur insisted he needed additional naval forces in the Southwest Pacific, Kinkaid firmly reminded him that Admiral King was unlikely to approve his request because the enemy fleet operated in other areas and because ships sent to MacArthur's zone were constantly exposed to land-based enemy bombers.

When Kinkaid's Seventh Fleet joined Halsey's Third Fleet off the Philippines, the two forces created one of the most impressive armadas ever seen. Yet, because of one glitch in the command setup, this conglomeration was almost embarrassed by an enemy plan devised in desperation. Kinkaid controlled his Seventh Fleet, but he held absolutely no authority over the forces protecting him—Halsey's Third Fleet.[20]

While Kinkaid quietly and steadily rose through the chain of command, William Frederick Halsey, Jr., plunged in with gusto. Few outside the Navy knew Kinkaid; Halsey's name and exploits filled headlines and dominated home front conversation.

Born in 1882, Halsey first served in destroyers after graduating as part of the Naval Academy's Class of 1904, but developed an interest in aviation and earned his wings in 1929 under then-Lieutenant Sprague. He gained home front acclaim in April 1942 when, on board the carrier *Enterprise* as commander of Task Force 16, Halsey transported Army Lt. Col. James H. "Jimmy" Doolittle and sixteen B-25 bombers within six hundred miles of Japan for Doolittle's daring raid on Tokyo. Though causing little substantive damage to Japan, the raid lifted American morale that had been shattered by Pearl Harbor and transformed Halsey into a public hero.

Within one month the Japanese fleet had moved into the Coral Sea off Australia's northeast coast. King and Nimitz had no choice but to send out a force to oppose this threat to Australia, but because Halsey was occupied with the Doolittle raid, he could not steam down to the Southwest Pacific in time to take part. Halsey bitterly regretted missing out on what became the world's first major clash between opposing aircraft carriers.

Halsey missed an even larger battle in June when he picked up a terrible rash from heat and strain. When he returned to Pearl Harbor to be briefed on an upcoming Japanese advance toward Midway, Nimitz immediately ordered him to the hospital. Instead of Halsey, still chagrined at watching the Battle of the Coral Sea from a distance, Nimitz sent Adm. Raymond A. Spruance to counter the Japanese. In early June, Spruance's aviators sank Yamamoto's four carriers in a crucial struggle that turned the war in favor of the United States.

While Spruance, a superb, calm commander who has been labeled the "Quiet Warrior" by his biographer, earned a decisive victory in history's largest aircraft carrier battle, Halsey lay flat on his back recovering from the rash. In less than forty days, he missed the only two carrier duels fought to date; battles that with only a bit of luck or better health *he* could have commanded. Halsey could do nothing but wait for his own crack at Japanese carriers. His only consolation rested in the knowledge that much fighting lay ahead. Surely he would sooner or later get his chance.

Halsey headed back to the Southwest Pacific where he relieved an ineffective Adm. Robert L. Ghormley as commander of South Pacific Forces in the Solomon Islands. For a time it looked as if American troops might be pushed off Guadalcanal, but Halsey's appearance and words quickly boosted morale. A *New York Times* headline boasted, "SHIFT TO OFFENSIVE IS SEEN IN SELECTION OF 'FIGHTING' ADMIRAL HALSEY AS COMMANDER IN THE SOUTH PACIFIC." Marines in muddy foxholes and civilians in comfortable American homes enthusiastically agreed with bombastic Halsey statements such as "The only good Jap is a Jap who's been dead six months" or that his main job was to "Kill Japs, kill Japs, then kill more Japs." Everyone loved this man who charged straight at the foe with everything in his arsenal and said of the enemy exactly what many people thought. After an early loss at the Battle of Santa Cruz Island, Halsey presided at a victory in the naval Battle of Guadalcanal and eventually turned around the American campaign in the Solomons.

When he was elevated to commander of the Third Fleet, Halsey controlled the most powerful accumulation of naval air power yet assembled. He intended to employ his carriers in typical fashion. "I believe in violating the rules," he boasted. "We violate them every day. We do the unexpected—we expose ourselves to shore-based planes . . . But, most important, whatever we do—we do fast!" [21]

Courageous words; exciting words. Perfect words for the press. In some ways Halsey perfected the art of the television byte years before it became a household word. He knew which phrases his men and public wanted to hear and delivered them with staccato speed—short, sweet, and to the point. The public and press loved the image Halsey created: he would crush the hated Japanese and safeguard the Pacific. In painting that picture, however, Halsey became a victim of his own press. The public and his men expected Halsey to chase after the enemy, therefore he would.

This was not the most effective way to command an entire fleet. Some officers grew disenchanted with Halsey's penchant for acting first and thinking later, especially when they compared Halsey's system to the organized conditions under Spruance. One officer mentioned that under Halsey "you never knew what you were going to do in the next five minutes or how you were going to do it." Another admitted, "My feeling was one of confidence when Spruance was there and one of concern when Halsey was there." The Japanese, who respected and feared Spruance as much as any other American admiral, agreed. One of Yamamoto's staff officers, Capt. Yasuji Watanabe, claimed that Spruance possessed an "air admiral's best character—strong, straight thinker, not impulsive fluctuating thinker." By late 1944, the desperation tactics and brash statements of 1942–43, designed to inject a hurried boost to morale, were no longer needed. The war had turned in the United States' favor and called for a more rigid approach to operations. The Leyte Gulf operation required a commander to be more structured than Halsey could be. [22]

In any event, Halsey yearned to grapple with the Japanese, carrier for carrier. Many of his contemporaries and more than a few junior officers, including Sprague, had had their shot at a carrier duel. He wanted his chance before the war ended.

Halsey was also deeply influenced by heated criticism of Spruance's actions at the Philippine Sea, where most aviators thought Spruance allowed the Japanese fleet to escape. Halsey agreed, and should the opportunity arise he was determined to chase after enemy carriers. Spruance might open himself to criticism, but Halsey would not.

Thus Halsey was primed for big game when he approached the Philippine campaign. His outlook solidified when Nimitz handed him the order that was, in effect, a free hand to leave the Leyte beachhead and pursue enemy carriers. Before he even entered battle, Halsey had determined that should enemy carriers appear, he would go after them, a dangerous presupposition for a commander to make. Rather than adapt his actions to events as they occurred, Halsey hoped events would unfold according to his wishes. With this attitude, a commander is more likely to mold events to a predetermined pattern than to examine them for what they truly are. Carriers, not protecting the Leyte beachhead, received Halsey's attention—precisely what Toyoda counted on.[23]

Born to an educated family in 1889, Vice Adm. Takeo Kurita absorbed his naval philosophy and training at the Japanese equivalent of Annapolis, the rigorous Etajima Academy located on the Inland Sea. After enduring a demanding oral interview, a horrendous series of physical and academic tests, and a thorough character check on not only him but his entire family, Kurita began a regimen that placed a premium on loyalty, discipline, and conformity while stifling initiative. Mass-produced from the same mold, young officers marched out of Etajima with shortcomings that hampered more than a few Pacific operations: an unwillingness to act without precise orders, a difficulty in adapting plans to unexpected events, a tendency to see only what lay before them rather than the entire strategic picture, and an aversion to making errors. They loved an operation so minutely detailed and planned that every single officer knew exactly what to do. The obvious flaw in this thinking, though, was its reliance on the enemy doing exactly what the plan assumed he would do.

Etajima also emphasized victory through decisive battles rather than a series of clashes that gradually wore down an opponent. Academy sports rewarded cadets who could win by one powerful action. In kendo, a challenger was knocked down with a single blow from a four-foot club. To win at botaoshi, a team of cadets had to yank down another team's flag pole employing any means necessary. The victor normally resorted to a mass rush in hopes of overwhelming the opponent.

As a result, Japanese strategists favored intricate operations that relied on deception, diversion, and division of the enemy to open the way for a knockout thrust toward the plan's main objective. Midway illustrated this philosophy, but it also underscored its shortcomings when Spruance was able to ignore diversionary Japanese forces and concentrate his strength against the main thrust.[24]

Kurita served on destroyers and cruisers after graduation, eventually rising to command of a unit protecting invasion transports in the Dutch East Indies. In 1942 he led the bombardment group that would have provided cover for the troops earmarked to invade Midway Island, but that operation failed before Kurita's ships fired a shot. He participated in the 14 October 1942 bombardment of American Marines on Guadalcanal, then later commanded the Second Fleet at the Battle of the Philippine Sea.

Kurita's career was marked by a disturbing tendency to doubt his mission's success, which in turn led to irresolution, timidity, and indecisiveness. During the Guadalcanal campaign, he pulled back his unit when four American torpedo boats charged toward him, and during the Battle of the Philippine Sea he had been one of the first commanders to advocate retreat. It was no surprise, then, that Kurita doubted the chances of Toyoda's plan for Leyte Gulf, where his powerful battleship and cruiser force was ordered to risk enemy air and surface attack to charge in against transports. Kurita, the Japanese admiral Sprague would go eye to eye with off Samar, started blinking before his ships left Lingga Roads.[25]

Actually, Kurita should have feared little, since his First Striking Force could throw more shells, large and small, at an enemy than any fleet afloat in either ocean. His ships carried frightening destructiveness, headed by the biggest, deadliest battleships ever to steam the oceans, the 70,000-ton *Yamato* and her sister ship *Musashi*. Cruising at the top speed of 27 knots, their main batteries of nine 18-inch guns belched 3,500-pound shells at an opponent from a distance no other vessel could match. Twelve 6-inch guns and 120 25-mm machine guns supplemented the main batteries. If any shells happened to pour in on either battleship, 16-inch-thick armor plate would deflect the intruding missiles. Leviathan by any definition, these two sea monsters alone could handle Sprague's tiny escort carriers.

Kurita carried far more power, however. The battleship *Nagato* packed eight 16-inch guns and twenty-six 5.5- and 5-inch guns, while the battleships *Kongo* and *Haruna* added eight 14-inch guns and twenty-two 6- and 5-inch guns. Twelve heavy and light cruisers and fifteen destroyers steamed as escorts and contributed a combined eighty 8-inch guns, over 150 5-inch guns, and more than two hundred torpedo tubes for firing the deadly Long

Lance torpedoes. Kurita's five battleships alone sported 112 guns *larger* than anything Sprague possessed.[26]

> They build a flight deck on a tanker hull,
>   Jam almost thirteen hundred men on board;
> They load it up with aviation gas,
>   With bombs, torpedoes, ammunition, fuel,
> And then, in case the poor guys have to fight,
>   What have they got? One stinkin' five-inch gun.[27]

So wrote an officer who served on an escort carrier, considered the minor leagues in comparison to Halsey's fast carriers. The puny vessels earned a variety of nicknames in their brief lifetime, none of them complimentary. Sailors joked, with only a halfhearted smile, that the designation letters for escort carriers, CVE, stood for "Combustible, Vulnerable, and Expendable," and derisively termed their ships "Crocks," "Tomato Cans," or "Kaiser's Creaking Coffins" after the man who built most of the escort carriers, Henry J. Kaiser. An odd sort of esprit de corps blossomed, however, that permitted criticism only from those who served in the escort navy. As one sailor wrote, "Woe be unto any outsider who even whispered such names about our wee vessels."[28]

Escort carriers appeared in response to the dangerous German U-boat peril in the Atlantic. President Roosevelt asked the Navy to devise a vessel that could be put to sea quickly for convoy escort and antisubmarine operations. This eventually led to the mass-produced Kaiser-class, or *Casablanca*-class, escort carriers. About half the size of Halsey's fast carriers, CVEs placed a 470-foot flight deck atop a merchant vessel hull only an alarming half-inch thick. One of Kurita's battleship or cruiser shells could tear through the feeble CVE hulls like a bullet shot through a paper bag, and escort carrier sailors wailed that they served on "two-torpedo ships—one in the side and one over the flight deck."[29]

Other complaints included engines that constantly broke down, metal plates improperly welded, a lack of air conditioning, and scant supplies. *Fanshaw Bay* seaman Christopher Carson later wrote, "I still wonder how we ever accomplished as much as we did. We were constantly handicapped by shortages of everything from toilet paper to machine guns; . . . I would personally hate to attest to how much equipment we had to beg, borrow, and steal just to get one hop off the deck."[30]

Armament placed on CVEs was practically an afterthought, since they were never intended to engage much more than enemy aircraft. A solitary

5-inch gun stared seaward from the stern, hardly the location to instill respect among an enemy as the ship could only fire if it was fleeing from its target. The diminutive shells could inflict barely a dent in the sides of Kurita's thick-skinned giants; while Kurita tossed car-sized shells at the Americans, Sprague could only respond with hubcap-sized projectiles—that is, if he could get within range. Sixteen 40-mm guns in twin mounts and twenty 20-mm guns at least made antiaircraft defense somewhat feasible. The 17-knot top speed for CVEs offered little hope of fleeing from Kurita's 35-knot ships. Escort carriers could neither stand with the enemy and fight nor turn heel and retreat. But then, they were not supposed to worry about that possibility. In theory at least, large Japanese surface forces would be kept far away by Halsey's fast carriers.[31]

Each CVE carried twelve to eighteen F4F Wildcat fighters and eleven to twelve TBF Avenger torpedo planes. Since escort carriers existed to provide air support for troops ashore, fly combat air patrol over transports, and defend against enemy submarines, their pilots had not even received training in attacking warships. CVE pilots, though they may have hoped to get a crack at an enemy carrier or battleship, considered the likelihood remote at best.[32]

Screening vessels for the CVEs posed far from awesome spectacles themselves. Mainly in place to attack Japanese submarines, three Fletcher-class destroyers, each sporting five 5-inch guns and ten torpedo tubes, and four smaller destroyer-escorts with two 5-inch guns and three torpedo tubes apiece protected Sprague's six escort carriers. Directed by Comdr. William Thomas on board the destroyer *Hoel,* Sprague's screen had never launched, or even practiced, an organized torpedo attack on surface vessels since the possibility for such a maneuver seemed remote. If serving on an escort carrier bore a lackluster reputation, providing the screen for CVEs was a step below. "Guarding six escort carriers was a letdown for us," explained Lt. Robert C. Hagen, gunnery officer for the destroyer *Johnston.* "We were out of the line of fire."[33]

Add the figures for available 5-inch guns and you get an idea of how outclassed Sprague's minuscule fleet would be when matched against Kurita. Sprague's thirteen ships could turn twenty-nine 5-inch guns on Kurita, approximately what the single Japanese battleship *Nagato* possessed. The muzzles of almost two hundred enemy 5-inch guns would stare back at Sprague, and they formed only a minor backup system of offense for Kurita's 170 potent 18-, 16-, 14-, 8-, and 6-inch guns, each of which could fire on Sprague long before the American ships steamed into 5-inch range.

On 12 October, Task Unit 77.4.3 steamed out of Manus along with Rear Adm. Jesse Oldendorf's Bombardment and Fire Support Group 77.2, for which Sprague would provide air cover. In addition to the *Fanshaw Bay,* Sprague's flagship, the unit consisted of the escort carriers *St. Lo, White Plains,* and *Kalinin Bay* screened by destroyers *Hoel, Johnston,* and *Heermann* and destroyer escorts *Dennis, John C. Butler, Raymond,* and *Samuel B. Roberts.* Four days later Sprague separated his unit from Oldendorf and headed for his assigned operating area east of the huge Philippine island of Samar, located along the center of the chain's eastern edge.[34]

A powerful typhoon impeded Sprague's progress the next day. Heavy sheets of rain propelled by 54-knot winds swept across the carriers and smaller destroyers, damaged a few aircraft, and forced a cancelation of the day's air operations. The commander of the *Samuel B. Roberts,* Lt. Comdr. R. W. Copeland, later remembered, "The seas were so rough and the ship rolled and pounded so badly that for the first two or three hours many of the men were afraid the ship would sink. For the next sixteen or eighteen hours many of them were so sick that they were afraid she wouldn't sink."[35]

Sprague skirted the typhoon's edge trying to remain on schedule. He finally had to swerve south to avoid even stiffer winds, necessitating a one-day delay in the scheduled 17 October air operations to soften the landing areas.[36]

On 18 October, Sprague positioned his unit east-southeast of Samar's southern edge in preparation for the day's strikes, which would officially open the Philippine campaign. Three escort carrier units, thirty to fifty miles apart, spread out along the Philippine coast. To the south, the escort carrier group commander and Sprague's immediate superior, Rear Adm. Thomas Sprague, took the helm of Taffy 1 off northern Mindanao. Fifty miles to his north, Rear Adm. Felix B. Stump's Taffy 2 floated close to Leyte Gulf, while Clifton Sprague guarded the northern approaches off Samar.[37]

The three Taffies opened operations with air strikes against Japanese air strips on Negros, Cebu, Mindanao, and Luzon. They flew 471 sorties in the two days before MacArthur's landing in which they dropped eighty-two tons of bombs and destroyed over sixty enemy aircraft. On 19 October, when the *Gambier Bay* and *Kitkun Bay* joined Sprague and brought Taffy 3 to its full strength of six escort carriers, three destroyers, and four destroyer escorts, Sprague's air groups were ready to make their presence felt.[38]

Each night Sprague shifted Taffy 3 to its night operating area in more open water fifty miles out to sea for better defense against Japanese submarines. After zigzagging through the night, Sprague moved closer to shore for the next day's flight operations so his aircraft would not have as far to fly. With little opposition offered by the Japanese, Sprague focused most of his energies into ensuring that more mundane, but vital, support operations and antisubmarine patrols performed at top level.[39]

Some in Taffy 3 hoped for a bit more action, but service in jeep carriers or destroyer escorts normally did not involve much combat. Like most of his shipmates, Sonarman 3d Class H. Whitney Felt of the *Samuel B. Roberts* had never seen his ship's guns take aim at an enemy ship or aircraft. "Most of us hoped that we'd at least see an enemy airplane. We never expected anything big, though."[40]

MacArthur started his triumphal return to the Philippines when four Army divisions stormed a ten-mile-wide front on Leyte beaches. That evening, American forces controlled a seventeen-mile-wide chunk of land, enabling MacArthur to wade ashore and utter his famous "I have returned" speech. By midnight the next day, 132,000 men supported by 200,000 tons of equipment had landed on Leyte, and a steady stream of supplies came ashore from the hundreds of supply transports. Within a day, only twenty-eight Liberty ships and twenty-five landing ships remained in the gulf of the hundreds that had poured in two days before.[41]

Sprague was satisfied with Taffy 3's contribution to the campaign's first week. The *Fanshaw Bay*'s VC-68 squadron alone had flown 245 sorties against land targets or for combat air and antisubmarine patrols and had gained more confidence with each day.[42]

Sprague occasionally squeezed in a chat with officers and men in an effort to keep morale high, particularly now that his ships operated in a war zone. Duane Iossi stood watch at his gun one time when Sprague walked over and started talking to him. The surprised youth muttered few words in reply, but after a short visit Sprague ended with "Keep up the good work."[43]

Sprague succeeded in restoring the escort carrier sailors' self-respect. Of all the measures he adopted in the days before Samar, that might have been his most vital, for when Kurita surprised everyone on 25 October, he faced men brimming with confidence instead of weakened by doubt. Carson wrote that "with Admiral Sprague these constant plaguing doubts of the jeep-sailor gave way to the confidence we had in him as a leader and as a personality who was working for our best interests."[44]

Before leaving, Kurita had to convince recalcitrant officers to enthusiastically support the mission. In a meeting with his division commanders and their staffs on his flagship, the heavy cruiser *Atago,* he indicated his awareness that a significant number of junior officers viewed the mission with great skepticism. Even though he held similar doubts, the usually shy commander explained how poorly the war had been going for Japan and how vital this assignment was for their nation's fate.

"Would it not be a shame to have the fleet remain intact while our nation perishes? I believe that Imperial Headquarters is giving us a glorious opportunity. You must remember that there are such things as miracles. What man can say that there is no chance for our fleet to turn the tide of war in a Decisive Battle?"

Even though Kurita pinned the mission's success to a miracle, his officers, many Etajima trained, relished the opportunity to strike a decisive blow against the enemy. Kurita left the room with loud cries of "Banzai" ringing in his ears.[45]

Kurita's fleet of battleships and cruisers departed Lingga Roads on 18 October, the same day Sprague's planes started softening the Philippine invasion area. Two days later he arrived at Brunei, Borneo, where he refueled for two days before steaming north for the Palawan Passage. Kurita planned to cross the Sibuyan Sea, fight his way through the San Bernardino Strait, and descend on Kinkaid's transports. The other three arms of Toyoda's steel pincers began closing on Leyte at the same time. Nishimura's Force C followed Kurita out of Brunei seven hours later, steamed north to the tip of Borneo, then headed east for Surigao Strait. Ozawa guided his decoy force out of Japan on 20 October, while Admiral Shima debouched from the Inland Sea shortly after receiving his 22 October orders to support Nishimura. Since the Japanese had recently switched its naval code and maintained radio silence, Nimitz's naval intelligence in Pearl Harbor never received a clear picture of the impending operation.[46]

American commanders were hardly handicapped from a lack of information, though, as reports poured in that something big had started. Within one day of Kurita's sailing, the two American submarines *Darter* and *Dace* located him off Palawan.

Here began an incredible string of errors, assumptions, and bad luck that, while severely rattling an already dubious Kurita, culminated with Sprague staring at pagoda masts. Kurita's journey up the Palawan Passage and through the Sibuyan Sea is reminiscent of the hapless victim in a slapstick comedy who, no matter where he turned, faced another pursuer. Yet somehow, he navigated his way through the opposition and popped out of San Bernardino Strait, battered, bruised, wet, exhausted, yet within sight of his goal.

Charge the initial errors to Kurita's account. His cruising disposition along Palawan begged an American submarine to attack. Instead of stationing escorting destroyers ahead of his fleet, Kurita placed them along the flanks of his two columns of battleships and cruisers. Incredibly, he positioned his own flagship *Atago* at the head of the left column. Any submarine fortunate enough to stumble onto the Japanese force needed only to approach from the unguarded front to line up a target in her periscope sights. Why a commander with Kurita's experience arranged his fleet in such careless fashion is difficult to fathom, but it raises serious concerns over his true commitment to the impending Leyte Gulf action. It is almost as though he were pleading for an attack that might justify his turning back to Brunei.

Submarines *Darter* and *Dace* fired the first shots in the early hours of 23 October. After spotting Kurita at 0116 and notifying their superiors, the two boats positioned for an attack. Comdr. David H. McClintock inched the *Darter* within 980 yards of the left column, aimed for the leading ship— Kurita's flagship *Atago*—and emptied her six bow tubes at 0632. McClintock immediately swung hard left and, as his initial spread of torpedoes ripped into the *Atago,* emptied his stern tubes on the second ship in line, the heavy cruiser *Takao,* which quickly burst into flames from two explosions. By 0634, McClintock started his descent to elude the inevitable depth charges.[47]

Brilliant orange flames punctuated the thick black smoke that enveloped Kurita's flagship, forcing the stunned leader to order the crew to abandon ship. He jumped overboard and swam toward a destroyer, which deposited the wet, shaken commander aboard the *Yamato.* In eighteen short minutes the *Atago* disappeared beneath the surface, taking with her 360 officers and men as well as Kurita's confidence. Though the *Takao* did not sink, the *Darter* inflicted enough damage that the heavy cruiser had to turn back to Brunei, escorted by two destroyers. Before he had steamed halfway to his objective, Kurita had lost four ships.[48]

"It looks like the Fourth of July out there!" shouted Comdr. Bladen D. Claggett, *Dace*'s skipper. "One is burning. The Japs are milling and firing all over the place. What a show! What a show!" Claggett added to Kurita's woes around 0656 by planting her own spread of four torpedoes directly into a third heavy cruiser, the *Maya.* At least one of the tin fish destroyed the *Maya*'s magazines and caused a series of devastating explosions. The *Maya,* which steamed just ahead of the *Yamato,* ripped apart as though it were made of paper. From the *Yamato,* Rear Adm. Matome Ugaki turned toward the *Maya,* "and after the spray and smoke had disappeared nothing of her remained to be seen." As the *Darter* dove to avoid depth charges,

Commander McClintock heard the *Maya* disintegrate in loud noises that sounded like "crackling cellophane."[49]

In twenty-four minutes Kurita had seen three heavy cruisers sunk or knocked out of the battle, endured an ocean swim to avoid drowning, and realized his approach had been broadcast to American forces off the Philippines. The encounter weakened Kurita, who the previous few days had been attempting to recover from a bout of dengue fever. Though he led a battered flotilla along Palawan and turned into the Sibuyan Sea with diminished hopes, he still retained enough power to brush aside most surface forces in existence. Each successive blow to his ships or his confidence, though, shook Kurita's ability to make sound decisions. Toyoda may have sensed this, for he dispatched a message during the submarine attack informing Kurita that although the enemy most likely knew he was headed toward the Philippines, he was to "EXECUTE ORIGINAL PLAN."[50]

More calamities harassed Kurita, this time delivered by Halsey's carrier air squadrons. By 0822 on 24 October, Halsey received word that Kurita had rounded Mindoro's southern tip and appeared headed toward San Bernardino Strait. Though no carriers were reported with Kurita, Halsey wasted little time in ordering his aircraft after the ships.[51]

Beginning at 1026, five quick air strikes stunned Kurita. For the next five and one-half hours, Halsey's aviators attacked with impunity, since the Japanese land-based air commander in the Philippines, Vice Adm. Shigeru Fukudome, had denied Kurita any land-based air cover in order to marshal his aircraft for strikes against American carriers. Almost one air attack per minute gave Kurita little time to pause or evaluate the situation. Barely had he turned his fleet in one direction to evade an American aircraft when a second would charge in from the opposite side. In a sign that the earlier submarine attacks shook the admiral, Kurita even ordered his battleships to fire their main batteries at aircraft ten miles away, a futile move made by a desperate man. "The small number of enemy planes shot down is regrettable," wrote Admiral Ugaki of the eighteen aircraft splashed by Kurita's antiaircraft guns.[52]

Two bomb hits shook the *Yamato* without inflicting much damage. At 1935 the *Yamato*'s sister ship, the *Musashi*, steaming directly behind Kurita's improvised flagship, sank with a thousand officers and men after absorbing an amazing nineteen torpedo and seventeen bomb hits. The heavy cruiser *Myoko* had to fall out of line two ships ahead of Kurita and return to Brunei when a torpedo damaged two shafts. After exiting the submarine attack

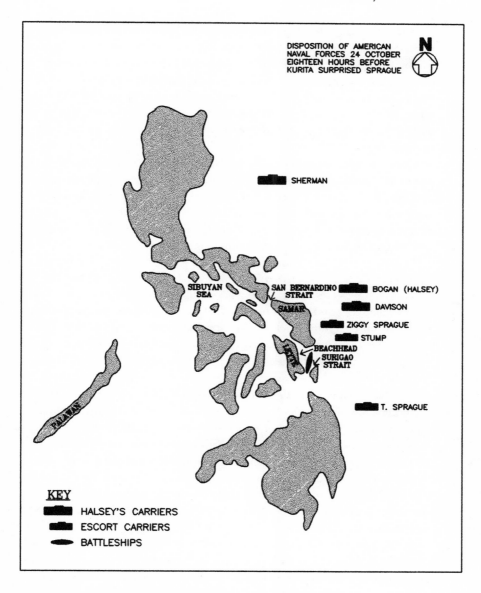

MAP 3. Disposition of American naval forces, 24 October 1944

shaken and minus five ships, Kurita watched American air power remove two additional ships from his arsenal, and he had not yet even faced an enemy surface vessel. He had to wonder that if his opponent could inflict this much damage so far from the center of his operations, what awaited him as he closed in on Leyte Gulf? Kurita's chief of staff, Admiral Koyanagi, himself twice wounded in this action, later wrote that he and Kurita expected air attacks, but this day's unrelenting assaults "were almost enough to discourage us."[53]

Kurita decided to temporarily reverse course to get away from Halsey's planes. By heading west, though, he threw off the fragile timetable dictated by Toyoda's rigid plan and ended all possibility of a joint action inside Leyte Gulf with Nishimura's Southern Force. That he realized this yet still steamed west for over an hour indicates the frustration he felt and the delicate state of mind with which he formed judgments.[54]

Toyoda and a halt in American air attacks prodded him back into action. "ALL FORCES WILL DASH TO THE ATTACK, TRUSTING IN DIVINE GUIDANCE" read a message from Tokyo. At 1714 Kurita once again headed for San Bernardino Strait. Maybe, with great amounts of luck, Kurita could charge through and do some damage inside Leyte Gulf. If a potent enemy surface force floated off the strait's eastern opening, however, Kurita knew he faced disaster.[55]

For that to happen, though, Halsey's Third Fleet had to be there. Within one hour of sighting Kurita's Center Force and launching Third Fleet planes over the Sibuyan Sea, Halsey received word of Nishimura's group approaching to the south. Since Oldendorf's battleships were already forming to counter that force, Halsey dismissed it from his mind and focused on the location of those elusive carriers. He felt certain the Japanese would not send large surface forces on such a major encounter without air support, yet no carriers had been spotted. Where in the world were they, the frustrated commander wondered.[56]

At 1512 Halsey started his countermoves by dispatching a "Battle Plan" to Mitscher, Vice Adm. Willis A. Lee, his battleship commander, and his task group commanders in which he informed everyone to be prepared to form Task Force 34 should it be needed. This force, specifically created to block Kurita's passage through San Bernardino Strait, would consist of four battleships, including Halsey's flagship, the *New Jersey,* two heavy cruisers, three light cruisers, and two divisions of escorting destroyers, under Lee's command. To ensure that his commanders understood that this message did

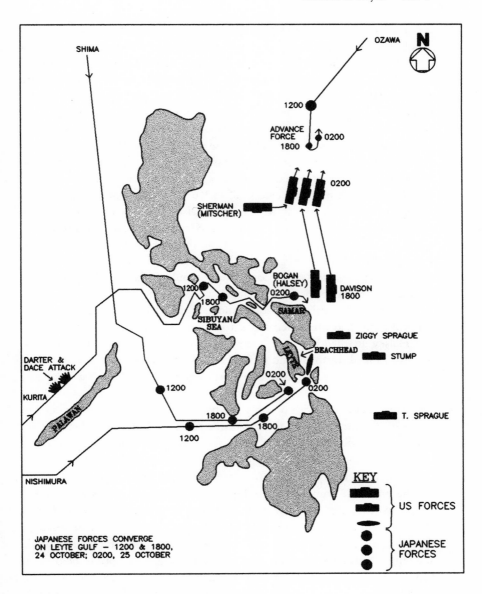

MAP 4. Japanese forces converge on Leyte Gulf.

not actually activate Task Force 34, but was sent merely as an alert that should the occasion arise, Task Force 34 would be formed, Halsey sent a second message via the TBS—Talk Between Ships. Directed to Admirals Bogan and Davison, from whose units Task Force 34 would be drawn, the message stated that "if the enemy sorties, TF 34 will be formed *when directed by me*." Until then, Third Fleet would continue operating as a unit.[57]

Though Halsey dispatched this only to his subordinate commanders, as is frequently the custom Kinkaid at Leyte and Nimitz at Pearl Harbor intercepted and read the messages. This started the first in a long string of assumptions that American commanders would make over the next twenty hours that almost handed Leyte Gulf to Kurita. Both Kinkaid and Nimitz *assumed* from Halsey's 1512 message that Halsey had formed Task Force 34 and that it was in position to guard San Bernardino Strait. Unfortunately, neither man could intercept Halsey's second message to Bogan and Davison since it was transmitted over the short-range TBS. Though their assumption was one that most any other commander would make, it still was only an assumption, not a verification of fact.[58]

On the eve of battle, two commanders charged with covering San Bernardino Strait had thus relegated it to secondary status. Kinkaid, thinking that Halsey guarded the strait, focused on Nishimura to the south. Halsey, in turn, looked north to find the unlocated enemy carriers. In the middle sat Sprague with his thin-skinned escort carriers—directly in Kurita's path.

Ozawa, burdened with possibly the harshest orders any commander can have—to sacrifice his own force—finally succeeded in getting Halsey's attention by sending two hybrid carriers, the *Ise* and *Hyuga,* south to make contact with the Americans. At 1640, Halsey received the welcome news that a force of enemy carriers bore down from the north.[59]

The impulsive commander paid lip service to proper procedure and discussed with his staff whether he should take the Third Fleet north, but in reality he had made up his mind long before. As he outlined them, he faced three options. He could wait off San Bernardino Strait for Kurita while allowing Ozawa to advance. Halsey discounted this option because it handed the initiative to Ozawa, who might be able to close on the Third Fleet and, in cooperation with Japanese airfields in the Philippines, shuttle bomb Halsey's ships. He could leave Task Force 34 off San Bernardino while taking the rest of the Third Fleet north to face Ozawa, but he feared this might leave him with two weak components that could be destroyed piecemeal. The third option, never really in doubt, was to engage Ozawa with his entire Third Fleet. In his memoirs, Halsey claimed he favored this choice because it placed the initiative with him, and should Kurita break out of San Bernardino, he believed Kinkaid possessed sufficient strength to deflect the Japanese. Even should Kurita dash into Leyte Gulf and fire on Kinkaid's transports, Halsey felt Kurita could do little more than mount a hit-and-run attack.[60]

Halsey relied heavily on pilot reports that Kurita had been seriously weakened in the Sibuyan Sea to justify his decision to abandon the strait. He later admitted those reports turned out to be "dangerously optimistic, but we had no reason to discredit them at the time." He should have, though, since pilots' claims of aerial kills were frequently exaggerated when compared to actual results. Instead, Halsey committed one of the most basic errors a commander can make—he determined ahead of time what he would do, then tried to fit the battle to conform to his wishes. His desire to get those carriers caused him to rationalize away facts that punched holes in his intentions.[61]

Halsey ignored a second crucial aspect—whether Ozawa's carriers formed a decoy, long a staple of Japanese plans. On 31 March, guerrilla forces extracted copies of Adm. Mineichi Koga's plans for future operations from two Japanese planes that had crashed in the Philippines. Koga, Toyoda's predecessor, planned to employ empty aircraft carriers to lure American carrier power away while other forces attacked the main objective. Nimitz had the plans copied and sent to every fleet commander in the Pacific. Spruance tied his carriers close to Saipan's beachhead at the Battle of the Philippine Sea because he feared such a decoy, yet the aggressive Halsey ignored the information. Two intelligence officers on the *New Jersey* even showed Halsey's staff secret documents supporting the notion that Halsey was being lured away, but nobody would listen.[62]

Halsey and his staff gave Third Fleet commanders fits the night of 24–25 October. Admiral Bogan personally contacted the *New Jersey* when he learned Kurita had turned again toward San Bernardino as a way of telling Halsey to reconsider, but Halsey's staff brushed him off with a curt response that they already had that information. Capt. James S. Russell, chief of staff to Davison, claimed later that "Halsey's action [in heading north with his entire force] was such an obvious mistake to Admiral Davison and me. Davison said, 'Jim, this doesn't look right to me.' I asked him if he wanted to say anything to Mitscher, but he replied no, that Mitscher would have more information. Halsey erred, but he wanted to get those carriers."[63]

When Admiral Lee shared his belief with Halsey's staff that Ozawa was a decoy, he received only a simple acknowledgment. Lee had noticed a Japanese fascination for decoy forces going back to his service in the Solomons, and according to his flag lieutenant, Lt. Gil Aertsen, "Lee thought we shouldn't trust the sons of bitches. He wanted to take his battleships and stand up and down in front of the straits." Aertsen added, "We thought we could clean them up."[64]

Mitscher thought Halsey was wrong, but refused to bother his superior. Mitscher's chief of staff, Capt. Arleigh Burke, thought the Northern Force was trying to decoy Halsey and wanted Mitscher to discuss it with Halsey. He and the staff had even developed a plan to retain Task Force 34 and one group of carriers off San Bernardino while sending the other carriers north, but Mitscher refused to carry the matter higher. "Well, I think you're right," answered Mitscher, "but I don't know you're right." He then ended the discussion by adding, "If [Halsey] wants my advice, he'll ask for it."[65]

Mitscher committed a blunder by remaining silent. More so than the other high-ranking officers who doubted Halsey that night, Mitscher's opinion carried weight. Had he been more forceful, he might have tempered Halsey's impulsiveness and succeeded in stationing Lee off San Bernardino. Instead, Mitscher's inaction at this crucial moment helped create the near-debacle off Samar.

When so many top subordinates disagree with their commander's action, it indicates that the commander sees something none of the other men notice or that the commander is making a huge error. Halsey fell into the latter category by allowing his emotions to rule his reason. He was the "Bull," the leader cheered by Guadalcanal Marines and hoisted to hero status by an adoring press, and by God the Japanese fleet was not going to elude him this time. Halsey, the admiral most of the American public associated with carrier air power, was not about to let this opportunity fall from his grasp. Halsey was willing to accept criticism, as long as it was for being overaggressive, not timid. Staring at the alternatives of guarding a static strait or jumping after enemy carriers, Halsey never hesitated.[66]

Halsey notified Nimitz and Kinkaid about 2000 that he was heading north, but the message's vague wording caused some to misconstrue its meaning. "STRIKE REPORTS INDICATE ENEMY FORCE SIBUYAN SEA HEAVILY DAMAGED. AM PROCEEDING NORTH WITH THREE GROUPS TO ATTACK ENEMY CARRIER FORCE AT DAWN." Kinkaid and Nimitz thought Halsey meant he was taking the three carrier groups but leaving behind Task Force 34, which they had erroneously assumed he had formed. Had they examined the message more carefully, they would have spotted clues that he was doing no such thing. The phrase "AM PROCEEDING NORTH" indicated he was going with them. Since his flagship, the *New Jersey*, was to be part of Task Force 34 when formed, this meant *all* ships were leaving San Bernardino. Even failing to notice that, Kinkaid and Nimitz should have realized that an admiral with Halsey's disposition would never sit off a strait in guard duty while sending other portions of his fleet to fight carriers.[67]

Thus Halsey, with an abundance of air power, steamed away from San Bernardino Strait as Kurita headed toward it, precisely what Toyoda had dreamed. The door to Leyte Gulf lay wide open for the First Striking Force. All that lay between the two was Sprague and his little escort unit.

Events now occurred that set the final stage. A slight change in any one might have altered 25 October, but fate, erroneous assumptions, and faulty decisions guaranteed this would not happen. Less than two hours after turning north, Halsey received a report placing Kurita off San Bernardino's western entrance. He ruled against turning back, believing Kinkaid could surely handle what must be the battle-weary Center Force. Shortly afterward, Kinkaid ordered Thomas Sprague to send out three daybreak searches over San Bernardino and Samar. Sprague in turn handed the responsibility to Admiral Stump's Taffy 2 at 0330 on 25 October. He received the order at 0430. Thirty minutes later Stump ordered the *Ommaney Bay* to carry out the task, but by the time the *Ommaney Bay* respotted its deck and launched the plane, Kurita had already opened fire on Taffy 3. Kinkaid also ordered five seaplanes to make a search of the area, but the plane going over San Bernardino arrived just before Kurita steamed into view.[68]

Finally, at 0412, Kinkaid sent the simple question that, if asked a few hours previously, could have produced a different outcome. Unconcerned about San Bernardino because he had heard nothing from Admiral Lee and his Task Force 34, whom he supposed to be watching the strait, Kinkaid asked his operations officer, Capt. Richard H. Cruzen, if there was anything he had forgotten in all the preoccupation with Nishimura in the Surigao Strait.

Cruzen answered, "Admiral, I can think of only one thing. We've never asked Halsey directly if Task Force 34 is guarding the San Bernardino Strait."

Kinkaid quickly approved a message informing Halsey of his heavy involvement in Surigao Strait and wondering if Task Force 34 stood guard off San Bernardino. Because of the command setup, the message had to be sent fifteen hundred miles to Manus, then relayed to Halsey. Kinkaid marked the dispatch urgent, but with events heating up all over the Philippines, Manus operators stacked dispatches in the order in which they arrived or simply grabbed one they thought looked important. Delays lasting hours occurred, and dispatches were often forwarded out of sequence.

As a result, shortly before the *Ommaney Bay*'s tardy search planes lifted from the deck, Halsey received Kinkaid's query. He quickly radioed a reply that floored Kinkaid. "NEGATIVE. TASK FORCE 34 IS WITH CARRIER GROUPS NOW ENGAGING ENEMY CARRIER FORCE." Partly because of Manus delays, caused by the flawed divided command, Kinkaid failed to have information he should have possessed long before. There was little he could do though, since by that time distress signals were pouring in from Clifton Sprague.[69]

Kurita entered the narrow, treacherous San Bernardino Strait in single file late on 24 October. As he rushed through at twenty knots, the weary admiral retained few hopes that he could burst into the Philippine Sea without a struggle. The enemy knew he had reversed course, and surely a large surface force awaited him at the eastern exit. Though hammered by American submarines and aircraft in the Sibuyan Sea, Kurita's force of four battleships, six heavy cruisers, two light cruisers, and eleven destroyers retained an awesome capacity for destruction. He would need it to sweep aside anything attempting to block his exit from San Bernardino.[70]

The operations officer on Kurita's staff, Comdr. Tonosuke Otani, prepared for battle as the twenty-three ships, with all crews at General Quarters, neared the eastern end. Rushing out of the strait around midnight, officers and men on each ship quickly looked about, expecting American shells to shatter the silence. When a few minutes passed with no sign of the Americans, officers breathed more normally. Could it possibly be that the plan had worked? Was this the miracle of which Kurita spoke?[71]

Kurita's chief of staff, Koyanagi, could hardly believe Halsey's battleships had not blocked the exit, for "a night engagement against our exhausted force would undoubtedly have been disastrous for us." Yet here they steamed, with the path to Leyte Gulf wide open. Through a combination of overconfidence, overreliance on exaggerated battle reports, faulty judgment, luck, and a string of erroneous assumptions, Kurita achieved his chance to inflict maximum damage to American forces in Leyte Gulf.[72]

"Thus the enemy missed an opportunity to annihilate the Japanese fleet,"

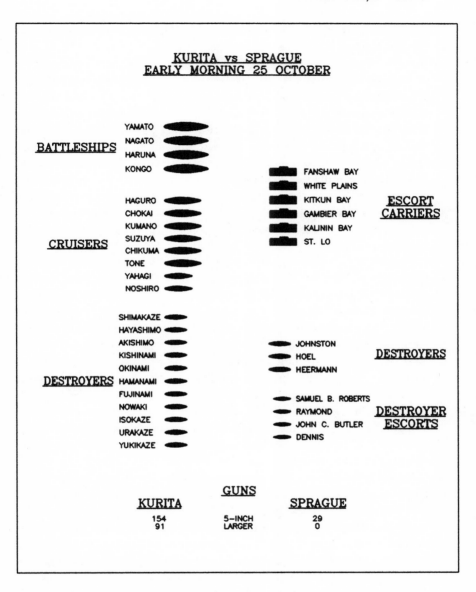

MAP 5. Comparison of Sprague's and Kurita's forces as the Japanese emerged from San Bernardino Strait

concluded Koyanagi. Kurita would now have his chance to do likewise to the Americans.[73]

For two hours the First Striking Force glided easterly through the calm waters with the ships forming widespread columns in a night search disposition. Nineteen of Kurita's twenty-three ships cruised in four columns ahead of his four battleships as an advance guard. The light cruiser *Yahagi* and her four escorting destroyers formed the easternmost column, while the light cruiser *Noshiro* and seven escorting destroyers comprised the western flank. Nestled between the two flanks steamed two lines of heavy cruisers—*Haguro* and *Chokai* to the left and *Kumano, Suzuya, Tone,* and *Chikuma* to the right. Aligned three miles behind Kurita's middle two columns followed the heavy hitters—battleships *Kongo* and *Haruna* on the right and *Nagato* and *Yamato* on the left.[74]

At 0300 Kurita altered course to the southeast for his final run on Leyte Gulf, still uncertain of his chances. Operations officer Otani believed "we would be completely destroyed before finishing with Leyte Gulf, but would do some damage." Unsettling reports poured in from the other Japanese forces. Nishimura radioed that he had fallen under brutal fire in Surigao Strait, casting doubt on his ability to enter Leyte Gulf, and a message one hour later from Shima indicated that he was retiring from the strait to save his force. The only remaining group, Ozawa's Northern Force, had been ominously silent. If Ozawa had turned back or been annihilated, Kurita could be charging headlong into loaded barrels with no chance of help, a thought that would hardly embolden a commander who had held small faith in the operation from its beginning and who had seen his enemy sweep aside five capital ships less than one day earlier.[75]

As dawn approached, Kurita started changing his ships from the night-time columnar position to a daylight circular formation, which proved more effective against air attacks. His battleships, cruisers, and destroyers had just begun maneuvering when Kurita spotted two enemy fighters. Suddenly, to Kurita's shock and dismay, ship masts appeared over the misty horizon, then the unmistakable outline of American carriers. These ships should not be there, but there they were, only sixty miles from Leyte Gulf, rising out of the early dawn like specters emerging from watery graves.

"We were quite taken aback when we met [Sprague's] force off Samar on the morning of the 25th," mentioned Koyanagi. Twenty miles distant, another commander received the shock of his life as well.[76]

→ CHAPTER TEN ←

"A Sighted Enemy Is a Dead Enemy"

O n the bridge of the *Fanshaw Bay* thirty-five miles east of Samar, Sprague started working on what appeared to be a busy day. He arrived earlier than normal—shortly before 0400—because he had to organize a schedule of strikes and patrols ordered by commander, Support Aircraft that "would keep my deck crews on the jump until sundown." In addition to the regular combat air patrols and antisubmarine patrols, photo and search missions had to be launched, as well as any emergency strikes required by MacArthur's forces fighting ashore.[1]

At least the past few days had been peaceful for Sprague. No enemy aircraft threatened his thin-skinned escort carriers, and Army troops on Leyte progressed satisfactorily. Any danger from the two units of the Japanese Navy that threatened Leyte seemed to have been cast aside—Oldendorf's battle line had only hours before annihilated Nishimura in the Surigao Strait, while Mitscher's carrier aircraft, preceded by the *Darter* and *Dace*, apparently crippled Kurita in the Sibuyan Sea. Thus Sprague started his day confident that nothing but long hours and frequent requests for air support would tax him. Besides, Kinkaid's powerful Seventh Fleet protected the southern approaches while Halsey's Third Fleet guarded the San Bernardino Strait to the north. Just the day before, Lt. Henry Burt Bassett of the *Gambier Bay* had flown his torpedo plane over a portion of Halsey's carriers directly north of the strait and "felt well-protected because this huge group was nearby." [2]

The skipper of the *Gambier Bay*, Capt. Walter Vieweg, described these early days off the Philippines as "uneventful in that we received no air attacks, and life was quite peaceful aboard ship." Most men appreciated the calm, but others were itching for a fight. Some officers and seamen aboard the destroyers and destroyer escorts had been disappointed in being assigned screening service to the "puny" jeep carriers instead of getting a fast carrier. In a conversation on a quiet 24 October night, the *Johnston*'s gunnery officer, Lt. Robert C. Hagen, shared his anguish with his commanding officer, Comdr. Ernest E. Evans, that the *Johnston* had participated in four invasions the past year without suffering so much as a scratch. "I wouldn't mind seeing a little action," added Hagen, who fretted that the active part of the war would leap-frog right over him. [3]

Sprague held no such concerns as an 0614 sunrise unfurled another lovely day. Mild northeasterly winds lightly buffeted a calm sea and gently nudged scattered cumulus clouds across the sky. Rain squalls dotted the horizon in a few spots, but none threatened to disrupt operations or greatly impede the eight-to-twelve-mile visibility. As usual, Sprague placed his ships on morning alert and launched eight search and patrol planes shortly before sunrise, but as a precaution he now ordered an additional six fighters into the sky at 0615. According to instructions by the task group commander, Rear Adm. Thomas Sprague, another two planes armed with torpedoes and two armed with 500-pound bombs stood ready for launch in case Oldendorf required assistance to the south. Confident that all was in order, Sprague took Taffy 3 off morning alert and sat down to enjoy a second cup of coffee. [4]

"Enemy surface force of four battleships, 8 cruisers, and eleven destroyers sighted twenty miles northwest of your task group and closing in on you at thirty knots." This message, radioed to the *Fanshaw Bay* by a young aviator flying antisubmarine patrol over Taffy 3, electrified Sprague and everyone else in the bridge and Flag Plot. Bolting out of his chair, Sprague bellowed into the squawk box, "Air Plot, tell him to check his identification." It angered Sprague that any pilot could make such an astonishing report when the only forces around Samar were his own Taffy 3 and Halsey's Third Fleet. "Now, there's some screwy young aviator reporting part of our own forces," thought a perturbed Sprague. "Undoubtedly, he's just spotted some of Admiral Halsey's fast battleships." Sprague had yet to learn that Halsey had turned north after Ozawa. [5]

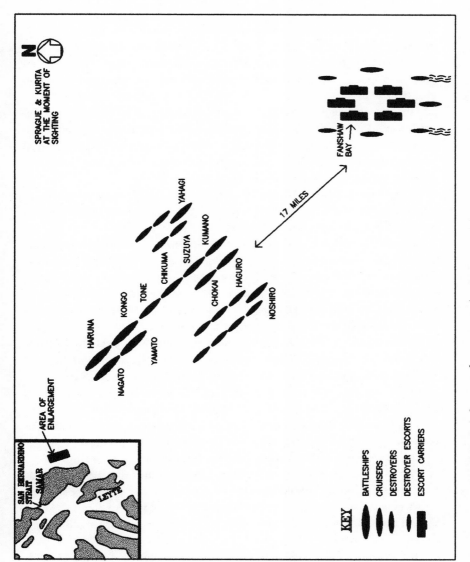

MAP 6. Sprague's and Kurita's forces at the moment of sighting

The young aviator, Ens. William C. Brooks, looked closer and radioed back at 0648 that this indeed was an enemy unit. He then added words that emitted shock waves about the *Fanshaw Bay*'s bridge. "Ships have pagoda masts." In rapid order more verification rolled in. Lt. Verlin Pierson, standing watch directly above the *Fanshaw Bay* bridge and scanning the horizon with his binoculars, yelled down, "Those ships look to us like Japanese battleships from here." The ship's combat information center reported ships only 16.5 miles away and heard Japanese chatter on its communication channel.[6]

"It's impossible! It can't be, it can't be!" exclaimed Sprague, yet any doubts still lingering in his mind dissipated when puffs of antiaircraft fire peppered the skies to the northwest, in Brooks's vicinity. Sprague realized at that moment that he "was on the spot," and vented his anger and astonishment at the flag officer he thought had been on watch.

"That son-of-a-bitch Halsey has left us bare-assed!" Sprague shouted, loud enough to be heard above the bridge by Lt. Vernon D. Hipchings, Jr., Sprague's visual fighter-director officer.[7]

Similar reactions of surprise and disbelief occurred on other Taffy 3 ships. On the destroyer escort *Samuel B. Roberts,* Sonarman 3d Class H. Whitney Felt called the executive officer, Lt. Everett E. Roberts, to the bridge when ships appeared to the north. Roberts identified the ships as Japanese, but never thinking they could be the Center Force, he assumed they were parts of the force destroyed by Oldendorf in Surigao Strait.

"Now hear this," he leisurely announced to the ship's personnel. "After you finish breakfast and before you relieve the watch, you might want to go astern and look back of us to see a remnant of the Japanese Navy."

Ship's members not on duty rushed topside to get a look. As one man hurried past the captain's quarters, the skipper, Lt. Comdr. R. W. Copeland, barked, "Lay to the topside hell! If there are any Japs out there sound the battle stations alarm and pass the word to man your battle stations!"[8]

On the escort carrier *Kalinin Bay,* the supply officer woke pilot Ens. Richard G. Altman from a sound sleep to inform him that Japanese ships were outside and he should prepare to take off in his torpedo plane. "I didn't believe him at first and stayed in my bed, but when he came back a second time and sounded extremely serious, I put on my clothes and rushed to the ready room."[9]

As antiaircraft fire chased Ensign Brooks about the sky, 14- and 16-inch shells that reminded one seaman of "long tree logs pointed at us with smoke puffing out," rumbled toward the escort carriers from Japanese battleships fifteen miles away. In seconds, salvos straddled the *White Plains* and splashed near the other carriers, producing multicolored geysers that lent a carnival atmosphere to the deadly dealings (each Japanese ship loaded its shells with a different color dye for spotting purposes). Sprague recalled that "In various shades of pink, green, yellow, and purple, the splashes had a kind of horrid beauty."[10]

Though Lieutenant Pierson thought the colorful splashes would make "a beautiful camera shot," he figured "we didn't have a ghost of a chance and that it would only be a matter of a few minutes until we would all be blown sky high." Sprague gave his force fifteen minutes at most. "What chance could we have—6 slow, thin-skinned escort carriers, each armed with only one 5-inch peashooter, against the 16-, 14-, 8-, and 5-inch broadsides of the 22 [sic] warships bearing down on us at twice our speed?" Sprague later stated that these opening minutes of battle were not like a bad dream or a nightmare, "for my mind had never experienced anything from which such a nightmare could have been spun . . . The thought that 6 of us would be fighting 22 Jap warships at gun range had never entered anyone's mind." Sprague believed his opponent would simply send a few cruisers to handle Taffy 3's ineffective challenge while continuing toward Leyte Gulf with the bulk of his force.[11]

Watching from the *Yamato*, Kurita agreed the battle would be short and victorious. Assuming the carriers were from Mitscher's fast carrier groups, Kurita changed course to 110° and radioed Combined Fleet, "BY HEAVEN-SENT OPPORTUNITY, WE ARE DASHING TO ATTACK ENEMY CARRIERS. OUR FIRST OBJECTIVE IS TO DESTROY THE FLIGHT DECKS, THEN THE TASK FORCE." Koyanagi called the surprise appearance of American carriers "a miracle. Think of a surface fleet coming up on an enemy carrier group. Nothing is more vulnerable than an aircraft carrier in a surface engagement." They appeared to be well on their way to proving a Japanese naval adage, "A sighted enemy is the equivalent of a dead enemy." After the war, in his heavily annotated 1947 copy of historian C. Vann Woodward's *The Battle for Leyte Gulf,* Sprague wrote in the margin alongside where Woodward quoted this proverb, "I thought so too."[12]

Sprague now rattled off a series of bold orders that deprived Kurita of the victory that appeared imminent. With Japanese salvos creeping closer to the *Fanshaw Bay* and the other five escort carriers, spraying their decks with showers of water, Sprague made decisions in these few crucial opening moments that set the tone for the entire battle, seized the initiative from Kurita, and forced the Japanese admiral to respond to his moves. Rarely in naval warfare has such an outgunned commander so dictated the course of battle.

Ironically, his first thought could have come straight from a Japanese military manual. He decided to sacrifice his force in hopes of drawing Kurita away from Leyte Gulf. "If we can get this [entire] task force to attack us, we can delay its descent on Leyte until help comes, though obviously the end will come sooner for us," Sprague reasoned. Suicidal tactics had been the enemy's forte throughout the war, but off Samar they would prove his undoing. To protect MacArthur and Kinkaid's forces inside Leyte Gulf, Sprague intended to expend himself and Taffy 3.

Determined to "give them all we've got before we go down," Sprague leaned over and started dictating orders to Taffy 3 over the TBS (Talk Between Ships), dominating the other excited voices with his control. Many officers used the network that morning, but according to those who could listen, "A calmer voice cut in to give commands" whenever Sprague spoke. Realizing that his classmate Tommy Sprague sat about one hundred thirty miles south by east and Rear Admiral Stump's Taffy 2 lay between them, Sprague shifted course at 0650 to 90° so Taffy 3, with the carriers forming a circle about twenty-five hundred yards in diameter and shielded by an outer screen of destroyers and destroyer escorts, would be heading away from Kurita and steaming into the wind. This would also allow his aviators to scramble into the air.[13]

Sprague, issuing frequent course changes to evade enemy salvos, ordered all ships up to full speed and hastened toward the shelter offered by a nearby rain squall. While desperately trying to reach the squall before Kurita's gunners zeroed in on his decks, Sprague put his only offensive weapons—his aircraft—into the foray. After requesting that Commander Whitehead, the Leyte air controller, return any Taffy 3 planes then on missions over the beachhead, Sprague ordered his escort carriers to launch every aircraft available and throw them at the enemy. When some captains objected that their fighters and torpedo planes were not loaded with the proper ammunition to attack the thick-skinned battleships and cruisers, Sprague's temper flared briefly.

"Get the damn things up!" he demanded. He needed time—time to reach the rain squall, time to think, and time for help to reach him. He did not care whether his aircraft carried the correct bombs or even none at all. He wanted them in the air to harass Kurita in any way they could. Besides,

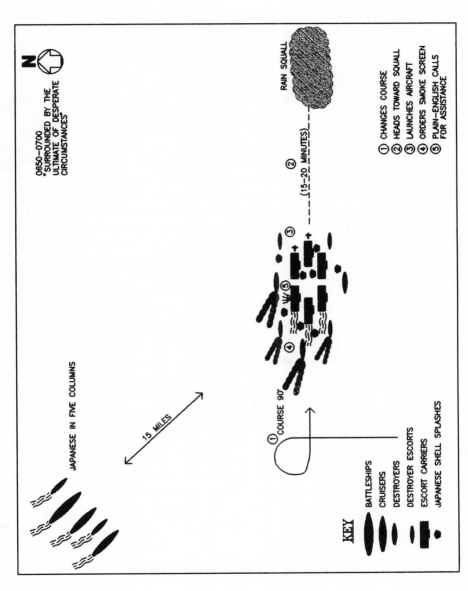

N

JAPANESE IN FIVE COLUMNS

15 MILES

RAIN SQUALL

(15–20 MINUTES)

① CHANGES COURSE
② HEADS TOWARD SQUALL
③ LAUNCHES AIRCRAFT
④ ORDERS SMOKE SCREEN
⑤ PLAIN–ENGLISH CALLS
   FOR ASSISTANCE

① COURSE 90°

KEY

BATTLESHIPS
CRUISERS
DESTROYERS
DESTROYER ESCORTS
ESCORT CARRIERS
JAPANESE SHELL SPLASHES

MAP 7. Sprague's initial moves

with enemy shells raining down, he had to get those gasoline-filled vehicles off the decks.[14]

He also needed something to protect Taffy 3 for fifteen minutes until it could disappear into the friendly rain and clouds of the nearby squall. At 0657 he told all commanders to begin making smoke that, with Taffy 3 steaming into the wind, would drift between the enemy and Taffy 3. In minutes, two types of smoke billowed from the destroyers and destroyer escorts—a white chemical smoke that poured out of large canisters and generators positioned on the ships' fantails, and a thicker black funnel smoke that drifted on top of the chemical smoke to create a double-layered curtain masking Taffy 3 from Kurita's guns.

The operations officer on Kurita's staff, Comdr. Tonosuke Otani, later admitted that Sprague's "use of smoke was skillful" as it severely hampered their ability to fire accurate salvos. Without radar equipment, the Japanese had no way of determining exactly where Sprague moved next, a chore made doubly difficult by their adversary's frequent course changes. Watching from the bridge of the *Samuel B. Roberts*, Lieutenant Commander Copeland admired what he stated was "one of the most effective smoke screens that any one on the *Roberts* had previously observed."[15]

As Sprague continued toward the rain squall, he broadcast a message in plain English appealing for assistance from any American forces in the area, but the only ones who could send immediate aid were Admirals Tommy Sprague and Felix Stump, who diverted portions of Taffy 1 and Taffy 2's air power to help their colleague. In trying to reassure Sprague that help was on its way, Stump's voice rose to such an unusually high pitch from the tension that Sprague and everyone else on the *Fanshaw Bay* bridge broke out in momentary smiles. "Don't be alarmed, Ziggy!" the excitable Stump rattled in a squeaky tone. "Remember, we're back of you—don't get excited—don't do anything rash!" Taffy 2 aircraft gave considerable support to Sprague throughout the long morning.[16]

Tommy Sprague, sitting closer to Leyte Gulf and thereby more involved with the beachhead, initially reacted with incredulity but dispatched whatever he could spare. Turning to his chief of staff, the rear admiral exclaimed about his friend to the north, "That damn fool can stir up more trouble than a small boy sticking his fish pole into a hornet's nests. Tell the boys to get out their flit guns and go help him."[17]

Kinkaid, whose ships were low on ammunition from their own fighting in Surigao Strait and who still cast a wary eye west toward the retreating Shima, could do little more than order Oldendorf's battleships and cruisers closer to Leyte Gulf. Even if he had sent Oldendorf north, it is doubtful he could have arrived in time to be of much help to Sprague.[18]

Sprague knew Halsey would receive his frantic appeal, but since the Third Fleet commander operated under Nimitz's jurisdiction, Sprague's message had to travel the tortuous route to Manus. Halsey would not read this dispatch for another hour.

Sprague mainly had to rely on his own craftiness, inadequately armed aircraft, and vulnerable surface vessels to fend off Kurita, whose faster ships steadily closed the range. As he continued toward the rain squall, now ten minutes away, Sprague felt the *Fanshaw Bay* rock and vibrate from near misses. He glanced over at the *White Plains,* his companion on the exposed rear flank, and saw enemy shells bracket the ship and dislodge a gigantic screen of water that almost completely shielded the ship from view.

"They're shooting at us in technicolor!" yelled a *White Plains* seaman in astonishment. Sprague wondered if his ships would reach the rain squall before Kurita destroyed them.

"At this point," wrote Sprague in his action report, "it did not appear that any of our ships could survive another five minutes of the heavy calibre fire being received, and some counteraction was urgently and immediately required. The Task Unit was surrounded by the ultimate of desperate circumstances."[19]

Amid shell splashes, nervous tension, and a communications network cluttered with excitable voices, Sprague shook off the surprise engendered by Kurita's stunning arrival to make no less than eight major decisions in the battle's first fourteen minutes. That he could fire off decisions so quickly was no mere fluke, but an inbred trait further refined by years in aviation.

At times of personal or professional crises, Sprague possessed the knack of immediately grasping the entire picture and knowing what to do without hesitation. He pursued Annapolis; he knew he wanted to marry Annabel after one meeting; he selected aviation; he outperformed most cohorts at Pearl Harbor; he safely veered the *Wasp* away from bombs. Each occurred, in part, because this inner sense—this intuition—guided him to the proper path.

A lengthy career in aviation gave Sprague quick reflexes, confidence in his talents, and the ability to trust his instincts. Though he became a pilot during aviation's infancy, when crashes killed or maimed an alarmingly high number of fliers, Sprague emerged unharmed. To do that, a pilot had to react rapidly, since a malfunctioning airplane allowed its pilot precious few moments to visualize a remedy; he had to believe that he could safely deal with any mission or emergency; he had to know that his first thoughts were correct thoughts. Remove any one of these traits, and the pilot soared into the heavens handicapped with doubts. Buttressed by his experience at Pearl Harbor, where he orchestrated a smooth-functioning defense among chaos, Sprague peered toward Kurita from the *Fanshaw Bay* bridge with confidence and responded as though he had been waiting all his life for precisely this moment.

A commander cannot risk the lives of hundreds of men strictly on something so nebulous as intuition, however. Sprague reacted so quickly because his intuition rested upon a firm foundation of *thought*—Sprague carefully considered his options before a battle ever started. He reacted quickly because he had already formulated his actions in rough form should his force come under attack. That is why he could act with the calm assurance of someone who knew what to do. Intuition is nothing more than the combination of previous experience steeled on the anvil of thought.

"Sprague was a cool customer," emphasized Lt. (jg) Henry A. Pyzdrowski, *Gambier Bay* pilot. "I got the impression he role played ahead of time and played this out, like he lay on his bunk and thought things through from every vantage. He must have done a lot of mental chess." A personal acquaintance of Sprague, historian Thomas Vaughan mentioned that "Sprague looked like he belonged in a library. He had a reflective nature and was always thinking." [20]

Thus when Kurita suddenly charged into view, thereby placing his battleships and cruisers against Sprague's vastly outgunned Taffy 3 in a battle for which there existed no tactics or previous rules, Sprague countered with his own moves. Lieutenant Hagen of the *Johnston* stated, "Sprague was an innovator and he learned quick. At Samar, he improvised and sort of grew into the battle." [21]

Sprague's personal conviction that when in a tough spot one must "pull up your socks and just do it" helped him now when he and Taffy 3 most needed it. No decision existed here for Sprague—only Taffy 3 stood between Kurita's devastating guns and MacArthur's vulnerable Leyte Gulf beachhead. Therefore he must get in the way and do whatever he could to harass the enemy leader. Though he assumed this meant death for many men and destruction for all his ships, since duty asked him to sacrifice Taffy 3, he would do it.

These thoughts allowed Sprague to act calmly, decisively, and aggressively. Seeing this from their commander, officers on board other ships acted in similar fashion. Sprague set the tone for the entire battle in its opening minutes, inspiring his officers to bold action by his own courageous tactics.

One officer wrote that of all the heroes produced in the Pacific war, "few can compare with the courage, coolness, and tactical genius of 'Ziggy' Sprague. His aggressiveness bewildered the Japanese and infected all his forces, surface and air." Their confidence originated with his confidence; their aggressiveness flowed out of his aggressiveness; their willingness to charge at Kurita started with his willingness to sacrifice.[22]

Had he reacted less decisively or exhibited panic in his words and deeds, Taffy 3 would have picked up those vibrations and would have fought less spiritedly. He did not. Though his inner thoughts told him Taffy 3 would be doomed within fifteen minutes, his actions let his men know they would successfully attack. He could have produced panic, indecision, and defeat with his words and deeds, for a commander either elevates his men to a higher level of action or drags them down to a tragic low, but Sprague never let doubts and fears seep through, only his confidence. This spirit spread throughout Taffy 3 and contributed to victory.

Fifteen miles across the water, Kurita carried out initial moves that, like Sprague's, affected the course of battle. When lookouts first spotted Sprague, Kurita was about to change his formation from the nighttime columnar disposition to the daylight circular formation. He now committed his first three errors. Instead of continuing to Leyte Gulf with most of his force while detaching a few cruisers to polish off Sprague, he turned his entire First Striking Force at Taffy 3. He possessed such incredible power that, had he chosen, Kurita could have both handled Sprague and steamed into Leyte Gulf to attack the beachhead.[23]

Kurita then sent out an order that threw his force into disarray. Rather than carefully drawing his cruisers and battleships into a battle line and placing his destroyers in front, he ordered General Attack, which gave each ship a free hand to charge Sprague. Since top speed varied among battleships, cruisers, and destroyers, Kurita's unit dissolved into an unorganized, piecemeal attack of individual ships or columns, instead of an orderly advance.

Observing that Sprague headed away from Samar in his attempt to reach the rain squall, Kurita elected to follow Sprague's course rather than veer southeast and cut him off from land. This was not a totally foolish move, for Kurita wanted to get in front of Sprague to deny him the wind advantage, but by cutting across, Kurita would have separated Sprague from Leyte Gulf and could have easily destroyed Taffy 3 before turning toward his main objective.

Why did Kurita err while Sprague could do little wrong? His Etajima naval training stifled initiative. When Kurita was faced with the choice of sticking with his mission or taking on Sprague, he was not sure what to do. Unlike Sprague, Kurita had not given much thought to varying scenarios. He had a mission to perform, but from the beginning he had not believed in Sho-1, and here he stared at a heaven-sent opportunity to destroy enemy carriers. With guts and initiative he might have accomplished both tasks, but Kurita lacked in those departments.

Recent events had impaired Kurita's judgment. Running the gauntlet of the South China Sea unnerved the Japanese admiral. He then steamed into narrow San Bernardino Strait, where he expected to face strong enemy opposition. Add to this the fact that he had slept little in the past few days, and you have a man likely to make mistakes. Rattled by events and lacking sleep, the frazzled commander made quick, impetuous decisions that hampered his force.

Neither commander had time to reflect on the situation and slowly formulate a response after lengthy consultation with trusted subordinates. The entire burden of action rested squarely with them, and at a time like this a commander must rely on his own knowledge, reflexes, and instincts. Because of their experiences and background, Sprague stood tall at Samar while Kurita stumbled.

Few men near Sprague on the *Fanshaw Bay* bridge gave Taffy 3 much hope. Japanese shells screamed overhead or plunged into the waters about Taffy 3 with increasing accuracy as the six slow-moving escort carriers and their little destroyer and destroyer escort guardians inched toward the rain squall. Shells smacked so close to the *Samuel B. Roberts* that Commander Copeland and anyone near him were drenched in minutes. Like a silent movie comedian trying to evade the Keystone Cops in a great chase, Sprague hastened east toward the welcome rain and mists.[24]

Kurita's unit, now charging in roughly five separate arms, rapidly closed on its quarry. In the middle, two columns of cruisers and one of battleships stood barely eleven miles away, protected on either flank by destroyers. The Japanese ships had gradually begun to split in an effort to trap Taffy 3. While the cruisers raced to the east to contain Sprague from heading farther out to sea and to prevent him from launching additional aircraft, the destroyers veered to the right so they could attack from the west. Simultaneously, Kurita's battleships maintained a steady course so they could pour shells on Sprague from astern. In his platform above Sprague, Lieutenant Hipchings watched the proceedings and thought of those desperate wagon trains surrounded by Indians so popularly depicted by Hollywood movies. Unfortunately, Taffy 3's dilemma was real.[25]

"Salvos were splashing thickly around all my ships" when Sprague finally entered the protective grasp of the rain squall at 0721. Thus shrouded from Kurita's big guns, for the first time since the opening salvos Sprague had time to evaluate events and plot his next moves. Thinking Halsey's Third Fleet still remained in the vicinity, Sprague believed he should draw Kurita farther away from San Bernardino "where somebody could smack him, for if we were going to expend ourselves I wanted to make it count," but the easterly course that enabled him to launch aircraft and get to the squall would not achieve this. He had to head south, keep Taffy 3 between the beachhead and the enemy, and bring Taffy 3 closer to the help that Sprague hoped was rushing from Leyte Gulf.[26]

Sprague quickly implemented what he called "a tough decision to make." He ordered a course change to 170°, almost due south, which placed him on a path toward Leyte Gulf. This courted disaster, for if Kurita was advancing to the southeast, Sprague would be turning Taffy 3 directly into his battleship and cruiser guns and setting his ships up for a frightful slaughter. Blinded by the rain squall, Sprague could not know for sure what his opponent had done, but he felt he had little choice but to veer south, leave the rain squall, and hope that Kurita had chosen unwisely.[27]

"I figured we'd be blown out of the water the instant we came out of the rain squall," Sprague later told reporters. To his astonishment, Kurita had not cut across to the southeast but had "stupidly followed us around the circle." Sprague's gamble purchased a valuable fifteen minutes for Taffy 3 who, shielded by the rain, was now steaming south while Kurita continued east. Kurita quickly caught on and turned his ships after Sprague, but the brief respite from enemy shelling allowed Sprague's commanders a chance to take stock of the situation.[28]

Lieutenant Pierson, close enough to Sprague throughout the battle to hear his words, described Sprague's course change to the south as "the order that saved us." Whereas most officers, according to Pierson, would have continued east and hoped for a miracle, Sprague took the bold path. "A miracle happened all right but the admiral sure helped the situation." For the first time in over thirty minutes Pierson, who earlier thought Taffy 3

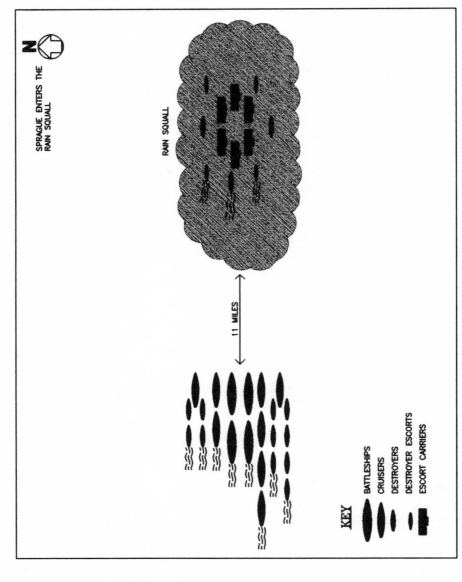

MAP 8. Sprague enters the rain squall.

was doomed, sensed that Sprague "might be able to get away with this after all." A second officer standing next to Pierson scoffed when hearing Pierson's sudden ray of hope. "Don't be silly," he retorted.[29]

Sprague could not afford to be optimistic. Looking to the north, he knew that within a very short time the speedier Japanese ships would have Taffy 3 under their guns from point-blank range.[30]

While Sprague juggled evasive tactics with one hand, he guided Taffy 3 planes with the other. His earlier order to get all aircraft off the decks resulted in a weird conglomeration of torpedo planes and fighters pouncing on Kurita in uncoordinated attacks from diverse altitudes, angles, and directions.[31]

By 0730, as Sprague veered south and emerged from the rain squall, almost one hundred fighters and torpedo planes began harassing Kurita with their torpedoes, bombs, and bullets. Kurita rarely faced more than a few at any moment, but like the driver of a vehicle being pestered by hornets, each sortie forced him to divert attention to the sky and away from Sprague.[32]

Lt. Comdr. R. S. Rogers, squadron commander of *Fanshaw Bay's* VC-68, completed three runs on the Japanese before using up his supply of ammunition. Unable to land and rearm, since by now Sprague had all escort carriers running with the wind and evading Japanese salvos, Rogers contacted Sprague and asked for further orders.

"Well, look," replied Sprague, "you just make dummy runs on the ships because every time you do, you draw fire away from my ships."

Rogers had mixed feelings about the order that, in effect, asked his aviators to sacrifice themselves to give Sprague's carriers more time. Fortunately, Sprague commanded courageous individuals who, taking their cue from Sprague's actions, cast aside personal safety and threw themselves at the enemy.

"Sprague had to give the order to make dummy runs," asserted Rogers. "It shows you the type of leader he was—he had his priorities in order and he did what he had to do. There's a time you've got to do things for the greater good, like falling on a grenade. This was one of those times."

Rogers's three dry runs—which he called "bloody frustrating!"—were typical of all the other pilots who attacked Kurita with little to throw at the oncoming Japanese battleships and cruisers. Dropping from ten thousand feet, Rogers headed for the nearest cruiser, realizing he lacked any ability to defend himself. "You know you can't shoot back and rattle the guy who is shooting at you. Psychologically, it's like getting into the ring with a good boxer and having your arms tied behind you."

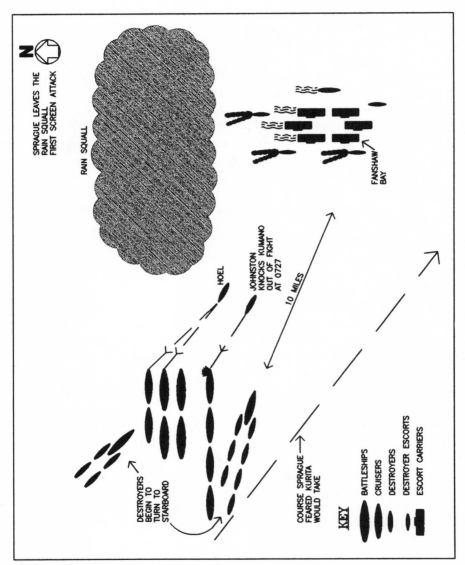

MAP 9. Sprague emerges from the rain squall.

Black puffs from antiaircraft shells blossomed directly in front of his fighter and tracers sped by his cockpit, but Rogers pushed on not once, but three times. Then, with a damaged aircraft, he flew ashore and landed safely at a Filipino airfield.[33]

Over at the *Gambier Bay*, Lt. (jg) Charles J. Dugan vaulted into the air and was immediately awed by the large number of enemy ships bearing down on Taffy 3. He wondered where Halsey's fast carrier pilots were, since attacking surface vessels was "their kind of work. We [escort carrier pilots] haven't been hired to fight the whole Jap fleet by ourselves." Nevertheless, he dove on a choice target, which turned out to be the *Yamato*, with scant knowledge of how a solitary fighter pilot should attack a battleship since his manuals "did not anywhere tell you where you should shoot a battleship with .50-caliber machine guns to mortally wound it."[34]

Taffy 3 aviators hampered Kurita more than they realized. Individually, an attack might accomplish little, but when added together they formed a crucial segment of Sprague's tactics in turning back Kurita. Since every Japanese captain had to assume each attacking aircraft carried bombs or torpedoes, they had to adopt evasive measures to safeguard their ships. In doing so, they threw Kurita's columns into disarray and slowed down his advance on Sprague.[35]

From twenty miles south of Sprague, Stump added available Taffy 2 planes to the fray as quickly as he could. Since most planes had already taken off on missions over the beachhead, Stump first had to recall them, land and rearm the aircraft, then get them back into the air in time to help Sprague. After this delay, which took about thirty minutes, Taffy 2 aircraft contributed to sinking three cruisers and buzzed about Kurita much of the morning until he withdrew.[36]

The ridiculous confusion that reigned in communications between Sprague and Kinkaid on one hand, and Sprague and Halsey on the other, almost negated the sublime bravery of Sprague, his ships' companies, and his air crews. Kinkaid's query whether Task Force 34 guarded San Bernardino Strait, sent out at 0412, failed to reach Halsey until shortly before 0700, as Kurita's first shells sped toward Sprague. Before now, Halsey assumed Kinkaid and other Seventh Fleet commanders understood that Halsey had Task Force 34 with him. He believed they would keep an air watch over the strait, but he now realized that Kinkaid must have intercepted the 1512 message about forming Lee's force. Halsey quickly sent a reply indicating that Task Force 34 headed north with his carriers.[37]

As Halsey grappled with this first disturbing dispatch, Kinkaid and Sprague blistered the air waves with five additional pleas for aid from the Third Fleet in just over thirty minutes. At 0707 Kinkaid dashed off a plain language dispatch that Japanese battleships and cruisers had Sprague under fire. Eighteen minutes later he sent a message indicating Sprague could not rely on assistance from Kinkaid's southern force by stating that Oldendorf's battleships were low on ammunition. He followed that at 0727 by radioing a plea, again in plain English to hasten its delivery, that Halsey send Lee's battle line south to Leyte Gulf and order a fast carrier air strike on Kurita. Kinkaid added a fourth message at 0739 emphasizing Sprague's immediate need for help from Third Fleet battleships, only four minutes after Sprague's own message, sent just as he emerged from the rain squall, that informed Halsey of the Japanese attack.[38]

Imagine Sprague's and Kinkaid's frustration when they failed to receive speedy replies to their desperate queries. Kinkaid's 0707 dispatch required seventy-five minutes to reach Halsey; his 0725 message took almost two hours; the 0727 message landed at Halsey's flagship ninety-three minutes later; and Sprague's 0735 plea took forty-seven minutes. By the time Halsey received any useful information from Sprague and Kinkaid, it was too late for his Third Fleet to play any significant part—he stood too far north to get back in time.[39]

In his copy of Woodward's book, Sprague wrote sarcastically of the time-consuming transmission of his pleas, "Staff work at its best."[40]

As Sprague led Taffy 3 out of the rain squall in his gamble to head south toward Leyte Gulf, heroic charges by brave men commanding the screening vessels dominated the battle. Their actions, which pitted small destroyers and destroyer escorts against cruisers and battleships, produced one of war's most gallant episodes.

CHAPTER ELEVEN

The Great Chase

Twenty-five miles southeast of Sprague Lt. Robb White, part of Nimitz's public relations staff, followed developments on Taffy 2's escort carrier *Natoma Bay*. Taking notes that he later included in a confidential report to Nimitz, he wrote that for Sprague, the "situation looks almost hopeless. . . ." Few people around White doubted that shells would soon fall about the *Natoma Bay,* and that if Sprague failed to deflect Kurita, "no one expects that any ship will be afloat when night falls." The Japanese force would brush aside Taffy 3, barrel over Taffy 2, then smash Taffy 1 as it raced into Leyte Gulf to bombard the beachhead and transports.[1]

Since Kurita's ships could power through the water at twice the speed of his own, Sprague knew that flight with his slow escort carriers was futile, but he had no other option. All he could do was head south, harass Kurita with air attacks, and hope that assistance came from Halsey or elsewhere, or that some unforeseen development altered the picture.

In minutes, the distance between the two forces had closed and a string of splashes, each one a bit nearer its target, indicated the enemy had started walking their shells toward the *Fanshaw Bay* and other escort carriers. Huge bubbling whirlpools twisted the surface near Sprague's flagship where shells

159

smacked into the water, while other shells zinged close by or exploded overhead, bouncing jagged shrapnel across the length of the deck.[2]

In a beautiful display of squeezing the maximum out of available resources, Sprague combined a variety of tactics to keep his ships afloat. Like prey battling a pack of hungry wolves as they close in for the kill, Sprague successively fended off challenges from three sides. He disregarded no tactic, no matter how hopeless it might appear, and succeeded in extricating his force from disaster because all those seemingly futile little moves blended to produce effective results. He utilized his interior lines. He maneuvered through his own smoke. He threw his destroyers and then his destroyer escorts at Kurita. He ordered his carriers to zigzag and to chase splashes (run toward the spot of the most recent splash because the next enemy shell would most likely hit elsewhere). He ordered his aircraft to hound Kurita with bombs, torpedoes, strafing, dry runs. He took advantage of the wind.[3]

"The most admirable thing about this battle was the way everything we had afloat or airborne went baldheaded for the enemy," wrote Samuel Eliot Morison in his volume on Leyte Gulf. Sprague epitomized that spirit and suffused it throughout Taffy 3, so surprising Kurita with his aggressiveness that the Japanese admiral exaggerated Sprague's strength—no one with inferior striking capacity would dare charge as recklessly as this—and concluded that strong American assistance must be close by. Sprague bluffed the daylights out of his opponent.[4]

"Racking my brains for some trick to delay the kill," Sprague decided "this was the time for my little group of seven escorts to charge our big tormentors," even though this meant he would be reducing the effectiveness of his smoke screen. For the next ninety minutes, Sprague's screen closed with Kurita in a succession of attacks that, while roughly coalescing into two separate actions, basically constituted a continuous series of individual or tandem assaults that diverted Kurita's focus from the carriers. Just when it seemed Kurita had warded off one destroyer and could turn his attention back to the carriers, a second destroyer or destroyer escort would dash out of the smoke.[5]

The charge of Sprague's screen comprises one of warfare's most glorious episodes. Though each of the three destroyers and four destroyer escorts contributed to the battle, and every man who stood on board one of Taffy 3's ships that stirring October morning has reason to thrust out his chest in pride, a few vessels shine for their heroic displays.

Destroyers *Johnston* and *Hoel* led the early charge. The *Johnston's* feisty skipper, Comdr. Ernest E. Evans, was a Cherokee Indian born to command in battle. More like Sprague than any other Taffy 3 commander, Evans possessed the ability to act quickly in an emergency.

Evans actually initiated the offensive shortly before receiving Sprague's order to attack. From 18,000 yards, he turned the 2,100-ton *Johnston* toward those cruisers and 70,000-ton battleships in Kurita's center that lobbed huge shells toward Sprague's carriers. The ship's tiny 5-inch guns rattled small shells off enemy superstructures while the *Johnston* closed through a shower of enemy salvos. From 9,000 yards Evans launched a spread of ten torpedoes at the cruiser *Kumano,* then sharply reversed course toward the carriers. At 0727, one of *Johnston's* torpedoes exploded against *Kumano's* bow and tore away a huge portion of the ship. The *Kumano,* slowed to twenty knots by the damage, veered out of line and ended her role in the melee. Together with the cruiser *Suzuya,* which had been earlier damaged by airplane attacks, the two ships watched the battle's remainder from afar.[6]

Other enemy guns turned on the *Johnston.* At 0730, three 14-inch and three 6-inch shells smashed into the ship with such force that her gunnery officer likened it to "a puppy being smacked by a truck." The blast tore off Commander Evans's clothes above the waistline and severed two fingers from his left hand, while scattering body parts and limbs among the dying men moaning on the blood-soaked deck.[7]

Though Sprague commanded a 360° view from the *Fanshaw Bay* bridge, he could only periodically follow the progress of his screen because of the smoke. What he could see—his six carriers surrounded by Japanese salvos— was none too encouraging.[8]

Knowing that Kurita's faster ships narrowed the gap separating the two forces every minute, at 0735 Sprague, with an amazing touch of humor considering the desperate situation he was in, ordered his escort carriers to "open up with peashooter [5-inch gun] on stern" as the enemy drew into range. He realized the impracticality of asking carriers with only one 5-inch gun each to challenge the array of weapons bearing down on them—in effect, he was employing his last line of defense, for after the small guns, what else could he throw at them?—but using a 5-inch gun was better than nothing at all. Maybe they would somehow inflict damage. Anyway, if he were doomed, he would exit with all guns blazing. As Sprague and others near him watched the *St. Lo* fire at an encroaching target, a veteran chief remarked, "They oughta fire that thing under water—we could use a little jet propulsion right now."[9]

Each carrier needed it to elude the many salvos peppering the sea about Taffy 3. Sprague shied from ordering sharp changes in course as these required his carriers to slow down while turning. Instead, he maintained as straight a path south as possible with smaller course changes along the way. Within that general framework, each carrier captain chased salvos that landed in his immediate area.[10]

Sprague thought the huge shells racing toward the *Fanshaw Bay* looked like enormous trucks. Screeching downward with frightening speed, they emitted sounds ranging from a whistling whine to an out-of-control rumbling boxcar and smacked into the sea with enough force to drench sailors on deck. More than once, Sprague followed a shell toward one of the other carriers and watched as its explosion created a giant geyser that enveloped the target.[11]

"You were in an arena of active noise, like you sat in the middle of a big opera show with sound coming from every side," recalled Hipchings. The staccato fire of machine guns and the slower whroomp of the solitary 5-inch gun added their own peculiar sounds to the deadly crescendo. Below Sprague, men hustled about the deck, pushing wheelbarrows brimming with bombs, rockets, or any other explosive material to the ship's edge where the flammable items were tossed overboard before one of Kurita's shells crashed through the *Fanshaw Bay*'s thin hull.[12]

While Sprague evaded salvos and the wounded Evans tried to extricate the *Johnston* from danger, Comdr. Leon S. Kintberger veered his destroyer, the *Hoel,* toward one of many targets he could have selected. Operating along the northeast corner of Sprague's disposition, Kintberger observed a column of battleships moving forward to his left and a line of cruisers advancing along the right. Deeming the battleships to be the more imminent threat, Kintberger closed at full speed to launch torpedoes. Rushing through shell splashes that soared 150 feet or more from the battleships' 18-, 16-, and 14-inch guns, Kintberger maintained his course even when a shell demolished his director platform near the bridge at 0725.

Two minutes later, after miraculously closing to within nine thousand yards, he launched five torpedoes at the lead battleship, *Kongo*. Before getting off the remaining five torpedoes, a 14-inch shell crashed into the *Hoel*'s after engine room, destroying the port engine and jamming the rudder hard right, and a third shell smacked aft, taking out the ship's electric steering. Undaunted, and manually steering his ship, Kintberger turned to the cruisers off his starboard side, maneuvered into position, and launched his last five torpedoes toward the column's lead cruisers.

As an officer later recalled, "With our ten 'fish' fired, we decided to get the hell out of there." With other Japanese battleships and cruisers threatening the *Hoel* from both sides, Kintberger reversed course in an attempt to reach the safety of the smoke screen.[13]

Evans and Kintberger ignored the long odds of a destroyer successfully closing on battleships and cruisers. Through desperate maneuvers both commanders achieved results they never imagined. The *Johnston's* torpedoes put one cruiser out of the action while the *Hoel's* torpedoes damaged a second, but more important was the impact on Kurita. The sudden appearance of two destroyers emerging from the smoke in almost-suicidal runs confused him. Instead of evaluating the threat for what it was, he imagined them to be larger, more destructive ships. The shaken admiral saw cruisers where destroyers and destroyer escorts existed. Sprague's turn southward out of the rain squall and his dispatch of the screen toward Kurita—desperate gambles adopted by a man who thought he had less than five minutes remaining—further confounded Kurita and made his next moves even more tenuous than they might have been.

Despite Sprague's countermoves, the Japanese continued to box in Taffy 3 on three sides. Two columns of destroyers, each led by one cruiser, steadily drew within ten thousand yards on Sprague's starboard side while four heavy cruisers—the *Chikuma, Tone, Haguro,* and *Chokai*—attempted to shut off any retreat eastward. Directly astern churned Kurita's battleships, pumping round after round at the six carriers from ranges between ten thousand and fifteen thousand yards, particularly the *Gambier Bay* and *Kalinin Bay,* who now occupied the vulnerable rear position of Taffy 3. The *Kalinin Bay's* chaplain, Elmer E. Bosserman, an avid hunter back home, scanned the situation and told others, "I now know what a squirrel feels like sitting up on the limb of a tree."[14]

Sprague maintained a tight circular formation for his six carriers, with his own *Fanshaw Bay* and *White Plains* occupying the southernmost spots, *Gambier Bay* and *Kalinin Bay* the northernmost, and *Kitkun Bay* and *St. Lo* the eastern and western sides. He edged the formation ten to twenty degrees from one side to the other, depending on which enemy column threatened him the most. Sprague later estimated that Kurita's ships fired salvos at two-second intervals for much of the battle.[15]

Watching the proceedings on board the *Gambier Bay,* Lieutenant Pyzdrowski of VC-10 was impressed with Sprague's ability to get six escort carriers moving as a unit through all the shells and sounds of the intense battle. "When you see six escorts working in harmony, rather than one drifting on its own, that is an example of leadership. It is hard for one ship to do what's right in the strain of battle, let alone six. Sprague had *command* of that task unit. These were definitely not helter-skelter movements. Also, Sprague cleverly took advantage of the smoke."[16]

With so many Japanese shells filling the air, Sprague could not long avoid damage to his carriers. At 0750, both the *Fanshaw Bay* and *Kalinin Bay* received hits, while near misses buffeted most every other carrier. An 8-inch shell struck the *Fanshaw Bay*'s bow, bounced through several bulkheads, and killed two crewmen and wounded two others before smashing through the ship's hull without exploding. Amazingly, the paper-thin hulls, jeered at so frequently by those who served on board, protected them now. Kurita's larger shells tore right through the hulls as if they did not exist.[17]

That first shell hit to Sprague's front and, according to Hipchings, "sounded like somebody had dropped a whole load of sheet metal. Most of their armor-piercing shells went through us and exploded overboard, sort of like firing a pistol through an empty shoebox. If every one that hit us exploded, we wouldn't be here today. Pure luck sure helps in battle."[18]

So does calm thinking. With his adversary still narrowing the gap and finding the range on his carriers, Sprague ordered his screen to make its second torpedo run. Again, Evans leaped into the fray with the *Johnston* and Kintberger supported with the *Hoel,* joined this time by Comdr. Amos T. Hathaway's destroyer, the *Heermann,* and Commander Copeland's tiny destroyer escort, the *Samuel B. Roberts.* Among them, these four skippers mounted charges rarely seen in naval action and further intimidated the weary Kurita.

Commander Copeland minced no words when informing his crew what they were about to do. He would take the *Samuel B. Roberts* into "a fight against overwhelming odds from which survival could not be expected, during which time we would do what damage we could." A bolder nor more terrifying sentence will not be found in any Taffy 3 action report; it epitomized the spirit flowing through the escort carriers and screen.[19]

"I thought our torpedo attack was hopeless," recalled Lt. Everett E. Roberts, Copeland's executive officer. "His announcement over the speaker gave us all cold chills, and one guy became so scared he ran to the back of the ship, which is senseless because you can't hide on an escort."[20]

At first Copeland waited for the other destroyer escorts to form up with him, since they were supposed to charge in as a unit, but after five minutes he got in line behind the *Hoel* and *Johnston* and started his run against the starboard side of the cruiser column. Plunging through heavy smoke, Copeland took the *Samuel B. Roberts* within four thousand yards of a heavy cruiser

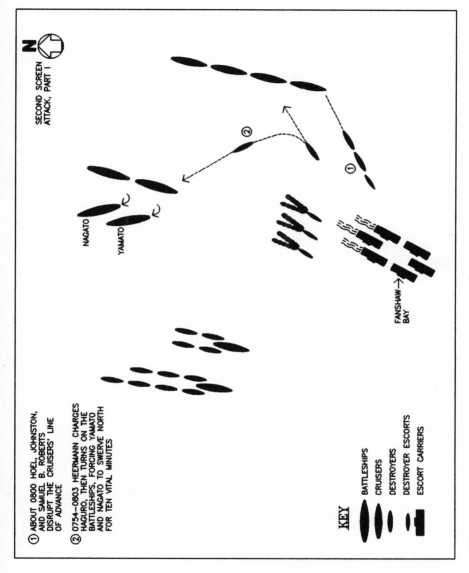

SECOND SCREEN
ATTACK, PART I

① ABOUT 0800 HOEL, JOHNSTON,
AND SAMUEL B. ROBERTS
DISRUPT THE CRUISERS' LINE
OF ADVANCE

② 0754–0803 HEERMANN CHARGES
HAGURO, THEN TURNS ON THE
BATTLESHIPS, FORCING YAMATO
AND NAGATO TO SWERVE NORTH
FOR TEN VITAL MINUTES

NAGATO

YAMATO

FANSHAW →
BAY

KEY

BATTLESHIPS

CRUISERS

DESTROYERS

DESTROYER ESCORTS

ESCORT CARRIERS

MAP 10. Second screen attack, Part I

and launched three torpedoes at 0800. Other Japanese ships swiftly turned on the little vessel, who returned fire with her 5-inch guns.

For the next fifty minutes, Copeland dueled with enemy cruisers at close range in a struggle reminiscent of David and Goliath. Darting about the agitated water at top speed, the *Samuel B. Roberts* slipped in and out of smoke in an attempt to avoid enemy shells and direct fire at additional cruisers. She steamed straight ahead without knowing what might suddenly appear out of the heavy smoke, and once raced so close to the *Heermann* that one crew member recalled, "We could have almost shaken hands with the other crew." Her two 5-inch guns blasted 608 shells at Kurita, and when the ammunition ran out, gun crews loaded star shells into the heated weapons. One gun crew dangerously fired six shells even after its air supply to the gas-ejection system was knocked out. On the seventh, the gun ripped apart in a mighty explosion that killed most of its crew. When other men rushed to help, they found Gunner's Mate 3d Class Paul H. Carr, with ghastly wounds from his neck to his thighs, cradling the last 5-inch shell in his arms and trying to load it in the demolished gun. Carr died soon after.[21]

Close by the *Samuel B. Roberts,* Commander Hathaway steered the *Heermann* in his own gallant charge at Kurita. The dash almost ended before it began, as in the smoke the *Heermann* barely avoided the above-mentioned collision as well as a second near miss with the *Hoel*. She closed on the heavy cruiser *Haguro,* unleashed seven torpedoes at the Japanese ship at 0754, then veered left to charge the battleship *Kongo.* For six minutes Hathaway boldly dueled both the *Haguro* and *Kongo,* then stood her ground when two more battleships joined the fray. Finally, at 0800, Hathaway selected one of his four assailants, the *Haruna,* as a target.[22]

"Buck, what we need is a bugler to sound the charge," he mentioned to his officer of the deck, Lt. Robert F. Newsome. As his 5-inch guns showered the startled battleship with shells, Hathaway closed on the *Haruna* and launched his final three torpedoes. Steering through so many near misses that he needed "a periscope with which to see over the wall of water," Hathaway quickly reversed course at 0803 to head back to the carriers.[23]

Good fortune smiled on the *Heermann,* for she emerged from this remarkable encounter with only minor scratches. Though her torpedoes missed their intended targets, they more than compensated by continuing directly toward Kurita's *Yamato.* Instead of turning toward the seven torpedoes to present the smallest possible target, the *Yamato*'s commanding officer, Rear Adm. Nobuei Morishita, mistakenly turned away from them. Hathaway's torpedoes quickly narrowed the distance as the ponderous battleship slowly turned and forced the embarrassed Morishita to steam north at top speed until the torpedoes ran out of fuel. The battleship *Nagato* followed the flagship in case it needed assistance.

For ten critical minutes Kurita's two most powerful ships headed away from the battle. By the time Hathaway's torpedoes slowed and dropped from sight, the action had moved so far to the south that the *Yamato* and *Nagato* had been as effectively removed from the battle as if a salvo had knocked them out.[24]

Sprague thus reaped far more benefits with his screen than he imagined when he ordered them in. Kurita later admitted that Sprague's continuous zigzagging and his screen's torpedo attacks completely disrupted the accuracy of his gunfire. While Kurita encountered few problems spotting Sprague's slow torpedoes, his ships had to veer wildly out of line to evade the missiles, thereby throwing Kurita's force into disarray and further splitting it apart. Kurita also emphasized that the smoke screen "was very serious trouble for us. It was exceedingly well used tactically."[25]

Kurita's chief of staff, Koyanagi, stated that retiring in the face of the enemy "is the most difficult of all tactics to execute successfully," and he praised Sprague's moves as "valiant and skillful. The enemy destroyers coordinated perfectly to cover the low speed of the escort carriers, bravely launched torpedoes to intercept us, and embarrassed us with their dense smoke screen." In comparison with Kurita's ships, which veered madly about the water, he admired how Sprague's carriers moved in unison. "I must admit admiration for the skill of their commanders."[26]

Sprague did not entertain such thoughts at the time, as Japanese shells began finding the range and inflicting heavy damage to his escort carriers. Damage-control teams fought oil and rising water deep in the *Kalinin Bay*'s bowels. In quick succession, Sprague saw one shell rip into the *Gambier Bay*'s flight deck, a second hit just off the port side, and a third tear into the carrier just below the water line, which flooded the forward engine room, slowed the carrier's speed to eleven knots, and forced the *Gambier Bay* out of formation.

"The Japs really poured it in then and we were being hit with practically every salvo," recalled Captain Vieweg. For one hour beginning at 0810, the *Gambier Bay* reeled from one hit every other minute.[27]

A string of shells spiraled into the *Fanshaw Bay* and created a sound with their impacts like two trains colliding head-on. One shell passed under the barrels of a 40-mm gun and tore away the face of the pointer, killing him instantly. The shell then bounced off the top forward edge of the gun shield and spun in pieces along the deck. The next missile shattered against the flight deck and damaged the catapult track and anchor windlass, killing one man and wounding two others, before penetrating Sprague's flag office, where it wounded Sprague's chief petty officer, Harold Moeller. Hipchings, who stood not far from Sprague and Moeller, stated the shell "clanked through, like a bowling ball bouncing through metal pins." Another shell tore into the catapult track, while two others exploded in the water on either side of the *Fanshaw Bay*. They propelled fragments through the hull, rocked the carrier from side to side, and inundated the flagship with columns of water that drenched anyone on deck. Damage control parties hastily brought minor flooding and a few fires under control, and the *Fanshaw Bay* was able to maintain operations and speed.[28]

While some "were wondering how much longer our luck could hold out," Sprague had a much different question on his mind. His ships had pulled off seemingly impossible missions for the past hour, but still he had heard nothing from Halsey, whose Third Fleet should have been within easy striking range. Where was Halsey, raged a bewildered Sprague.[29]

Back at Pearl Harbor, Admiral Nimitz had been concerned about Halsey's whereabouts since early in the morning. If his ships stood off San Bernardino, Nimitz should have received a dispatch by now from Halsey informing him of action against the enemy, since the Center Force was expected to exit about midnight. So far, no message had arrived. Nimitz asked his assistant chief of staff, Capt. Bernard Austin, if he had seen any dispatches from Halsey, but Austin replied that Nimitz had been handed every incoming message. Austin added that no one seemed exactly sure where Task Force 34 stood.

As the morning unfolded, Nimitz quizzed Austin twice more about messages from Halsey. Austin finally suggested that Nimitz directly ask Halsey about his battleships, but Nimitz refrained since he did not want to interfere with his commanders on the scene. He would await developments a bit longer and hope Halsey had not dangerously exposed Sprague's northern flank by taking Task Force 34 with him.[30]

Halsey was getting angrier about all the reminders streaming into his flagship that he was needed elsewhere. About 0830, twenty minutes after learning of Oldendorf's victory in Surigao Strait, Halsey was handed

Sprague's 0735 plea for aid as well as Kinkaid's dispatch that Japanese ships had closed within fifteen miles of Sprague's Taffy 3. Halsey wondered how Kinkaid had allowed Sprague to get surprised like this and could not believe that Sprague's own search planes had not spotted Kurita. Halsey relaxed, though, since he assumed Tommy Sprague's eighteen escort carriers packed enough strength to fend off Kurita until Oldendorf's battleships arrived from the south.[31]

Halsey's disposition soured eight minutes later when another Kinkaid dispatch, this one more urgent and emphatic, stated "SITUATION CRITICAL, BATTLESHIPS AND FAST CARRIER STRIKE WANTED TO PREVENT ENEMY PENETRATING LEYTE GULF." Halsey could hardly believe that a fellow commander urged him to send his carrier planes south when he was about to engage the enemy in a carrier duel, his first and probably only opportunity of the war to attain one of his prize goals.[32]

Forgetting his mission of protecting the beachhead from enemy attack in favor of Nimitz's addendum to hasten after Japanese carriers, Halsey ordered Vice Adm. John S. McCain's Task Group 38.1, then fueling far to the east, to immediately head back toward Leyte Gulf, a meaningless response since McCain's carriers could never close the distance in time to harm Kurita.[33]

Halsey's actions bothered two of Nimitz's fleet intelligence officers. Lt. W. J. Holmes monitored the series of messages bouncing among Sprague, Kinkaid, and Halsey and wondered where Halsey placed Task Force 34. At first Holmes assumed it stood off San Bernardino, but he could not recall reading a dispatch from Halsey that clearly stated it was there. By telephone he informed his superior, Comdr. Edwin T. Layton, who exploded in anger at the news and concluded that Halsey must have taken the force with him. When Holmes suggested Halsey had signaled Lee visually to remain at San Bernardino, Layton abruptly answered, "I doubt it" and slammed down the phone.[34]

On board the Third Fleet fast carrier *Franklin*, Rear Admiral Davison and his chief of staff, Capt. James S. Russell, gave Sprague little hope of escaping Kurita. "When we got Ziggy's message," explained Russell, "we knew he was in a bad spot because we thought Lee should have been detached. Admiral Davison and I almost had the feeling toward Halsey, 'What the hell, we told you so!' "[35]

Lt. Robb White, the CinCPac public relations staff member observing events off Samar from Taffy 2's *Natoma Bay*, reflected the pessimistic mood prevailing on his carrier by writing in his notebook the men "are wishing that aid would come and knowing that it will not . . . the great and famous Task Force 38 [Halsey] is far to the north. No help is coming."[36]

White's sarcasm was more than matched by Sprague's handwritten comments in his Woodward history. When the historian wrote that despite receiving Sprague's and Kinkaid's messages for aid, Halsey maintained a northerly course, Sprague added, "Can you beat it?" Two pages later, Sprague filled almost the entire right margin alongside Woodward's description of Halsey sending McCain to his aid, "McCain's planes didn't get to my area until after noon and the battle was over a good three hours and then they nearly attacked us and were only diverted at the last moment by CIC on the *Fanshaw*." The obvious disgust in Sprague's words for Third Fleet actions on 25 October rings loud and clear.[37]

Sprague's thirteen ships, his crews, and his airmen performed valorously, but they could not contain Kurita's superior strength indefinitely. Wherever the smoke permitted Sprague a clear view of events, he observed Kurita's cruisers grasping the upper hand. One and one-half miles to the northeast, the *Gambier Bay* steamed on one engine and steadily fell behind the formation, making her easy prey for the *Chikuma* and other heavy cruisers. Salvos straddled the *Kitkun Bay*, while enemy cruisers pumped fourteen hits into the *Kalinin Bay*, which Sprague thought "was getting the worst working over."[38]

These ships formed Sprague's port side and it is here that Kurita's four heavy cruisers concentrated in an effort to cut off his retreat. The *Tone* and *Chikuma* churned in the vanguard, followed by the *Haguro* and *Chokai,* each discharging a deafening stream of 8- and 5-inch salvos at Sprague's battered unit from steadily diminishing ranges. To keep his carriers afloat, at 0826 Sprague radioed his screen, then operating to his starboard, to "INTERCEPT HEAVY CRUISER COMING IN ON PORT QUARTER." He also ordered Taffy 2 and Taffy 3 aviators to abandon whatever targets they had selected and swarm on the cruisers, whose shells hit so often and so close that Sprague thought Taffy 3's demise "seemed inevitable."[39]

The situation worsened when Commander Hathaway reported the *Heermann's* torpedo tubes empty, and similar messages from other ships brought the same dismal news. "As I listened," wrote Hathaway, "it became evident that there wasn't a torpedo among us. Anything we could do from now on would have to be mostly bluff."

Not one of the ships to starboard carried a torpedo. They could do little more now than bounce 5-inch shells off the thick-skinned cruisers as the larger ships advanced to finish the kill. Hearing this information, a radioman on the *White Plains* muttered, "The situation is getting a little tense, isn't it?"[40]

Despite the demoralizing responses, Sprague's retort cleared the issue of what to do next. "EXPEDITE!" he ordered his screen.

Hathaway veered toward the enemy, trying to remain optimistic about his mission. "We were opposed by a total of thirty-eight 8-inch guns and about twenty 5-inch. Our entire strength on the *Heermann* consisted of five 5-inchers. I had one thing in my favor: a splendid range. Those cruisers made beautiful targets for our little guns at 12,000 yards; we made a difficult target for their big ones."[41]

Once again part of his unit threw itself against the enemy in a sacrificial manner. The *Heermann, Samuel B. Roberts, Dennis, John C. Butler,* and *Johnston* quickly turned from their starboard positions and charged straight across the carriers' circular formation to interpose their feeble power between Sprague and Kurita. Watching from the *Fanshaw Bay,* Sprague knew that some of these men would not live to see their families, but he had no other choice but to send them in.

On the platform directly above Sprague, Lieutenant Pierson stared at the little destroyers and destroyer escorts as a man might gaze at a condemned criminal plodding to his execution. "My heart went out for those guys as they headed straight across into certain death without a seconds [*sic*] hesitation." Focusing on one of the ships, Pierson turned to another officer standing near him and remarked, "Look at that little DE committing suicide, Mac."[42]

Only one screen ship did not participate in this dauntless attack. Trapped by the *Kongo* and several heavy cruisers after expending her ten torpedoes, the *Hoel* reeled from blow after blow from 5-, 8-, and 14-inch shells. At least forty hits rocked the vessel, who gamely replied with five hundred 5-inch shells. At 0830, as Sprague sent in the rest of the screen, Japanese shells knocked out the *Hoel*'s remaining engine and stopped it in the water. With fires ravaging the ship, now replete with dents, shell holes, blood, and body parts, Kintberger ordered his crew to abandon ship. As survivors grasped floating debris and watched with saddened eyes, the *Hoel* sank at 0855. Only 82 crew members, including Commander Kintberger, survived out of the 353.[43]

The other six ships rushed to deflect the cruisers from Sprague's carriers. The destroyer escorts *John C. Butler* and *Dennis* continued to lay smoke as they cut astern of the *Fanshaw Bay* to the port quarter, where the destroyer

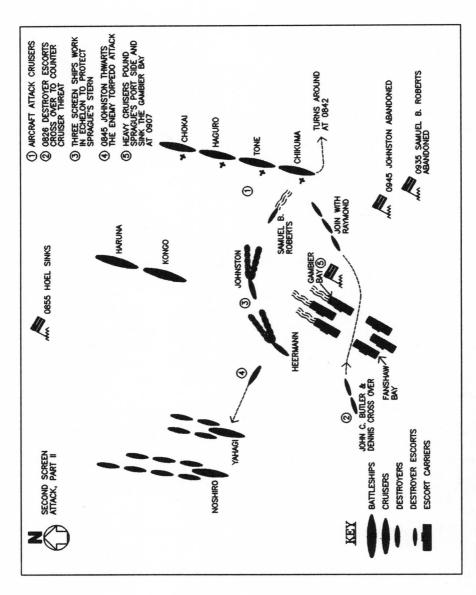

N

SECOND SCREEN
ATTACK, PART II

① AIRCRAFT ATTACK CRUISERS
② 0826 DESTROYER ESCORTS
   CROSS OVER TO COUNTER
   CRUISER THREAT
③ THREE SCREEN SHIPS WORK
   IN ECHELON TO PROTECT
   SPRAGUE'S STERN
④ 0845 JOHNSTON THWARTS
   THE ENEMY TORPEDO ATTACK
⑤ HEAVY CRUISERS POUND
   SPRAGUE'S PORT SIDE AND
   SINK THE GAMBIER BAY
   AT 0907

CHOKAI
HAGURO
TONE
CHIKUMA

TURNS AROUND
AT 0842

0855 HOEL SINKS

HARUNA
KONGO

①

SAMUEL B.
ROBERTS

0945 JOHNSTON ABANDONED

0935 SAMUEL B. ROBERTS
ABANDONED

JOHNSTON

③

JOIN WITH
RAYMOND

GAMBIER
BAY ⑤

HEERMANN

④

FANSHAW
BAY

②

JOHN C. BUTLER &
DENNIS CROSS OVER

YAHAGI

NOSHIRO

KEY

BATTLESHIPS
CRUISERS
DESTROYERS
DESTROYER ESCORTS
ESCORT CARRIERS

MAP 11. Second screen attack, Part II

escort *Raymond* joined them. Together, the three centered their fire on the lead cruiser, *Chikuma,* which turned around at 0842 under a hail of 5-inch shells and accurate air attacks. The heavy cruiser *Tone* stepped up and landed three hits on the *Dennis* that forced her to retire at 0902.[44]

The *Heermann* formed with the *Samuel B. Roberts* and *Johnston* and worked in echelon to protect Sprague's stern to give him time to retreat. As two ships steamed in a wide circle, the third spread smoke and fired her 5-inchers from the van position, all the time absorbing a horrible beating from enemy shells. The exposed vessel then cut back through the smoke while another ship took her place on the firing line and repeated the operation.[45]

Shells whistled and splashed ever closer to the *Fanshaw Bay* and every other ship afloat. Copeland yelled, "All engines back full!" when one 14-inch shell splashed barely fifty yards astern. The sudden reversal almost backed her stern under water, but momentarily saved the destroyer escort as three shells wobbled overhead and smacked into the water one hundred yards dead ahead, just where the ship would have been without the reversal. Copeland no sooner eluded death from one threat, however, than another pounced on him. As Copeland ordered "All engines ahead flank," three successive 8-inch shells walloped the little vessel. Gradually, Kurita's force tightened the noose about Taffy 3.[46]

"I heard the whine of shells as they came closer to the ship," recalled Sonarman Felt of the *Samuel B. Roberts.* "That first shell hit, and then an explosion and tremendous shaking, as if a giant had grabbed hold of the ship and given it a good shaking." The *Samuel B. Roberts* ground to a quick halt. Copeland glanced about his ship and saw only "dead and wounded men everywhere. The ship was hopelessly battered up." Copeland ordered the crew off at 0935, and thirty minutes later the stout destroyer escort disappeared under the surface.[47]

As one valiant ship slipped beneath the waves, another rushed by on its final run. Shortly before he left the sinking *Samuel B. Roberts,* Copeland watched the *Johnston* speed by to intercept enemy destroyers threatening Sprague on the starboard quarter. Copeland later wrote that Commander Evans looked as battered as his destroyer, with his clothes torn off to the waist and "covered with blood. His left hand was wrapped in a handkerchief." As the *Johnston* raced by less than one hundred feet away, "he turned a little and waved his hand at me. That's the last I saw of him. . . ."[48]

That may have been the final time anyone not on the *Johnston* saw Commander Evans. For more than thirty minutes Evans swerved the *Johnston* from one side of the formation to the other, first battling cruisers to the port, then destroyers to starboard in what Lieutenant Hagen described as "a somewhat desperate attempt to keep all of [the Japanese ships] from closing the carrier formation." As a result, enemy ships from both flanks turned their guns on the *Johnston* with such accuracy and volume that the "ship was getting hit with disconcerting frequency throughout this period."[49]

When Evans spotted the heavy cruiser *Chikuma* trying to finish off the damaged *Gambier Bay,* he shouted to his gunnery officer, "Commence firing on the cruiser, Hagen." He hoped this would divert some of the cruiser's attention to the *Johnston* and give the imperiled escort carrier time to scurry away, but the Japanese warship never wavered until Hathaway's *Heermann* joined the attack.[50]

Two heavy cruisers pulled to within ten thousand yards of the *Fanshaw Bay,* where they pumped forty to fifty broadsides at the carrier. Shells fell so close to the flagship, whistling directly over the bridge or crashing only yards astern, that Pierson thought, "They are really pouring it on us, or I should say all around us." Sprague figured the end would come shortly, since all his enemy had to do was move in closer and sink each escort at point-blank range, but for some reason they held at ten thousand yards. The puzzled Sprague later wrote, "I never did figure out why they didn't close to 5,000 and polish us off."[51]

Other carriers faced equally grave situations. Though her 5-inch gun put up a feeble opposition, Capt. John P. Whitney ordered the *Kitkun Bay*'s gun crew to maintain a continuous fire to boost his men's morale, who would be encouraged in that "at least we were throwing something at the enemy." Since the cruisers and destroyers remained outside their range, the carrier's 40-mm and 20-mm gun crews watched helplessly. One 40-mm battery officer sarcastically mentioned to his men, "It won't be long now, boys. We're sucking them into 40-mm range."[52]

The *Gambier Bay* was not as fortunate. Though the *Johnston* and *Heermann* had drawn off part of the cruiser fire, the *Gambier Bay* had sustained too much damage to last much longer. With her speed rapidly dwindling, Japanese ships administered the coup de grâce as they passed two thousand yards to her port. Captain Vieweg ordered the carrier abandoned at 0850, seventeen minutes before she capsized to port.[53]

A new threat stalked Sprague's starboard quarter at 0845 when the light cruiser *Yahagi* and four destroyers formed for the only organized Japanese torpedo attack of the battle. Evans hastened across with the *Johnston* to inter-cept before the ships could get into proper range for launching.[54]

"We felt like little David without a slingshot," recalled gunnery officer Hagen of the ship's charge. *Johnston* gun crews pumped 5-inch shells toward the five ships at an incredible rate, twelve of which hit the *Yahagi*. Though the 5-inch shells were only a nuisance to the enemy cruiser and destroy-ers—Hagen compared shooting at the Japanese with his 5-inch guns to "bouncing paper wads off a steel helmet"—they forced the ships to swerve out of their paths and release their torpedoes from 10,500 yards, much far-ther than the Japanese intended. By the time the missiles caught up to Sprague's carriers, the speed had so diminished they could be easily avoided. Amazingly, an entire torpedo attack had been turned back by a solitary, battered destroyer. The gutsy Evans proudly strutted about his bridge, ex-claiming in triumph, "Now I've seen everything!"[55]

The Japanese took their revenge upon the pesky *Johnston*. Enemy cruisers and destroyers gradually circled the destroyer and pumped a stream of shells that shook the trapped vessel and practically lifted her out of the water, forcing Evans to order the ship abandoned at 0945. When the *Johnston* sank twenty-five minutes later, sailors in the water observed a Japanese com-mander standing stiffly on his destroyer bridge, hand raised to his forehead in a touching tribute to a gallant foe.[56]

Sprague, who had watched his ships and airplanes swat Kurita away for almost two hours when he at first gave his force fifteen minutes to survive, glimpsed a ray of optimism. "To me it was a miracle that under such terrific fire for that length of time only one carrier had suffered a crippling hit. Two others had suffered several hits and three others none at all. And all of my six carriers, except the *Gambier Bay,* were able to make their maximum speed." He turned to his chief quartermaster, William Morgan, and ex-claimed, "By God, I think we may have a chance."[57]

Other signs, however minuscule, pointed to the same possibility. Six *White Plains* 5-inch shells smacked into the heavy cruiser *Chokai* shortly before *Kitkun Bay* airplanes scored repeated hits. The *Chokai* swerved sharply to the right, lumbered five hundreds yards, then erupted in a mighty explosion and sank in five minutes. Sprague even received a report, which later turned out to be false, that friendly carrier planes approached from less than sixty miles to the southwest.[58]

* * *

Halsey, 350 miles to the north in hot pursuit of Ozawa, remained totally oblivious to the stirring events off Samar. A flurry of Kinkaid and Sprague messages had alerted him to Kurita's presence along Samar's eastern coast, but Halsey assumed Kinkaid could quickly dispatch the threat with forces already at his command. He knew nothing of Sprague's feisty defense. Instead, he centered his attention on smashing Ozawa's carriers.

A new batch of messages started arriving, which finally awoke Halsey to the dangerous predicament to the south. Like a bucket of cold water dumped over his head, the communiqués prodded him to action, albeit belatedly. A message in plain English from Kinkaid started the ball rolling at 0900 when the commander of the Seventh Fleet pleaded, "ENEMY FORCE ATTACKING OUR CVES COMPOSED OF 4 BATTLE-SHIPS, 8 CRUISERS, AND X OTHER SHIPS. REQUEST LEE PRO-CEED TOP SPEED COVER LEYTE. REQUEST IMMEDIATE STRIKE BY FAST CARRIERS."

A second dispatch twenty-two minutes later sent the first shock waves coursing through the old warhorse. Until now, Halsey assumed Kinkaid could ward off Kurita with his escort carriers until Oldendorf's battleships arrived, but this message informed Halsey that Oldendorf's battleships were low on ammunition. Halsey angrily wondered why his compatriot waited so long to radio this important information, which might have altered his handling of the Third Fleet, until he noticed the message had been sent at 0725, almost two hours earlier.

Despite receiving news that admittedly stunned him, Halsey nevertheless continued after Ozawa with his entire Third Fleet. His response to Kinkaid simply restated his earlier order sending McCain to Leyte, but the Third Fleet commander failed to release either Lee's battleships or any of Mitscher's carrier groups. Those tempting enemy carriers were already coming under fire from Third Fleet aircraft, and shortly he would arrive to finish Ozawa with his battleships and cruisers. He was not about to let the Japanese carriers go now that he had them firmly in his grasp.[59]

"Here I was on the brink of a critical battle, and my kid brother was yelling for help around the corner," Halsey later stated of the frustration at feeling someone tug at his sleeve from behind while he tended to something in front. "There was nothing else I could do, except become angrier." His intense desire to get a crack at enemy carriers, bolstered by Nimitz's dictum, had blinded him to the fact that protecting his kid brothers—Kinkaid and Sprague—was precisely his mission.[60]

* * *

Nimitz became more anxious as the morning unfolded. Had Task Force 34 been left at San Bernardino Strait, Nimitz figured Halsey would have ordered Lee to attack Kurita, yet all Halsey did was direct McCain to assist Kinkaid. Nimitz concluded that Lee must still be with Halsey, but if so, why did Halsey retain the battleships instead of releasing them south? Finally overcoming his reluctance to interfere with his commanders, Nimitz ordered Captain Austin to draw up a question asking Halsey the location of Task Force 34.

One of the war's most controversial messages followed. Nimitz hoped the dispatch would prod Halsey into sending Lee south, but the temperamental Third Fleet commander misinterpreted its meaning. With padding added to confuse Japanese interceptors, Nimitz's dispatch asked, "WHERE IS RPT WHERE IS TASK FORCE THIRTY-FOUR RR THE WORLD WONDERS." The final three words confused communicators on the *New Jersey*, who left in the phrase in case it was part of Nimitz's message. When Halsey received the note shortly after 1000, he instantly took it as an embarrassing reprimand from his superior.[61]

"I was stunned as if I had been struck in the face," Halsey later wrote in his memoirs. "The paper rattled in my hands. I snatched off my cap, threw it on the deck, and shouted something that I am ashamed to remember. Mick Carney [his chief of staff] rushed over and grabbed my arm: 'Stop it! What the hell's the matter with you? Pull yourself together!' "[62]

Halsey's vituperative reaction to Nimitz's message indicates two threads running through Halsey's mind—how much he wanted to get a crack at those carriers, and his guilt, conscious or not, that he placed a higher priority on the carriers than he did on protecting Leyte Gulf. One who acts with a clear conscience does not normally get as flustered as the shaken Halsey did over this message, but his bitter response points to his uncertainty over the propriety of turning north.

Nimitz's missive finally shook Halsey into action, though he appeared in no great rush. Seventy-five minutes elapsed between the time he received Nimitz's message and the time he ordered his ships south, and although he could do little to assist Sprague from 350 miles away and notified Nimitz he could not arrive until 0800 the next day, it shows how hesitant he was to turn away from Ozawa's carriers. "I turned my back on the opportunity I had dreamed of since my days as a cadet," Halsey subsequently mourned.[63]

Sprague saw events a bit differently. Reading Woodward's account of Halsey turning to the south, Sprague angrily commented of his cohort who reversed course too late to be of any help, "Might just as well have stayed there or gone back to Pearl." When Woodward later quoted Halsey's regret that he was abandoning his golden opportunity, Sprague retorted, "His golden opportunity had been lost the day before" when he failed to block Kurita's exit from San Bernardino Strait. In Sprague's opinion, Halsey abandoned his proper post and permitted Kurita to sneak in on Leyte Gulf, thereby imperiling Taffy 3 and costing numerous lives.[64]

By the time Halsey smashed his hat to the deck, the incredible developments off Samar took one more bizarre twist. Suddenly, after more than two hours of fighting amid screeching shells, plunging aircraft, acrid smoke, and straining engines, silence settled over Sprague and Taffy 3. Kurita had reversed course.

"God damn it, boys, they're getting away," yelled a signalman near Sprague, who stared across the waters at Japanese sterns. Still in disbelief, Sprague waited until Taffy 3 and Taffy 2 aircraft also reported that Japanese ships were leaving. First the *Haguro* broke off. Then the *Tone*. A third message related that the battleships were heading northeast. When the *Fanshaw Bay* Combat Information Center confirmed that the entire Japanese fleet was pulling away, Sprague let out a yell of delight.

"I could not believe my eyes, but it looked as if the whole Japanese fleet was indeed retiring," wrote Sprague. "At best, I had expected to be swimming by this time, along with all my crews. . . ." Though elated, Sprague cautioned his men, "Stay on your toes and stay alert. We're not out of the woods yet."[65]

But they were, at least from Kurita's unit—thanks to faulty communications, a weary commander, poor judgment, and Sprague's aggressive tactics. Unable to contact his cruisers or destroyers because the *Yamato*'s radiotelephones failed, Kurita was unaware how close his ships were to finishing Taffy 3. Weary from incessant air attacks and bothersome torpedo charges, Kurita readily agreed when Koyanagi recommended that Kurita "discontinue this chase. There's still Leyte Gulf to attack." He sent a recall signal at 0911, "RENDEZVOUS, MY COURSE NORTH, SPEED 20."[66]

Why Kurita turned away when he seemingly had Sprague in his grasp has intrigued participants and historians for years, not so much for its mystery as for its stupidity. The Japanese commander defended his action with a lengthy list of reasons, chief among them being his counterpart's aggressive moves. The torpedo attacks forced Kurita to take evasive action that further dispersed his ships, slowed his advance, and hampered his tactical control. Taffy 2 and Taffy 3 aviators not only sank three heavy cruisers but kept Kurita from focusing all his attention on Sprague. Sprague's deft use of smoke so effectively hid his carriers from confused Japanese gunnery officers and obstructed Kurita's view that Sprague wrote in Woodward's book, "The smoke saved us."[67]

The above reasons started with Sprague and forced Kurita to react. The Japanese commander's timidity produced the rest. Though doubtless containing some validity, the following rationalizations illuminate Kurita's exhausted mental state more than they support his actions. He imagined Halsey's fast carriers in front of him instead of escort carriers, and thus he better retreat before being trapped. He thought Sprague's ships steamed at thirty knots rather than their actual seventeen, thereby making it difficult to contain them. He intercepted Kinkaid's and Sprague's calls for aid, which meant powerful surface forces could be arriving any moment. Nishimura had been wiped out and he had heard nothing from Ozawa, so he had better scurry away. Half his force had been destroyed without his even entering Leyte Gulf, so what use was there in continuing into an area where American land and carrier aircraft would most probably be waiting in abundance. Even if he burst into the gulf, what damage could he inflict since most of the transports had been unloaded anyway. If he had to fight the enemy, he preferred doing so on the open sea where he had room to maneuver than in the confines of Leyte Gulf. He was low on fuel.[68]

These are the thoughts of a weary man commanding an operation in which he had little faith. Against this frame of mind, Sprague's decisiveness produced results he could never have dreamed. Had Sprague acted as tentatively as Kurita, he would have doomed Taffy 3 and opened the path for Kurita to create havoc inside Leyte Gulf.

Instead, doubts and fears dominated Kurita, who lost a battle he should have won. After the war, both he and Koyanagi admitted they should have continued. After learning that Ozawa had successfully lured Halsey from the area, Kurita mentioned, "I see now that it was very regrettable that I did not push on at the time." Koyanagi added, "I was astonished to learn that our quarry had been only six escort carriers, three destroyers, and four destroyer escorts." He contended that had he and Kurita realized this, they would have charged onward "and we would have annihilated the enemy . . . Giving up pursuit when we did amounted to losing a prize already in hand."[69]

Kurita spent the next three hours steaming north, then west and southwest, then again north while he vacillated between crashing into Leyte Gulf or chasing after another reported American carrier force. Finally deciding he had accomplished all he could, Kurita withdrew from the battle area and headed toward San Bernardino Strait.[70]

CHAPTER TWELVE

Kamikazes and Controversy

W hile Kurita agonized over his next step, Sprague enjoyed the first taste of serenity since dawn brought the Japanese fleet three long hours ago. At 0952 the *Fanshaw Bay* Log registered the welcome sentence, "Japanese forces reported fading to the north off the radar screen." Crew members standing on the flight deck below Sprague emitted such a boisterous cheer that Pierson claimed "it could be heard in Tokyo. We began to relax a bit and start thinking about food." Sprague ordered nourishment taken to each battery, and shortly a steady stream of oranges, apples, coffee, and sandwiches coursed to the weary crew. At the same time, he turned the escort carriers into the wind to land circling aircraft.[1]

On board the four other surviving carriers, commanders gave haggard men a brief rest and checked on the condition of their ships and crew. The *Kalinin Bay*'s chaplain, Elmer Bosserman, left the bridge to help with the wounded, and in the course of his work he came across one dying man who quietly mumbled that he had not yet been baptized. "I looked around, but there was no water available, so I used the only thing I could under the circumstances and baptized him with his own blood."[2]

Suddenly, just as Sprague and most everyone else started to think their tribulations had ended, nine enemy airplanes approached below radar level

181

at 1049. Taffy 3 fighters splashed four of the intruders, but five others droned steadily toward the carriers. The first aircraft climbed rapidly and dove at the *Kitkun Bay* from several thousand feet, braving antiaircraft fire on its descent. Hundreds of anxious officers and men on the nearby carriers, including Sprague, followed the plane as it dropped lower and lower and wondered why the pilot had not released his bomb. Suddenly, the enemy pilot plunged toward the *Kitkun Bay*'s bridge, crashed into the ship's port catwalk, and exploded in a bright fireball that somersaulted into the sea.[3]

Sprague had witnessed one of the first organized kamikaze attacks of the war. Devised by Vice Adm. Onishi Takijiro, commander of the First Air Fleet, as an answer to the growing Japanese deficiency in weaponry and skilled aviators, kamikazes combined frugality—one plane, one pilot—with the national spirit of sacrifice and pointed them straight at an American ship. For the rest of the war, this special unit exacted a bloody toll on the U.S. Navy and instilled fear wherever they appeared.[4]

As the first kamikaze tumbled into the sea from the *Kitkun Bay*, another charged toward the *Fanshaw Bay* from her starboard quarter. Sprague hardly had to turn his eyes to locate the aggressor, since the *Kitkun Bay* lay in the same direction. A heavy stream of *Fanshaw Bay* antiaircraft fire converged near the Zero, which finally burst into flames, spun wildly to the sea, and exploded less than twelve yards from the *Fanshaw Bay*'s fantail, spraying debris over the after part of the flight deck. A second suicide plane also fell victim to the flagship's guns.[5]

Two other kamikazes pounced on the *White Plains*. One barreled into the carrier between the port catwalk and the water and injured eleven crew members. Antiaircraft fire damaged the other, which then veered toward the *St. Lo* and sped directly into the carrier's flight deck. An enormous explosion caused raging fires that ignited torpedoes and bombs stored on the hangar deck. Sprague watched a second explosion hurl large portions of the flight deck high into the air and create a ball of flames that soared two hundred feet into the sky. At 1056 Sprague sent the surviving ships of his screen to stand by the mortally wounded *St. Lo* and rescue survivors. Within half an hour, the hapless carrier disappeared under the surface.[6]

The brief Japanese attack left observers numbed. Though many in Taffy 3 had just emerged from a three-hour battle in which they had exhibited the same willingness to die as the Japanese pilots, this was different. These pilots purposely selected a target and expended their lives in shocking style, whereas Sprague's men retained a slim hope of survival. Now they stood on what basically were enormous floating bull's-eyes. Apprehensive sailors started scouring the skies for signs of further attacks.[7]

Another welcome lull settled across Taffy 3 during which additional aircraft landed on board various carriers. Sprague stripped his four surviving carriers of their destroyer and destroyer escort screen as well as their combat air patrol so those units could help locate survivors from the *St. Lo, Gambier Bay,* and other sunken Taffy 3 ships. Though normally a dangerous, almost foolhardy move in a combat area, Sprague believed that his men floating in the sea needed the ships and planes more than his carriers did. As he wrote in his Woodward copy,"I dispatched all my 4 remaining escorts to pick up the survivors and had none left [for his carriers]. I felt we had been through so much that nothing forthcoming could be any worse."[8]

A second kamikaze attack at 1110 almost proved him wrong. Before the *Fanshaw Bay* could land all the planes circling overhead, more enemy aircraft rushed in from astern. One American torpedo bomber pilot reported he was almost out of fuel and had to land, but Sprague waved him off so the *Fanshaw Bay* could prepare for the suicide planes. One *Fanshaw Bay* officer later stated that it "must have been difficult for the admiral to have to refuse him a safe landing on our friendly flight deck." The pilot headed away and made an emergency landing in the water.[9]

No kamikazes came after the *Fanshaw Bay* this time, but her guns helped knock down one that flew directly over the flagship and headed toward the *Kitkun Bay.* Her antiaircraft gunners hit the plane several times before the *Kitkun Bay*'s guns tore off both its wings and sent it spinning to the sea fifty yards short of the *Kitkun Bay*'s port bow.[10]

The *Kalinin Bay* suffered the heaviest damage of this raid when two kamikazes smacked into her almost simultaneously, one causing minor damage to the flight deck and the other demolishing a 20-mm gun mount when it hit the after port stack. "The kamikazes hit the flight deck, crumbled, then fell overboard," explained Bosserman. "I was numb—I didn't think this could be happening."[11]

Like the first onslaught, this attack ended within minutes. Though rescue operations and alerts preoccupied Sprague for the rest of the day, Taffy 3's battle off Samar ended when the final kamikaze tore into the *Kalinin Bay.* Sprague led his four escort carriers—battered, bruised, but victorious—off stage.

"Retired to the southward with no DD or DE screen," stated the *Fanshaw Bay*'s Log at 1115. Sprague, convinced just hours before that Taffy 3 had only fifteen minutes' grace, could not believe they had survived.[12]

"The failure of the enemy main body and encircling light forces to completely wipe out all vessels of this Task Unit," Sprague wrote in his action report, "can be attributed to our successful smoke screen, our torpedo counter-attack, continuous harassment of enemy by bomb, torpedo, and strafing attacks, timely maneuvers, and the definite partiality of Almighty God."[13]

Not as successful were the rescue operations to pick up Taffy 3 survivors from the five sunken ships. Even though Morison labels them "in general, well done," a series of assumptions, sighting errors, and divided command caused tired, oil-covered men to remain in shark-infested waters two days after they should have been rescued.[14]

Sprague notified Kinkaid each time one of his five ships sank and re- quested that the Seventh Fleet commander organize search and rescue oper- ations. When no search ships appeared, Sprague stripped Taffy 3 of its screen for eight hours—a bold move with enemy ships prowling in the vicinity— and ordered them to concentrate on the area where the *St. Lo* went down. The *Heermann, Dennis, Butler,* and *Raymond* searched the sea for four hours and picked up almost eight hundred men from the *St. Lo.*

"This desperate expedient [stripping his screen]," he explained in a mild rebuke of Kinkaid in his action report, "was made necessary by the absence of any rescue effort from other sources." Inundated with the pressures of withdrawing his damaged escort carriers from a battle area and of retrieving aircraft, Sprague left further rescue attempts in the hands of others and trusted they would be properly carried out.[15]

They were not. The staff of Taffy 2's commander, Admiral Stump, re- ceived a search plane's report at 1230 indicating several hundred men in the water, but the location given by the plane was twenty to forty miles south of where the men floated. Stump notified Kinkaid, and by 1530 the first organized search and rescue operation headed out from Leyte Gulf—to the incorrect position. Aircraft could have greatly assisted the operation by widening the search area, but most such planes were employed looking for downed aviators closer to Leyte Gulf.[16]

To top it off, divided command transformed haphazard rescue efforts into a tragedy. After the battle, destroyers from Rear Adm. O. C. Badger's Task Group 34.5 hunted the waters off Samar for crippled Japanese ships but, since Badger was part of Halsey's Third Fleet, they knew nothing of Taffy 3 survivors floating in the area and left without looking. Since the destroyers belonged to Halsey and not to the Seventh Fleet, Kinkaid was unaware of Badger's presence and thus did not request their assistance.[17]

While confusion reigned at the top, Sprague's men in the water suffered. Shivering from cold at night and burning from the blazing sun by day, men grimaced as the warm salt water lapped at their wounds. Sonarman Felt floated with thirty-five other survivors from the *Samuel B. Roberts* and believed that the time in the water was worse than the battle. "We all felt we'd be rescued immediately, since there were so many ships in Taffy 1 and Taffy 2. A plane flew over us on October 25 and wiggled its wings as a sign he'd spotted us, but nothing came. The next day morale was getting low, and by the second night it seemed hopeless. The third morning, only twenty of the thirty-five were still alive." [18]

Shipmate Jack Yusen, seaman 2d class, who floated alongside a raft with a different group, also preferred battle to the sea. "The second day was terrible because of the sharks. We'd see their fins come along, and then the sharks would dive and approach. When you couldn't see their fins you knew they were coming for you. It was such a helpless, useless feeling! At least during the battle we could do something, but not really here. We men in the water turned around to face the sharks and, while other men in the raft grabbed on, kicked our legs to keep the sharks away.

"The sharks would go out a ways, then slowly start in again. One guy's leg was bit off and he bled so much that we had to cut him loose to get rid of all the sharks he was attracting. He was almost dead anyway, but he floated away from the raft and let all the sharks get him.

"One twelve-foot shark swam right by me. I kept perfectly still and thought, 'This is it. I'll never see my family.'" [19]

Men in the water experienced bitterness and betrayal. After enduring the horrible three-hour clash with Kurita, they now had to wait while hundreds of ships and planes apparently searched elsewhere or forgot all about them. Even the few aircraft that flew overhead ignored them. Commander Copeland wrote in his action report that at least those planes could have dropped more rafts, water, and medical supplies, but nothing arrived. Some men wondered where Halsey had been and how he let this happen. [20]

For the first time in his career, Sprague received harsh criticism from men he commanded. Understandably upset as they warded off sharks, exposure, and abandonment, some charged that Sprague ignored his duties by failing to send even one destroyer escort to their relief.

"We always wondered where was the rescue effort," recalled William Mercer, seaman 2d class on the *Johnston*. "A lot of us were blaming Halsey for not being there to help us. We also blamed Sprague since he was our admiral and knew where we were. We felt like we were kind of left in the water." [21]

After the war, Lt. Thomas Stevenson, communications officer on the

Samuel B. Roberts, learned one possible explanation why no help followed after his group was spotted by a torpedo bomber. When Stevenson related the story to an aviator at a Taffy 3 reunion, the man replied that he had been the pilot, had wiggled his wings, but since he was under strict radio silence he could not send the position. By the time he landed, he could not remember the exact location.

"That first night in the water was a downer," mentioned Stevenson. "Nobody came. Why didn't Sprague send one ship after us? One ship could have saved a lot of lives."[22]

Unaware that Sprague had no more ships to send and that he had been occupied with kamikaze attacks, reported sightings of enemy aircraft and submarines, not to speak of getting his own aircraft back on board damaged escort carriers, these men naturally directed their anger at the most likely candidate, a feeling some retain even to this day. Though Sprague erred in trusting that Kinkaid would dispatch search teams and in not asking for confirmation that such teams had been formed, when one examines all that Sprague had done to help his men, it is hard to find what additional steps he could have taken under the circumstances.

Upon whom does Sprague place the blame? In his copy of Woodward, he wastes little time getting to the point. "This was a disgrace and I blame Kinkaid who promised rescue ships on my demand."[23]

At 1711, Kinkaid finally ordered Lt. Comdr. J. A. Baxter to lead two patrol craft and five gunboats to the battle area. Baxter's force arrived the next day, and after a day-long search finally located some survivors from the *Gambier Bay* at 2229. Through the night and on into the following day, Baxter's ships plucked more than eleven hundred numbed, exhausted sailors from the sea, including Jack Yusen.[24]

"By the third morning [27 October] I had started to lose hope and thought I couldn't get through another day. Suddenly, someone yelled that a ship was approaching, and when I saw the American flag—what a feeling! The ship came closer and someone on board yelled through a megaphone, 'Who won the World Series?' With most of us covered with oil, they weren't sure if we were Japanese. We all shouted, 'St. Louis, Goddammit!'"[25]

By rescuing as many men as they did, Baxter's ships avoided a major disaster that could have cut short the careers of high-ranking officers, possibly including Sprague. Lieutenant Hagen from the *Johnston* estimated that forty-five officers and men from his ship alone died in the water. He added that another ninety-two who were seen in the water, including heroic

Commander Evans, were never found. Had rescue ships arrived one day later, "there would have been no survivors of this ship." Rather than stir up a controversy amid an enormous American victory, however, the matter was allowed to quietly fade away.[26]

Until sunset, Sprague landed, refueled, and rearmed seventy Taffy 3 planes that pursued the fleeing Kurita and damaged the *Tone* and *Nagato* before they reached San Bernardino Strait. Afterwards, Halsey's aircraft chased Kurita as he scurried west and sank the light cruiser *Noshiro*. When Kurita finally steamed outside of Halsey's reach, only fourteen of his original thirty-two ships remained.[27]

At sunset, after receiving a report that fifty enemy aircraft approached, Sprague alerted his lookouts to watch the horizon for low-flying torpedo bombers. Pierson scanned the sky from his *Fanshaw Bay* berth directly above Sprague and worried that without escorts the carriers would not stand "a ghost of a chance" against such a strong force. Happily, the report proved erroneous.[28]

At 2000, three destroyers arrived from Leyte Gulf to provide protection for Sprague's unescorted carriers. His surviving screen, bursting with *St. Lo* survivors, transported the wounded to hospital ships, refueled, then headed to the Palaus for repairs.[29]

Kinkaid acknowledged Sprague's heroic efforts in a message sent that afternoon by describing the encounter with Kurita as "a magnificent performance" for which "my admiration knows no bounds. You have carried a load that only fleet carriers could be expected to carry." More meaningful for Sprague, however, was the outpouring of affection toward him by the *Fanshaw Bay* crew, many of whom fifty years later still credited Sprague's cool maneuvering off Samar with saving their lives. In recognition, the men took up a collection to purchase a silver smoking set engraved with the words "Admiral C. A. F. Sprague, From Ship's Company, U.S.S. FANSHAW BAY, Remembering Oct. 25, 1944." The *Fanshaw Bay* crew also sent a delegation to the ship's captain, Capt. D. P. Johnson, with a request that the battle flag flying atop the escort carrier during the encounter be presented to Admiral Sprague. Rarely do officers and seamen so warmly honor an admiral. "I was deeply affected I can assure you," Sprague later told friends.[30]

The next day brought a mixture of humor, sadness, and gratefulness. Rushing out of the sea cabin very early in the morning, Sprague tripped over a seaman who had flopped to the flight deck and fallen sound asleep.

The startled Sprague righted himself, apologized to the equally startled sailor, then took a closer look and said, "Ordnanceman," and rushed on to his busy schedule. The man was William Carson, the aviation ordnanceman Sprague had told before the battle to get his rest wherever he could.[31]

At 1030 Sprague attended funeral services for the four *Fanshaw Bay* crew members killed in action on 25 October. After the somber ceremony, Sprague ordered course for Woendi, one of the Schouten Islands off New Guinea's northwest coast, where his four carriers and accompanying destroyers would fuel for the passage to Manus. The *Kalinin Bay's* engineer officer summed everyone's relief by writing in the engineering log as the ships limped toward back areas, "Steaming as before, thanks be to God."[32]

Sprague stopped at Woendi for one day to refuel and drop off wounded at the base hospital, then departed for Manus at 0540 on 30 October. After a two-day passage, he guided his unit into Manus for a six-day layover.[33]

Official duties and reports kept Sprague busy at Manus, especially a 4 November meeting at Kinkaid's headquarters in Hollandia with Tommy Sprague and Felix Stump. Tommy Sprague took the opportunity to tease his classmate about the benefits of having battled Kurita in such a fierce encounter. "Well, God damn it, now you have an excuse. When people ask you what is the matter with your face, you can always blame it on the battle and they won't know that you looked exactly that way before the battle." As far as is known, Sprague did not share with Kinkaid his feelings about the bungled rescue operations.[34]

Sprague left Manus with his force on 7 November for the lengthy trans-Pacific voyage to San Diego, which included two days in Pearl Harbor. Along the way, Sprague conducted two awards ceremonies during which he handed out one letter of commendation, five Air Medals, one Bronze Star, and twenty-two Purple Hearts for actions off Samar. At one ceremony, his humorous remarks helped lift the spirits of men who had been through the tribulations of 25 October.

"Men, I have only two regrets. First, that I'm not a French admiral and two that you aren't Waves." Aviation Ordnanceman Carson claimed, "We really needed that kind of remark to clear the air of the gloom and doom consequent to battle."[35]

When the four escort carriers and screen arrived in San Diego on 27 November, Sprague rewarded the officers and men of his flag staff by locating more spacious quarters for them on Coronado Island and granting time off. Everyone needed a break to soothe nerves worn thin by battle and constant readiness.[36]

Controversy over Halsey's decision to take Task Force 34 north quickly overshadowed the marvelous performance of Sprague and Taffy 3 at Samar and led to a semiofficial suppression of criticism that buttressed Halsey's career while minimizing praise of Sprague. The adverse effects continue even fifty years later, when Sprague's name is known by practically no one outside the Navy or the small circle of Pacific historians interested in Leyte Gulf. Even there, some historians muddy the waters by passing over Sprague's role or crediting his achievements to Thomas Sprague or Kinkaid.

Certain facts about Leyte Gulf and Samar remain indisputable. Japan absorbed a resounding defeat from which her Imperial fleet never recovered. Over ten thousand Japanese died. Four aircraft carriers, three battleships, and eighteen cruisers and destroyers were sunk in the four battles off the Philippines at the cost of three thousand American lives, one light carrier, two escort carriers, two destroyers, and one destroyer escort. The Japanese suffered such tragic losses that Admiral Ozawa, the only Japanese commander to successfully carry out his mission, stated, "the surface force became strictly auxiliary, so that we relied on land forces, special attack, and air power."[37]

For his crucial role at Samar, the Navy awarded Sprague the Navy Cross and cited his "personal courage and determination in the face of overwhelming enemy surface gunfire and air attack." The award also credited as being instrumental in turning back the Japanese Sprague's "stubborn defense and damage inflicted on the enemy ships by ships and aircraft of his command." After Sprague repeatedly pestered the awards board, the thirteen Taffy 3 ships eventually received the Presidential Unit Citation for its "courageous determination and the superb teamwork of the officers and men."[38]

That was all, for Halsey, Kinkaid, King, and Nimitz grabbed the spotlight from Sprague and Taffy 3 before the smoke of battle settled on 25 October. At 2126, barely twelve hours after kamikazes slammed into Taffy 3, Halsey radioed Nimitz, "It can be announced with assurance that the Japanese navy has been beaten, routed, and broken by the Third and Seventh Fleets." Though he participated in only portions of the far-flung battle, Halsey upstaged his fellow commanders and announced the victorious news as though his had been the directing hand. King planned to withhold the message from the press until an evaluation of the battle afforded a more comprehensive view, but when MacArthur released his own victory bulletin to the

Reuters News Agency, President Roosevelt read Halsey's notice to the press corps at 6:00 P.M. Washington time on 25 October.[39]

The first name, then, that the American public associated with the glorious naval victory off the Philippine Islands was Halsey's, not Kinkaid's or Oldendorf's, and certainly not Sprague's. An American home front, already accustomed to Halsey's wartime heroics and braggadocio, again fell to his spell.

Less than one hour after dispatching his victory announcement, Halsey wired a top-secret message to Nimitz and King that attempted to justify his chase to the north on the grounds that because of damage inflicted in the Sibuyan Sea, Kurita "could no longer be considered a serious menace to the Seventh Fleet." Thus no reason existed for him to guard San Bernardino Strait, and when Ozawa was spotted, he took his fleet in hot pursuit.[40]

That Halsey felt compelled to send such a self-serving message so soon after the battle indicates the doubts that plagued his mind. Had he more confidence in the propriety of his tactics, Halsey would not have seen any need to defend himself.

Nimitz wrestled with this matter for three days before sending a letter to King marked PERSONAL and TOP SECRET in which he concluded that by sending his message, "Halsey feels that he is in a defensive position. . . ." While he approved of most decisions made at Leyte Gulf, Nimitz regretted that Halsey had not left Lee's battleships behind to protect the northern approaches. "It never occurred to me that Halsey, knowing the composition of the ships in the Sibuyan Sea, would leave San Bernardino Strait unguarded, even though the Jap detachments in the Sibuyan Sea had been reported seriously damaged." In words that are remarkably similar to Sprague's, Nimitz then attributed success at Samar to "special dispensation from the Lord Almighty."[41]

Nimitz clearly condemns Halsey in this letter and agrees with Sprague that the Third Fleet commander left Taffy 3 high and dry, though he refuses to acknowledge any personal responsibility in the matter. Nimitz wrote that he never imagined Halsey would allow Kurita to freely exit San Bernardino Strait, but he should have. Nimitz issued the order giving Halsey permission to concentrate on enemy carriers, and everyone, including Nimitz, knew that when handed a choice between watching a strait and attacking carriers, Halsey would opt for the latter. Nimitz stumbled in giving Halsey a free hand at Leyte Gulf.

King added his own harsh words about Halsey. Sprague's classmate Jocko Clark happened to be in King's Washington, D.C., office when news came in that Halsey had left San Bernardino Strait unguarded. King, known far and wide for his volcanic temper, erupted in such a profane tirade that Clark later claimed he had never seen King angrier. After examining battle reports, King told Nimitz the next month that Halsey needed a rest. He then sent his chief of staff, Vice Adm. Savvy Cooke, to Kinkaid with the message that the Seventh Fleet commander had done nothing improper at Samar and recommended that Kinkaid be promoted to a four star admiral. Within one month of Samar, both Nimitz and King concluded that Halsey had erred.[42]

By the time Halsey visited King in Washington the following January, King had tempered his anger and slightly changed his assessment. When Halsey mentioned he had made a mistake off Samar, King told him, "You've got a green light on everything you did."[43]

This statement served two purposes. King wanted to assuage Halsey's feelings while protecting himself. Deeper analysis of Leyte Gulf would assuredly focus criticism on the divided command and on Nimitz's decision that Halsey could make enemy carriers his prime target, two aspects in which King had a hand. His determination that the Navy not be relegated to a secondary role under MacArthur influenced the Joint Chiefs of Staff's decision to implement the former, and as Nimitz's superior he was aware of the latter. He could not be overly critical of either of those actions without condemning himself.[44]

Kinkaid, whose forces had borne the brunt of Kurita's sudden appearance, naturally castigated Halsey. He believed Halsey failed in his mission of keeping the Japanese fleet away from Leyte Gulf and missed a chance to annihilate Kurita as he emerged from San Bernardino Strait.[45]

In a preliminary action report, submitted four days after the battle, Sprague asserted that the enemy plan "came dangerously close to succeeding" because Halsey abandoned San Bernardino Strait. "It *was* essential that the Third Fleet be removed" so Kurita could steam down untouched. Since Taffy 3 had never been handed the responsibility of watching the strait, "in the absence of any information that this exit was no longer blocked, it was logical to assume that our northern flank could not be exposed without ample warning." Terming his and Taffy 3's survival "remarkable almost to the point of being unexplainable," Sprague stated that the enemy plan failed mainly because of "the decision of the Jap commander to retreat at the time he did." He also gave his own unit credit, praising in particular the "skill, the unflinching courage, the inspired determination to go down fighting" of his officers and men.[46]

A week later, Sprague submitted a more comprehensive action report that contained harsher words about Halsey's role on 25 October. Taffy 3 and supporting aircraft "alone turned back the major body of the Japanese Fleet" and saved Leyte Gulf. Answering a recent Halsey declaration that he was not willing to risk his fast carriers by moving them within range of shore to provide combat air patrol over the objective area, Sprague admitted that an escort carrier did not carry the same strategic value as a fast carrier, but typically added that "the loss of personnel is of equal importance." He urged that unless definite control of the air is already established, escort carriers should not be employed in a situation where they have to provide both air coverage ashore and over their own vessels, unless "we are willing to deliberately sacrifice the ships and men." A unit of six escort carriers simply did not possess the air strength to accomplish both. He ended by recommending that land forces plan to use their own air support within forty-eight hours of the assault and that carriers be withdrawn. "This is especially true in view of the current success of the enemy in eliminating carriers with suicide dives." [47]

Before the waters had calmed off Samar, then, commanding officers rushed to defend their actions in regard to the battle. A heated controversy appeared to be brewing, one that could rend the Navy and deflect attention from its prime purpose—the defeat of Japan. Nimitz, who had seen the debilitating effects of the Sampson-Schley controversy when he attended the Academy and vowed he would never let that happen should he be in charge, stepped in and quashed further criticism of Halsey, Kinkaid, or any of the other major players at Leyte Gulf. He not only refused to allow public criticism, especially of Halsey, but quickly moved to eliminate harsh judgments from official records that one day might be made public. When the head of his analytical section, Capt. Ralph C. Parker, sharply condemned Halsey in the first official CinCPac report of Leyte Gulf, Nimitz rejected it and ordered Parker to write a second, less critical version. "What are you trying to do, Parker, start another Sampson-Schley controversy? Tone this down," a miffed Nimitz wrote across the report's cover page. [48]

Nimitz's edict tended to stifle open debate about Halsey. Sprague's only public account, which appeared in the April 1945 issue of *American Magazine* with the Navy's permission, praised Kurita's daring for navigating the treacherous San Bernardino Strait at night, but never mentioned Halsey's role. In the ten remaining years of his life, out of loyalty to the Navy Sprague refused to publicly condemn Halsey. He had done his duty. He would now remain silent, and thus out of the spotlight. [49]

Flattering accounts of the popular Halsey blossomed shortly after war's end. A 1946 biography made the fantastic assertion that when Kurita surprised everyone by heading back toward San Bernardino Strait following his battering in the Sibuyan Sea, escort carriers "managed to occupy [Kurita's fleet] until Halsey could tear back with some of his big, new battleships and put it to rout permanently." According to this book, the gallant Halsey charged in with his battleships and saved MacArthur's troops from "slaughter," while Sprague (who is not named) "occupied" the enemy. Though high-ranking officers inside the Navy knew what happened at Leyte Gulf, this distortion of the truth bolstered Halsey's reputation among the American public as the bold warrior who arrived to save the day.[50]

Four other books added fuel to the controversy, which was confined mainly to naval historians and battle participants. Historian C. Vann Woodward's 1947 book, *The Battle for Leyte Gulf,* the first scholarly account of the battle, supported Halsey's contention that he was correct in chasing after enemy carriers. Though he praises Taffy 3's actions, Woodward never interviewed Sprague to get his views of 25 October.[51]

That same year Halsey defended his actions at Leyte Gulf, embellished his image among the American public, and propelled the controversy among historians and participants to new heights with seven widely read *Saturday Evening Post* installments based on his best-selling autobiography, which also appeared in 1947. Claiming that when he reviewed the Leyte Gulf material he could hardly bring himself to write, "so painfully does it rankle still," Halsey asserted that his main mission off the Philippines was offensive—to get the enemy carriers—not to protect Kinkaid's Seventh Fleet. He blamed the divided command for his inability to either attack Kurita off Samar or finish Ozawa off Cape Engano. Rather than admit any responsibility for allowing Kurita to sneak up on Sprague, Halsey wondered "how Kinkaid had let 'Ziggy' Sprague get caught like this." It was Kinkaid's search planes that failed to stop Kurita, not the Third Fleet.[52]

"I suspect you had to loosen your collar when reading Bull's account of the battle," Adm. Raymond A. Spruance teased Kinkaid. The stung Seventh Fleet commander shot back. He wrote to Capt. Arleigh Burke, Mitscher's chief of staff at the time of Leyte Gulf, "I had kept quiet on the subject for nearly three years because I believed a controversy would do the Navy no good and I declined . . . until Halsey's seventh installment appeared in the *Saturday Evening Post.*" Stating that he owed it to his Seventh Fleet, Kinkaid tore into Halsey's accusation that Kinkaid had failed to properly keep the strait under observation. Halsey failed by leaving San Bernardino Strait, he asserted, and thereby abandoned his primary mission of protecting the Seventh Fleet.[53]

The dispute not only turned Kinkaid and Halsey, two old friends, into enemies, but caused Admiral King to rebuke Halsey for openly criticizing Kinkaid and the divided command. In his memoirs five years later, King chastized Halsey for heading north, but tempered it by also directing criticism at Kinkaid for not adequately searching San Bernardino Strait.[54]

Halsey was hurt that fellow officers could so harshly attack his aggressive tactics and wondered if it would not have been better if the more conservative Spruance "had been with Mitscher at Leyte Gulf" and thus closed the strait to Kurita, while he "had been with Mitscher in the Battle of the Philippine Sea," where Spruance had been roundly condemned for remaining close to the beachhead rather than head out to sea after Japanese carriers. Halsey made this remark more as a wishful concession to get critics off his back, but it indicated that the doubts that first surfaced with his 25 October messages to Nimitz continued to haunt him.[55]

In 1958, three years after Sprague's death, Adm. Samuel Eliot Morison dedicated Volume XII of his monumental *History of United States Naval Operations in World War II,* the volume covering Leyte Gulf, to Sprague, the man who "took the rap in the Battle off Samar. . . ." Morison could have selected any number of officers, including Halsey or Kinkaid, but he chose Sprague because of his personal bravery and because he "was the sort of officer who is known as 'all Navy,' dedicated to his profession, thorough and conscientious." Morison stated that the struggle near Samar "had no compeer in this war," and called Sprague's victory over Kurita "forever memorable, forever glorious." Though this boosted Sprague's reputation among historians, Sprague was still a relatively unknown figure outside the Navy.[56]

Nimitz contained this controversy as much as possible. In 1959, historian E. B. Potter prepared a textbook for midshipmen called *Sea Power: A Naval History.* Potter concluded that Halsey had gravely erred at Leyte Gulf and included a damning indictment in his early draft, stating that "Halsey had made the wrong decision. In the light of what we now know, there can be no question about that." When asked for his reaction, Nimitz suggested the words be eliminated and that Potter let the reader draw his own conclusion based on the facts that were given. Once again, Nimitz had come to Halsey's defense in an effort to avoid a Sampson-Schley debacle.[57]

Though the dispute continues, there is little doubt that much of the blame for Taffy 3 being caught by surprise rests on Halsey's shoulders. Halsey saw what he wanted to see, not what actually was there. Instead of keeping an open mind to evaluate events, he saw only carriers. He wanted that elusive battle with enemy flattops, and when Ozawa steamed into view he charged after him. Rather than going through a rational assessment of what to do, Halsey relied on assumptions that favored what he wanted to do anyway. He assumed that his pilots' exaggerated damage reports were accurate and that Kurita, badly mauled in the Sibuyan Sea, would continue his retirement. When Kurita reversed course and headed toward San Bernardino Strait, he first assumed Oldendorf's battleships could rush from Surigao Strait and help, then assumed Thomas Sprague's sixteen escorts could handle the threat.

All Halsey needed to do was leave one portion of his immense force off San Bernardino Strait. While his detached unit destroyed Kurita's ships in piecemeal fashion as they exited San Bernardino Strait, Halsey could have taken the remainder of his Third Fleet and pursued and destroyed Ozawa almost at leisure.

Kinkaid received much abuse for the lack of an adequate air search over San Bernardino Strait, but that is a moot point. All commands knew long before the Japanese admiral arrived off Samar that Kurita had reversed course and was heading toward the strait. Had Halsey fulfilled his mission and guarded the strait, air searches from Kinkaid's Seventh Fleet would have been unnecessary. Kinkaid's main fault was in not seeking at a much earlier time a definite answer from Halsey as to the whereabouts of Task Force 34. With that information in hand, Kinkaid could have positioned the Taffies farther to sea and diverted properly armed aircraft to the strait.

Nimitz must accept his share of the blame for ordering Halsey to make enemy carriers his primary objective, which only confused what had been clear-cut areas of responsibility. Halsey maneuvered his ships according to this order, while Kinkaid and Sprague operated according to a different set of instructions. Even Nimitz's son, a lieutenant commander in the Navy, told his father the evening of 25 October that in issuing Halsey this order, he gave him an open hand to abandon the beachhead.

"It's your fault," he told his father. Admiral Nimitz curtly ended the discussion by answering, "That's your opinion."[58]

The most important factor, however, was the catastrophic division of command. None of the above would have occurred had one man been firmly in charge, whether it was MacArthur or Nimitz. With the complicated command system, messages from one command to another took too long to reach their destination; one arm did not know what the other was doing; confusion reigned over air searches; and Taffy 3 men drowned off Samar. Remove division of command as a factor and the other tragic problems are eliminated.

Another individual, far from the scene and light-years away from the naval world, clearly saw this within weeks of the battle. In an extraordinarily touching letter, written to Sprague by the father of a sailor lost on the *Gambier Bay,* Mr. A. L. Arpin of Crowley, Louisiana, poured out a stream of emotion while placing the blame for his son's death at Sprague's feet. Though there is no record of Sprague's reply, the correspondence must have bothered him deeply, for he had long regarded his men's safety as paramount. Although Mr. Arpin incorrectly blames Sprague, his keen perception of what occurred that day off Samar shines from every phrase.

Dec. 1st 1944
Rear Admiral C. A. F. Sprague
U.S. Navy Washington D.C.

Dear Sir:

I note your interview given to the A.P. concerning the battle of the Philippines Oct. 24th. You mention that not one of our vessels were damaged. From previous press reports I understand that there were two battles, one on the 25th in which the PRINCETON was lost. Also the St. Lo and the Gambier Bay and several others not mentioned in the interview.

Since Oct. 25th I have sought by many letters and telegrams to learn something of our only son, Radioman on the Gambier Bay, Louis W. Arpin 275 00 30. Not till the 14th of Nov. was I advised that he was missing and no further information.

One account of the battle of the 25th stated that it was a complete surprise. That the Jap fleet started west on the 24th, reversed its course, and not having been watched by air or surface scouts, emerged next morning in the middle of our unprotected carriers. The Gambier Bay, the first attacked, was as the correspondent put it, "cold turkey."

I don't know Admiral if you have any sons in the service but if so and under a like situation I think you would be critical. I on my part wonder WHY the Japs were not watched and were permitted to surprise our carriers which were unprotected and why were they practically unprotected?

You say 600 on the Gambier Bay were saved. All I know is that my son was not saved. And you don't mention how many were in the crew so we don't know how many were lost. Presumably there must be some good reason why this information is not given to the public and to fathers and mothers. BUT I can't imagine what that reason is.

An account given by one boy who drifted four days and landed on Samar was that our boys were in the water in the midst of the Jap fleet and the Japs threw hand grenades at them. That is damd [*sic*] unpleasant to contemplate and my thought is that that is how my boy died. And WHY? I feel that it is because you did not watch the Jap Fleet and prevent this surprise and slaughter. It does seem that after Pearl Harbor we should not have too many surprises.

Maybe you won't like this letter but just consider that it comes from a father and mother who because of the loss of their only son, now have no further interest in life. It is one thing to lose a son in a fight where he has a chance and is doing something for his country but it is entirely a different matter to know that he was caught in a trap and didn't have a chance and nothing to show for his having sacrificed himself.

Maybe you won't reply to this letter but I think it well that you should know how at least one father feels.

Sincerely yours, A. L. Arpin[59]

Sprague rarely discussed the matter with family members. As stated before, however, he left a confidential written record on the pages of Woodward's book where he felt free to express his views. While every other commander had a stake in shifting blame elsewhere, Sprague had no need to do this since he had pulled his unit out of danger and won a surprising victory. His words thus ring truer than those from Halsey, Nimitz, or Kinkaid.

Sprague heatedly ripped into Halsey for leaving San Bernardino Strait unguarded and thereby exposing Taffy 3. When Woodward wrote that Kinkaid assumed Halsey had left Task Force 34 behind, Sprague added in the margin, "And everybody else did." Of Halsey's informing Nimitz he was heading north, Sprague wrote, "The message said 3 groups would proceed north. I presumed Sherman, Davison, and Bogan were the ones meant and that T.F. 34 would still guard San Bernardino. So did Kinkaid. So did Nimitz." [60]

Halsey rushed north with his entire force because Ozawa dangled a few tempting carriers in his face. Woodward quoted Ozawa as saying his first mission was to act as a decoy for Halsey. Sprague added alongside, "He certainly accomplished his mission." Another subject of debate is why Halsey failed to return to Leyte Gulf when information arrived that Kurita had once again steamed toward San Bernardino. Halsey claimed he relied on his pilots' damage reports that stated that Kurita had been badly damaged, a rather lame excuse according to Sprague, who believed a commander could not depend on their accuracy and that Halsey should have been aware of this tendency. Sprague wrote: "This overestimating of enemy damage was prevalent thru out our air groups. the [sic] worst was the *Shangri-La* group [which Sprague later commanded] who destroyed more planes than the Japs built during the war."[61]

Because of this rash decision to continue north, Halsey missed the opportunity to pounce on a vulnerable Kurita as his ships emerged in single file from the strait. Sprague wrote: "What a set up for T.F. 34"—a moan about the fumbled chance. When Halsey finally turned back toward Leyte Gulf, he rushed ahead with his fastest battleships, the *Iowa* and *New Jersey,* in an effort to cut off Kurita's retreat. In other words, he left behind one portion of the Third Fleet to attack with a second portion, exactly what he claimed he could not do earlier with Task Force 34. An astonished Sprague could only scribble in the margin, "Spectacular but meaningless."[62]

Sprague reserved his harshest criticism of Halsey for the book's final page, when Woodward cited Kurita's hesitation and lack of resolve as major factors affecting Samar's outcome. Woodward concluded, "What was needed on the flag bridge of the *Yamato* on the morning of the 25th was not a Hamlet but a Hotspur—a Japanese Halsey instead of a Kurita."

Near this sentence, which cast Halsey in the hero's role, Sprague added twelve devastating words that summarized how the commander of Taffy 3 felt about his higher-ranking cohort. "If he [Kurita] had been a Halsey he would have been missing entirely."[63]

If Sprague so resolutely guided Taffy 3 away from oblivion off Samar in what has been termed an epic of the war, why is he known to almost no one other than Taffy 3 survivors and a few interested historians? Had the other main American character in this drama been someone other than the popular Halsey, Sprague might have received the praise due him. How does one tear down a hero without causing a larger controversy or without harming morale? The American public needed Halsey on the front lines, combating the enemy in its behalf. Even MacArthur, no staunch friend of the Navy, quashed criticism of "the Bull" in his headquarters.[64]

The Navy also needed Halsey on the front lines. Who else in the Pacific had the charisma and influence with the press that Halsey possessed? Not Nimitz. Certainly not the talented but quiet Spruance. Halsey's utterances

This photograph, frequently misidentified by historians as showing Sprague during the Battle of Samar, actually was taken on 21 March 1944. It pictures Sprague on the bridge of the *Wasp*.

The USS *Wasp* in April 1944, painted in wartime camouflage

This picture, taken at about 1424 on 19 June 1944 during the dive-bombing attack on the *Wasp*, shows a flaming Japanese plane plunging down (*lower center*) aft of the ship, a Japanese dive-bomber (*upper center*) diving on the *Wasp*, phosphorous bomb explosions (*upper right and lower left center*) over the *Wasp*, and a battleship (*right center*) in the distance.

Adm. William F. "Bull" Halsey, Jr., the Navy's dominant Pacific hero, was itching to get a crack at enemy carriers. (*Courtesy U.S. Naval Institute Collection*)

Vice Adm. Thomas C. Kinkaid, Sprague's superior, commanded the Seventh Fleet, which was given the task of supporting Gen. Douglas MacArthur's operations in the Philippines. (*Courtesy U.S. Naval Institute Collection*)

Vice Adm. Takeo Kurita was Sprague's opponent in the fighting off Samar. (*Courtesy U.S. Naval Institute Collection*)

Sprague's flagship during the fighting off Samar, the USS *Fanshaw Bay* (CVE-70)

Early in the fighting, a destroyer and a destroyer escort lay smoke to shield Sprague's six escort carriers from Kurita's battleships and cruisers.

Enemy salvos fall close to one of Sprague's escort carriers.

Shell splashes and smoke partially hide four Taffy 3 ships in this photograph taken from the *White Plains.*

A Japanese suicide plane just seconds before crashing into the *White Plains* and injuring eleven men. The escort carrier was able to continue on her own.

A kamikaze misses the *Fanshaw Bay*'s fantail by less than twelve yards
during the fighting off Samar.

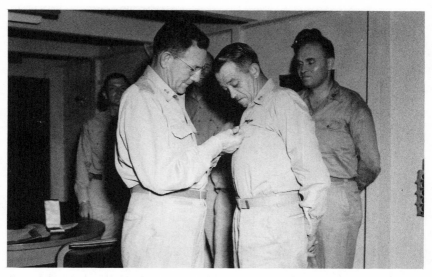

Rear Adm. Calvin T. Durgin pins the Navy Cross on Sprague on board the *Fanshaw Bay* for his direction of Taffy 3 on 25 October 1944.

Rear Admiral
Sprague in Kodiak,
Alaska, during his
time as comman-
dant, Seventeenth
Naval District, and
commander,
Alaskan Sea
Frontier

Sprague enjoyed the opportunities that service in Alaska offered. Here he returns from an obviously successful fishing trip.

Sprague (*left*), wearing an electronically heated flight suit, walks to the B-29 aircraft, Lonesome Polecat, for his 12 November 1950 flight over the North Pole.

Sprague (*back row, second from right*) is photographed with the crew of the Lonesome Polecat shortly before heading to the North Pole.

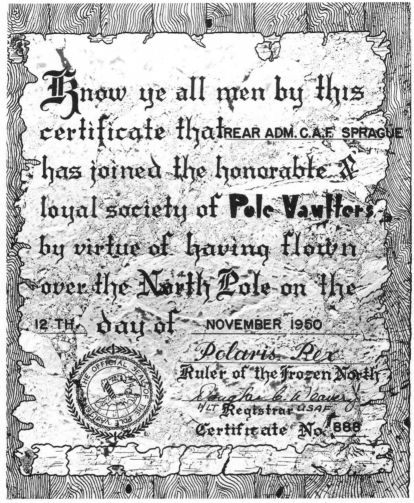

Know ye all men by this certificate that REAR ADM. C.A.F. SPRAGUE has joined the honorable & loyal society of **Pole Vaulters** by virtue of having flown over the North Pole on the 12TH day of NOVEMBER 1950

Polaris Rex
Ruler of the Frozen North

1/LT Registrar USAF

Certificate No. 888

THE OFFICIAL SEAL OF THE POLE VAULTERS

Humorous certificate given to Sprague by members of the Lonesome Polecat. He could laugh after the event, but Sprague experienced some uneasy moments during the sixteen-hour flight.

Sprague welcomes Thomas E. Dewey, the prominent American politician
and presidential candidate, to Alaska.

The guided missile frigate USS *Clifton Sprague* (FFG–16) steams down Maine's Kennebec River on her way to sea in February 1980.

one day made banner headlines the next. In the Pacific, where MacArthur loved to control press releases and dominate news coverage, Halsey kept the Navy on the front pages.

More than once King toyed with the idea of removing Halsey, but he always shied away because of Halsey's popularity. "The men are crazy about him," King would tell staff members, "and they will follow him anywhere." Besides, it is easier to forgive a commander when he errs on an offensive mission, particularly when the commander's side is victorious.[65]

That Halsey could not easily be shoved out of the spotlight is illustrated by the fact that Halsey later led the Third Fleet into two separate typhoons that mauled his ships and killed over eight hundred men, yet he remained in command. Secretary of the Navy James Forrestal at first demanded Halsey's resignation, but King convinced him that such a step would hurt American morale and aid the enemy. If avoidable deaths and fierce storms could not remove Halsey, certainly a victory at Leyte Gulf could not.[66]

Sprague never helped his own cause. Modest by nature, he believed an officer simply performed his duties and moved on to the next challenge. Publicity was not important to Sprague, who detested the political game so loved by some officers, where a man with lofty aspirations built a following and reputation, then directed his actions toward achieving whatever goal he had in mind.

Historian Thomas Vaughan, Daniel's brother, discussed Leyte Gulf with Sprague one evening, and not once did Sprague take any credit. "From what he told me, you'd think he was in charge of nothing more than a ward room," explained Vaughan. "He was embarrassed with publicity and would only respond that he only did what he was supposed to do."[67]

Ironically, in helping save Halsey's reputation at Leyte Gulf, Sprague ensured that scant praise would come for himself. Accolades still poured in to Halsey, particularly from the public, and the Navy rode along the crest with him. Every word of praise given to Sprague, though, meant one less for Halsey. Make Sprague the hero, and you transform Halsey into a bungler. Thus it was in the Navy's interests to retain Halsey in the hero's role. Sprague said little in public and not much more in private.

Even when a few glowing words trickled in for Sprague, they often were handed to his Academy classmate Thomas Sprague, the commander of Task Group 77.4 and Clifton Sprague's immediate superior. Confusion over the two Spragues existed for much of their careers, and as the higher-ranking man at Samar, Thomas Sprague benefited from the publicity. Vice Adm. Calvin T. Durgin, who later became Deputy Chief of Naval Operations

(Air), told Sprague after the war that "all the people of the United States gave Tommy all the credit but we who had the straight dope knew that you should have been given all the credit for the heroic work done by your boys in the CVE's."[68]

Historians sometimes credit Tommy Sprague with the victory off Samar since he held overall command, while failing to even mention Clifton Sprague. Even as late as 1994, World War II historian Gerhard L. Weinberg incorrectly placed Thomas Sprague with Taffy 3 off Samar. Clifton Sprague's name appears nowhere in the book's one thousand pages.[69]

Of the many factors preventing Sprague from receiving his fair share of the acclaim, politics probably hurt the most. To protect his Navy from the divisive effects of another Sampson-Schley controversy, Nimitz clamped such a tight lid on criticism that some officers who disagreed with Halsey refused to openly discuss the battle. Both Nimitz and King refrained from castigating Halsey because by doing so, they would be criticizing themselves as well.[70]

Naval aviation could suffer should the Navy look bad. Sentiment for a separate military force in charge of all aviation matters, including naval aviation, had been slowly gaining momentum. King, as well as all naval aviators—including Sprague—vehemently argued against removing carrier air power from the Navy, and a public relations staff was organized to showcase naval aviation. Anything that cast the Navy in a poor light was avoided or swept under the rug. Ironically, in part Sprague failed to receive the acclaim due him *because* of naval aviation, something he had devoted his entire career to building.[71]

World events, particularly in Europe, also shoved Sprague and Leyte Gulf off center stage. Allied troops smashed through France as they neared the Rhine in the eagerly awaited final assault on Hitler. The bitter Battle of the Bulge monopolized headlines, while dominant personalities such as MacArthur, Patton, and Eisenhower stamped their imprints across America's front pages. Against this and impending Pacific operations, Leyte Gulf receded to the back pages of newspapers.

The men of Taffy 3 waged a long struggle to gain recognition for their commander, who they asserted has been overshadowed by Halsey and unnoticed by their nation. In 1947 Christopher Carson, a former *Fanshaw Bay* crew member, wrote Adm. Frederick C. Sherman a lengthy letter in which he extolled the benefits of serving on board an escort carrier. He included warm words for Sprague.

"The high light of my jeep-carrier-career was aboard the USS *Fanshaw*

Bay when we had the good fortune to draw Admiral C. A. F. Sprague as our Task Force C.O. After serving through the now famous 'Battle Off Samar' under him, I don't believe there's a more fine or courageous officer in the United States Navy. I can never hope to express how much the men of our outfit admired and adored that man. Whether or not he places the reason with God for our narrow squeak and consequent escape; I shall always place it with him."[72]

Fanshaw Bay Ordnanceman William M. Carson summed up the general sentiment held by Taffy 3 members toward Sprague when he wrote, "He had the gift of making the sum of the parts add up to alot more than the whole. Part of leadership I guess is bringing out the best in people and focusing their energies on worthwhile and mutually beneficial goals. Whatever it is he had it in spades." Carson then added, "The Halseys of this world may add the drama to war but it is the Spragues who win the battles."[73]

Shipmate Christopher Carson said it best in a letter to Sprague: "We would have gone to hell and back twice for you."[74]

What happened to Kurita following Samar? Censured by the Imperial Navy for calling off his attack with victory in his grasp, Kurita was shunted away from the active areas of the war and appointed president of the Etajima Naval Academy in December 1944. His career never recovered from his timid display off Samar.[75]

⇢ CHAPTER THIRTEEN ⇠

The War Winds Down

S prague's hectic schedule continued in the weeks after Samar. In addition to compiling action reports and tending to his normal duties, Sprague had the pleasant task of preparing for his first trip home since bringing out the *Wasp* earlier in the year.

Though Sprague worked long hours, he possessed a wartime aide who watched carefully over him. In a letter to Annabel shortly after Samar the aide, Lt. Comdr. Charles Cunningham, referred to the "prodigious amount of work" Sprague tackled and said that "although he is, I believe tired, he looks well. He hasn't lost his marvelous sense of humor and it has been grand for all of us."

Cunningham reassured Annabel that he constantly pestered her husband to alleviate his job's pressures by going out for walks when ashore, but he needed her help for one other matter. "One of my duties as Flag Lieutenant is to run the mess, and I am afraid in this I have run you a very poor second. I wish that you would send me a few suggestions of his favorite dishes."

The aide wanted Annabel to realize the esteem in which her husband was held in the Pacific for what he had achieved off the Philippines. Sprague's orchestration of the outgunned escorts has "stirred me, in fact [has] stirred us all and I wanted to write to you to tell you how proud we all are of him, and what a wonderful job he has been doing. When I say this, I speak not only of his staff, but of every officer and man under his command.

"I wanted very much to have you know this, because I know how proud you and Courtney and Pat are of him. I don't know what the home papers have to say about recent events, but there isn't a doubt in my mind as to what history books will say when the facts are out. There isn't a man among us and I have talked with many who doesn't feel the same way I do."[1]

In early December, Sprague stopped at Pearl Harbor, then continued on to Washington to give an official report about Samar to Admiral King. Though the Navy's top commander knew the volatile Halsey should have protected Sprague's northern flank, he refrained from criticizing the home front hero to avoid stirring up a controversy.[2]

After completing official business in Washington, Sprague headed toward Philadelphia for a welcome four-day leave with his family. The exhausted admiral's appearance stunned Patricia, who noticed huge black circles under his eyes. "It looked like someone had punched him in both eyes," she later recalled. "After he rested, they went away, but God, what a sight at first!"[3]

Sprague quickly settled into a relaxed routine. Conversation steered away from Leyte Gulf—Annabel and the girls knew Sprague would say no more than that he had simply done his job. They preferred to discuss more immediate concerns, such as Annabel's query whether Sprague had brought with him his gasoline and food ration coupons. "Here I am home from death's door," Sprague laughed, "and all your mother wants are my ration coupons!"[4]

Rather than view him as a hero, the family treated Sprague as they always had—as a father and husband who had come home for a brief visit. "When he came home from Leyte," mentioned Courtney, "we didn't know he was famous or anything. I just thought to myself, 'Well, he's home, and soon he'll go back.'"[5]

A bit of acclaim began coming Sprague's way, yet he never once gave himself credit for what happened off Samar. In a lengthy interview with a Philadelphia newspaper, Sprague admitted he thought his escort carriers had little chance to escape the Japanese forces. "As the British say, it was a spot of bother," explained the admiral, who called the battle's outcome a "miracle." He predicted that because the American Navy so thoroughly destroyed the Imperial fleet in the four actions off the Philippines, the Japanese Navy would "never be back in force" during this war.[6]

When pressed to name heroes of Samar, Sprague swung the spotlight to his escort carrier pilots. He asked one reporter in November to praise the Taffy aviators because "They were wonderful" off Samar. The next month, he labeled escort carrier pilots "the hottest boys in the sky . . . I can't possibly praise highly enough the work those fellows, taking off from those little flattops, are doing. They're right in there. They form a parasol over the heads of landing troops. They land and take off from flight decks right in among the troop ships, not miles away. They've got guts, and there isn't a flier anywhere who can beat them."[7]

Unfortunately, most mention of the carrier war in hometown newspapers focused on the exploits of fast carriers and their aviators. Sprague agreed that fast carriers bore the war's offensive naval brunt, but he also attempted to inform the public that escort carriers and the people who served on board performed a vital function as well.

A 22 January 1945 article in *Life* magazine about the new breed of American admirals cast more notice toward Sprague. These admirals, according to the article, accurately foresaw early in their careers the crucial role naval aviation would play, and jumped in at aviation's beginnings. Of the twenty or so admirals mentioned, Sprague and his three Academy classmates stood out prominently.[8]

Sprague had to leave by the middle of the month to resume his command. From San Diego, he wrote his sister he would try to get Japanese souvenirs for nephew Rick Harvey, but added that his nephew might be expecting too great a sacrifice. "I could have gotten a Jap machine gun at Saipan if I was willing to exchange a quart of bourbon. I could have given a quart, but it looked better than the machine gun to me."[9]

Sprague assumed command of Carrier Division 26, on board the *Natoma Bay* for the 19 February 1945 invasion of Iwo Jima, where his unit provided close air support for the Marines ashore. Moving his flag back to the *Fanshaw Bay,* Sprague commanded the same unit off Okinawa, where his ships once more battled kamikaze attacks. Sprague's signalman, Robert Carew, recalled one time when Sprague walked onto the captain's bridge and noticed that a metal frame had been welded nearby to hold a rubber raft for the captain. When Sprague asked the captain what the raft was for, the officer answered, "In case we have to abandon ship." Upset that this officer thought of his personal safety and angered about the negative signal this sent to the crew, Sprague mentioned it was very thoughtful for the captain to be thinking of Sprague's welfare. Casting an icy gaze toward the captain, Sprague then wondered, "What're you going to use?"[10]

On another occasion, Sprague followed a Japanese land-based aircraft as it scouted high above the reach of his guns and above the top altitude of his Wildcats. The plane circled awhile, then headed over Okinawa. Just then an escort carrier containing Corsairs, which could fly at higher altitudes than the Wildcats, joined the formation. Sprague told Carew to get word over to the new carrier to launch a few Corsairs, send them to maximum altitude, and be alert for the Japanese aircraft. Not long after, a Corsair pilot shouted "Tally-ho!" as a flaming enemy plane plunged seaward. A pleased Sprague mentioned to Carew, "I knew he'd be back for another look before going home."[11]

In a personal letter Rear Adm. Calvin Durgin, Sprague's immediate superior, thanked Sprague for giving unquestioning support to any request made. "As Division Commander your ships and squadrons always met every problem and every demand in a most outstanding manner. Many times you carried out these demands when a less determined or courageous commander would have said the task was impossible." Durgin added that Sprague's "efficient handling of ships, courage and leadership in battle, spunk under most trying conditions, and willingness to take on any task" made it an honor for Durgin to command. In recognition of his work off Okinawa, Sprague received a second Gold Star in lieu of a Third Legion of Merit.[12]

He also received promotion to fast carrier command when he was named commander of Carrier Division 2 in May with flag on the *Ticonderoga*. The normally reserved Sprague wrote Annabel on 15 May, "Well your old man has reached an assignment which is just about tops in the Navy. At any rate it is as far as I can go as a Rear Admiral." He explained he would receive a task group, which now placed him "in line for greater jobs in the future, if I make good here. Pray for me."

He also told Annabel about a revealing meeting at Ulithi with Halsey, the first time Sprague and his controversial cohort crossed paths since Leyte Gulf. While Sprague idly chatted with two old friends, Ted Sherman and Shorty Gillette, Halsey approached.

In describing the chance meeting, Sprague used words intended only for Annabel's eyes. The letter thus illuminates his true convictions about Halsey's actions off Leyte Gulf as well as spotlights Halsey's own doubts of his role in the affair.

The gentleman who failed to keep his appointment last October came up to me and said, "Zeegee, I didn't know whether you would speak to me or not." I said, "Why Admiral Bill, I'm not mad at you." He said, "I want you to know I think you wrote the most glorious page in American Naval History that day."

Halsey continued to heap praise on Sprague in front of Sherman and Gillette, who nodded his head vigorously in agreement, while Sprague stood there awkwardly. He told Annabel that Halsey's words were "so flattering it was embarrasing [sic]. All I could mumble was 'I hope your praise is deserved.'"[13]

Sprague moved his flag to the *Ticonderoga* on 1 June, eager to employ his expertise with a fast carrier unit before the war ended. Hitler's Germany had surrendered on 7 May, and the Japanese appeared to have little naval strength left to throw at the Americans. He had told Annabel in mid-May of his feeling that the war would end shortly. If he was correct, he would be heading home before getting a chance to command fast carriers.[14]

Before he settled in as commander, Carrier Division 2, Sprague attended a dinner marking the *Ticonderoga*'s first anniversary. When he spied the menu, he knew he could not let pass the opportunity to tweak his wife and daughters. The scrumptious menu listed roast beef au jus, roast brown potatoes, and broccoli, but Sprague knew his family, still rationed in America, would instantly notice the strawberry ice cream, birthday cake, and candy. In case they had trouble spotting the items, Sprague drew arrows pointing to them and scribbled on the menu, "It is just the mean streak in me that causes me to send this along." He good-naturedly rubbed it in further by asking, "How are the lambs neck stews?"[15]

A second letter sent out about the same time was not as pleasant. Railway Express Agency mailed Sprague a bill for $1.32 to cover the delivery cost for a government package sent to him while at Gulf Sea Frontier headquarters in Miami. The ludicrous letter asked Sprague to clear up the matter, which dated to 8 October 1942. Sprague could hardly believe such time and expense had been wasted on a minor matter and wondered, with sarcasm barely concealing his anger, if—"since the tourist season in Miami should be over by now"—they could send one of their "bright young employees over to the Dupont [sic] building and get the matter straightened out." He requested they refrain from using limited mail facilities for such trivial details. Apparently his rebuke worked, for he heard no more about the matter.[16]

Most of Sprague's energies from May through July went into bombing attacks on enemy targets at Okinawa and the three Japanese home islands of Kyushu, Honshu, and Hokkaido in preparation for the invasion of Japan itself. By mid-August, Sprague had been designated one of the four task group commanders in Vice Adm. John Towers's Task Force 38—Tommy Sprague, John Ballentine, and Arthur Radford were the other three—whose responsibility would be to bomb targets around Tokyo and north-eastern sections of Japan.[17]

After atom bombs destroyed Hiroshima on 6 August and Nagasaki on 9 August, Sprague maintained normal air strikes against Japanese military and industrial targets while the Japanese government negotiated the war's conclusion. At 0635 on 15 August, while the *Ticonderoga* steamed 151 miles off Honshu's eastern coast and after aircraft had already been launched for a morning strike against Tokyo, Sprague received word from Nimitz that Japan had accepted peace terms and that all offensive operations should cease.[18]

For the next eleven days Sprague's aviators kept a close watch on Japanese airfields and military installations, located American prisoner of war camps, and dropped bundles of food and clothing to their incarcerated countrymen. Four days after the formal 2 September surrender ceremony, Sprague sailed on waters every American naval officer yearned to navigate since 7 December 1941. "Entered Tokio on *Ticonderoga*," he wrote. In a humorous vein four days later, Sprague mailed some captured Japanese flags to his nephew Rick, explaining, "I got them by storming Hirohito's palace in as intrepid an assault as I've ever heard tell of."[19]

The war ended in a fitting manner for Sprague. Present at Pearl Harbor when Japanese naval air power almost muscled the United States out of the war, he gazed across Tokyo Bay's waters toward a vanquished enemy from the decks of a fast carrier that was not even afloat when war opened. One of only a few aviators to command a ship at the scene of the war's start and its conclusion, Sprague had participated in and contributed to American naval aviation's triumph. That he failed to get much of a chance to command fast carriers in combat was out of his hands. Few of Sprague's contemporaries rose to such a level, and only three of his classmates matched or surpassed his wartime record.

→ CHAPTER FOURTEEN ←

Final Duties

Athough Sprague's naval career continued for another six years after the end of World War II, and he was embroiled in at least one momentous occasion, his final years became a footnote to his war service. Other commands awaited him, including a fast carrier task force, but the focus of his major contributions would remain in the Pacific. The shadow of Leyte Gulf, in particular, rarely receded from view as various historians began examining the controversial battle.

In November 1945 Sprague returned to the West Coast on board the fast carrier *Bennington*. The next month he traveled to Washington, where he attended a meeting with other naval leaders at the White House. His initial impressions of Harry Truman, who assumed the presidency after Franklin Roosevelt's death, were most likely swayed by family leanings toward the Republican party, but they were not far from the views held by a large segment of the American public. "He is a much better looking man than his pictures would indicate. The feeling you have when you leave is that you feel sorry for the guy, a feeling you shouldn't have, I believe, for a President of the U.S.A." In the course of time, Truman would prove both Sprague and the public wrong.[1]

* * *

In February 1946, Sprague received orders to San Diego as commander of Navy Air Group 1.6 of Joint Task Force 1 with flag on board the carrier *Shangri-La*. For the next six months Sprague supervised naval aviation forces involved in Operation Crossroads, the enormous military undertaking that dropped two atom bombs on Bikini Atoll in the Marshall Islands. Though he coordinated the photography of the explosions and air-sea rescue units, Sprague's main responsibilities centered on drones—pilotless F6F Hellcat fighter aircraft that controllers guided through the enormous mushroom-shaped cloud to measure turbulence, record the tests on movie film, and gather radioactive dust.[2]

Sprague's experimental work, dating back to the 1920s tests to perfect arresting gear, and his strong emphasis on proper training made him an ideal commander for the units assembling in the San Diego area. In less than five months his men had to learn the intricacies of an operation so complex that one reporter likened it to "a football player throwing a forward pass, then running down the field to catch it himself. . . ."[3]

According to the operational blueprint, four F6F Hellcat drones would catapult off the *Shangri-La* forty miles southeast of Bikini Atoll. Control aircraft—two for each drone—would then take over and guide the drones within twenty miles of Bikini, where the drones would proceed on their own through the swirling radioactive cloud at altitudes of 10,000, 15,000, 20,000, and 28,000 feet. When the drones emerged through the other side, eight new control aircraft would intercept them and guide them to a safe landing at Roi Island, 180 miles to the southeast.[4]

Sprague frequently had to divert his attention from preparing his units at San Diego to handling an aggressive press. Each aspect of the Bikini tests received heavy scrutiny from a national press corps that, at times, leveled a serious charge at the Navy. Leaving administrative details of everyday training to subordinates, Sprague attempted to stem criticism of his Navy, but in doing so he had to step into an arena the normally quiet man preferred to avoid—the national spotlight.

The charge, stating that the Navy would favorably rig the test results to guarantee a role for the Navy in the postwar world, stemmed from war's end, where the U.S. Navy found itself in an almost unchallenged position. Ships of the Japanese Navy, the only fleet besides that of friendly England capable of taking on the United States, dotted the ocean's floor in hundreds of locations from the Gilbert Islands to Japan, and no other hostile nation possessed a navy powerful enough to challenge the U.S. Navy. Some people, inside and outside the military, wondered what, if any, role the Navy should play. If the Bikini tests proved the atom bomb's frightening potency, critics wondered why the nation holding a monopoly on atomic weapons should even bother to maintain a powerful navy.[5]

Sprague answered the charge in an 8 May press conference with forty newspaper, newsreel, and radio reporters on board the *Shangri-La*. Calling the criticism "nonsense," Sprague explained that the purpose of the June–July tests was "the impersonal collection of data," including the blast's effects on surface ships. Analysis "may or may not change the form of our naval weapons," but whatever the outcome, the Navy would do nothing to shade the tests in its favor. As further evidence that the results would be impartially evaluated, Sprague emphasized, the entire operation would be observed by over two hundred reporters who would act as the eyes and ears of the public. "They will be allowed to see, record and relay every aspect of the tests consistent with security and national safety. Our orders are to lay the cards on the table."[6]

Sprague invited the newsmen to a 9 May rehearsal of his drone unit, the final in a series of over twenty practice runs he put his men through before heading to Bikini. As Sprague and the newsmen watched, a radio-controlled drone catapulted off the *Shangri-La* to its mother plane, which directed it in a series of climbs and turns before sending it to within fifty feet of the newsmen. The successful run, which one reporter called "a dramatic example of precision and timing," ended with the mother aircraft guiding the drone to a safe landing at Brown Field near San Diego.[7]

Sprague's task group left San Diego shortly after the final rehearsal so Sprague could arrive in time for a planned 26 June conference of commanders on Bikini. Four days later, with Sprague and Task Group 1.1.2 a distant fifty miles from the epicenter, a B-29 delivered the first atom bomb from an altitude of thirty thousand feet. A second bomb, detonated underwater, shook Bikini Lagoon the next month.[8]

The bombs also shook the U.S. Navy, for the venerable carrier *Saratoga* was sunk by the new weapon while a second, the *Independence,* was badly damaged. Though the unmanned carriers had been placed close to the epicenter as part of the tests, many in the Navy doubted that they would be harmed. Aircraft carriers now appeared vulnerable to a weapon that could be delivered by a single bomber, causing budget-conscious politicians in postwar America to favor reductions in the Navy while shifting funds to the Air Force. Naval aviation, in particular, seemed in jeopardy of being dominated by an Army Air Force wielding the atom bomb. Sprague sensed that dramatic changes might loom for the Navy. In a conversation with his future son-in-law, Daniel Vaughan, Sprague said of Bikini, "It's all over. It's a different world now. The ships don't mean as much." [9]

Sprague received a Gold Star in lieu of a fourth Legion of Merit for his work in Operation Crossroads. The citation praised a familiar trait, as Sprague "soundly prepared the Navy Air Group for its difficult duties. . . ." It added an ominous note, however, by honoring him for "Training the operating personnel to follow the intricate Air Plan necessitated by rigid radiological safety provisions in an operating area of tremendous potential danger. . . ." In other words, he drilled safety measures into his men because of the unknown consequences of atomic radiation. Although radiation's effects would become a source of heated controversy fifty years later, Sprague never appeared overly concerned at the time nor mentioned it to any family member afterwards. His airmen approached no closer than twenty miles of the bomb, and even that was thirty miles closer than Sprague and the *Shangri-La* were situated. [10]

One month after Operation Crossroads, Sprague was named chief of Naval Air Basic Training at Corpus Christi, where he succeeded classmate Jocko Clark. The Navy again took advantage of Sprague's expertise in training and his skill in teaching aviation to others (dating from the 1929–31 stint at the Naval Academy) to develop a solid corps of naval aviators in the postwar world.

Sprague first tackled a personal issue before diving into his air training responsibilities. Since Leyte Gulf, he had been in possession of the battle flag given him by the *Fanshaw Bay* crew. Sprague wanted the memento to reside in a more public location, since he believed his unit had fought an action that would one day be considered epic. On 26 September he wrote a letter to Rear Adm. Aubrey W. Fitch, then the superintendent of the Naval Academy, offering the flag to the Academy's museum. Sprague said that although he would always cherish the flag, "I believe it merits a place in the trophy room, as an item of future historical value, and I believe the Naval Academy is the place for it. . . ."

Sprague felt the flag deserved special treatment because "For about two hours and a quarter my outfit was subjected to a most merciless bombardment. Never in the history of naval warfare has any force suffered such a pounding, Windy Corner at Jutland was a zephyr compared with it." Despite the fierce opposition, his unit had emerged victorious and thus deserved recognition. Kurita fled because of "my destroyers, my planes, the wonderful support of the planes from Felix Stump's unit, a major factor, and the support of Tommy Sprague's planes. . . ."

Sprague implored Fitch to respond honestly whether he also felt the flag should reside in honor at Annapolis, and asked him not to think "I am trying to pose as a hero for I must confess I have never had a happier moment in my life than the one when the action was broken off." Not feeling totally comfortable with what he feared could be seen as self-promotion, Sprague asked Fitch to keep the letter confidential.

One remarkable paragraph stands above the rest of this beautiful letter. The man who preferred to accomplish his duties without fanfare wrote, "Our Navy for reasons that are clear to me and possibly to you too, has never played up this action to any extent. . . ." This confidential correspondence was about as public a forum as Sprague would use to propound his belief that the Navy purposely clamped a lid on criticism of Halsey. Taffy 3 could not be honored without detracting from Halsey or possibly splitting the Navy into two camps, therefore its heroic role could not be fully acknowledged. Then Sprague added, "I am convinced that history will accord the proper place for [Taffy 3] in the decisive actions of the war, probably a half century or so after I have passed on."[11]

Fitch replied within a week that he would love to have the flag permanently reside at the Academy, "because it will serve as an inspiration to the Brigade of Midshipmen and to all the future midshipmen so long as our country continues to exist." He promised it would occupy a place of honor with other historic flags at the museum.[12]

Sprague quickly shipped the flag to Fitch along with a handwritten note that he apparently intended to be included in any display. His words this time are more formal than his usual letters, but they convey his feelings toward the men who fought at Leyte Gulf.

> May our Navy always show the dogged determination that characterized the officers and men of my group, on ship and in the air and characterized those aviators sent to my assistance from the jeep carriers of Rear Admiral Thomas Sprague and Rear Admiral Felix Stump. Against heavy odds they turned back the Japs that day with considerable loss to the Imperial Japanese Navy.
>
> And for those officers and men of my force who did not return from that engagement but who gave their lives for their country, may their sacrifice be an inspiration to our young future naval officers.[13]

These are noble words from a brave man, designed to instill pride and a sense of duty among midshipmen who would walk the paths of Annapolis for years to come. Sprague's flag remains at the Academy's museum. Unfortunately, it rests inside a storage container in a back room, far from the Navy memorabilia that currently regale visitors as they pace the museum's floors.[14]

On 19 November 1946, Sprague participated as commentator in a nationally broadcast NBC radio program covering the inactivation of his former aircraft carrier, the *Wasp*. During the fifteen-minute program, Sprague explained how the ship quickly established "a fighting reputation among the ships of the Navy second to none" during the Battle of the Philippine Sea by shooting down five enemy aircraft. He emphasized that neither the aircraft, the ship, nor any commanding officer had been responsible for the *Wasp*'s outstanding record, which "now lives in tradition and history for the honor of all men who know the sea." He placed that honor on those "fine men" who served aboard the *Wasp*.[15]

Shortly afterward, Sprague's name appeared in the midst of an issue that threatened not merely to split the Navy into two camps, but possibly to eliminate naval aviation in its entirety. During the latter stages of the war, support had grown for the establishment of a separate Air Force with responsibility for all aviation concerns, including those handled by the Navy. Some proponents of an autonomous Air Force even wondered what value, other than ferrying supplies and men overseas, remained in keeping an independent Navy. Who, they asked, formed a naval threat in the atomic age? The two nations most likely to challenge the United States—the Soviet Union and China—did not possess strong maritime fleets.[16]

Naval aviators, who battled their way past battleship advocates during the lean 1920s and 1930s to create the carrier air arm that played so prominent a role in the Pacific war, now saw another struggle loom on the home front. Instead of the gun club, Air Force adherents threatened to clamp a lid on naval aviation. At the least, a separate Air Force could divert funds earmarked for the Navy. At its worst, the Air Force could absorb naval aviation.[17]

High-ranking officers in the Navy gradually drifted into one of two camps—those who saw a separate Air Force as a certainty and thus threw their weight behind it, hoping by their support to keep naval aviation in the hands of the Navy, and those who opposed it. Sprague's classmate Forrest Sherman supported the new military department and persuaded Adm. Chester Nimitz, now Chief of Naval Operations, to add his endorsement. Classmate Jocko Clark vehemently opposed the idea along with Vice Adm. Arthur W. Radford, Nimitz's Deputy Chief of Naval Operations (Air).[18]

Nimitz, with his aversion to any controversy threatening to divide the Navy, tried to contain the rift before it became public. Thus, when an article written by the respected military correspondent Hanson W. Baldwin appeared in the Sunday *New York Times* on 26 January 1947, a concerned Nimitz reacted immediately. Titled "Air Dispute Remains," Baldwin's article explained that a group of naval aviators strongly objected to the Navy Department's apparent willingness to support an independent Air Force. Baldwin labeled the opposition a "revolt" and listed eight prominent names as leaders of the movement, including Adm. John H. Towers, then commander in chief of the Pacific Fleet, Radford, Clark, and Sprague.[19]

Two days after the article appeared, Nimitz fired off a confidential letter to each man named by Baldwin. Nimitz stated that information in the article obviously came from meetings between Nimitz and Secretary of the Navy James Forrestal, and he asked them if they knew how such material became available to the reporter. Sprague had no idea how the leak occurred. When he queried each member of his staff whether they had any pertinent knowledge, they unanimously answered in the negative, which Sprague recorded in a checklist he penciled in at the bottom of Nimitz's letter. On 4 February Sprague replied by letter that while he had once briefly met Baldwin at Kwajalein during Operation Crossroads, Sprague had "had no contact with him of any description on any subject at any time" and therefore could not provide Nimitz with any helpful information.[20]

The storm passed over in July, when the Unification Act created a separate U.S. Air Force but retained a naval air arm. Sprague and the others named in Baldwin's article suffered no consequences over the issue. Jocko Clark and Felix Stump, for example, commanded major naval units during the Korean War and retired as full admirals, while Sprague's assignments placed him in positions of ever-increasing responsibilities. Other than being an avid supporter of naval aviation, Sprague never determined exactly how his name came to appear in Baldwin's article.[21]

When not embroiled in controversy, Sprague implemented one measure at Corpus Christi that contributed to pilot safety while producing a more capable aviator. Since his days as a student pilot at Pensacola, novice naval aviators trained in biplanes. This practice continued, with the support of most veteran flight instructors, even though the fliers would operate nothing but monoplanes throughout their years in the Navy. Lighter biplanes were supposedly less exacting to fly and allowed a greater margin of error for the neophyte airmen. Sprague, however, thought such training in biplanes instilled bad habits that needed to be expunged when switching the student to monoplanes. This was particularly true in emergencies, he contended, when student aviators developed one set of reactions that could be dangerous if used in a similar emergency with a monoplane. Why train in biplanes, he wondered, when the pilot would eventually be switched to a monoplane?

Beginning in March 1947, Sprague conducted experiments in which one hundred student aviators trained in monoplanes. The results so justified his beliefs that even flight instructors dropped their objections. According to a Navy Department release, Sprague's change "will give the Navy a better aviator in a shorter period of time, and at less cost." [22]

In January 1948 Sprague was redesignated as commander of Naval Air Advanced Training at Corpus Christi. Four months later new orders returned him to sea as commander of Carrier Division 6 on board the aircraft carrier *Kearsarge*. After nineteen months in Texas, the Spragues' longest stay at one location in ten years, Sprague was off to the sea one final time. [23]

This command would be an easy wind-up for Sprague's career. Carrier Division 6 headed for a four-month, 20,000-mile tour of the Mediterranean Sea as part of the nation's effort to show support for the Greek and Turkish governments in their battle against communist factions. Much of Sprague's schedule revolved around official courtesy visits in various ports and in sightseeing. [24]

Two stops typified his tour in the Mediterranean. Accompanied by the destroyer *Massey*, Sprague and the *Kearsarge* arrived at Tripoli, Libya, on 23 June for a six-day visit. Few serious matters crossed his desk. Other than holding one press conference and warning his men that tension between the Arab and Jewish factions in Tripoli could flare, Sprague found himself entertaining dignitaries on board the *Kearsarge* or being entertained on shore. Eleven of twelve items logged in his visit report concerned such light matters of protocol, which must have taxed the patience of a man more at home with close friends than with government dignitaries. The twelfth item—his press conference—lasted barely five minutes as Sprague gave reporters only a few nuggets of information. In response to a question about possible maneuvers in the Mediterranean, Sprague replied, "We always have to practice or the pilots will get stale." Most often though, as with the query whether his visit had anything to do with the turbulent Mideast situation, Sprague gave no comment. "I am not a diplomat," he admonished, "I'm only a naval officer." [25]

A four-day visit across the Mediterranean to Naples, Italy, differed only in the number of official visits and functions Sprague endured. On Saturday, 3 July, he called on five dignitaries, received three visits, and attended a special dinner. [26]

Sprague spent as much time as possible visiting tourist attractions, especially Rome, which he described in a letter to Annabel as "a wonderful place and you would have to live there a year to see all that it contains." His sightseeing also enabled him to employ his devilish wit in letters and cards back home. He wrote of Pompeii that "They have been evacuating this place for 200 years and still at it or about as long as it takes Court to make up her bed." From Argostoli, Greece, he teased Annabel by warning his daughters, "Don't tell Mother but the ladies here want me to stay. The town went into mourning when I pulled out." [27]

Sprague's cruise ended in early October when the carrier *Franklin D. Roosevelt* arrived to replace the *Kearsarge*. Sprague steamed home for his last three years of duty, served partly in sunny California and partly in Alaska. [28]

On 1 January 1949 Sprague became commander, Naval Air Bases, Eleventh and Twelfth Naval Districts, based at the Naval Air Station on Coronado Island near San Diego. He had been given his choice of either this post or duty in Bermuda, and selected Coronado after Annabel indicated her preference for the location. [29]

In Sprague's year as commander, little of importance occurred on the military level. The highlight in family matters was the 3 December 1949 marriage of Courtney to Daniel Vaughan, a rising ophthalmologist from the San Francisco area. When Courtney informed her parents she was to be married, Annabel gushed with the usual excitement, but Sprague suddenly quieted and said nothing to his daughter. The next morning, apparently after letting the news sink in, Sprague watched Courtney walk down the stairs and said, "Here comes the bride"—his way of stating he approved of the union.

"He said it simply, just like he did after Pearl Harbor when he told his men they were 'all right for my money,'" explained Courtney. "Then he handled just about everything for the wedding, including writing the invitations."

Sprague felt an instant rapport with his son-in-law and told his sister Dorothea that he was a wonderful young man despite the fact that he voted for the Democrats. Long fond of golf, Sprague beamed about Dan's accomplishments in amateur golf in the Bay Area.

The marriage ceremony took place at the Navy Chapel in San Diego. Never fond of organized religion or church services, an impatient Sprague let the chaplain know through body language that he should waste no time. "He wanted the wedding to last about two minutes," recalled Daniel

Vaughan. "That poor chaplain was under a gun. Ziggy, his boss, sat in the second row staring at him as if saying, 'Get going!' "[30]

Sprague ended his duties at Coronado in February 1950 and indicated on his fitness report that he desired either the post of commander of Naval Air Forces in the Atlantic or a return to Pensacola as commander of Naval Air Training. Instead, he relieved Rear Adm. Frank Wagner as commandant of the Seventeenth Naval District and commander of the Alaskan Sea Frontier headquartered on Kodiak Island. The Alaskan Sea Frontier, with borders skirting those of the communist Soviet Union, demanded a calm leader, for shortly before Sprague's appointment the Soviet Union startled U.S. officials by successfully testing its own atomic weapon. The days of atomic monopoly ended, ushering in an age of fragile relations and delicate diplomacy. The Alaskan Sea Frontier assumed greater importance than ever and needed the guidance of someone who would not be rattled into a rash decision that could send the world spinning closer to its first atomic confrontation.[31]

Alaska offered few of the benefits to which Annabel had grown accustomed, and she had little fondness for the location. Sprague, however, reveled in the superb fishing provided by the streams and bays and took advantage of his wife's discomfort for some gentle teasing. In a November letter to Courtney he claimed "we now have our winter supply of blubber in hand. Your mother went out in a kaiak [sic] and in 45 minutes, single handed, returned with the biggest whale since Baranoff the Prince of Alaska landed one 2 lbs. heavier in 1857. This astonished the natives but was no surprise to me for you know mother has been blubbering all her life. She is now chewing on some seal hides making me a pair of shoes. A good mother and a good wife . . . Well so much for the gay fast life in Alaska."[32]

Three days after writing the letter, Sprague participated in one of the scariest flights of his lengthy career. The Air Force's 375th Weather Reconnaissance Squadron planned its 375th weather flight over the North Pole for 12 November 1950, and asked Sprague to accompany the flight as honorary commander. The squadron flew to the North Pole and back every other day to track the paths of cold air masses that formed over the icy Arctic region and swooped down on Canada and the contiguous forty-eight states.[33]

Sprague did not worry about the flight, and even joked about the turbulent weather in a letter a few days before taking off. "Come Sunday, I'm flying over the North Pole," he wrote Courtney. "You'd think by this time, I'd be staying home and tending to my hooked rugs. I've always gotten a big laugh during my career in bad weather by saying, 'Well, I wouldn't send my mother-in-law up in weather like this.' Ask Dan if he wants me to take Annabel along."[34]

The joking ended Sunday at 0650 when Sprague, sporting an electronically heated flight suit over heavy clothes, joined the thirteen-man crew of a B-29 called the Lonesome Polecat. He sat transfixed as the plane lumbered down the cold, 14,600-foot runway and lifted off into a snowstorm nearing blizzard proportions. The B-29 flew a route known as the Ptarmigan Track, named after a bird common to those regions. As the aircraft flew at just over eighteen thousand feet, Sprague peered through breaks in the clouds and was surprised to see open water ninety miles north of Point Barrow. As the plane flew on, drift ice covered more of the water until it gradually led into the polar ice cap.[35]

Though he showed no signs of alarm and afterward told the press the flight went smoothly, Sprague felt so uneasy for much of the trip that he later told his son-in-law that he thought he was going to get killed. The plane often had to fly blindly through storm clouds, piloted by airmen about whom he knew little. He realized that few navigational aids existed in a region blanketed with ice—no checkpoints to look for, no radio stations or beacons to rely on, a magnetic field that wreaked havoc on compasses.[36]

After reaching the North Pole, making Sprague the first admiral to fly over that landmark spot, the Lonesome Polecat headed home in darkened skies. Weather information from Eielson Air Force Base, from which they had taken off, indicated the snowstorm had worsened while they were gone. The storm had become so intense that Eielson flight controllers had to talk the B-29 down to a safe, though nerve-wracking, landing. The fifteen-hour fifty-five-minute flight covered 3,500 miles, 70 percent over ice.[37]

A diplomatic Sprague publicly termed the flight his greatest thrill in aviation since earning his wings. As for the crew, he warmly stated, "I certainly take my hat off to those boys. That's real flying!" Even though the Air Force presented Sprague an official "Pole Vaulters" certificate the next day in a ceremony attended by Secretary of the Air Force Thomas K. Finletter and Assistant Army Secretary Earl D. Johnson, Sprague was simply happy that the exacting flight was over.[38]

Sprague spent the following twelve months training the forces of his command so they would be more prepared for conflict with the Soviet Union. At the same time, he and Annabel began planning their retirement location. Sprague had always hoped to retire to his childhood love, Rockport, but the toll of an active military life and the thought of warmer climes vaulted Southern California to the forefront. Before Sprague's Alaskan duty ended, Annabel returned to San Diego, purchased a lot on Alameda Boulevard in Coronado, and hired a contractor to build their retirement home. Sprague faced comforting years in the sun, with family and friends at hand and the Pacific Ocean only a stone's throw away.[39]

CHAPTER FIFTEEN

Final Years

On 9 August 1951 Sprague requested voluntary retirement in a letter to Secretary of the Navy Daniel Kimball. After thirty-four years, four months, and four days of service—fifteen of those years at sea—during which he received sixteen awards and citations, Sprague separated from the Navy he loved, finally to spend time with Annabel and his daughters. Sprague logged his last flight on 2 October and officially retired on 1 November 1951. As was the custom of the time, the Navy advanced him to vice admiral at retirement in recognition of his Navy Cross.[1]

For the first time since their marriage, Clifton and Annabel Sprague owned a spot they could call home. Gone were the trains transporting family and possessions to yet another town; gone were the long separations; gone were the worries about each other's well-being. Sprague quickly adapted to the slowed pace of retirement at Coronado and enjoyed such ordinary tasks as working around the house or putting in a large brick patio in the backyard. He read history and biographies, followed baseball—the Boston Red Sox had always been his favorite team—and boxing, and relaxed with close Navy friends who lived nearby.[2]

"I was amazed how easily he adjusted to retirement," mentioned Courtney. "He was completely relaxed and happy, as though he thought the Navy life was over and now he goes on to the next thing."[3]

Family matters, so long absent over his thirty-four-year career, occupied a greater proportion of his life. Patricia married Travis Reneau in Coronado on 15 February 1952, then remained in the San Diego area, meaning that Sprague would eventually have grandchildren nearby. Whenever he wanted to see Courtney and Daniel Vaughan in San Jose, he and Annabel would drive up for a short visit, see the grandchildren, then return to Coronado the same day.

"He wasn't the kind who'd stay overnight," explained Daniel. "Everything was quick. One time in San Francisco, he picked up Courtney and me for dinner, drove us to the restaurant, we all ate, he drove us back—all within 1½ hours."[4]

His fatherly concern crossed over into aviation affairs whenever a member of his family had to fly. Before they boarded the aircraft, Sprague studied the weather forecasts and talked to the pilots to determine their level of professionalism. He wanted to ensure that his family flew in the safest possible manner.[5]

Sprague also became interested in politics. He never voted while in the Navy, since he believed he owed his loyalty to whomever was the president and since he had never lived at a permanent address. In Coronado, though, he felt free to express his views, which leaned toward the Republican party, and to cast his vote. Nephew Rick Harvey recalled seeing Sprague at the height of the Army–Senator Joseph McCarthy hearings setting up a card table in downtown Coronado, urging passersby to sign a petition protesting *Time* magazine's coverage of the episode. A strong supporter of the Wisconsin Republican, Sprague considered the weekly newsmagazine's reporting too critical of the senator.[6]

Life continued in smooth fashion for four years. In March 1955, Sprague added a wing to their home and transformed the garage into a separate bedroom. Against better judgment, for Navy physicians informed him at his retirement that he had a weak heart, Sprague moved all his furniture into the new bedroom himself. A few days later, while Annabel stitched a dress, Sprague shuffled to the bedroom and stretched out. When Annabel asked him if something was wrong, Sprague could not answer. She rushed to his side and asked if he was sick, at which Sprague feebly nodded his head. Annabel quickly summoned a physician, who called an ambulance to take him to nearby Coronado Hospital. At Sprague's request, he was moved to the Naval Hospital in San Diego.

Sprague never recovered. He lay in the hospital in an oxygen tent another two weeks, upset that he could do nothing to improve. During one visit from friend Ella Yanquell, Sprague slowly turned his head, pointed at all the tubes protruding from his body, and said, "Oh, look at what they have done to me, Ella!" He had successfully faced many crises throughout his life, but this was one he could not conquer. On 11 April 1955, the 59-year-old Sprague died from a massive heart attack.[7]

Sprague was buried two days later with full military honors and in the presence of numerous high-ranking officers, at Fort Rosecrans National Cemetery in San Diego. The cemetery proved a fitting location for an old sea dog like Sprague. Situated on a small piece of land that juts into the water, the cemetery is flanked by San Diego Bay on one side and the Pacific Ocean—the setting of his military triumphs—on the other. The man who so loved the water now lay in land daily caressed by salty breezes and ocean waves.

As Sprague's body was lowered into its grave, a fifteen-gun salute boomed from North Island Naval Air Station, and each U.S. Navy ship at anchor in San Diego Harbor lowered its flag to half mast. Fittingly, among the ships to honor Sprague that day was the *Wasp*, his first major seagoing command, which arrived in San Diego Harbor only six hours after the death of her first commander.[8]

Obituary notices appeared in newspapers across the nation, and both *Time* and *Newsweek* noted his passing. Secretary of the Navy Charles S. Thomas sent polite condolences to Annabel, while Adm. Frederick C. Sherman labeled Sprague's direction at Leyte Gulf "a masterpiece of fighting skill and cool courage in the face of overwhelming odds [that] will go down in history as one of the proudest moments of the U.S. Navy." John A. Roosevelt, who served under Sprague on board the *Wasp*, wrote that "I feel the loss not only of a great leader but also a friend."[9]

Recognition for Sprague's achievements has come slowly. In an article titled "Most Dramatic Sea Battle in History" for the 24 October 1954 *New York Times* magazine, Hanson Baldwin mentioned Sprague's role, but did not single him out more than other leaders. Four years later Samuel Eliot Morison dedicated his narrative of Leyte Gulf to Sprague and wrote, "Modest and retiring by nature, he used to give his senior, Rear Admiral Thomas Sprague, all the credit for stopping Kurita off Samar; but 'Tommy' Sprague, with equal generosity, ascribes the victory to his junior."[10]

The Navy gave official recognition on 16 February 1980 by launching a guided missile frigate named the *Clifton Sprague*. Constructed by the Bath Iron Works Corporation of Bath, Maine, the ship was commissioned 21 March 1981. Though Sprague probably would have been embarrassed by the honor, he would have liked the design of the ship's coat-of-arms and motto. Placed on a red field, representing Sprague's courage under fire, the coat-of-arms bore blue and white zigzag lines for his nickname above a lion that symbolizes his qualities as a leader. Lightning bolts in the lion's paws represent his command of aircraft carriers, while clouds refer to Sprague's navigational skills at Samar where he hid behind a smoke screen and in a rain squall. Wings, standing for his career in naval aviation, rest above three stars signifying Sprague's rank and flank a cross in honor of his Navy Cross. "Nunc Paratus"—Latin for "Ready Now"—summarizes Sprague's philosophy of command.[11]

The most significant boost to Sprague's reputation came neither from historians nor from the Navy, but from the pen of a novelist. In 1978 the noted author Herman Wouk, who had earlier published the classic novel of the sea, *The Caine Mutiny,* wrote a fictionalized account of World War II called *War and Remembrance* in which he devoted six chapters to events surrounding Leyte Gulf. In vivid style he described Sprague's instantaneous reactions to Kurita's surprise appearance, the stunning charge of Sprague's destroyers and destroyer escorts, and Halsey's abandonment of San Bernardino Strait. He then tapped Sprague on the shoulder when handing out responsibility for the victory.

> The real "solution" of Leyte Gulf is that Ziggy Sprague, an able American few remember or honor, frustrated the SHO plan and saved Halsey's reputation and MacArthur's beachhead. He held up Kurita for six crucial hours: two and a half hours in the running fight, and three and a half hours in regrouping. After midday, proceeding into the gulf was a very iffy shot.[12]

The novel gained a widespread audience, formed the basis of a major television miniseries, and gave Sprague family members tremendous satisfaction. "When I read Wouk's book, I thought that finally someone got it right!" stated Daniel Vaughan.[13]

Events of more recent years indicate that Sprague's achievements at Leyte Gulf, while gaining some attention, are still obscured by Halsey's name, MacArthur's fame, and the war in Europe. In 1985, Sprague was inducted into the Carrier Aviation Hall of Fame on board the *Yorktown,* now a naval museum at Patriots Point, in Charleston, South Carolina. But when Dr.

Stanley Falk, a noted Pacific war historian, printed a comprehensive review of books dealing with Leyte Gulf in the Fall 1988 issue of *Naval History,* Sprague's name is found nowhere. The review repeatedly refers to Halsey, MacArthur, Kinkaid, Kurita, and Ozawa but relegates Sprague's role to two sentences that conclude, without naming Sprague, "the tiny carrier group managed to fight off and delay the Japanese."[14]

Annabel lived another thirty-two years before dying in her sleep in San Diego on 22 July 1987. She was buried beside her husband in Fort Rosecrans National Cemetery, sharing not only his final resting spot but the serene view of the Pacific Ocean.[15]

When asked how Sprague would want to be remembered, family members mention qualities such as performance under adverse conditions, doing his job without worrying about being a hero, integrity, honesty, and concern for his men. Perhaps, though, the words Sprague would most appreciate came from a *Fanshaw Bay* seaman. In a 21 September 1947 letter to Sprague, Christopher W. Carson thanked him "for saving our necks" at Samar. Carson then extended an offer that sums up the deep feelings Sprague's men carried then—and still carry today—toward their commander. "If you ever need any help of any kind," the seaman stated to the admiral, "my address is below. Please don't hesitate to call on me."[16]

Clifton Sprague, the midshipman whose fellow classmates at Annapolis called a true-blue comrade, could ask for no more appropriate remembrance.

Awards

1. NAVY CROSS for the 25 October 1944 action off Samar.
2. LEGION OF MERIT MEDAL for his command of the *Wasp*.
3. GOLD STAR in lieu of the Second Legion of Merit for the Morotai landings.
4. GOLD STAR in lieu of the Third Legion of Merit for the Iwo Jima and Okinawa operations.
5. GOLD STAR in lieu of the Fourth Legion of Merit for Operation Crossroads.
6. PRESIDENTIAL UNIT CITATION to Task Unit 77.4.3, the escort carriers and screen he commanded off Samar.
7. The guided missile frigate USS *Clifton Sprague* (FFG–16) is launched at Bath, Maine, on 16 February 1980.
8. Inducted into the CARRIER AVIATION HALL OF FAME in Charleston, South Carolina, on 13 October 1985.

→ NOTES ←

ONE: "The Crowd Will Cheer"

Most of the material for this chapter comes from the Sprague family. Foremost are the letters and documents from the Clifton A. F. Sprague Collection housed in Monte Sereno, California, to which I was given free access (the collection will be donated to the Naval Historical Center in Washington, D.C., upon publication of this biography). The collection consists of Sprague's official records, personal papers, flight logs, official and personal correspondence, and an extensive photographic section. I relied heavily on this source throughout my book.

His daughters, Courtney Sprague Vaughan and Patricia Sprague Reneau, wrote a 1992 family biography of their father, *Remembered and Honored*. The book is a valuable source and the daughters were very gracious in allowing me to examine an early draft of the book.

Family members shared relevant information with me during lengthy interviews. Especially helpful for this chapter was Sprague's sister, Dorothea Sprague Harvey, who filled in some gaps of her brother's youth and education.

1. Reneau and Vaughan, *Remembered and Honored,* 1–2 (hereinafter cited as Reneau/ Vaughan); Josephine Heinzelman letter to Patricia Reneau, 6 June 1981.
2. Reneau/Vaughan, 2; Heinzelman letter to Reneau.
3. Reneau/Vaughan, 2.
4. Reneau/Vaughan, 3–4.
5. Reneau/Vaughan, 4–5; Dorothea Sprague Harvey letter to Patricia Reneau, 7 January 1980.
6. Ibid.
7. Reneau/Vaughan, 5; Harvey letter to Reneau.
8. Author's interview with Dorothea Harvey, 25 October 1991; Reneau/Vaughan, 5–6.
9. Dorothea Harvey interview; Reneau/Vaughan, 7.
10. Dorothea Harvey interview.
11. Author's interview with Daniel Vaughan, 11 December 1993.
12. Dorothea Harvey interview.
13. Heinzelman letter to Reneau; Reneau/Vaughan, 5.
14. Harvey letter to Reneau; Dorothea Harvey interview.
15. Reneau/Vaughan, 5.

16. Milton Public Schools' 1910 Graduation Exercises program; Reneau/Vaughan, 7–8; Harvey letter to Reneau.
17. Reneau/Vaughan, 8–9.
18. Dorothea Harvey interview.
19. Harold P. Drisko letter to Courtney Vaughan, 4 May 1976; Reneau/Vaughan, 9; author's interview with Anne Thompson, 27 January 1993.
20. Gerhard Rehder letter to Courtney Vaughan, 20 April 1976; Roxbury Latin School Official Records.
21. Drisko letter to Vaughan, 27 April 1976; Drisko letter to Vaughan, 4 May 1976; *The Tripod,* Roxbury Latin's school newspaper, 1913.
22. Drisko letters to Vaughan, 27 April and 4 May 1976.
23. Drisko letter to Vaughan, 27 April 1976; Reneau/Vaughan, 10.
24. Laurin Hall Healy and Luis Kutner, *The Admiral,* 28; Reneau/Vaughan, 11.
25. Reneau/Vaughan, 11–12.
26. Reneau/Vaughan, 12; Victor Blue, chief of the Bureau of Navigation, letter to Clifton Sprague, 20 December 1913.
27. Frank Plumley letter to Clifford [*sic*] Sprague, 30 March 1914; Carroll Page letter to Clifton Sprague, 7 April 1914; Reneau/Vaughan, 12.
28. Reneau/Vaughan, 13–14; Page letter to Clifton Sprague, 20 May 1914.
29. Reneau/Vaughan, 14; author's interview with Courtney Vaughan, 16 August 1991.

T W O : "A Friend Once, a Friend Always"

I supplemented material from the Clifton A. F. Sprague Collection with Sprague's official Naval Academy file and editions of the Academy yearbook, *Lucky Bag,* for the years he attended, 1914–17. The friendly and expert assistance I received from staff members at the Naval Academy's Chester W. Nimitz Library made my research in Annapolis much easier than it might have been.

1. Howarth, *To Shining Sea,* 275; Fleming, "School for Sailors," 98.
2. Sweetman, *The U.S. Naval Academy,* 158.
3. Puleston, *Annapolis,* 135–37; Ageton, "Annapolis, Mother of Navy Men," 1502; Lewis, "Description of the United States Naval Academy," 1461; Duval, *Guide to Historic Annapolis and U.S. Naval Academy,* 52; Fleming, "School for Sailors," 90–99.
4. Reneau/Vaughan, 15; Clifton A. F. Sprague Annapolis File (hereinafter cited as Sprague Annapolis File); Potter, *Admiral Arleigh Burke,* 10; Stevens, *Annapolis,* 307–12.
5. Eller, "Navy Life Begins," 1521–22; Stevens, *Annapolis,* 307–12; Reneau/Vaughan, 15.
6. *Regulations of the U.S. Naval Academy,* 94–115.
7. Sprague Annapolis File.
8. Reneau/Vaughan, 16.
9. Ibid.; *Lucky Bag,* 1915.

10. Ibid.
11. Lovette, *School of the Sea,* 112; Reneau/Vaughan, 17.
12. Reneau/Vaughan, 15, 17–18.
13. Sweetman, *The U.S. Naval Academy,* 160.
14. Buell, *The Quiet Warrior,* 11–13.
15. Sweetman, *The U.S. Naval Academy,* 159; Stevens, *Annapolis,* 314; Gallery, *Eight Bells, and All's Well,* 32; Ageton, "Annapolis, Mother of Navy Men," 1511; Potter, *Nimitz,* 51; Buell, *The Quiet Warrior,* 13.
16. *Annual Register of the U.S. Naval Academy,* 1915, 1916, 1917.
17. Potter, *Nimitz,* 49.
18. Fleming, "School for Sailors," 96–97.
19. Alden, "The Changing Naval Academy: A Retrospect of Twenty-five Years," 498; Potter, *The United States and World Sea Power,* 411–12; Howarth, *To Shining Sea,* 267–68; Potter, *Nimitz,* 53.
20. Potter, *Nimitz,* 53.
21. *Lucky Bag,* 1918; Reneau/Vaughan, 15 (fn).
22. Ibid.
23. Ibid.
24. Courtney Vaughan interview; Patricia Reneau interview.
25. Courtney Vaughan interview.
26. Reneau/Vaughan, 19–20.
27. Clifton Sprague to Dorothea Sprague, undated letter.
28. Sweetman, *The U.S. Naval Academy,* 167–68.
29. Ibid.; Puleston, *Annapolis,* 120.
30. Reneau/Vaughan, 20.
31. Marshall, *The American Heritage History of World War I,* 204; Link, *Woodrow Wilson and the Progressive Era,* 274.
32. Link, *Woodrow Wilson and the Progressive Era,* 281–82; Marshall, *The American Heritage History of World War I,* 205–6.
33. Lovette, *School of the Sea,* 112; Bolander, "The Naval Academy in Five Wars," 43.
34. Reneau/Vaughan, 21; Clifton Sprague to Hazel Sprague, undated letter.
35. Sweetman, *The U.S. Naval Academy,* 168–69.
36. Bolander, "The Naval Academy in Five Wars," 43; Reneau/Vaughan, 21–23.

THREE: "A Pleasure to Serve"

Most of the material for this chapter came from the Naval Historical Center in Washington, D.C., or from the Sprague family. The most valuable source proved to be the official file for the USS *Wheeling* located in the Ships' Histories Section of the Naval Historical Center.

1. Mooney, *Dictionary of American Naval Fighting Ships, Vol. VIII,* 248 (hereinafter cited as *Dictionary*).
2. Ibid.; "Historical Sketch of the USS *Wheeling*" (Ships' Histories Section, Naval Historical Center, 13 July 1923), 1 (hereinafter cited as "Historical Sketch"); "His-

tory of the USS *Wheeling*" (Ships' Histories Section, Naval Historical Center, 13 June 1955), 1 (hereinafter cited as "History").

3. "Historical Sketch," 1.
4. "Historical Sketch," 1; "History," 3; *Dictionary*, 248.
5. Gunner's Mate 1st Class Leroy W. Kolster to Clifton Sprague, 2 December 1944; "Listing of Decorations and Citations, Vice Admiral C. A. F. Sprague," in the Clifton Sprague Collection.
6. "Historical Sketch," 2–3; *Dictionary*, 249.
7. "Historical Sketch," 3; *Dictionary*, 249; "History," 3.
8. "Historical Sketch," 3; *Dictionary*, 249; Dorothea Harvey interview.
9. "Historical Sketch," 4.
10. Ibid.; Reneau/Vaughan, 4; Dorothea Harvey interview.
11. "Historical Sketch," 4–7; *Dictionary*, 249; "History," 3.
12. "Historical Sketch," 7; "History," p. 3; "Listing of Decorations and Citations, Vice Admiral C. A. F. Sprague"; Kolster letter to Sprague.
13. Reneau/Vaughan, 26.

FOUR: The Emerging Commander

Interviews with family members, supplemented by his daughters' biography and material from the Clifton A. F. Sprague Collection, form the core of this chapter. An extensive interview that stretched over two sessions with Adm. James Russell, who served with Sprague on board the carrier *Yorktown* in the 1930s, yielded excellent material. Sprague's Flight Logs for this period were of immense help.

1. Reneau/Vaughan, 28.
2. Van Deurs, *Wings for the Fleet*, 97, 103; Caras, *Wings of Gold*, 39.
3. Author's interview with Adm. James Russell, 14 April 1992; Woodhouse, "U.S. Naval Aeronautic Policies, 1904–1942," 174; Reneau/Vaughan, 30; Tomlinson, "Flying Blind," 19; Sprague's Naval Aviator Certification.
4. Patricia Reneau interview; Courtney Vaughan interview; author's interview with Daniel Vaughan, 11 December 1993.
5. Reneau/Vaughan, 29.
6. Arnold, *Global Mission*, 16; Coffey, *Hap*, 61.
7. Van Deurs, *Wings for the Fleet*, 4; Gallery, *Eight Bells, and All's Well*, 72–73; Adm. James Russell interview; Tomlinson, "Flying Blind," 19.
8. Sprague Flight Log, 1921, 1922, 1923.
9. Reneau/Vaughan, 30–31.
10. Ibid., 31.
11. Ibid., 28; Arpee, *From Frigates to Flat-Tops*, 160.
12. Reynolds, *Admiral John H. Towers*, 44, 106; Woodhouse, "U.S. Naval Aeronautic Policies, 1904–1942," 167, 174; Wukovits, "Nothing Is Impossible," 57.
13. Courtney Vaughan interview.
14. Arpee, *From Frigates to Flat-Tops*, 121; Potter, *The United States and World Sea Power*, 591–92; Reynolds, *Admiral John H. Towers*, 190.

15. Arpee, *From Frigates to Flat-Tops*, 121.

16. Reynolds, *Admiral John H. Towers*, 176, 194–95; Wragg, *Wings Over the Sea*, 58; Arpee, *From Frigates to Flat-Tops*, 109; Howarth, *To Shining Sea*, 331, 344.

17. Reneau/Vaughan, 34–35; Deputy Chief of Naval Operations (Air) and the Commander, Naval Air Systems Command, *United States Naval Aviation, 1910–1970*, 55 (hereinafter cited as *Naval Aviation, 1910–1970*); Caras, *Wings of Gold*, 79–80.

18. Turnbull and Lord, *History of United States Naval Aviation*, 268–69; Reneau/Vaughan, 39; Johnson, *Fly Navy*, 133.

19. Weekly News Letter from Lt. Comdr. D. C. Ramsey, week ending 8 June 1929, in Records of the Superintendent, General Correspondence, Support Facilities Box No. 2, Folders No. 2, 3, 4 in the Admiral Nimitz Collection, Nimitz Library, U.S. Naval Academy (hereinafter cited as Weekly News Letter).

20. Weekly News Letter, 8 June 1929 and 15 June 1929; Lord, *Incredible Victory*, 142–46.

21. Weekly News Letter, 8 June 1929 and 15 June 1929; Navy News Release, 3 September 1951, in the Aviation File of the Admiral Nimitz Collection; Arpee, *From Frigates to Flat-Tops*, 156–58; Turnbull and Lord, *History of United States Naval Aviation*, 268–69.

22. Sprague Flight Log, 25 June 1929; Halsey and Bryan, *Admiral Halsey's Story*, 51–52; Potter, *Bull Halsey*, 123–25; Reneau/Vaughan, 39–40.

23. Reneau/Vaughan, 31; C. A. F. Sprague, "Duties Performed" Card, in the Clifton Sprague Collection.

24. Sprague, "Duties Performed"; Reneau/Vaughan, 36; Stern, *The Lexington Class Carriers*, 112–14; *Naval Aviation, 1910–1970*, 52.

25. Reneau/Vaughan, 36; Sprague, "Duties Performed"; Patricia Reneau interview.

26. Poolman, *Allied Escort Carriers of World War II in Action*, 217; "Vice Admiral Clifton A. F. Sprague," Sprague Biographical File, Naval Historical Center, Washington, D.C.; Reynolds, *Famous American Admirals*, 323.

27. Reynolds, *Admiral John H. Towers*, 215.

28. Stern, *The Lexington Class Carriers*, 119; Arpee, *From Frigates to Flat-Tops*, 154.

29. Reynolds, *Admiral John H. Towers*, 217–18.

30. Wilson, *Slipstream*, 129.

31. Johnson, *Fly Navy*, 138–41; Wilson, *Slipstream*, 135.

32. Arpee, *From Frigates to Flat-Tops*, 155–56; *Naval Aviation, 1910–1970*, 63–64.

33. Reneau/Vaughan, 40–41; Rear Adm. E. H. Eckelmeyer letter to Henry Pyzdrowski, 17 March 1989.

34. Eckelmeyer letter to Pyzdrowski.

35. Ibid.

36. Ibid.; Reneau/Vaughan, 36, 42, 44; author's interview with Rear Adm. E. H. Eckelmeyer, 27 September 1993.

37. Author's interview with Daniel Vaughan, 11 December 1993.

38. "Sprague Blazes Aerial Trail," undated, unnamed newspaper article in the Clifton Sprague Collection; Reneau/Vaughan, 42–43.

39. Reneau/Vaughan, 42.

40. Ibid., 44.

41. Ibid., 46; Letter of Commendation, Capt. Aubrey Fitch to Lt. Comdr. Sprague.

42. Reneau/Vaughan, 52; Stern, *The Lexington Class Carriers,* 61–62.

43. Stern, *The Lexington Class Carriers,* 116, 150; author's interview with Adm. James H. Russell, 14 April 1992.

44. Sprague Flight Log, November 1937; Courtney Vaughan interview; Admiral Russell interviews, 14 April and 21 April 1992; Reneau/Vaughan, 55.

45. *Dictionary,* 534.

46. Adm. George W. Anderson letter to Courtney Vaughan, 12 March 1979.

47. Ibid.

48. Admiral Russell interviews.

49. Reneau/Vaughan, 57–58.

50. Ibid., 58–59.

51. Ibid., 59; "*Patoka* Placed in Commission," untitled, undated newspaper article in the Clifton Sprague Collection; "Christmas, 1939," the Christmas roster and menu of the *Patoka.*

52. Reneau/Vaughan, 61.

53. George S. Hausen letter to Patricia Reneau, 24 March 1981; Reneau/Vaughan, 61.

54. George S. Hausen letter to his grandmother, 2 April 1940; Frank Stewart letter to Patricia Reneau, 10 February 1981.

55. Hausen letter to Reneau; Hausen letter to grandmother; Stewart letter to Reneau, Reneau/Vaughan, 63–65.

56. Reneau/Vaughan, 65–67; Hausen letter to Reneau; Stewart letter to Reneau.

57. Reneau/Vaughan, 31.

58. Bruccoli, *Some Sort of Grandeur,* 17.

59. Reneau/Vaughan, 32; Dorothea Harvey interview.

60. Ibid.

61. Daniel Vaughan interview.

62. Reneau/Vaughan, 32–33.

63. Ibid., 33–34.

64. Ibid., p. 37; Courtney Vaughan interview; Patricia Reneau interview.

65. Reneau/Vaughan, 40; Dorothea Harvey interview; Courtney Vaughan interview.

66. Reneau/Vaughan, 40.

67. Bruccoli and Duggan, *Correspondence of F. Scott Fitzgerald,* 451; Mellow, *Invented Lives,* 450–51; Reneau/Vaughan, 53.

68. F. Scott Fitzgerald letter to Annabel Sprague, 10 September 1936, in Bruccoli, 448–450.

69. Courtney Vaughan interview; Reneau/Vaughan, 69.

70. Bruccoli, *Correspondence of F. Scott Fitzgerald,* 544, 601; Turnbull, *Scott Fitzgerald,* 305.

71. Mellow, *Invented Lives,* 451; Daniel Vaughan interview; Courtney Vaughan interview; Patricia Reneau interview.

FIVE: "All Right for My Money"

Official records from the Naval Historical Center heavily supplemented the Clifton Sprague Collection for this chapter. Sprague's action reports were particularly valuable.

I also received important information from the men who served with Sprague on the *Tangier*. They provided clues on his style of command as well as added a human element to 7 December.

1. Reneau/Vaughan, 67–68; Courtney Vaughan interview; Patricia Reneau interview.
2. Clifton Sprague letter to Courtney Sprague, 23 September 1947.
3. Patricia Reneau interview; Reneau/Vaughan, 60.
4. Reneau/Vaughan, 68.
5. Lt. (jg) Leon J. Kehoe, Ret., letter to the Chief of Naval Operations, 3 May 1954.
6. Clifton Sprague letter to Comdr. D. Ketcham, 30 April 1941; Ketcham letter to Clifton Sprague, 2 May 1941.
7. Kehoe letter to the Chief of Naval Operations; *Dictionary, Volume VII*, 40–41.
8. Reynolds, *Famous American Admirals*, 325.
9. Wesley L. Larson letter to Patricia Reneau, 10 February 1981; author's interview with Larson, 15 April 1992; author's interview with Richard L. Fruin, Jr., 25 April 1992.
10. Author's interview with Joseph Mapes, 9 April 1992; author's interview with C. A. Wilkinson, Jr., 20 April 1992; Reneau/Vaughan, 73; Roster of Officers, USS *Tangier*, 1 December 1941.
11. Richard L. Fruin interview; Joseph Mapes interview.
12. Author's interview with Leonard Barnes, 4 April 1992; Richard L. Fruin interview; Joseph Mapes interview.
13. Wesley L. Larson interview; Leonard Barnes interview; author's interview with John Hughes, 24 April 1992.
14. John Hughes interview.
15. Author's interview with Robert Isacksen, 3 April 1992.
16. Robert Isacksen interview; Joseph Mapes interview.
17. Leonard Barnes interview; C. A. Wilkinson interview.
18. Courtney Vaughan interview, 16 August 1991; Leonard Barnes interview; Richard L. Fruin interview.
19. Richard L. Fruin interview.
20. Reneau/Vaughan, 75; Daniel Vaughan interview.
21. Costello, *The Pacific War, 1941–1945*, 118–19; Morison, *The Two-Ocean War*, 46; Fuchida and Okumiya, *Midway: The Battle That Doomed Japan*, 25.
22. Reneau/Vaughan, 75; Costello, *The Pacific War*, 120–21.
23. Robert Isacksen interview; Reneau/Vaughan, 75–76.
24. Costello, *The Pacific War*, 120–21.
25. Wesley Larson interview; Reneau/Vaughan, 76–77; author's interview with Robert Munroe, 23 February 1993.
26. Costello, *The Pacific War*, 124.

27. Morison, *Two-Ocean War,* 49; Costello, *The Pacific War,* 129–32; Fuchida, *Midway,* 26–27; Fuchida, "I Led the Air Attack on Pearl Harbor," 53–55.

28. C. A. F. Sprague, commanding officer, USS *Tangier* (AV-8), to commander in chief, Pacific Fleet, "Official Report on the Pearl Harbor Air Raid, January 2, 1942" (hereinafter cited as Clifton Sprague to CinCPac, 2 January 1942); Costello, *The Pacific War,* 133–34; Reneau/Vaughan, 77; Morison, *History of the United States Naval Operations in World War II, Volume III: The Rising Sun in the Pacific, 1931–April 1942,* 102–3.

29. Morison, *Two-Ocean War,* 54; Hough, *The Longest Battle; the War at Sea, 1939–1945,* 70.

30. Costello, *The Pacific War,* 134; Morison, *Two-Ocean War,* 56, 60.

31. Richard L. Fruin interview.

32. Larson letter to Reneau, 10 February 1981; Wesley L. Larson interview.

33. Leonard Barnes interview; Richard L. Fruin interview; Joseph Mapes interview; C. A. Wilkinson Private Monograph, 1977.

34. Costello, *The Pacific War,* 135; Leonard Barnes interview; Clifton Sprague to CinCPac, 2 January 1942.

35. Clifton Sprague to CinCPac, 2 January 1942.

36. Wesley Larson interview; Larson letter to Reneau.

37. Clifton Sprague to CinCPac, 2 January 1942; G. H. DeBaun, executive officer, to C. A. F. Sprague, commanding officer, "Report of Engagement between the USS *Tangier* (AV-8) and Japanese Airplanes on December 7, 1941," 11 December 1941 (hereinafter cited as DeBaun Report); Lord, *Day of Infamy,* 69; W. B. Fletcher, "U.S.S. *Tangier*," personal narrative.

38. Author's interview with John F. Dore, 22 July 1993.

39. Clifton Sprague to CinCPac, 2 January 1942; Wesley Larson interview; Morison, *Two-Ocean War,* 59; Costello, *The Pacific War,* 136.

40. Wesley Larson interview; Leonard Barnes interview.

41. John Hughes interview.

42. DeBaun Report; Morison, *The Rising Sun in the Pacific,* 102; Costello, *The Pacific War,* 137.

43. Clifton Sprague to CinCPac, 2 January 1942; Costello, *The Pacific War,* 139; Morison, *The Rising Sun in the Pacific,* 115; R. A. West, RM1c, USS *Tangier* (AV-8), "Notes of Surprise Attack by Japanese Planes on Pearl Harbor, T.H., as Taken by R. A. West, RM1c while at General Quarters Station on Bridge," 7 December 1941 (hereinafter cited as West Notes).

44. Leonard Barnes interview.

45. Costello, *The Pacific War,* 139; Morison, *The Rising Sun in the Pacific,* 115; Richard L. Fruin letter to Admiral Hansen, 27 May 1947; Wesley Larson letter to Clifton Sprague, 15 June 1946; G. H. DeBaun letter to Rick Dillard, 16 June 1979.

46. Fuchida, *Midway,* 30–31; Costello, *The Pacific War,* 139; Morison, *Two-Ocean War,* 67; Clifton Sprague to CinCPac, 2 January 1942.

47. Clifton Sprague to CinCPac, 2 January 1942; West Notes.

48. Walter F. Hamelrath letter to Patricia Reneau, 25 May 1987.

49. Clifton Sprague to CinCPac, 2 January 1942; DeBaun Report.

50. Fruin letter to Hansen; Clifton Sprague letter to Bennett Oden, 29 May 1943; Clifton Sprague to CinCPac, 2 January 1942.

51. Clifton Sprague to CinCPac, 2 January 1942; West Notes; Richard L. Fruin interview.

52. Clifton Sprague to CinCPac, 2 January 1942.

53. Ibid.; Sprague letter to Oden; DeBaun letter to Dillard.

54. Belote and Belote, *Titans of the Sea,* 13; Costello, *The Pacific War,* 139–40.

55. Costello, *The Pacific War,* 140–43; Fuchida, *Midway,* 31; Morison, *Two-Ocean War,* 67; Belote and Belote, *Titans of the Sea,* 13.

56. Wilkinson Monograph; Lord, *Day of Infamy,* 165–66; Fletcher narrative; *Tangier* Deck Log.

57. West Notes; author's interview with Orban R. Chambless, 8 April 1992.

58. West Notes; John Dore interview.

59. Wilkinson Monograph; West Notes; Morison, *Two-Ocean War,* 68; Richard L. Fruin interview; Richard L. Fruin letter to Rick Dillard, 3 May 1979.

60. Richard L. Fruin interview; Fruin letter to Dillard.

61. DeBaun Report; DeBaun letter to Dillard.

62. Clifton Sprague to CinCPac, 2 January 1942; Clifton Sprague, commanding officer, USS *Tangier* (AV-8), to commander in chief, Pacific Fleet, "Reports of Individual Ships Concerning Meritorious Action of Personnel," 4 February 1942 (hereinafter cited as Clifton Sprague to CinCPac, 4 February 1942).

63. C. A. F. Sprague to Secretary of the Navy, 7 July 1946; C. W. Nimitz, commander in chief, Pacific Fleet to C. A. F. Sprague, commanding officer, USS *Tangier* (AV-8), 12 May 1942; Clifton Sprague to CinCPac, 4 February 1942; C. A. F. Sprague to Rear Adm. Robert A. Theobold, president of the Board of Awards, 21 March 1942; Larson letter to Reneau.

64. Sprague letter to Oden; Clifton Sprague letter to Dorothea Harvey, 2 February 1942; Sprague message to the USS *Tangier* Officers and Crew, 8 December 1941.

65. Hamelrath letter to Reneau; Leon J. Kehoe letter to Annabel Sprague, 12 April 1955; Adm. P. N. Bellinger, ComAirPac, commander, Patrol Wing Two to C. A. F. Sprague, Letter of Commendation, 25 December 1941; Joseph Mapes interview, 9 April 1992.

66. Richard R. Lingeman, *Don't You Know There's A War On?* 26; Reneau/Vaughan, 92.

67. Reneau/Vaughan, 92–93.

68. Ibid.

69. Clifton Sprague letter to Dorothea Harvey.

70. Hough, *The Longest Battle,* 79.

SIX: "We Might Have Made It"

As is true for most chapters, while official government records formed the skeleton of the story, letters and documents in the Clifton Sprague Collection and interviews with family and *Tangier* crew members fleshed out the narrative.

1. West Notes; author's interview with Henry Frietas, 8 April 1992.
2. West Notes.
3. Ibid.
4. Ibid.; John Toland, *Infamy*, 18.
5. Schultz, *Wake Island*, 10–11; Wukovits, "A Nation's Inspiration," 34.
6. Butcher, "Admiral Frank Jack Fletcher, Pioneer Warrior or Gross Sinner?" 71.
7. Andrews, "The Defense of Wake," 10; Lundstrom, "Frank Jack Fletcher Got a Bum Rap," 24; Layton, Pineau, and Costello, *And I Was There*, 331; C. A. Wilkinson interview, 7 April 1992; Larson letter to Reneau; Joseph Mapes interview; Wesley Larson interview; Morison, *The Rising Sun in the Pacific*, 226–27.
8. Schultz, *Wake Island*, 68–69; Morison, *The Rising Sun in the Pacific*, 235–36; Heinl, *Soldiers of the Sea*, 329–30.
9. Heinl, *Soldiers of the Sea*, 329; Larson letter to Reneau; Schultz, *Wake Island*, 86–87.
10. Morison, *The Rising Sun in the Pacific*, 242.
11. Ibid., 242–43; author's interview with Norris G. Edwards, 21 July 1993; C. A. Wilkinson interview.
12. Norris G. Edwards interview; Wilkinson Monograph, 17.
13. Norris G. Edwards interview; Heinl, *Soldiers of the Sea*, 332.
14. Heinl, *Soldiers of the Sea*, 332; Schultz, *Wake Island*, 92–93.
15. Schultz, *Wake Island*, 93, 99; Robert Isacksen interview; Heinl, *The Defense of Wake*, 38; Wukovits, "A Nation's Inspiration," 34; Heinl, *Soldiers of the Sea*, 331.
16. Morison, *The Rising Sun in the Pacific*, 243, 250–51; Schultz, *Wake Island*, 110–11.
17. Robert Isacksen interview; copy of order in the Clifton Sprague Collection.
18. Schultz, *Wake Island*, 107, 110–11; Morison, *The Rising Sun in the Pacific*, 250.
19. Morison, *The Rising Sun in the Pacific*, 244; Schultz, *Wake Island*, 107; Reneau/Vaughan, 103.
20. Wukovits, "A Nation's Inspiration," 36; Heinl, *Soldiers of the Sea*, 332–33; Morison, *The Rising Sun in the Pacific*, 251–52.
21. Andrews, "The Defense of Wake," 73, 78; Schultz, *Wake Island*, 144–45; Morison, *The Rising Sun in the Pacific*, 252.
22. John Dore interview; Richard Fruin interview; Henry Frietas interview; Robert Isacksen interview; Heinl, *Soldiers of the Sea*, 332–33.
23. Layton, Pineau, and Costello, *And I Was There*, 346–47; Morison, *The Rising Sun in the Pacific*, 253–54; Robert J. Casey, *Torpedo Junction*, 36–37.
24. Schultz, *Wake Island*, 145; Clifton Sprague's handwritten comment on Fletcher order in the Clifton Sprague Collection; Morison, *The Rising Sun in the Pacific*, 254.
25. John Dore interview.
26. Larson letter to Reneau; Fletcher Narrative; Clifton Sprague message to crew, 12 December 1941 in the Clifton Sprague Collection.
27. Larson letter to Reneau.
28. Wesley Larson interview; Joseph Mapes interview; Henry Frietas interview.
29. Joseph Mapes interview.
30. Wilkinson Monograph; Reneau/Vaughan, 104; Fletcher Narrative.
31. Clifton Sprague letter to Dorothea Harvey.
32. Clifton Sprague letter to Annabel Sprague, 9 February 1942; Reneau/Vaughan, 104–5.

33. Kehoe letter to the Chief of Naval Operations; History of the *Tangier,* in ship's file at Naval Historical Center, 3 (hereinafter cited as History of *Tangier*); Fletcher Narrative.

34. Kehoe letter to the Chief of Naval Operations; Richard L. Fruin letter to Rick Dillard, 15 November 1978; G. H. DeBaun letter to Rick Dillard, 16 June 1979; Clifton Sprague to the Flag Officer Commanding Australian Squadron, 18 March 1942.

35. History of *Tangier,* 3; Kehoe letter to the Chief of Naval Operations.

36. Fletcher Narrative.

37. Norris Edwards interview.

38. Ibid.

39. Kehoe letter to the Chief of Naval Operations.

40. Norris Edwards interview; Kehoe letter to the Chief of Naval Operations.

41. Hamelrath letter to Reneau.

42. Clifton Sprague letter to Dorothea Harvey.

SEVEN: Atlantic Interlude

The Gulf Sea Frontier is an under-researched area of World War II that awaits a definitive account, although Michael Gannon filled part of the void with his excellent *Operation Drumbeat* in 1990. Besides that book and the Clifton Sprague Collection, I relied upon a fine organizational history written in 1946 by Lt. (jg) John A. Reynolds, *History of the Gulf Sea Frontier.*

1. Reneau/Vaughan, 106.

2. Michael Gannon, *Operation Drumbeat,* 347–48; Morison, *The Two-Ocean War,* 108–9.

3. Hough, *The Longest Battle,* 54–55.

4. Adams, *1942: The Year That Doomed the Axis,* 70, 74; Morison, *The Two-Ocean War,* 115; Buell, *Master of Sea Power,* 264–65; Morison, *The Battle of the Atlantic,* 137.

5. Gannon, *Operation Drumbeat,* 349–50; Adams, *1942: The Year That Doomed the Axis,* 73, 75.

6. Reynolds, *History of the Gulf Sea Frontier,* 97, 222; Morison, *The Two-Ocean War,* 121.

7. Gannon, *Operation Drumbeat,* 389.

8. Ibid., 347; Reynolds, *History of the Gulf Sea Frontier,* 27–28.

9. Reynolds, *History of the Gulf Sea Frontier,* 27–28.

10. Gannon, *Operation Drumbeat,* 350–57; Vaeth, *Blimps & U-Boats,* 27–28; Rear Adm. James Dudley letter to Patricia Reneau, 19 June 1981.

11. Morison, *The Battle of the Atlantic,* 138; Bishop, "'Hooligan's Navy': Coastal Pickets at War," 46–48; Gannon, *Operation Drumbeat,* 351–53; Morison, *The Two-Ocean War,* 131.

12. Gannon, *Operation Drumbeat,* 385–86; Adams, *1942: The Year That Doomed the Axis,* 77–78; Reynolds, *History of the Gulf Sea Frontier,* 230–32.

13. Reynolds, *History of the Gulf Sea Frontier,* 121–22; Dudley letter to Reneau.
14. Dudley letter to Reneau.
15. Adams, *1942: The Year That Doomed the Axis,* 78; Howarth, *To Shining Sea,* 425.
16. Reynolds, *History of the Gulf Sea Frontier,* 122–45; Gannon, *Operation Drumbeat,* 388.
17. Dudley letter to Reneau; Reneau/Vaughan, 113–14; Reynolds, *History of the Gulf Sea Frontier,* 147.
18. Reynolds, *Famous American Admirals,* 74–75, 306–7, 325–26.
19. Author's interview with Henry Pyzdrowski, 2 October 1993.

EIGHT: Seek Out and Destroy Our Foe

The most important sources for this chapter were the *Wasp's* official records, most of which can be found on microfilm #NRS 1981-9, which contains the carrier's war history, diary, and official reports. I made frequent use of the ship's newsletter, *Waspirit.* In addition to providing a refreshing and informative look at life on board the *Wasp,* it reflected the crew's wait-and-see attitude toward their new commander and their eventual acceptance of Sprague. Interviews with *Wasp* pilots and crew added relevant detail.

1. *Dictionary, Volume VIII,* 148; "U.S.S. *Wasp*: World War II History," 1 (hereinafter cited as "*Wasp*: History"; Marvin H. Bender, *The Mighty Stinger,* 12.
2. *Waspirit,* 15 July 1944, 1.
3. Author's interview with Robert P. Daly, 23 February 1993; Reneau/Vaughan, 117; "*Wasp*: History," 1.
4. *Waspirit,* 18 May 1944, 7; *Waspirit,* 15 July 1944, 8; Comdr. Charles C. Cunningham letter to Annabel Sprague, 21 April 1955.
5. *Waspirit,* 18 May 1944, 7.
6. *Waspirit,* 15 July 1944, 8.
7. Reneau/Vaughan, 117; Eleanor Roosevelt letter to Captain Sprague, 4 December 1943.
8. *Dictionary,* 148; "*Wasp*: History," 2.
9. "*Wasp*: History," 3.
10. Reneau/Vaughan, 121–22.
11. *Waspirit,* 15 July 1944, 7; "*Wasp*: History," 3–4.
12. *Waspirit,* 15 July 1944, 7.
13. Ibid., 8; John A. Roosevelt letter to Mrs. C. A. F. Sprague, 13 April 1955.
14. *Waspirit,* 15 July 1944, 8.
15. "*Wasp*: History," 4–5; Reneau/Vaughan, 125–26.
16. "*Wasp*: History," 5; Bender, *The Mighty Stinger,* 12.
17. Bender, *The Mighty Stinger,* 14; "Wasp: History," 6.
18. "*Wasp*: History," 6–8; Bender, *The Mighty Stinger,* 15.
19. Reynolds, *The Fast Carriers,* 154.
20. "*Wasp*: History," 9; Bender, *The Mighty Stinger,* 16; Y'Blood, *Red Sun Setting,* 217.
21. "War Diary—Period 1 May–31 May 1944," 4 (hereinafter cited as "War Diary"); "*Wasp*: History," 10.

22. Bender, *The Mighty Stinger,* 16.

23. Ibid., 16–17.

24. "War Diary, 19 May 1944"; *Wasp* Action Report, Attack on Marcus and Wake Islands, 1 June 1944 (hereinafter cited as Action Report).

25. Action Report; author's interview with Robert Carew, 25 February 1992.

26. Action Report.

27. Ibid.; "War Diary, 19–20 May 1944."

28. Robert Carew interview.

29. *Waspirit,* 15 July 1944, 7.

30. "War Diary, 23 May 1944"; Action Report.

31. Action Report.

32. Report from commander, Carrier Division Five to commander in chief, U.S. Fleet, 3 June 1944; Reynolds, *The Fast Carriers,* 154.

33. Reneau/Vaughan, 128.

34. Wukovits, "Every Move Seen," 31–32.

35. Morison, *New Guinea and the Marianas,* 174, 412–15.

36. *Wasp* Action Report, Attack on the Marianas, June 1944, 3 (hereinafter cited as Marianas Action Report).

37. Marianas Action Report, 3; Fulton, "Tail-End Charlie" (hereinafter cited as Fulton Log); Belote and Belote, *Titans of the Sea,* 297; Y'Blood, *Red Sun Setting,* 31–33; Morison, *New Guinea and the Marianas,* 157.

38. Morison, *New Guinea and the Marianas,* 213–19; Spector, *Eagle Against the Sun,* 306–7.

39. Ibid.

40. Marianas Action Report, 3; "War Diary," 4; Hough, *The Longest Battle,* 319–21; Y'Blood, *Red Sun Setting,* 35–45; Belote and Belote, *Titans of the Sea,* 297.

41. Y'Blood, *Red Sun Setting,* 44–45.

42. Marianas Action Report, 3–4; "War Diary," 4; Y'Blood, *Red Sun Setting,* 46–47.

43. Marianas Action Report, 4; Fulton Log, 8–9; Morison, *New Guinea and the Marianas,* 243.

44. Winton, *War in the Pacific,* 126; Spector, *Eagle Against the Sun,* 308.

45. Buell, *The Quiet Warrior,* 263–64, 270–72; Holmes, *Double-Edged Secrets,* 178–80.

46. Marianas Action Report, 4.

47. Collier, *The War in the Far East, 1941–1945,* 444–45; Potter and Nimitz, *Triumph in the Pacific,* 85–86; Spector, *Eagle Against the Sun,* 308.

48. Belote and Belote, *Titans of the Sea,* 302–4.

49. Dull, *A Battle History of the Imperial Japanese Navy (1941–1945),* 305; Morison, *New Guinea and the Marianas,* 258; Spector, *Eagle Against the Sun,* 309.

50. Reneau/Vaughan, 165.

51. Marianas Action Report, 4; Morison, *New Guinea and the Marianas,* 265–66.

52. Winton, *War in the Pacific,* 128; Morison, *New Guinea and the Marianas,* 265–67; Y'Blood, *Red Sun Setting,* 106; Costello, *The Pacific War,* 480; Spector, *Eagle Against the Sun,* 309.

53. Marianas Action Report, 4; Taylor, *The Magnificent Mitscher,* 227; Y'Blood, *Red Sun Setting,* 132.

54. Morison, *New Guinea and the Marianas,* 269; Bender, *The Mighty Stinger,* 25.

55. Marianas Action Report; Belote and Belote, *Titans of the Sea,* 317–18; Morison, *New Guinea and the Marianas,* 269–70.
56. Marianas Action Report; Morison, *New Guinea and the Marianas,* 269–71.
57. Marianas Action Report; Y'Blood, *Red Sun Setting,* 112; author's interview with Everett Fulton, 27 November 1993; Fulton Log, 10.
58. Marianas Action Report.
59. Morison, *New Guinea and the Marianas,* 271–72.
60. Robert Daly interview, 11 November 1993; Marianas Action Report; Morison, *New Guinea and the Marianas,* 272; Y'Blood, *Red Sun Setting,* 133.
61. Marianas Action Report; Y'Blood, *Red Sun Setting,* 133; Bender, *The Mighty Stinger,* 26.
62. Bender, *The Mighty Stinger,* 26; Marianas Action Report.
63. Bender, *The Mighty Stinger,* 26; Robert Carew interview, 18 February 1992.
64. Marianas Action Report; Bender, *The Mighty Stinger,* 26; Robert Carew interview, February 18, 1992.
65. Robert Carew interview, February 18, 1992; Bender, *The Mighty Stinger,* 26–27; Robert Carew letter to the author, 8 November 1991.
66. Marianas Action Report.
67. Ibid.; Everett Fulton interview.
68. Morison, *New Guinea and the Marianas,* 278; Y'Blood, *Red Sun Setting,* 138, 228–29; Marianas Action Report; Bender, *The Mighty Stinger,* 28.
69. Marianas Action Report; Bender, *The Mighty Stinger,* 28–29; Morison, *New Guinea and the Marianas,* 283–84.
70. Robert Daly interview, 11 November 1993.
71. Fulton Log, 11.
72. Marianas Action Report; Everett Fulton interview.
73. Y'Blood, *Red Sun Setting,* 153–54; Spector, *Eagle Against the Sun,* 310–11; Morison, *New Guinea and the Marianas,* 292; Marianas Action Report.
74. Author's interview with Al Walraven, 22 November 1993; Everett Fulton interview; Belote and Belote, *Titans of the Sea,* 334, 337.
75. Spector, *Eagle Against the Sun,* 311; Fulton Log, 11; Robert Daly interview, 6 January 1994.
76. Morison, *New Guinea and the Marianas,* 292; Y'Blood, *Red Sun Setting,* 153–54; Al Walraven interview.
77. Fulton Log, 12; Y'Blood, *Red Sun Setting,* 153–54; Marianas Action Report.
78. Belote and Belote, *Titans of the Sea,* 352.
79. Fulton Log, 16.
80. Everett Fulton interview; Fulton Log, 12–13.
81. Everett Fulton interview; Fulton Log, 13; Y'Blood, *Red Sun Setting,* 179.
82. Bender, *The Mighty Stinger,* 30; Morison, *New Guinea and the Marianas,* 301; Al Walraven interview; Robert Daly interview, 11 November 1993.
83. Fulton Log, 16; Spector, *Eagle Against the Sun,* 311.
84. Spector, *Eagle Against the Sun,* 311; Morison, *New Guinea and the Marianas,* 302; Marianas Action Report; Robert Daly interview, 11 November 1993.
85. Marianas Action Report; Everett Fulton interview; Fulton Log, 14.
86. Cunningham letter to Annabel Sprague; author's interview with Donald Duggan, 24 February 1992; Robert Daly interview, 11 November 1993.

87. Robert Daly interview, 11 November 1993; Fulton Log, 16.

88. Marianas Action Report; Marianas "War Diary"; Bender, *The Mighty Stinger,* 30–31; Robert Daly interview, 11 November 1993; Fulton Log, 16.

89. Author's interview with Vice Adm. Walter D. Gaddis, 20 November 1993; Robert Daly interview, 11 November 1993.

90. Everett Fulton interview; Fulton Log, 16.

91. Spector, *Eagle Against the Sun,* 311; Marianas Action Report; Y'Blood, *Red Sun Setting,* 234–35.

92. Fulton Log, 16.

93. Reynolds, *The Fast Carriers,* 202–3; Marianas Action Report; Marianas "War Diary."

94. Fulton Log, 16–18.

95. Fulton Log, 18; Marianas "War Diary."

96. Marianas "War Diary"; Marianas Action Report.

97. Marianas Action Report; Morison, *New Guinea and the Marianas,* 300–301; Okumiya and Horikoshi, *Zero,* 321; Hough, *The Longest Battle,* 325.

98. Marianas Action Report; "Recommendation for Awards," C. A. F. Sprague, commanding officer, to commander, Task Force 58, 29 June 1944 (hereinafter cited as "Awards").

99. "Awards."

100. Ibid.

101. Marianas Action Report.

102. C. A. F. Sprague, commanding officer, to Mrs. Lucy Clifton, 3 January 1944; C. A. F. Sprague, commanding officer, to Mr. Walter S. Crawford, 16 February 1944.

103. C. A. F. Sprague, commanding officer, to Mrs. Lyra Bridges, undated.

104. Reneau/Vaughan, 238; Marianas Action Report; "Admiral Sprague Decorated," New York *Herald Tribune,* 14 January 1945; "Adm. Sprague Honored for Heroism in Pacific," Philadelphia *Inquirer,* 15 January 1945.

105. *Waspirit,* 15 July 1944, 7; Robert Carew interview, 25 February 1992; Everett Fulton interview.

106. Y'Blood, *Red Sun Setting,* 211–12; Spector, *Eagle Against the Sun,* 312; Buell, *The Quiet Warrior,* 277.

107. Potter, *Bull Halsey,* 271–72; Hough, *The Longest Battle,* 325.

108. Marianas "War Diary."

109. Ibid.; Marianas Action Report.

110. Marianas "War Diary"; Philadelphia *Inquirer,* 15 January 1945.

111. Marianas "War Diary"; Y'Blood, *The Little Giants,* 103.

112. "*Wasp*: History," 101; Comdr. W. J. Slattery to Clifton Sprague, 23 February 1945.

113. John A. Roosevelt letter to Annabel Sprague; *Waspirit,* 15 July 1945, 1.

NINE: Prelude to Leyte

In this and the next three chapters, I made heavy use of the action reports filed by the thirteen ships comprising Taffy 3, all of which can be found on microfilm #NRS 1979-4, "Taffy 3 in Samar Phase of Battle for Leyte Gulf," available from the Naval Historical

Center. Stephen Howarth's fine chapters in his book, *Men of War: Great Naval Leaders of World War II*, shed light on the Japanese naval training at Etajima. Interviews and papers from the Sprague Collection also gave valuable information.

1. Sprague Flight Log, 18 August 1944; Y'Blood, *The Little Giants,* 102–3.
2. Sprague Flight Log, 19 August 1944; Ship's Log, *Fanshaw Bay,* 28 August and 10 September 1944 (hereinafter cited as *Fanshaw Bay* Log).
3. War Diary, commander, Carrier Division 25 (hereinafter cited as War Diary, Com-CarDiv 25); Bulkley, *At Close Quarters,* 368–70; Morison, *Leyte,* 25–27; Y'Blood, *The Little Giants,* 103–6.
4. Morison, *Leyte,* 25; Y'Blood, *The Little Giants,* 107–8.
5. William Carson letter to the Sprague sisters, September 1989; Y'Blood, *The Little Giants,* 71; Christopher Carson letter to Adm. Frederick C. Sherman, 31 August 1947.
6. William Carson letter to the Sprague sisters.
7. *Fanshaw Bay* Log, 3 October 1944; War Diary, ComCarDiv 25; Y'Blood, *The Little Giants,* 107–8; Blair, *Silent Victory,* 712; Morison, *Leyte,* 27; Roscoe, *United States Destroyer Operations in World War II,* 413–14.
8. War Diary, ComCarDiv 25; *Fanshaw Bay* Log, 7 October 1944; Y'Blood, *The Little Giants,* 107–8.
9. Lewin, *The American Magic,* 253; Potter, *Nimitz,* 327; Woodward, *The Battle for Leyte Gulf,* 26; Costello, *The Pacific War,* 501–2.
10. Woodward, *The Battle for Leyte Gulf,* 26–27; Potter and Nimitz, *Triumph in the Pacific,* 111–12.
11. Potter, *Nimitz,* 325; Mason, *The Pacific War Remembered,* 267.
12. Potter, *Nimitz,* 325.
13. Potter, *Bull Halsey,* 290.
14. Potter and Nimitz, *Triumph in the Pacific,* 104; Reynolds, *The Fast Carriers,* 262.
15. Woodward, *The Battle for Leyte Gulf,* 21.
16. Potter and Nimitz, *Triumph in the Pacific,* 104–6; Spector, *Eagle Against the Sun,* 428–29; Morison, *Leyte,* 190.
17. Evans, *The Japanese Navy in World War II,* 360.
18. United States Strategic Bombing Survey No. 227, "Interrogation of Vice Admiral Tokusaburo Ozawa, 30 October 1945" (hereinafter cited as USSBS); USSBS No. 47, "Interrogation of Vice Admiral Takeo Kurita, 16, 17 October 1945."
19. Evans, *The Japanese Navy in World War II,* 377.
20. Leary, *We Shall Return!,* 114–54; Howarth, *Men of War,* 331–48; James, *The Years of MacArthur: Volume II, 1941–1945,* 358.
21. Woodward, *The Battle for Leyte Gulf,* 29.
22. Larrabee, *Commander in Chief,* 391; Spector, *Eagle Against the Sun,* 423; Forrestel, *Admiral Raymond A. Spruance,* 56.
23. Howarth, *Men of War,* 229–43; Young, *The World Almanac of World War II,* 551–52.
24. Howarth, *Men of War,* 111–24.
25. Toland, *The Rising Sun,* 682–83; Stewart, *The Battle of Leyte Gulf,* 42–43.
26. Toland, *The Rising Sun,* 683; Leckie, *Delivered From Evil,* 791; Morison, *Leyte,* 162–63; Young, *The World Almanac of World War II,* 422–34.

27. Dix, *Missing Off Samar,* 12.
28. Costello, *The Pacific War,* 512; Christopher Carson letter to Sherman.
29. Ross, *The Escort Carrier Gambier Bay,* 19; Karig, Harris, and Manson, *Battle Report: The End of an Empire,* 385; Y'Blood, *The Little Giants,* 10–17, 34–35.
30. Y'Blood, *The Little Giants,* 34–35, 99; Christopher Carson letter to Sherman.
31. Y'Blood, *The Little Giants,* 34–35; Steinberg, *Return to the Philippines,* 60.
32. Steinberg, *Return to the Philippines,* 60; Morison, *Leyte,* 244–45.
33. Stewart, *The Battle of Leyte Gulf,* 147–48; author's interview with Robert C. Hagen, 12 February 1994; Young, *The World Almanac of World War II,* 434; Grove, *Sea Battles in Close-Up,* 212.
34. *Fanshaw Bay* Action Report; "History of the U.S.S. *Kalinin Bay.*"
35. *Fanshaw Bay* Action Report; Copeland and O'Neill, *The Spirit of the "Sammy-B,"* 57.
36. *Fanshaw Bay* Action Report.
37. Y'Blood, *The Little Giants,* 123; Morison, *Leyte,* 243.
38. Y'Blood, *The Little Giants,* 123–28; *Gambier Bay* Action Report.
39. Copeland and O'Neill, *The Spirit of the "Sammy-B,"* 64.
40. Author's interview with H. Whitney Felt, 7 February 1994.
41. Costello, *The Pacific War,* 502–3; Howarth, *To Shining Sea,* 458.
42. *Fanshaw Bay* Action Report.
43. Duane Iossi letter to the author, February 1994; author's interview with Al Hopkins, 12 April 1993.
44. Christopher Carson letter to Sherman.
45. Toland, *The Rising Sun,* 683–84.
46. Morison, *Leyte,* 168; Toland, *The Rising Sun,* 684; Potter and Nimitz, *Triumph in the Pacific,* 106; Costello, *The Pacific War,* 504.
47. Morison, *Leyte,* 170–72.
48. Costello, *The Pacific War,* 504–5.
49. Smith, *The United States Navy in World War II,* 847; Potter and Nimitz, *Triumph in the Pacific,* 107; Morison, *Leyte,* 172; Costello, *The Pacific War,* 504.
50. Costello, *The Pacific War,* 505.
51. Ibid.; Morison, *Leyte,* 175.
52. Morison, *Leyte,* 184–87.
53. Ibid., 186; Evans, *The Japanese Navy in World War II,* 356, 364.
54. Morison, *Leyte,* 187–89; Toland, *The Rising Sun,* 690–91.
55. Morison, *Leyte,* 189; USSBS, "Kurita"; Costello, *The Pacific War,* 508.
56. Costello, *The Pacific War,* 505–6.
57. Halsey and Bryan, *Admiral Halsey's Story,* 214; Potter, *Bull Halsey,* 293.
58. Potter, *Bull Halsey,* 293–94; Howarth, *Men of War,* 344.
59. Spector, *Eagle Against the Sun,* 431; Costello, *The Pacific War,* 508.
60. Halsey and Bryan, *Admiral Halsey's Story,* 216–17.
61. Ibid., 216.
62. Lewin, *The American Magic,* 248; Winton, *Ultra in the Pacific,* 184.
63. Adm. James Russell interview, 21 April 1992; Potter, *Bull Halsey,* 297–98; Morison, *Leyte,* 195–96.
64. Karig, *The End of an Empire,* 379–80.

65. Cant, "Bull's Run"; Potter, *Bull Halsey,* 297; Adm. James Russell interview, 21 April 1992; Morison, *Leyte,* 195–96.

66. Morison, *Leyte,* 194.

67. Potter, *Bull Halsey,* 296–97.

68. Woodward, *The Battle for Leyte Gulf,* 83–84; Reynolds, *The Fast Carriers,* 271–72; Morison, *Leyte,* 245; Potter, *Bull Halsey,* 301.

69. Potter, *Bull Halsey,* 300–301; Mason, *The Pacific War Remembered,* 273.

70. USSBS, "Kurita"; Morison, *Leyte,* 186.

71. USSBS, "Kurita"; USSBS No. 170, "Interrogation of Commander Tonosuke Otani, 26 October 1945."

72. Evans, *The Japanese Navy in World War II,* 365.

73. Ibid.

74. Y'Blood, *The Little Giants,* 154.

75. Potter and Nimitz, *Triumph in the Pacific,* 124–25; Evans, *The Japanese Navy in World War II,* 373.

76. Karig, *End of an Empire,* 387; USSBS No. 149, "Interrogation of Rear Admiral Tomiji Koyanagi, 24 October 1945."

TEN: "A Sighted Enemy Is a Dead Enemy"

Taffy 3 action reports continue to play a prominent role, but they are now supplemented by two pieces that, taken together, form the closest we get to actually interviewing Clifton Sprague. Regrettably, no historian thought to interview him in the first ten years after the battle. His death in 1955 precluded any opportunity to draw information out of Sprague that no other commander could possibly possess, for only he commanded at Samar.

However, shortly after Leyte Gulf, with the Navy's approval he published an account of the battle, written by Lt. Philip H. Gustafson, USN, that appeared in the April 1945 issue of *American Magazine.* Though obviously withholding much information for security reasons, Sprague shared some of the thoughts and decisions he experienced that day.

The second source is more valuable, for here we have Sprague's honest thoughts, given with no fear of reprisal or of harming anyone since he did not intend the remarks to be published. When he read C. Vann Woodward's 1947 book, *The Battle for Leyte Gulf,* Sprague annotated numerous pages with his opinions and reactions to what Woodward wrote. The book has remained in Courtney Vaughan's possession since her father's death and has not been used by any historian, biographer, or researcher until now. As I read Sprague's annotated copy of Woodward, I received the impression I was listening to his deepest thoughts and sharing a conversation with him. Combined with his magazine article, and further supplemented by family reminiscences, we can construct a picture of the battle seen through Sprague's eyes.

1. Rear Adm. C. A. F. Sprague, as told to Lt. Philip H. Gustafson, "The Japs Had Us on the Ropes," 258 (hereinafter cited as Sprague/Gustafson; all page numbers come from the copy printed in Appendix C of Reneau/Vaughan, 258–64); Pierson, "The Battle Off Samar," 2.

2. Author's interview with Capt. Henry Burt Bassett, 2 February 1994.

3. *Gambier Bay* Action Report; Hagen and Shalett, "We Asked for the Jap Fleet— and Got It," 9–10 (hereinafter cited as Hagen/Shalett).

4. Rear Adm. Clifton A. F. Sprague, "Action against the Japanese Main Body off Samar Island, 25 October 1944, Special Report of," 29 October 1944 (hereinafter cited as Sprague Action Report); *Fanshaw Bay* Action Report; *Fanshaw Bay* Log; Stewart, *The Battle of Leyte Gulf*, 149.

5. Sprague/Gustafson, 258.

6. Ibid., 258–59; Pierson, "The Battle Off Samar," 2; *Fanshaw Bay* Log.

7. Pierson, "The Battle Off Samar," 2; Sprague/Gustafson, 259; author's interview with Vernon Hipchings, Jr., 31 January 1994.

8. H. Whitney Felt interview; Elbert Gentry letter to Lloyd Gurnett, reprinted in *Samuel B. Roberts* Association newsletter, 1 July 1985.

9. Author's interview with Adm. Richard G. Altman, 24 January 1994.

10. Sprague/Gustafson, 259; Gentry letter to Gurnett.

11. Pierson, "The Battle Off Samar," 2–3; Sprague/Gustafson, 259.

12. Sprague's comments in Woodward, 173; Toland, *The Rising Sun*, 704; Steinberg, *Return to the Philippines*, 60.

13. Morison, *Leyte*, 252; Dix, *Missing off Samar*, 17; Sprague Action Report.

14. Sprague Action Report; Sprague/Gustafson, 260; Robert Hagen interview.

15. Sprague Action Report; *Samuel B. Roberts* Action Report; USSBS, "Otani"; Copeland and O'Neill, *The Spirit of the "Sammy-B,"* 68.

16. Sprague/Gustafson, 260; Morison, *Leyte*, 252.

17. C. A. F. Sprague message to Thomas Sprague, October 1944 and Thomas Sprague reply, in the Clifton Sprague Collection.

18. Potter and Nimitz, *Triumph in the Pacific*, 120.

19. Morison, *Leyte*, 252–53; Sprague Action Report.

20. Daniel Vaughan interview; Henry Pyzdrowski interview.

21. Robert Hagen interview.

22. Reneau/Vaughan, 256.

23. Morison, *Leyte*, 248; Evans, *The Japanese Navy in World War II*, 367.

24. Copeland and O'Neill, *The Spirit of the "Sammy-B,"* 72.

25. Vernon Hipchings interview; Roscoe, *United States Destroyer Operations in World War II*, 425.

26. Sprague/Gustafson, 260–61.

27. Sprague/Gustafson, 261; Sprague's comments in Woodward, 172.

28. Navy Department Press Release, "Interview with Rear Admiral C. A. F. Sprague," 30 November 1944; Sprague/Gustafson, 261.

29. Pierson, "The Battle Off Samar," 5.

30. Sprague/Gustafson, 261.

31. Woodward, *The Battle for Leyte Gulf*, 187.

32. Stewart, *The Battle of Leyte Gulf*, 155; Morison, *Leyte*, 279.

33. Author's interview with Richard Rogers, 3 October 1993.

34. Y'Blood, *The Little Giants*, 166.

35. Mason, *The Pacific War Remembered*, 270.

36. Morison, *Leyte*, 286; Spector, *Eagle Against the Sun*, 437.

37. Halsey and Bryan, *Admiral Halsey's Story*, 218.
38. Morison, *Leyte*, 293–94; Mason, *The Pacific War Remembered*, 275–76.
39. Morison, *Leyte*, 294.
40. Sprague's comments in Woodward, 143.

ELEVEN: The Great Chase

1. Confidential Report of Lt. Robb White, USNR, Public Relations, CinCPac, on board *Natoma Bay*, 25 October 1944, Aviation History Files, Naval Historical Center, pp. C2–3 (hereinafter cited as White Report).
2. Sprague/Gustafson, 261.
3. Navy Department Press Release, "Interview with Rear Admiral C. A. F. Sprague," 30 November 1944.
4. Morison, *Leyte*, 255.
5. Sprague/Gustafson, 261; Copeland and O'Neill, *The Spirit of the "Sammy-B,"* 71.
6. *Johnston* Action Report; Y'Blood, *The Little Giants*, 173–74; *Fanshaw Bay* Action Report.
7. Hagen/Shalett, 72; *Johnston* Action Report; Robert Hagen interview; Y'Blood, *The Little Giants*, 173–74.
8. Sprague/Gustafson, 261–62; Vernon Hipchings interview.
9. Sprague Action Report; Sprague/Gustafson, 261.
10. Author's interview with Rear Adm. Richard Ballinger, 2 February 1994; Sprague/Gustafson, 261–62.
11. Pierson, "The Battle Off Samar," 3; author's interview with Thomas Vaughan, 11 December 1993.
12. Pierson, "The Battle Off Samar," 3; Vernon Hipchings interview.
13. Toland, *The Rising Sun*, 705; Roscoe, *United States Destroyer Operations in World War II*, 427.
14. Sprague/Gustafson, 261–62; author's interview with Reverend Elmer E. Bosserman, 25 January 1994; Morison, *Leyte*, 276.
15. Sprague/Gustafson, 262.
16. Henry Pyzdrowski interview.
17. *Fanshaw Bay* Action Report; *Fanshaw Bay* Log.
18. Vernon Hipchings interview.
19. *Samuel B. Roberts* Action Report.
20. Author's interview with Capt. Everett E. Roberts, Jr., 2 February 1994.
21. *Samuel B. Roberts* Action Report; Roscoe, *United States Destroyer Operations in World War II*, 428–29; H. Whitney Felt interview.
22. Toland, *The Rising Sun*, 705–6.
23. Karig, *The End of an Empire*, 389; Woodward, *The Battle for Leyte Gulf*, 180.
24. Y'Blood, *The Little Giants*, 176; Steinberg, *Return to the Philippines*, 73.
25. USSBS, "Kurita"; Spector, *Eagle Against the Sun*, 437.
26. Evans, *The Japanese Navy in World War II*, 373.
27. *Gambier Bay* Action Report; Toland, *The Rising Sun*, 706.

28. *Fanshaw Bay* Action Report; Vernon Hipchings interview; author's interview with William Mercer, 22 February 1993; Y'Blood, *The Little Giants,* 184–85.

29. *Kitkun Bay* War History, 17 November 1944.

30. Potter, *Nimitz,* 336–39.

31. Halsey and Bryan, *Admiral Halsey's Story,* 218–20; Potter and Nimitz, *Triumph in the Pacific,* 122.

32. Halsey and Bryan, *Admiral Halsey's Story,* 218–20; Morison, *Leyte,* 293–94; Cant, "Bull's Run."

33. Morison, *Leyte,* 293–94.

34. Holmes, *Double-Edged Secrets,* 192.

35. Adm. James Russell interview.

36. White Report, C3.

37. Sprague comments in Woodward, 143, 145.

38. Sprague/Gustafson, 262; *Kitkun Bay* War History; Y'Blood, *The Little Giants,* 182.

39. Sprague Action Report; Morison, *Leyte,* 268.

40. Morison, *Leyte,* 268; Smith, *The United States Navy in World War II,* 872.

41. Sprague Action Report; Steinberg, *Return to the Philippines,* 61–62.

42. Pierson, "The Battle Off Samar," 6.

43. Toland, *The Rising Sun,* 706; Roscoe, *United States Destroyer Operations in World War II,* 427; Y'Blood, *The Little Giants,* 177; Dix, *Missing off Samar,* 29.

44. Y'Blood, *The Little Giants,* 177–78; Morison, *Leyte,* 268–69.

45. Copeland and O'Neill, *The Spirit of the "Sammy-B,"* 85.

46. Ibid., 87–88.

47. Ibid., 95; H. Whitney Felt interview; Roscoe, *United States Destroyer Operations in World War II,* 429.

48. Copeland and O'Neill, *The Spirit of the "Sammy-B,"* 97.

49. *Samuel B. Roberts* Action Report.

50. Toland, *The Rising Sun,* 706.

51. *Fanshaw Bay* Action Report; Sprague/Gustafson, 262; Pierson, "The Battle Off Samar," 7.

52. *Kitkun Bay* War History; Karig, *The End of an Empire,* 395.

53. *Gambier Bay* Action Report; Sprague/Gustafson, 262.

54. Morison, *Leyte,* 272.

55. Hagen/Shalett, 10, 74; Morison, *Leyte,* 272–73; Toland, *The Rising Sun,* 707; *Fanshaw Bay* Action Report; Sprague Action Report.

56. William Mercer interview; Morison, *Leyte,* 274; Toland, *The Rising Sun,* 707.

57. Sprague/Gustafson, 263; Courtney Vaughan interview.

58. Pierson, "The Battle Off Samar," 8; Morison, *Leyte,* 284–85.

59. Potter, *Bull Halsey,* 302–3; Halsey and Bryan, *Admiral Halsey's Story,* 218–20.

60. Halsey and Bryan, *Admiral Halsey's Story,* 220; Cant, "Bull's Run."

61. Potter, *Nimitz,* 338–40.

62. Halsey and Bryan, *Admiral Halsey's Story,* 220.

63. Ibid., 220–21; Potter, *Bull Halsey,* 304.

64. Sprague comments in Woodward, 147.

65. Sprague/Gustafson, 263; Pierson, "The Battle Off Samar," 8–9; Robert Carew interview, 25 February 1992.

66. Toland, *The Rising Sun*, 707; Morison, *Leyte*, 280, 297.
67. Sprague comments in Woodward, 173; Morison, *Leyte*, 275.
68. USSBS, "Kurita"; Morison, *Leyte*, 299; USSBS No. 149, "Interrogation of Rear Admiral Tomiji Koyanagi, 24 October 1945"; Evans, *The Japanese Navy in World War II*, 381–83.
69. Evans, *The Japanese Navy in World War II*, 368; Cant, "Bull's Run."
70. Morison, *Leyte*, 297; Y'Blood, *The Little Giants*, 193; Evans, *The Japanese Navy in World War II*, 381.

TWELVE: Kamikazes and Controversy

1. *Fanshaw Bay* Log; Pierson, "The Battle Off Samar," 9.
2. Reverend Elmer Bosserman interview.
3. *Fanshaw Bay* Log; Sprague Action Report; Morison, *Leyte*, 302–3; Toland, *The Rising Sun*, 707–8.
4. Spector, *Eagle Against the Sun*, 440–41.
5. *Fanshaw Bay* Action Report; Pierson, "The Battle Off Samar," 10.
6. *Fanshaw Bay* Log; Toland, *The Rising Sun*, 707–8; Morison, *Leyte*, 302–3; Sprague Action Report; Pierson, "The Battle Off Samar," 10; Costello, *The Pacific War*, 518.
7. Reverend Elmer Bosserman interview.
8. Sprague's comments in Woodward, 211.
9. Pierson, "The Battle Off Samar," 10; Morison, *Leyte*, 303.
10. *Fanshaw Bay* Action Report; Y'Blood, *The Little Giants*, 218.
11. Y'Blood, *The Little Giants*, 218; Reverend Elmer Bosserman interview.
12. *Fanshaw Bay* Log.
13. Sprague Action Report.
14. Morison, *Leyte*, 312.
15. Sprague Action Report; Morison, *Leyte*, 313.
16. Morison, *Leyte*, 313–14; Y'Blood, *The Little Giants*, 235–39; *Johnston* Action Report.
17. Morison, *Leyte*, 314.
18. H. Whitney Felt interview; Dix, *Missing off Samar*, 36–37, 43.
19. Author's interview with Jack Yusen, 28 April 1992.
20. *Samuel B. Roberts* Action Report; author's interview with John Dudley Moylan, 7 February 1994.
21. William Mercer interview, 9 February 1994; author's interview with Thomas Stevenson, 7 February 1994.
22. Thomas Stevenson interview.
23. Sprague comments in Woodward, 216.
24. Stewart, *The Battle of Leyte Gulf*, 190; Morison, *Leyte*, 314–16.
25. Jack Yusen interview.
26. *Johnston* Action Report.
27. Navy Department News Release, "Interview with Rear Admiral C. A. F. Sprague," 30 November 1944; Toland, *The Rising Sun*, 713–14; Potter and Nimitz, *Triumph in the Pacific*, 130.

28. Pierson, "The Battle Off Samar," 12.

29. Morison, *Leyte,* 304; Y'Blood, *The Little Giants,* 218–19.

30. Potter, *Nimitz,* 343; Adm. C. A. F. Sprague to Adm. A. W. Fitch, Jr., 26 September 1946; Reneau/Vaughan, 185–86.

31. William Carson letter to the Sprague sisters.

32. *Fanshaw Bay* Log, 26 October 1944; "History of the U.S.S. *Kalinin Bay.*"

33. *Fanshaw Bay* Log, 27 October–1 November 1944.

34. Sprague Flight Log, November 1944; C. A. F. Sprague letter to Dorothea Harvey, 18 December 1944.

35. *Fanshaw Bay* Log, 7–27 November 1944; William Carson letter to the Sprague sisters.

36. Al Hopkins interview.

37. Costello, *The Pacific War,* 518–19; USSBS, "Ozawa."

38. Rear Adm. Clifton A. F. Sprague Navy Cross Citation; Task Unit 77.4.3 Presidential Unit Citation.

39. Potter, *Nimitz,* p. 343.

40. Ibid., 343–44.

41. Ibid., 344.

42. Larrabee, *Commander in Chief,* 409; Cant, "Bull's Run"; Reynolds, *The Fast Carriers,* 280.

43. Halsey and Bryan, *Admiral Halsey's Story,* 226.

44. Buell, *Master of Sea Power,* 451.

45. Leary, *We Shall Return!,* 142–43; Mason, *The Pacific War Remembered,* 273–74.

46. Sprague Action Report.

47. Commander, Task Unit 77.4.3, to commander in chief, U.S. Fleet, "Action Report—Leyte Operation—12 October through 27 October 1944," 6 November 1944; Commander, Task Unit 77.4.3, to commander, Task Group, "Lessons Learned from Operation of CVE's in Leyte Operation," 4 November 1944.

48. Potter, *Nimitz,* 344.

49. Sprague/Gustafson, 259; Courtney Vaughan interview.

50. Jordan, *Born to Fight,* 180.

51. Courtney Vaughan interview.

52. Halsey and Bryan, *Admiral Halsey's Story,* 218; Potter, *Bull Halsey,* 371.

53. Leary, *We Shall Return!,* 142; Adm. Thomas C. Kinkaid letter to Capt. Arleigh Burke, 4 December 1947; Adm. Thomas C. Kinkaid letter to Rear Adm. Richard Cruzen, 15 August 1947; Adm. Raymond A. Spruance letter to Adm. Thomas C. Kinkaid, 21 August 1947. All letters cited are found in the personal papers of Adm. Thomas C. Kinkaid.

54. King and Whitehill, *Fleet Admiral King,* 580; Potter, *Bull Halsey,* 371–72.

55. Taylor, *The Magnificent Mitscher,* 265.

56. Morison, *Leyte,* ix–x, 338.

57. Potter, *Bull Halsey,* 380–81.

58. Potter, *Nimitz,* 343.

59. A. L. Arpin letter to C. A. F. Sprague, 1 December 1944.

60. Sprague comments in Woodward, 81, 143.

61. Ibid., 129, 155.

62. Ibid., 88, 217.

63. Ibid., 235.

64. James, *The Years of MacArthur,* 564–65.

65. Buell, *Master of Sea Power,* 451–52.

66. Morison, *Leyte,* 308.

67. Thomas Vaughan interview.

68. Vice Adm. C. T. Durgin letter to Vice Adm. Clifton Sprague, 8 November 1954.

69. Weinberg, *A World At Arms,* 854–55.

70. Cant, "Bull's Run"; Buell, *Master of Sea Power,* 451–52.

71. Reynolds, *The Fast Carriers,* 217.

72. Christopher Carson letter to Sherman.

73. William Carson letter to Bill William, 1 August 1989.

74. Christopher Carson letter to Rear Adm. C. A. F. Sprague, 21 September 1947.

75. Reynolds, *The Fast Carriers,* 283–84.

THIRTEEN: The War Winds Down

1. Reneau/Vaughan, 165.

2. Ibid., 154; Buell, *Master of Sea Power,* 450–52; Courtney Vaughan interview.

3. Patricia Reneau interview.

4. Reneau/Vaughan, 154.

5. Author's interview with Fred Harvey, 25 October 1991; Courtney Vaughan interview.

6. "Sprague Tells how his Baby Carriers Withstood 2½ Hours of Jap Fire," name of newspaper unknown, December 1944.

7. "Battle of Samar didn't end when Nip fleet tried to run," article written on board the *Fanshaw Bay* by United Press reporter Richard W. Johnston, 13 November 1944; "'Hottest Boys in the Sky,' Admiral Calls CVE Pilots," Philadelphia *Inquirer,* December 1944.

8. *Life,* January 22, 1945.

9. C. A. F. Sprague letter to Dorothea Harvey, 18 December 1944.

10. Reneau/Vaughan, 168–70; Robert Carew letter to the author, 8 November 1991.

11. Carew letter to the author.

12. Rear Adm. Calvin Durgin letter to C. A. F. Sprague, 1 November 1945.

13. C. A. F. Sprague letter to Annabel Sprague, 15 May 1945.

14. Ibid.

15. First Anniversary Menu.

16. Railway Express Agency letter to C. A. F. Sprague, 13 March 1945; C. A. F. Sprague to Railway Express Agency, 10 June 1945.

17. Reynolds, *Admiral John H. Towers,* 507.

18. *Big "T",* 2.

19. Ibid., 13; Sprague list of commands in Clifton Sprague Collection; Reynolds, *The Fast Carriers,* 375–77; Naval Historical Center interview of Adm. Gerald F. Bogan, 147; C. A. F. Sprague letter to Dorothea Harvey, 10 September 1945.

FOURTEEN: Final Duties

Material from the Clifton Sprague Collection, particularly family correspondence, provided helpful information for Sprague's last years of active service. Contemporary newspaper accounts and interviews conducted by the author were also useful.

1. C. A. F. Sprague letter to Dorothea Harvey, 6 December 1946; Reneau/Vaughan, 173; Reynolds, *Admiral John H. Towers,* 515.
2. Reneau/Vaughan, 176–77; "Shangri-La Sails for Test of the Bikini 'Drones'," San Francisco *News,* 9 May 1946 (hereinafter cited as "Shangri-La Sails"); Operation Crossroads, Press Release #4, 15 February 1946 and Press Release #39, 17 April 1946.
3. "Shangri-La Sails."
4. Ibid.
5. Reynolds, *The Fast Carriers,* 395–96; "Bikini Bound," San Francisco *Chronicle,* 9 May 1946 (hereinafter cited as "Bikini Bound").
6. "Atom Tests Won't Be Rigged for Navy," San Francisco *News,* 8 May 1946; "Bikini Bound"; "Shangri-La Sails."
7. "Shangri-La Sails"; "Reporter Sees Robot Planes Take Off From Bomb Test Ship," Los Angeles *Examiner,* 9 May 1946.
8. Sprague Flight Log, 26 June 1946; Reneau/Vaughan, 180–81.
9. Daniel Vaughan interview; Reynolds, *The Fast Carriers,* 395–96.
10. Gold Star in lieu of the fourth Legion of Merit Citation, in Clifton Sprague Collection.
11. C. A. F. Sprague letter to Aubrey W. Fitch, 26 September 1946.
12. Fitch letter to Sprague, 2 October 1946.
13. Sprague letter to Fitch, 7 October 1946.
14. Author's interview with James Cheevers, senior curator at the Naval Academy Museum, 25 March 1994.
15. Reneau/Vaughan, 188–89.
16. Schratz, "The Admirals' Revolt," 65; Reynolds, *The Fast Carriers,* 215.
17. Reynolds, *The Fast Carriers,* 217.
18. Clark with Reynolds, *Carrier Admiral,* 249–50; Reynolds, *The Fast Carriers,* 396.
19. Baldwin, "Air Dispute Remains."
20. Chester W. Nimitz letter to C. A. F. Sprague, 28 January 1947; Sprague letter to Nimitz, 4 February 1947.
21. Reynolds, *The Fast Carriers,* 396.
22. Navy Department Release, 1 August 1947.
23. Reneau/Vaughan, 203.
24. Ibid., 205.
25. Ibid., 205–6; Report of Operational Visit to Tripoli, Libya, 1 July 1948.
26. Report of Operational Visit to Naples, Italy, 4 August 1948.
27. Reneau/Vaughan, 207–8; postcard from C. A. F. Sprague to his daughters, 6 July 1948.
28. Reneau/Vaughan, 208.
29. Ibid., 209.

30. Daniel Vaughan interview; Courtney Vaughan interview.
31. Fitness Report, 1 March 1949 to 1 February 1950; Daniel Vaughan interview; McCullough, *Truman,* 748–49; Reneau/Vaughan, 214.
32. C. A. F. Sprague letter to Daniel and Courtney Vaughan, 9 November 1950.
33. Reneau/Vaughan, p. 215; Phillips, "Polar Communities," 10–11.
34. Reneau/Vaughan, 216.
35. Ibid.; Seventeenth Naval District Press Release, 14 November 1950; Phillips, "Polar Communities," 10–11.
36. Phillips, "Polar Communities," 13; Press Release, 14 November 1950; Daniel Vaughan interview.
37. Phillips, "Polar Communities," 13; Press Release, 14 November 1950; Reneau/Vaughan, 216.
38. Press Release, 14 November 1950; Reneau/Vaughan, 216–17; "B-29 'Recon' Flies over North Pole," UP dispatch, 12 November 1950.
39. Reneau/Vaughan, 218.

FIFTEEN: Final Years

All the material for Sprague's final years came from the Clifton Sprague Collection and interviews with family members.

1. Reneau/Vaughan, 218–19; Sprague Discharge Papers; Sprague Flight Log, 2 October 1951.
2. Ibid., 221; Daniel Vaughan interview.
3. Courtney Vaughan interview.
4. Reneau/Vaughan, 222; Daniel Vaughan interview.
5. Daniel Vaughan interview.
6. Courtney Vaughan interview; Daniel Vaughan interview; Fred Harvey interview.
7. Author's interview with Ella Yanquell, 25 March and 1 April 1992; Reneau/Vaughan, 223.
8. Reneau/Vaughan, 223–24.
9. New York *Times,* 12 April 1955; *Time,* 25 April 1955; *Newsweek,* 25 April 1955; Charles S. Thomas letter to Annabel Sprague, 19 April 1955; Frederick C. Sherman letter to Annabel Sprague, 17 April 1955; John A. Roosevelt letter to Annabel Sprague.
10. Hanson Baldwin, "Most Dramatic Sea Battle in History"; Morison, *Leyte,* x.
11. Commissioning Program of the *Clifton Sprague,* 21 March 1981.
12. Wouk, *War and Remembrance,* 1285.
13. Daniel Vaughan interview.
14. Falk, "Leyte Gulf: A Bibliography of the Greatest Sea Battle," 60–61.
15. Reneau/Vaughan, 227.
16. Fred Harvey interview; Daniel Vaughan interview; Courtney Vaughan interview; Patricia Reneau interview; Christopher Carson letter to Sprague.

→ BIBLIOGRAPHY ←

PRIMARY SOURCES

Naval Historical Center
Action Reports: *Tangier, Wasp, Fanshaw Bay, Kalinin Bay, St. Lo, White Plains, Gambier Bay, Kitkun Bay, Heermann, Hoel, Johnston, Dennis, John C. Butler, Raymond, Samuel B. Roberts*

Clifton A. F. Sprague Collection

Commander, Carrier Division 6 Records

Navy World War II Records

Officer Biography Section

Personal Papers of Admiral Thomas C. Kinkaid

Photographic Section

Ships' Histories Section

U.S. Government Microfilm Records: #NR-A 124 USS *Tangier* Log; #NRS 1981-9 *Wasp* History, Diary, Reports; #NRS 1979-4 Taffy 3 in Samar Phase of Battle for Leyte Gulf; #NRS 1975-8 Joint Task Force One, Operation Crossroads

The Naval Academy
Records of the Superintendent, U.S. Naval Academy, General Correspondence, Support Facilities, SERIES: Naval Air Facilities, Box No. 2, Folders No. 2, 3, 4

United States Naval Academy Aviation File, located in the Admiral Chester W. Nimitz Collection, Admiral Nimitz Library

Miscellaneous Records
Clifton A. F. Sprague Collection, privately held (soon to reside at the Naval Historical Center)

Norwich University Transcripts

Reverend Elmer E. Bosserman Collection, privately held

Robert C. Hagen Collection, privately held

Roxbury Latin School Transcripts

Interviews: Family and Friends
HARVEY, DOROTHEA SPRAGUE, sister, 25 October 1991

HARVEY, FRED, nephew, 25 October 1991

RENEAU, PATRICIA SPRAGUE, daughter, 18 August 1991

VAUGHAN, COURTNEY SPRAGUE, daughter, 16 August 1991

VAUGHAN, DANIEL, son-in-law, 11 December 1993

VAUGHAN, THOMAS, historian, 11 December 1993

YANQUELL, ELLA, family friend, 25 March 1992; 1 April 1992

Interviews: Military Personnel
ALTMAN, ADM. RICHARD G., *Kalinin Bay* torpedo plane pilot, 24 January 1994

BALLINGER, REAR ADM. RICHARD, *Gambier Bay* executive officer, 2 February 1994

BARNES, LEONARD, *Tangier* seaman 1st class, 4 April 1992

BASSETT, CAPT. HENRY BURT, *Gambier Bay* torpedo plane pilot, 2 February 1994

BOSSERMAN, REVEREND ELMER E., *Kalinin Bay* chaplain, 25 January 1994

CAREW, ROBERT, Clifton Sprague's signalman from 1943 to 1945, 18 February 1992, 25 February 1992

CHAMBLESS, ORBAN R., *Tangier* and *Samuel B. Roberts* signalman, 8 April 1992

CHEEVERS, JAMES, Naval Academy Museum senior curator, 25 March 1994

DALY, ROBERT P., *Wasp* communications officer, 23 February 1993, 11 November 1993, 6 January 1994

DERWOYED, DANIEL, *Raymond* water tender 3d class, 21 February 1994

DORE, JOHN F., *Tangier* ensign, 22 July 1993

DUGGAN, DONALD, *Wasp* water tender, 24 February 1992

ECKELMEYER, REAR ADM. E. H., Squadron VP-8 aviator, 27 September 1993

EDWARDS, NORRIS G., *Tangier* storekeeper 1st class, 21 July 1993

FELT, H. WHITNEY, *Samuel B. Roberts* sonar operator 3d class, 7 February 1994

FOSTER, REAR ADM. JOHN, JR., *Lexington* aviator, 15 November 1993

FRIETAS, HENRY, *Tangier* boat engineer, 8 April 1992

FRUIN, RICHARD L., *Tangier* medical officer, 25 April 1992

FULTON, EVERETT, *Wasp* dive-bomber pilot, 27 November 1993

GADDIS, VICE ADM. WALTER D., *Wasp* assistant gunnery officer and gunnery officer, 20 November 1993

GARBO, NUNZIO, *Tangier* chief boatswain's mate, 20 July 1993

GRIFFIS, THOMAS, *Tangier* Marine master sergeant, 29 April 1992

GUTTMAN, PAUL, *Fanshaw Bay* combat photographer, 1 February 1994

HAGEN, ROBERT C., *Johnston* gunnery officer, 12 February 1994

HART, J. D., *Fanshaw Bay* cook 3d class, 22 February 1993

HATHAWAY, CAPT. AMOS T., *Heermann* commanding officer, 11 November 1993

HEDDING, VICE ADM. TRUMAN, deputy chief of staff for Adm. Marc Mitscher, 30 September 1993

HIPCHINGS, VERNON D., JR., *Fanshaw Bay* visual fighter-director officer, 31 January 1994

HOPKINS, ALFRED, *Fanshaw Bay,* 12 April 1993

HUGHES, JOHN, *Tangier* ensign, 24 April 1992

ISACKSEN, ROBERT, *Tangier* petty officer 3d class, 3 April 1992

JIRACEK, ROBERT, *Tangier* photographer, 1 April 1992

KASTAN, ROBERT L., *Fanshaw Bay* boatswain's mate 2d class, 8 March 1993

LARSON, WESLEY, *Tangier* boatswain, 15 April 1992

LUPO, THOMAS, *Fanshaw Bay* aviator, 3 March 1994

MAPES, JOSEPH, *Tangier* crewman, 9 April 1992

MERCER, WILLIAM, *Johnston* crewman, 22 February 1993, 9 February 1994

MOYLAN, JOHN DUDLEY, *Samuel B. Roberts* sonar officer, 7 February 1994

MUNROE, ROBERT, Clifton Sprague's orderly on the *Tangier,* 23 February 1993, 19 July 1993

PACE, CAPT. JOHN, *John C. Butler* commanding officer, 15 November 1993

PREDMORE, WOODY, *Fanshaw Bay* flag yeoman 2d class, 22 February 1993, 24 February 1993

PYZDROWSKI, HENRY, *Gambier Bay* aviator, numerous contacts

ROBERTS, CAPT. EVERETT E., JR., *Samuel B. Roberts* executive officer, 2 February 1994

ROGERS, RICHARD, commander, Composite Squadron 68 on the *Fanshaw Bay,* 3 October 1993

RUSSELL, ADM. JAMES, *Yorktown* officer, 14 April 1992, 21 April 1992

SCHWENKE, JAMES, *Tangier* yeoman, 7 April 1992

STEVENSON, THOMAS, *Samuel B. Roberts* communications officer, 7 February 1994

WALRAVEN, ALBERT T., JR., *Wasp* dive-bomber pilot, 22 November 1993

WILKINSON, C. A., JR., *Tangier* storekeeper 3d class, 7 April 1992, 20 April 1992

YUSEN, JACK, *Samuel B. Roberts* seaman 2d class, 21 April 1992, 28 April 1992

SECONDARY SOURCES

Books and Major Sources

Adams, Henry H. *1942: The Year That Doomed the Axis*. New York: McKay, 1967.

Annual Register of the United States Naval Academy, 1915, 1916, 1917.

Arnold, H. H. *Global Mission*. New York: Harper, 1949.

✓ Arpee, Edward. *From Frigates to Flat-Tops*. Chicago: Lakeside Press, 1953.

Baldwin, Hanson. *Battles Lost and Won*. New York: Harper and Row, 1966.

Belote, James H., and William M. Belote. *Titans of the Sea*. New York: Harper and Row, 1975.

Bender, Marvin H. *The Mighty Stinger*. Russell, Kans.: No publisher, no date.

Bennett, Geoffrey. *Naval Battles of World War II*. New York: McKay, 1975.

Big "T", Magazine of the USS *Ticonderoga*.

✓ Blair, Clay, Jr. *Silent Victory*. New York: Lippincott, 1975.

Bruccoli, Matthew J. *Some Sort of Grandeur: The Life of F. Scott Fitzgerald*. New York: Harcourt Brace Jovanovich, 1981.

Bruccoli, Matthew J., and Margaret M. Duggan, eds. *Correspondence of F. Scott Fitzgerald*. New York: Random House, 1980.

✓ Buell, Thomas B. *The Quiet Warrior: A Biography of Admiral Raymond A. Spruance*. Boston: Little, Brown, 1974.

✓ ———. *Master of Sea Power: A Biography of Fleet Admiral Ernest J. King*. Boston: Little, Brown, 1980.

✓ Bulkley, Capt. Robert J., Jr. *At Close Quarters: P. T. Boats in the United States Navy*. Washington, D.C.: Naval Historical Center, 1962.

✓ Caras, Roger A. *Wings of Gold*. New York: Lippincott, 1965.

✓ Casey, Robert J. *Torpedo Junction*. New York: Bobbs-Merrill, 1942.

Chastain, Bob, and Bill Mercer, writers and eds. *The Fighting and Sinking of the USS Johnston (DD-557) as Told by her Crew*. The *Johnston/Hoel* Association, 1991.

✓ Clark, Adm. J. J., with Clark G. Reynolds. *Carrier Admiral*. New York: McKay, 1967.

Coffey, Thomas. *Hap*. New York: Viking Press, 1982.

? Collier, Basil. *The War in the Far East, 1941–1945*. New York: Morrow, 1969.

Copeland, Rear Adm. Robert W., and Jack O'Neill. *The Spirit of the "Sammy-B."* Independently published, no date.

✓ Costello, John. *The Pacific War, 1941–1945*. New York: Quill Books, 1982.

✓ Cutler, Thomas J. *The Battle of Leyte Gulf, 23–26 October 1944*. New York: HarperCollins, 1994.

✓ Daniels, Josephus. *Our Navy at War*. New York: Doran, 1922.

Deputy Chief of Naval Operations (Air) and the Commander, Naval Air Systems Command. *United States Naval Aviation, 1910–1970*. Washington, D.C.: Department of the Navy, 1970.

Dix, John C. W. *Missing off Samar.* Pocahontas Press, 1949.

Dull, Paul S. *A Battle History of the Imperial Japanese Navy (1941–1945).* Annapolis: Naval Institute Press, 1978.

Duval, Ruby R. *Guide to Historic Annapolis and U.S. Naval Academy.* Baltimore: Norman, Remington, 1926.

Evans, David C., ed. *The Japanese Navy in World War II: In the Words of Former Japanese Naval Officers.* Annapolis: Naval Institute Press, 1986.

Fletcher, W. B. "USS *Tangier.*" Narrative written by ship's cook 2d class.

Forrestel, Vice Adm. E. P. *Admiral Raymond A. Spruance, USN: A Study in Command.* Washington, D.C.: Director of Naval Historical Center, 1966.

Fuchida, Mitsuo and Masatake Okumiya. *Midway: The Battle That Doomed Japan.* Annapolis: U.S. Naval Institute, 1955.

Fulton, E. P. "Tail-End-Charlie." The Personal Log of Ensign Everett P. Fulton, *Wasp* dive-bomber pilot.

Gallery, Rear Adm. Daniel V., USN (Ret.). *Eight Bells, and All's Well.* New York: Norton, 1965.

Gannon, Michael. *Operation Drumbeat.* New York: HarperCollins, 1990.

Grove, Eric. *Sea Battles in Close-Up.* Annapolis: Naval Institute Press, 1993.

Halsey, Fleet Admiral William F., and J. Bryan III. *Admiral Halsey's Story.* New York: McGraw-Hill, 1947.

Healy, Laurin Hall, and Luis Kutner. *The Admiral.* Chicago: Ziff-Davis, 1944.

Heinl, Robert Debs, Jr. *Soldiers of the Sea.* Annapolis: U.S. Naval Institute, 1962.

———. *The Defense of Wake.* Washington, D.C.: Historical Section, Division of Public Information, Headquarters, U.S. Marine Corps, 1947.

"History of the USS *Tangier.*" Monograph in the Ships' History File at the Naval Historical Center, Washington, D.C.

Holmes, W. J. *Double-Edged Secrets.* Annapolis: Naval Institute Press, 1979.

Hough, Richard. *The Longest Battle: The War at Sea, 1939–45.* New York: Morrow, 1986.

Howarth, Stephen. *To Shining Sea.* New York: Random House, 1991.

Howarth, Stephen, ed. *Men of War: Great Naval Leaders of World War II.* London: Weidenfeld and Nicolson, 1992.

James, D. Clayton. *The Years of MacArthur: Volume II, 1941–1945.* Boston: Houghton Mifflin, 1975.

Johnson, Brian. *Fly Navy: The History of Naval Aviation.* New York: Morrow, 1981.

Jordan, Ralph B. *Born to Fight: The Life of Admiral Halsey.* Philadelphia: McKay, 1946.

Karig, Walter, Lt. Earl Burton, and Lt. Stephen L. Freeland. *Battle Report: The Atlantic War.* New York: Farrar and Rinehart, 1946.

Karig, Walter, Russell L. Harris, and Frank A. Manson. *Battle Report: The End of an Empire.* New York: Rinehart, 1948.

Kenney, George C. *General Kenney Reports*. New York: Duell, Sloan and Pearce, 1949.

King, Ernest J., and Walter Muir Whitehill. *Fleet Admiral King: A Naval Record*. New York: Norton, 1952.

Larrabee, Eric. *Commander in Chief*. New York: Harper and Row, 1987.

Layton, Rear Adm. Edwin T., USN (Ret.), with Capt. Roger Pineau, USN (Ret.) and John Costello. *And I Was There*. New York: Morrow, 1985.

Leary, William M., ed. *We Shall Return!: MacArthur's Commanders and the Defeat of Japan*. Lexington: University Press of Kentucky, 1988.

Leckie, Robert. *Delivered From Evil*. New York: Harper and Row, 1987.

Lewin, Ronald. *The American Magic*. New York: Farrar Straus Giroux, 1982.

Lingeman, Richard R. *Don't You Know There's A War On?* New York: Putnam, 1970.

Lord, Walter. *Day of Infamy*. New York: Holt, 1957.

———. *Incredible Victory*. New York: Harper and Row, 1967.

Lovette, Leland P. *School of the Sea*. New York: Stokes, 1941.

Link, Arthur S. *Woodrow Wilson and the Progressive Era*. New York: Harper and Row, 1954.

Lucky Bag. Naval Academy Yearbook, 1915, 1916, 1917, 1918.

Marshall, S. L. A. *The American Heritage History of World War I*. New York: American Heritage, 1964.

Mason, John T., Jr., ed. *The Pacific War Remembered*. Annapolis: Naval Institute Press, 1986.

McCullough, David. *Truman*. New York: Simon and Schuster, 1992.

Mellow, James R. *Invented Lives: F. Scott and Zelda Fitzgerald*. Boston: Houghton Mifflin, 1984.

Miller, Nathan. *The Naval Air War, 1939–1945*. Annapolis: Naval Institute Press, 1991.

Mizener, Arthur. *The Far Side of Paradise*. Boston: Houghton Mifflin, 1951.

Mooney, James L., ed. *Dictionary of American Naval Fighting Ships, Volumes VII, VIII*. Washington, D.C.: Naval Historical Center, 1981.

Morison, Samuel Eliot. *The Two-Ocean War*. Boston: Little, Brown, 1963.

———. *History of United States Naval Operations in World War II, Volume I: The Battle of the Atlantic, September 1939–May 1943*. Boston: Little, Brown, 1950.

———. *History of United States Naval Operations in World War II, Volume III: The Rising Sun in the Pacific, 1931–April 1942*. Boston: Little, Brown, 1965.

———. *History of United States Naval Operations in World War II, Volume VIII: New Guinea and the Marianas, March 1944–August 1944*. Boston: Little, Brown, 1964.

———. *History of United States Naval Operations in World War II, Volume XII: Leyte, June 1944–January 1945*. Boston: Little, Brown, 1958.

———. *History of United States Naval Operations in World War II, Volume XIV: Victory in the Pacific, 1945*. Boston: Little, Brown, 1975.

Navy Department, Bureau of Navigation. *Examination Papers for Admission to the United States Naval Academy.* Washington, D.C.: Government Printing Office, 1920.

Okumiya, Masatake, and Jiro Horikoshi. *Zero.* New York: Dutton, 1956.

Pierson, Lt. Verling. "The Battle Off Samar." Personal recollections.

Poolman, Kenneth. *Allied Escort Carriers of World War II in Action.* Annapolis: Naval Institute Press, 1988.

Potter, E. B. *Bull Halsey.* Annapolis: Naval Institute Press, 1985.

———. *Nimitz.* Annapolis: Naval Institute Press, 1976.

———. *Admiral Arleigh Burke.* New York: Random House, 1990.

Potter, E. B., ed. *The United States and World Sea Power.* Englewood Cliffs, N.J.: Prentice-Hall, 1955.

Potter, E. B., and Chester W. Nimitz, USN. *Triumph in the Pacific: The Navy's Struggle Against Japan.* Englewood Cliffs, N.J.: Prentice-Hall, 1963.

Puleston, Capt. W. D. *Annapolis.* New York: Appleton-Century, 1942.

Raven, Alan. *Essex-Class Carriers.* Annapolis: Naval Institute Press, 1988.

Regulations of the United States Naval Academy, Parts I And II, 1911. Washington, D.C.: Government Printing Office, 1911.

Reneau, Patricia Sprague and Courtney Sprague Vaughan. *Remembered and Honored: Clifton A. F. "Ziggy" Sprague.* Santa Cruz, Calif.: Privately published, 1992.

Reynolds, Clark G. *Admiral John H. Towers: The Struggle for Naval Air Supremacy.* Annapolis: Naval Institute Press, 1991.

———. *The Fast Carriers: The Forging of an Air Navy.* Annapolis: Naval Institute Press, 1968.

———. *Famous American Admirals.* New York: Van Nostrand Reinhold, 1978.

Reynolds, Lt. (jg) John A. *History of the Gulf Sea Frontier (February 6, 1942–August 14, 1945).* Miami: Headquarters, Gulf Sea Frontier, 1946.

Roscoe, Theodore. *United States Destroyer Operations in World War II.* Annapolis: U.S. Naval Institute, 1953.

Ross, Al. *The Escort Carrier Gambier Bay.* Annapolis: Naval Institute Press, 1993.

Schultz, Duane. *Wake Island.* New York: St. Martin's Press, 1978.

Smith, S. E., ed. *The United States Navy in World War II.* New York: Quill Books, 1966.

Spector, Ronald H. *Eagle Against the Sun.* New York: Free Press, 1985.

Steinberg, Rafael. *Return to the Philippines.* Alexandria, Va.: Time-Life Books, 1979.

Stern, Robert C. *The Lexington Class Carriers.* Annapolis: Naval Institute Press, 1993.

Stevens, William Oliver. *Annapolis.* New York: Dodd, Mead, 1937.

Stewart, Adrian. *The Battle of Leyte Gulf.* New York: Scribner, 1979.

Sulzberger, C. L. *The American Heritage Picture History of World War II.* New York: American Heritage, 1966.

Sweetman, Jack. *The U.S. Naval Academy: An Illustrated History.* Annapolis: Naval Institute Press, 1979.

Taylor, Theodore. *The Magnificent Mitscher.* Annapolis: Naval Institute Press, 1991.

Toland, John. *Infamy.* Garden City, N.Y.: Doubleday, 1982.

———. *The Rising Sun.* New York: Random House, 1970.

Trimble, William F. *Admiral William A. Moffett.* Washington, D.C.: Smithsonian Institution Press, 1994.

Turnbull, Andrew. *Scott Fitzgerald.* New York: Scribner, 1962.

Turnbull, Archibald D., and Clifford L. Lord. *History of United States Naval Aviation.* New Haven: Yale University Press, 1949.

Vaeth, J. Gordon. *Blimps & U-Boats.* Annapolis: Naval Institute Press, 1992.

Van der Vat, Dan. *The Pacific Campaign.* New York: Simon and Schuster, 1991.

Van Deurs, Rear Adm. George, USN (Ret.). *Wings for the Fleet.* Annapolis: Naval Institute Press, 1966.

———. *Anchors in the Sky.* San Rafael, Calif.: Presidio Press, 1978.

Weinberg, Gerhard L. *A World At Arms.* Cambridge: Cambridge University Press, 1994.

Weisgall, Jonathan M. *Operation Crossroads: The Atomic Tests at Bikini Atoll.* Annapolis: Naval Institute Press, 1994.

Wilkinson, C. A. Private Monograph. 1977.

Willmott, H. P. *The Barrier and the Javelin.* Annapolis: Naval Institute Press, 1983.

Wilson, Eugene E. *Slipstream: The Autobiography of an Air Craftsman.* New York: McGraw-Hill, 1950.

Winton, John. *Ultra in the Pacific.* Annapolis: Naval Institute Press, 1993.

———. *War in the Pacific.* New York: Mayflower Books, 1978.

Woodward, C. Vann. *The Battle for Leyte Gulf.* New York: Macmillan, 1947.

Wouk, Herman. *War and Remembrance.* New York: Pocket Books, 1978.

Wragg, David. *Wings Over the Sea: A History of Naval Aviation.* New York: Arco, 1979.

Y'Blood, William T. *The Little Giants: U.S. Escort Carriers Against Japan.* Annapolis: Naval Institute Press, 1987.

———. *Red Sun Setting: The Battle of the Philippine Sea.* Annapolis: Naval Institute Press, 1981.

Young, Brigadier Peter, ed. *The World Almanac of World War II.* New York: Pharos Books, 1981.

Articles

"Admiral Sprague Decorated." New York *Herald Tribune,* 14 January 1945.

"Admiral Sprague Honored for Heroism in Pacific." Philadelphia *Inquirer,* 15 January 1945.

Ageton, Lt. Arthur A. "Annapolis, Mother of Navy Men." U.S. Naval Institute *Proceedings* 61, 10 (October 1935): 1499–1514.

Alden, Carroll Storrs. "The Changing Naval Academy: A Retrospect of Twenty-five Years." U.S. Naval Institute *Proceedings,* 55, 6 (June 1929): 495–501.

Andrews, Peter. "The Defense of Wake." *American Heritage,* 38, 5 (July/August 1987): 65–80.

"Atom Tests Won't Be Rigged for Navy." San Francisco *News,* 8 May 1946.

"B-29 'Recon' Flies over North Pole." United Press report, 12 November 1950.

Baldwin, Hanson W. "Air Dispute Remains." New York *Times,* 26 January 1947.

———. "Most Dramatic Sea Battle in History." New York *Times* Magazine, 24 October 1954.

———. "Greatest & Last Battle of a Naval Era," *Time,* 26 October 1959, 16–18.

"Bikini Bound." San Francisco *Chronicle,* 9 May 1946.

Bishop, Eleanor C. "'Hooligan's Navy': Coastal Pickets at War." *Naval History,* 6, 2 (Summer 1992): 46–48.

Bogan, Vice Adm. Gerald F. "The Navy Spreads Its Golden Wings." U.S. Naval Institute *Proceedings* 87, 5 (May 1961): 97–101.

Bolander, Louis H. "The Naval Academy in Five Wars." U.S. Naval Institute *Proceedings* 72, 4 (April 1946): 35–45.

Butcher, Lt. Comdr. M. E., USN. "Admiral Frank Jack Fletcher, Pioneer Warrior or Gross Sinner?" *Naval War College Review* 40, 1 (Winter 1987): 69–79.

Cant, Gilbert. "Bull's Run: Was Halsey Right at Leyte Gulf?" *Life,* 14 November 1947.

Coletta, Paolo E. "Annapolis and Naval Air." *Shipmate* (November 1984).

Craven, Capt. T. T. "Naval Aviation." U.S. Naval Institute *Proceedings* 46, 2 (February 1920): 181–91.

Deac, Wilfred P. "The Battle off Samar." *American Heritage* XVIII, 1 (December 1966): 20–23, 95–100.

Eller, Lt. E. M. "Navy Life Begins." U.S. Naval Institute *Proceedings* 61, 10 (October 1935): 1515–28.

Falk, Stanley L. "Leyte Gulf: A Bibliography of the Greatest Sea Battle." *Naval History* 2, 4 (Fall 1988): 60–61.

Fleming, Thomas. "School for Sailors." *American Heritage* 41, 3 (April 1990): 90–99.

Hagen, Lt. Robert C., and Sidney Shalett. "We Asked For the Jap Fleet—and Got It." *Saturday Evening Post,* 26 May 1945: 9–10, 72–76.

Halsey, Fleet Admiral William F., Jr. "The Battle for Leyte Gulf." U.S. Naval Institute *Proceedings* 78 (May 1952): 487–95.

Heinl, Lt. Col. R. D., Jr. "We're Headed for Wake." *Marine Corps Gazette* (June 1946): 35–38.

Holloway, Adm. J. L., Jr. "Recollections, 1915–1920." *Shipmate* (April 1984): 17–19.

"'Hottest Boys in the Sky,' Admiral Calls CVE Pilots." Philadelphia *Inquirer,* December 1944.

Johnston, Richard W. "Battle of Samar Didn't End When Nip Fleet Tried to Run." United Press article, 13 November 1944.

Lewis, Charles Lee. "Description of the United States Naval Academy." U.S. Naval Institute *Proceedings* 61, 10 (October 1935): 1443–67.

Lundstrom, John B. "Frank Jack Fletcher Got a Bum Rap." *Naval History* 6, 2 (Summer 1992): 22–27.

Patrick, Midshipman K. W. "Midshipmen Cruises." U.S. Naval Institute *Proceedings* 61, 10 (October 1935): 1545–51.

Phillips, Reynolds. "Polar Communities." *Boeing Magazine* (December 1950): 10–13.

Prados, John. "The Spies at the Bottom of the Sea." *MHQ: The Quarterly Journal of Military History* 6, 2 (Winter 1994): 38–47.

Schratz, Capt. Paul R. "The Admirals' Revolt." U.S. Naval Institute *Proceedings* 112, 2 (February 1986): 64–71.

"Shangri-La Sails for Test of the Bikini 'Drones'." San Francisco *News,* 9 May 1946.

Small, Lt. Dorothy L. "Catapults Come of Age." U.S. Naval Institute *Proceedings* 80, 10 (October 1954): 1113–17.

Small, Midshipman Ernest G. "The U.S. Naval Academy: An Undergraduate's Point of View." U.S. Naval Institute *Proceedings* 30, 12 (December 1912): 1397–1403.

"Sprague Blazes Aerial Trail." Name and date unknown, in Clifton A. F. Sprague Collection.

Sprague obituaries: *Newsweek,* 25 April 1955; New York *Times,* 12 April 1955; *Time,* 25 April 1955.

Sprague, Rear Adm. C. A. F., as told to Lt. (jg) Philip H. Gustafson. "The Japs Had Us on the Ropes." *American Magazine* (April 1945).

"Sprague Tells how his Baby Carriers Withstood 2½ Hours of Jap Fire." Newspaper unknown, December 1944.

Stevenson, Jack. "Academy Aviation Training in Forty-Sixth Year." *Log* (28 March 1972): 34–35.

Sufrin, Mark. "Survival Cannot be Expected." *Military History,* 40–48.

Tate, Rear Adm. Jackson R. "We Rode the Covered Wagon." U.S. Naval Institute *Proceedings* 104, 10 (October 1978): 62–69.

Tomlinson, Capt. Daniel W. "Flying Blind." *Shipmate* (December 1977): 19–22.

Weisgall, Jonathan M. "Bikini 'Witch's Brew.'" U.S. Naval Institute *Proceedings* 120, 2 (February 1994): 78–81.

Wheeler, Gerald E. "Naval Aviation's First Year." U.S. Naval Institute *Proceedings* 87, 5 (May 1961): 89–95.

Woodhouse, Henry. "U.S. Naval Aeronautic Policies, 1904–42." U.S. Naval Institute *Proceedings* 68, 2 (February 1942): 161–75.

Wukovits, John F. "Nothing Is Impossible." *American History Illustrated* (June 1984): 56–63.

———. "A Nation's Inspiration." *World War II* (September 1992): 30–37.

———. "Every Move Seen." *World War II* (May 1991): 30–37.

→ INDEX ←

263

➔ ABOUT THE AUTHOR ⬅

John F. Wukovits is a teacher/writer from Trenton, Michigan, who specializes in the Pacific War. After graduating from the University of Notre Dame, Wukovits received his Master's in History from Michigan State University. Since 1968 he has taught history, literature, and writing to junior high school students. He currently instructs at Monguagon Middle School in Trenton.

Mr. Wukovits has written extensively about the U.S. conflict with Japan. His work has appeared in a variety of reference works and in the 1992 title *Men of War: Great Naval Leaders of World War II,* for which he contributed a biographical essay on Adm. Raymond Spruance. Earlier this year, the Marine Corps Historical Center published Wukovits's account of the battle of Okinawa as part of its fiftieth anniversary series of World War II battle histories. Two essays—profiles of Admirals George Dewey and William Halsey—will soon appear in Naval Institute Press collections. In addition, Mr. Wukovits has written more than one hundred articles for twenty-five different national publications, including *Naval History, World War II, The Journal of Military History, Naval War College Review,* and *Air Power History.*